Using Organizational Culture to Resolve Business Challenges

Gerardo Reyes Ruiz
Center for Naval Higher Studies (CESNAV), Mexico

A volume in the Advances in Human Resources Management and Organizational Development (AHRMOD) Book Series

IGI Global
PUBLISHER of TIMELY KNOWLEDGE

Published in the United States of America by
IGI Global
Business Science Reference (an imprint of IGI Global)
701 E. Chocolate Avenue
Hershey PA, USA 17033
Tel: 717-533-8845
Fax: 717-533-8661
E-mail: cust@igi-global.com
Web site: http://www.igi-global.com

Library of Congress Cataloging-in-Publication Data

Names: Reyes Ruiz, Gerardo, 1971- editor.
Title: Using organizational culture to resolve business challenges / edited by Gerardo Reyes Ruiz.
Description: Hershey, PA : Business Science Reference, [2023] | Includes bibliographical references and index. | Summary: "Using Organizational Culture to Resolve Business Challenges, edited by Gerardo Reyes Ruiz, provides a transformative solution to the challenges faced by SMEs. This groundbreaking book offers a collection of real success stories from around the world, demonstrating how organizational culture played a pivotal role in the resilience and triumph of these enterprises during the pandemic. By exploring these case studies, readers gain invaluable insights and practical strategies to cultivate and leverage organizational culture for navigating change and driving sustainable growth"-- Provided by publisher.
Identifiers: LCCN 2023029640 (print) | LCCN 2023029641 (ebook) | ISBN 9781668465677 (hardcover) | ISBN 9781668465684 (paperback) | ISBN 9781668465691 (ebook)
Subjects: LCSH: Corporate culture. | Organizational behavior.
Classification: LCC HD58.7 .U85 2023 (print) | LCC HD58.7 (ebook) | DDC 658.3/14--dc23/eng/20230623
LC record available at https://lccn.loc.gov/2023029640
LC ebook record available at https://lccn.loc.gov/2023029641

This book is published in the IGI Global book series Advances in Human Resources Management and Organizational Development (AHRMOD) (ISSN: 2327-3372; eISSN: 2327-3380)

British Cataloguing in Publication Data
A Cataloguing in Publication record for this book is available from the British Library.

Advances in Human Resources Management and Organizational Development (AHRMOD) Book Series

Patricia Ordóñez de Pablos
Universidad de Oviedo, Spain

ISSN:2327-3372
EISSN:2327-3380

MISSION

A solid foundation is essential to the development and success of any organization and can be accomplished through the effective and careful management of an organization's human capital. Research in human resources management and organizational development is necessary in providing business leaders with the tools and methodologies which will assist in the development and maintenance of their organizational structure.

The **Advances in Human Resources Management and Organizational Development (AHRMOD) Book Series** aims to publish the latest research on all aspects of human resources as well as the latest methodologies, tools, and theories regarding organizational development and sustainability. The **AHRMOD Book Series** intends to provide business professionals, managers, researchers, and students with the necessary resources to effectively develop and implement organizational strategies.

COVERAGE

- Disputes Resolution
- Employee Benefits
- Diversity in the Workplace
- Strategic HRM
- Personnel Policies
- Executive Compensation
- Corporate Governance
- Worker Behavior and Engagement
- E-Human Resources Management
- Executive Education

IGI Global is currently accepting manuscripts for publication within this series. To submit a proposal for a volume in this series, please contact our Acquisition Editors at Acquisitions@igi-global.com or visit: http://www.igi-global.com/publish/.

The Advances in Human Resources Management and Organizational Development (AHRMOD) Book Series (ISSN 2327-3372) is published by IGI Global, 701 E. Chocolate Avenue, Hershey, PA 17033-1240, USA, www.igi-global.com. This series is composed of titles available for purchase individually; each title is edited to be contextually exclusive from any other title within the series. For pricing and ordering information please visit http://www.igi-global.com/book-series/advances-human-resources-management-organizational/73670. Postmaster: Send all address changes to above address.

Titles in this Series

For a list of additional titles in this series, please visit: http://www.igi-global.com/book-series/

HR Analytics in an Era of Rapid Automation
Radha Yadav (CHRIST University, India) Mudita Sinha (CHRIST University, India) and Joseph Varghese Kureethara (CHRIST University, India)
Business Science Reference • © 2023 • 359pp • H/C (ISBN: 9781668489420) • US $225.00

Policies, Protocols, and Standards for Professionalism in a Diverse Work Environment
Christiana Bevier (Purdue University Global, USA) Barry Regan (Purdue University Global, USA) and Carolyn N. Stevenson (Purdue University Global, USA)
Business Science Reference • © 2023 • 324pp • H/C (ISBN: 9781668473085) • US $225.00

Measuring the Effectiveness of Organizational Development Strategies During Unprecedented Times
Kyla Latrice Tennin (College of Doctoral Studies, University of Phoenix, USA & Forbes School of Business, USA & World Business Angels Investment Forum (WBAF)-G20, USA & Lady Mirage Global, Inc., USA)
Business Science Reference • © 2023 • 345pp • H/C (ISBN: 9781668483923) • US $250.00

Role of Human Resources for Inclusive Leadership, Workplace Diversity, and Equity in Organizations
Caglar Dogru (Ufuk University, Turkey)
Business Science Reference • © 2023 • 421pp • H/C (ISBN: 9781668466025) • US $240.00

Global Citizenship and Its Impact on Multiculturalism in the Workplace
Randa Diab-Bahman (Kuwait College of Science and Technology, Kuwait) and Abrar Al-Enzi (Gulf University for Science and Technology, Kuwait)
Business Science Reference • © 2023 • 300pp • H/C (ISBN: 9781668454367) • US $240.00

Talent Acquisition and Retention Strategies in Global Startups
Neetima Agarwal (Symbiosis International University, India) Leo Paul Dana (Kingston University, UK) and Sujata Khandai (Amity University, India)
Business Science Reference • © 2023 • 305pp • H/C (ISBN: 9781668475140) • US $250.00

IGI Global
PUBLISHER of TIMELY KNOWLEDGE

701 East Chocolate Avenue, Hershey, PA 17033, USA
Tel: 717-533-8845 x100 • Fax: 717-533-8661
E-Mail: cust@igi-global.com • www.igi-global.com

Table of Contents

Preface xiii

Chapter 1
Scientific/Technological Human Resources as a Success Factor in the Organizational Culture of SMEs: A Longitudinal Study for a Maquiladora Company 1
Gerardo Reyes Ruiz, Center for Higher Naval Studies (CESNAV), Mexico

Chapter 2
Institutional Policymaking and Its Implications in the Analysis of Institutional Change 35
José G. Vargas-Hernandez, Tecnológico Superior de Jalisco, Mexico
Omar C. Vargas-González, Tecnológico Nacional de México, Cuidad Guzmán, Mexico

Chapter 3
Organisational Philosophy and Culture: Human Capital as Pivot, Women as Fulcrum 60
Catherine Hayes, University of Sunderland, UK

Chapter 4
Development and Validation of the Scale of Intergenerational Conflict in Organizations 86
María de Lourdes Elena García Vargas, Universidad Autónoma del Estado de Hidalgo, Mexico
Maria Teresa De la Garza, Universidad Tecnológica de Celaya, Mexico
Gerardo Reyes Ruiz, Center for Superior Naval Studies (CESNAV), Mexico

Chapter 5
Institutional Change and Institutionalization 107
José G. Vargas-Hernandez, Tecnológico Superior de Jalisco, Mexico
Omar C. Vargas-González, Tecnológico Nacional de México, Ciudad Guzmán, Mexico

Chapter 6
Organizational Change Models in Practice: The Case of Michelin Group........132
Umut Uyan, Munzur University, Turkey

Chapter 7
Power Structure as a Guide to Organizational Culture: OC Strategies for Adapting to Change 146
K. S. S. Kanhaiya, Steel Authority of India Limited, India

Chapter 8
Conflict Management in Organisations of Emerging Economies: A Literature Review and Future Research Agenda 170
Nirma Sadamali Jayawardena, O.P. Jindal Global University, India
Darshana Jayawardena, National School of Business Management, Sri Lanka

Chapter 9
The Role of Organizational Culture on Women's Leadership in Organizations in Switzerland 185
Silvena Dencheva Yordanova, Varna University of Management, Bulgaria
Vahid Asghari, Varna University of Management, Bulgaria

Chapter 10
The Effect of Work and Family Conflict on Life Satisfaction: Gender Concept..205
Selda Coşkuner Aktaş, Hacettepe University, Turkey

Chapter 11
From Resistance to Readiness: Leveraging Neuroscience Perspectives for Successful Change Management in the Manufacturing Sector 222
Ashlita Florence Lopez, CHRIST University (Deemed), India
Sebin Joy, CHRIST University (Deemed), India
Arti Arun Kumar, CHRIST University (Deemed), India

Compilation of References 247

About the Contributors 294

Index 297

Detailed Table of Contents

Preface xiii

Chapter 1
Scientific/Technological Human Resources as a Success Factor in the Organizational Culture of SMEs: A Longitudinal Study for a Maquiladora Company 1
Gerardo Reyes Ruiz, Center for Higher Naval Studies (CESNAV), Mexico

Globalization demands better prepared students and Mexico should not remain indifferent to these demands. Thus, the objective of this case study is to show first-hand information to understand the problems that currently exist in terms of the formation of scientific and technological human capital in the State of Tlaxcala, Mexico. The results obtained through this research work will help to understand the importance generated by these human resources to build a successful and fundamental organizational culture for any Mexican company that today bets on cutting-edge innovation, especially all those that are generated in the States of Mexican Republic with less generation of these specialized human resources. The local public policy efforts made by local companies for the adoption of scientists and technologists in this geographical area of Mexico are also glimpsed.

Chapter 2
Institutional Policymaking and Its Implications in the Analysis of Institutional Change 35
José G. Vargas-Hernandez, Tecnológico Superior de Jalisco, Mexico
Omar C. Vargas-González, Tecnológico Nacional de México, Cuidad Guzmán, Mexico

This study has the purpose of analyzing the implications of institutional policymaking in the analysis of institutional change. The analysis departs from the assumption that the analysis of institutional policymaking is a framework to design and implement institutional change. The method used is the meta cognitive-analytic-descriptive based on the conceptual-theoretical and empirical review of the literature on these issues. It is concluded that the analysis of institutional change must be supported by a framework of a policymaking development.

Chapter 3
Organisational Philosophy and Culture: Human Capital as Pivot, Women as Fulcrum 60
Catherine Hayes, University of Sunderland, UK

This chapter considers the ongoing issues faced in relation to gender discrimination and change in relation to global recovery from the COVID-19 pandemic. A theoretical approach is adopted to consider the agency women are afforded within the context of leadership generally and change management, specifically. These debates are contextualised within global higher education and examined through theoretical lenses of influence, such as neoliberalism, which have impacted so much on the context specificity of change management in higher education and the cultures within which it has influenced so greatly. The recent global COVID-19 pandemic is used as a vehicle by which to drive thinking around concepts, which have had such an impact on women during this time, such as emotional labour, systemic equity, and structural inequality. The chapter concludes with a consideration of organisational structures and the agency that this has afforded women both historically and within the leadership challenges they currently face.

Chapter 4
Development and Validation of the Scale of Intergenerational Conflict in Organizations 86
María de Lourdes Elena García Vargas, Universidad Autónoma del Estado de Hidalgo, Mexico
Maria Teresa De la Garza, Universidad Tecnológica de Celaya, Mexico
Gerardo Reyes Ruiz, Center for Superior Naval Studies (CESNAV), Mexico

The study validates a scale that allows the exploration of intergenerational conflict in organizations. To validate the questionnaire, the descriptive statistics of the sample are obtained, Cronbach's alpha and Pearson's correlations between variables are calculated, an exploratory factor analysis is performed with the SPSS software. A first-order confirmatory factor analysis is performed with the AMOS software, and the Dillon-Goldstein rho (or composite reliability) is calculated to verify the internal consistency of the indicators for each latent variable. The result is that all the acceptance criteria have been met, the Rho de Dillon-Goldstein is acceptable, the first factor (opening of the generation gap) is 0.85, and the second factor (limitations for intergenerational work) is 0.78, so the model obtained the required validation quality.

Chapter 5
Institutional Change and Institutionalization 107
José G. Vargas-Hernandez, Tecnológico Superior de Jalisco, Mexico
Omar C. Vargas-González, Tecnológico Nacional de México, Ciudad Guzmán, Mexico

This study has the purpose to analyze the implications between institutional change and institutionalization. It departs from the assumption that some institutional change theories provide through different framework perspectives to explain and analyze the different strengths and challenges of the institutionalization processes. The methods used are the meta-cognitive analytical descriptive based on the conceptual, theoretical, and analytical literature review. As it had been assumed, the study concludes in that institutional change theoretical frameworks lead to provide the intellectual tools to describe, explain, and analyze the strengths and challenges posed by the institutionalization processes.

Chapter 6
Organizational Change Models in Practice: The Case of Michelin Group........ 132
Umut Uyan, Munzur University, Turkey

In a competitive business environment, it is vital that firms consider implementing techniques to cope with constant change to remain competitive and survive. Most change initiatives, however, suffer from several difficulties and are often hampered by resistance, primarily caused by fear of adopting new practices or concern about competence. As a result, such initiatives could result in unintended consequences. In fact, they might result in irreversible situations, impairing the dynamics of an organization. Michelin Shanghai underwent an organizational change initiative to enhance its competitiveness. The initiative resulted in significant improvements in the company's productivity and profitability as well as increased employee satisfaction. The main objective of the study is to understand the organizational change dynamics of Michelin Shanghai Co. The chapter also attempts to evaluate challenges encountered during the process and critically analyze the leadership approaches that were applied by Mr. Ballarin (plant manager of Michelin Co.) based on related theories.

Chapter 7
Power Structure as a Guide to Organizational Culture: OC Strategies for Adapting to Change 146
K. S. S. Kanhaiya, Steel Authority of India Limited, India

Organizational culture is a crucial element for the success of any organization. It encompasses shared beliefs, values, attitudes, and assumptions that influence how members perceive and respond to situations. Power structure affects the organizational culture significantly, including how employees behave, communicate, and collaborate. This chapter explores the advantages and disadvantages of different power structures, their relationship with organizational culture, and their impact on organizational adaptability to change. Organizational culture strategies are essential for adapting to change. Providing an overview of different types of strategies, their advantages, and disadvantages, the chapter emphasizes the importance of aligning power structures with organizational culture strategies. A case study is also included, and the chapter highlights the significance of understanding the power structure's influence on organizational culture strategies and the importance of an aligned approach. The chapter concludes by suggesting future research directions in the field.

Chapter 8
Conflict Management in Organisations of Emerging Economies: A Literature Review and Future Research Agenda 170
Nirma Sadamali Jayawardena, O.P. Jindal Global University, India
Darshana Jayawardena, National School of Business Management, Sri Lanka

The purpose of this chapter is to provide an overview on conflict management strategies within the emerging economies via a detailed literature review. The study of organisational conflicts in emerging economies is a very rare research topic. This study was able to identify four major gaps in this area. Firstly, the topic organisational conflict research focuses more on organizational behaviour and occupational psychology research with less consideration on human resource management. Secondly, a majority of these studies has been conducted in Western and European countries with less focusing on the Asian context and emerging economies. Thirdly, few studies used the mixed research methodology to investigate the scenarios which provides more accurate findings. Fourthly, few studies analysed perspectives of both employees and employers since the majority of the existing studies used the perspective of either employee or the employer.

Chapter 9
The Role of Organizational Culture on Women's Leadership in Organizations in Switzerland 185
Silvena Dencheva Yordanova, Varna University of Management, Bulgaria
Vahid Asghari, Varna University of Management, Bulgaria

Each organization is defined by its own culture, formed by the key stakeholders. For some companies, it is considered as male culture being aggressive, whereas other companies tolerate different organizational beliefs. For sure, the organizational culture reflects on the values of all its members. It affects human resource practices also. How people are selected in interviews and how their career planning is performed reflects also the company values. It is considered that the performance of the companies measured by the revenues and turnover of staff depend on the leaders in the organization. The following hypotheses have been formulated: 1. Women's leadership positively affects the organizational culture of organizations based in Switzerland. 2. Women's leadership positively affects organizational values of organizations in Switzerland. 3. Women's leadership positively affects organizational conditions of organizations in Switzerland. 4. Women's leadership positively affects the organizational environment of organizations based in Switzerland.

Chapter 10
The Effect of Work and Family Conflict on Life Satisfaction: Gender Concept 205
Selda Coşkuner Aktaş, Hacettepe University, Turkey

The purpose of this study is to examine the effect of gendered aspects of work and family conflict on life satisfaction. The data were collected from two major public universities in Turkey, and 349 dual-earner family members were reached by using random sampling method. The study employed linear regression analysis to predict the effect of work and family conflict on women's and men's life satisfaction. The regression analysis model explained 21% of the life satisfaction of women while it explained 20% of the life satisfaction of men. According to the findings, women's life satisfaction was predicted by both strain-based work-to-family conflict and strain-based family-to-work conflict. The life satisfaction of men, however, was only predicted by strain-based family-to-work conflict. In light of the results, the contribution of the study to the literature was highlighted.

Chapter 11
From Resistance to Readiness: Leveraging Neuroscience Perspectives for Successful Change Management in the Manufacturing Sector 222
Ashlita Florence Lopez, CHRIST University (Deemed), India
Sebin Joy, CHRIST University (Deemed), India
Arti Arun Kumar, CHRIST University (Deemed), India

Change initiatives often encounter resistance from employees, impeding successful implementation. Leveraging insights from neuroscience can provide valuable guidance in navigating this resistance and promoting readiness for change. Social experiences in a work environment affect the brain positively or negatively. By understanding the brain's response to change, change managers can create a supportive environment and communicate accordingly. This study examines the impact of social experiences on readiness to change among employees in the manufacturing sector from a neuroscience perspective. SCARF is a neuroscience-based model that evaluates five dimensions of social experiences such as status, certainty, autonomy, relatedness, and fairness. This quantitative study is based on data collected from different manufacturing organisations. The results of this study provide insights into how change managers can address these social domains to promote successful change initiatives and improve employee readiness to change.

Compilation of References 247

About the Contributors 294

Index 297

Preface

In today's rapidly changing and interconnected global landscape, the success of organizations hinges on several critical factors, including human capital, training, technology transfer, and above all, organizational culture. As the Editor of this reference book *Using Organizational Culture to Resolve Business Challenges*, I am delighted to present a compilation of insights and success stories that shed light on the pivotal role of organizational culture, particularly in the context of Small and Medium Enterprises (SMEs).

SMEs play a crucial role in the economic growth and employment generation of nations across the world. Despite facing chronic challenges like excessive bureaucracy and limited support from governments, their resilience and determination cannot be understated. This book seeks to explore how some of these companies achieved excellence and weathered the storm, finding innovative solutions through their organizational cultures.

Within the Latin American context, SMEs represent a significant portion of businesses, often comprising over 90% of companies in several countries. However, they face numerous hurdles, from lack of specialized personnel to difficulties accessing cutting-edge technology and financing. It is evident that a strong and dynamic organizational culture can be a driving force behind their success, enabling them to adapt, thrive, and make a positive impact on both their communities and the broader economy.

The COVID-19 pandemic brought unprecedented challenges, forcing companies worldwide to reassess their strategies and operational models. It accelerated the need for organizational culture to become a guiding force that influences decision-making, fosters adaptability, and promotes resilience. Through this book, we aim to showcase a diverse range of success stories from SMEs that were able to navigate the pandemic's uncertainties and emerge stronger due to their unique organizational cultures.

Total quality principles are instrumental in shaping an organization's culture. As the world experiences paradigm shifts, companies must embrace new ways of working to remain competitive. This book delves into the various elements that constitute organizational culture, such as control systems, power structures, symbols, rituals, and stories, all of which play a role in shaping an organization's identity and behavior.

The primary objective of this book is to provide a compelling collection of global success stories from SMEs during the COVID-19 pandemic. By analyzing these real-world examples, readers will gain insights into how these companies effectively integrated their organizational cultures to confront and overcome the challenges brought about by the pandemic.

In today's interconnected world, the demands of globalization require educational systems to prepare students with skills that transcend borders. The opening chapter of this edited reference book sets the stage by highlighting Mexico's need to address these demands. Chapter 1 delves into the challenges faced in forming scientific and technological human capital in the State of Tlaxcala, Mexico. It presents firsthand insights into the issues impeding the creation of this crucial resource. The chapter's results offer a deep understanding of the significance of such human resources in building a thriving organizational culture within Mexican companies. The focus extends to those operating in states with less access to these specialized talents, shedding light on local public policies and efforts by companies to embrace scientists and technologists.

Chapter 2 embarks on an exploration of institutional policymaking and its implications for understanding institutional change. Through a meta-cognitive-analytic-descriptive approach, the chapter analyses the link between policymaking and the framework of institutional change. It asserts that effective institutional change requires a robust framework rooted in policymaking development. This chapter contributes a conceptual and empirical foundation to the discourse around institutional change and its driving forces.

Amid the ongoing repercussions of the COVID-19 pandemic, Chapter 3 takes a gender-focused perspective on institutional change. This chapter examines how women's agency intersects with leadership and change management, particularly in the context of global higher education. Theoretical lenses like Neoliberalism provide insights into how systemic equity, emotional labor, and structural inequality have impacted women during the pandemic. Drawing from this, the chapter reflects on the agency women historically possessed within organizational structures and the challenges they currently confront in leadership roles.

Chapter 4 introduces a validated scale designed to explore intergenerational conflict within organizations. This chapter intricately validates the questionnaire through a range of statistical analyses and confirms its applicability. With an emphasis on generational gaps and limitations in intergenerational work, the validated model contributes a significant tool for organizations grappling with the complexities of intergenerational dynamics.

Building upon the concepts of institutional change and institutionalization, Chapter 5 delves into theoretical frameworks that aid in understanding the strengths and challenges of institutionalization processes. Through meta-cognitive analytical methods, this chapter provides a comprehensive review of these frameworks, illustrating their role in deciphering the intricacies of institutionalization. By anchoring the study in theoretical foundations, the chapter enriches the discourse on organizational change and its lasting impact.

Organizational adaptability to change is a cornerstone of survival in competitive business environments. Chapter 6 presents a case study of Michelin Shanghai's successful organizational change initiative. This initiative not only bolstered the company's productivity and profitability but also improved employee satisfaction. Through an in-depth analysis, the chapter uncovers the dynamics of this organizational change and scrutinizes the leadership approaches applied. The insights garnered contribute to a deeper understanding of effective change management strategies.

Chapter 7 delves into the intricate relationship between power structures, organizational culture, and adaptability to change. By examining various power structures' advantages and disadvantages, this chapter highlights their role in shaping organizational culture and its capacity to embrace change. The chapter underscores the importance of aligning power structures with culture strategies and offers a case study to emphasize this alignment's significance.

Chapter 8 undertakes a unique exploration of conflict management strategies within emerging economies. It highlights gaps in existing research, especially in the context of organizational behavior, occupational psychology, and Human Resource Management. This chapter provides insights into the distinctive challenges faced in these economies, emphasizing the need for mixed research methodologies and perspectives from both employees and employers.

Chapter 9 examines the impact of women's leadership on organizational culture in Swiss organizations. Through formulated hypotheses, the chapter delves into the influence of women's leadership on various organizational facets, from culture and values to conditions and environment. This chapter's insights contribute to the ongoing dialogue around gender, leadership, and their impact on organizational dynamics.

The focal point of Chapter 10 is the examination of gendered aspects of work-family conflict and their influence on life satisfaction. By analyzing data from Turkish universities, the chapter delves into the predictors of life satisfaction for women and men. This chapter's findings emphasize the varied effects of strain-based work-to-family conflict on the life satisfaction of both genders.

The concluding chapters explore the neuroscientific dimensions of change readiness. Chapter 11 dives into how social experiences in the workplace influence employees' brain responses to change. Drawing from the SCARF model, the chapter identifies five critical dimensions—status, certainty, autonomy, relatedness, and fairness—that shape employees' readiness for change. By understanding and leveraging these dimensions, change managers can enhance their initiatives' success and promote employee readiness for transformation.

I firmly believe that this book contributes an innovative perspective to the existing literature on organizational culture and its impact on SMEs. As we delve into previously unexplored territory, I hope this work sparks new ideas and inspires further research in the field. By studying these success stories, educators and students alike will find valuable material to enhance their learning experiences and foster a deeper understanding of the intricate relationship between organizational culture and business success.

I extend my gratitude to all the contributors whose valuable insights and experiences have enriched this book. Their firsthand accounts offer a rare glimpse into the practical application of organizational culture as a catalyst for growth and survival during turbulent times.

This book is intended for a diverse audience, including educators, scholars, business leaders, managers, and entrepreneurs, as well as professionals in various industries. Its real-world case studies and novel proposals are designed to engage stakeholders from different backgrounds and foster dynamic discussions on organizational culture and its impact on business outcomes.

In conclusion, *Using Organizational Culture to Resolve Business Challenges* seeks to inspire readers to embrace a culture-driven approach to navigate through the complexities of the modern business landscape successfully. As we explore these remarkable stories of triumph and resilience, I am confident that this book will make a meaningful contribution to the understanding and appreciation of organizational culture's far-reaching influence on the world of business.

Gerardo Reyes Ruiz
Center for Naval Higher Studies (CESNAV), Mexico

Chapter 1
Scientific/Technological Human Resources as a Success Factor in the Organizational Culture of SMEs:
A Longitudinal Study for a Maquiladora Company

Gerardo Reyes Ruiz
https://orcid.org/0000-0003-0212-2952
Center for Higher Naval Studies (CESNAV), Mexico

ABSTRACT

Globalization demands better prepared students and Mexico should not remain indifferent to these demands. Thus, the objective of this case study is to show first-hand information to understand the problems that currently exist in terms of the formation of scientific and technological human capital in the State of Tlaxcala, Mexico. The results obtained through this research work will help to understand the importance generated by these human resources to build a successful and fundamental organizational culture for any Mexican company that today bets on cutting-edge innovation, especially all those that are generated in the States of Mexican Republic with less generation of these specialized human resources. The local public policy efforts made by local companies for the adoption of scientists and technologists in this geographical area of Mexico are also glimpsed.

DOI: 10.4018/978-1-6684-6567-7.ch001

INTRODUCTION

In today's globalized world, the role of human capital, training, and technology transfer are increasingly recognized as key elements in the success of companies. Since the nineties of the last century, these elements have been fully identified in multiple works and different ways (Nataraajan and Chawla, 1994; Grosse, 1996; Bessant and Rush, 1995). In Mexico, Small and Medium Enterprises (SMEs) generally have negative characteristics such as low financing, high failure rates, partners acting as managers, the labor force being satisfied with relatives, accounting management without professionals, lack of an administrative and productive structure, lack skilled labor, have a null level of innovation and training, and present a high dependence on large companies. The quality of university graduates in the area of science and engineering and their incorporation in SMEs is a critical success factor for those companies that wish to venture into the generation of value beyond simple maquila processes, i.e., the creation of an organizational culture (Keogh and Galloway, 2004; Martín, Segredo and Perdomo, 2013).

The sector where most SMEs venture into is the commercial sector, followed by services and finally manufacturing: This behavior shows that few SMEs venture into the latter sector due to a lack of technology, financing, and qualified professionals in their workforce (Saavedra and Hernández, 2008). By not having an evaluation and planning in the creation of SMEs, it is deduced that they will lack specialized professionals in the workforce. Rubio and Aragón (2002) found that competitive success factors in SMEs vary from one country to another. However, these authors argue that the two elements coincide in different countries. The first element refers to the quality of human resources in the company; the level of knowledge, skills, and behaviors, of the workforce are elements that can determine the success of SMEs.

Regarding the first element, a study on maquiladoras in Mexico (Carrillo, 2007) mentions that human resources in Mexico have limitations, for example, insufficient professional labor, especially engineers (basic sciences), low qualification of university students, as well as low identification of these with the company. In addition to the above, higher education does not provide the necessary amount of skilled labor, especially scientists and engineers that the economy requires (Sala-I-Martin et al., 2009). On the other hand, many SMEs justify their lack of science and technology professionals on the associated costs and size. Studies show that SMEs are reluctant to hire professional graduates and provide training to existing employees. This latter dynamic limits the ability of SMEs to exploit new knowledge, resulting in a clear lack of innovation, which has been considered a transcendental factor in organizational culture (Bowen, Lloyd and Thomas, 2004; Acosta, 2015).

Research on this topic (Torre, 2014; Guisan and Neira, 2001) also addresses how human resources trained in the area of science and engineering influence economic growth and welfare in countries around the world, these studies include companies of different sizes, for example, Castelblanco and Robledo (2014) mention that innovation is a key and fundamental factor for the economic development of countries: In their article, these researchers develop an algorithm to determine the importance and intrinsic relationship of some indicators in science and technology with the growth of Gross Domestic Product (GDP). Another research (Syeda-Masooda, Oakey and Kippling, 1999) already raised the serious underutilization of science and technology graduates in the SME sector in the United Kingdom; it explores the potential of absorbing the so-called "know-how" of science and technology graduates in this sector by taking into account the attitudes of these graduates towards the option of employment in SMEs. These studies illustrate the importance of skilled labor, at all levels, as this is a key element and determinant for the success of organizations and/or companies that have intrinsically created a robust organizational culture (Calderón and Serna, 2009).

Although organizational culture indeed emphasizes some human values, philosophy, myths, and various concepts that the members of a given company share (Serrate, Portuondo, Sánchez and Suarez, 2014), it is also true that this culture is not palpable. That is, all these factors can only be observed indirectly and, at best, their effects and/or consequences in companies can be understood (Edwards, 2013). Culture cannot exist without human beings, which is why human resources are the most important element in a company. Human resources are so important that the Cambridge Ultimate Business Dictionary defines organizational culture as the attitudes and working conveniences agreed upon among the employees of a company (Cambridge University Press, 2023). Undoubtedly, organizational culture is complex and dynamic, but human resources favor multiple aspects that favor organizational culture, such as talent, diversity, and inclusion. In addition, if these human resources are specialized then some factors of organizational culture that can benefit are innovation, productivity based on new technologies, decision making, strengthening of interactions between employees, and an improvement in the perception that employees have of their company, to name a few (Nazarian et al., 2017).

The transcendence and relevance of this study on the organizational culture of SMEs lie in the importance of their specialized human resources. This human capital, seen as a whole, and through an economy based on the level of knowledge, is a key element that not only favors the economic, social, scientific, and technological development of a given country or region but also allows for generating the foundations for a robust business culture (National Economic Council 2011; Araújo and Teixeira, 2014). However, the intellectual human resources available to a country are limited, and even more so those considered to be of high level. Therefore, it is of utmost importance to know the specialized intellectual pool that a given country or region has and will have since today's young people will undoubtedly be responsible for and leaders of some Mexican SMEs.

BACKGROUND

Culture" is defined by multidimensional and holistic approaches, including artistic, social, political, and educational expressions. The term "culture" refers to a relatively solid set of beliefs, values, and behaviors practiced and shared by society. This conception is derived from social anthropology as a framework for understanding "primitive" societies (Kotter and Heskett, 1992) and used in the context of organizations through the development of motivated personnel, committed to a common set of values, beliefs, and assumptions (Denison, 1996) cited by Garcia, Hernandez, Vargas and Cuevas (2012). The term culture refers to the understanding of the arts, sciences, and other intellectual achievements; applied to the organization it is the individual belief and practice influenced by the social context in which the company operates. Guberman, Fournier, Belleau, Beeman and Gervais (1994) consider some factors that affect organizations and particularly their organizational culture, these are: 1) the structure and manner of management, 2) reporting to the members of the organization, 3) reporting to salaried workers, 4) reporting of personal life, and 5) reporting to management. In addition to these factors, the availability of resources, business line, country of origin of the owners and decision-makers, organizational and hierarchical structure, level of education of the staff as a whole, regiбn, and location of the company can also be considered.

Marcondes-Leite and Cristiane de Oliveira (2014) point out that organizational culture is a set of characteristics pre-established and determined by the company, being these, beliefs, values, ethics, principles, and norms that, in turn, have an influence on the behavior of the organization's members for the achievement of the organization's final results. The expression "organizational culture" encompasses the functioning and formal organization of work, the division and assignment of work, the hierarchy of members, the distribution of power, and certain values and representations of the organization's members (Guberman et al., 1994). In addition to the above, for Robbins and Coulter (2005), organizational culture is an important characteristic of a learning organization and includes some aspects such as strong mutual relationships, a sense of community, and caring. Dextras (2014) states that the concept of organizational culture has been the subject of a large number of works that diverge between the definition adopted and the types of culture, this is partly because of the elements that characterize this concept and, in particular, the fact that it is elusive, complex, paradoxical, dynamic and abstract. In this sense, Lima, Fleith de Medeiros, Carvalho and Meurer (2013) state that organizations need to perpetuate the set of assumptions that represent their image and identity, using organizational management and communication strategies, which contributes to the dissemination and promotion of culture within the organizations, being able to ensure the appropriation of such culture or identity in people within the organization itself.

For Wu (2008), organizational culture is considered the sum of the decisions made in the past or the interactions between the critical mass of the organization. Dextras (2014) defines organizational culture from two perspectives: a) The "symbolic" current, which refers to the conception of organizational culture as a social construct, formed by visions of the world, as part of symbolisms contributed from the social culture itself, being this more than simple habits or unreasoned ways of acting and revolving around more structured products such as strategic plans (financial, marketing, purchasing, sales, growth, etc.), production programs, development projects (personnel, infrastructure, infrastructure, etc.), production programs, development projects (personnel, infrastructure, etc.), production programs, development projects (personnel, infrastructure, research), among others; b) The "functionalist" current states that organizational culture can be influenced and/or motivated by top management, where senior decision-makers define and/or redefine the symbolic means on which organizational culture is based, such as attitudes, beliefs, behavioral norms, perceptions, assumptions and values.

Organizational Culture Models (OCM)

There are several models to establish the dimensions of organizational culture, but it is essential to use one that focuses on the search for the key cultural dimensions. No model is completely inclusive or correct, but the one selected must describe the reality accurately, be valid and also be able to integrate and organize most of the proposed dimensions (Hernández, Fernández and Baptista, 2010) and, above all, that through its study and application, the desired results are obtained. To generate the measurement instrument, it was considered that organizational culture is generally formed by the assumptions that people have and by the interpretations they make of situations and that personnel tend to act as they think. It is also considered that the essence of management by top-level decision-makers involves a clear understanding of where an organization's efforts should be directed to obtain results at the lowest cost. For this to happen, it is important to have a broad understanding of the ideal and real organizational culture as perceived by the members of the organization and to generate strategies to arrive at the optimal culture.

Studies on Organizational Culture

The studies to know the organizational culture in Mexico by García, Hernández, Vargas, and Cuevas (2012) consider the dominant and preferred organizational culture in the educational field under the Competent Values Model (CVM) of Cameron and Quinn (2010), according to this model the products presented in the two institutions denominated as recent and old creation showed a mixture of values in their quadrants, resulting predominantly in the two institutions the current market culture and as preferred culture the clan culture in the recently created university and adhocratic in the old university. The authors considered the CVM to be useful because of its ample evidence; the evaluation instrument (OCAI) allowed them to know the cultures of the institutions so that the managers could organize their competencies to change, thus providing them with the possibility of becoming efficient, productive, and competitive organizations. In the Colombian context, Martinez (2010) conducted an exploratory study on organizational culture and performance with a sample of 11 companies (nine in the manufacturing sector, one in the extractive sector, and one in the financial sector). His research showed that companies are framed in the sense of "mission", which is associated with the variables of sales growth, profitability and return on assets, employee satisfaction, overall company performance, and innovation rating.

Measuring Organizational Culture

The analysis of organizational culture requires a variety of instruments and strategies to approach the object of study (Scott et al., 2003), generating importance and great interest on the part of some academics and political agents in carrying out a quantitative measurement of organizational culture (Scott, 2005). Some measurement methods are presented below:

Observation-based approach, either simple or composite.
Determining values, beliefs, symbols, rituals, stories, and ceremonies.
Through the use of non-probabilistic sampling techniques such as accidental or convenience, intentional, typical case, and expert, among others.
The evaluation of the organizational philosophy and structure and the organizational management system (vision, mission, values, policies, objectives, goals, goals, actions, etc.).

In this context, Scott et al (2003) made a complete review of the different measurement instruments that exist in the literature and that have shown good results in the measurement of organizational culture (Table 1).

Table 1. Instruments for measuring organizational culture

Name and Key References	Culture Dimensions and Outcome Measurements	Strengths	Limitations
Competing Values Framework - Competency value framework (Cameron & Freeman, 1991; Gerowitz et al., 1996; Gerowitz, 1998).	Organizational climate, leadership style, personnel union system (synergic), prioritization of objectives. Assessment of results in different types of culture, described as clans, adhocracy, hierarchy, and types of markets. Usually, each organization has more than one type of culture.	Simple and quick to complete, high degree of validation, used in multiple studies, solid theoretical basis, validates the congruence and strength of organizational culture.	Few classifications of the types of organizations.
Quality Improvement Implementation Survey - Quality Improvement Implementation Survey (Shortell et al., 2000).	Organizational character, management style, cohesion, prioritization of objectives, and rewards. Assessment of results in four different types of organizational culture: group, development, hierarchy, and rational.	Simple and quick to complete, a high degree of validation, used by leading teams, adds the dimension of rewards.	Limited classification of types of organizations.
Organizational Culture Inventory - Organizational Culture Inventory (Cooke & Lafferty, 1987; Thomas et al., 1990, Seago, 1997; Ingersoll et al., 2000).	Shared norms and expectations that guide the thinking and behavior of group members, resulting in 12 styles of thinking of individuals within the group: humanistic-serving, affiliative, permissive, conventional, dependent, avoidant, oppositional, power-hungry, competitive, competent/perfectionist, performer, autonomous. The analysis of these 12 styles results in three factors - personal/safety culture, satisfaction culture, and work/safety culture.	Good validation spectrum, widely used, graphical illustration of the results.	Analysis of results on a limited number of aspects of culture, initial printing that is lengthy and difficult to complete, under copyrights, and can be costly to use.
Harrison's Organizational Ideology Questionnaire - Harrison's Organizational Ideology Questionnaire (Harrison, 1975; Ott, 1989; Litwinenko & Cooper, 1994).	Validates the ideology of the organization in terms of potential orientation, roles, tasks, and individuals.	A good level of validity covers existing and preferred cultures.	Limited types of organizational culture.

continues on following page

Table 1. Continued

Name and Key References	Culture Dimensions and Outcome Measurements	Strengths	Limitations
Practice Culture Questionnaire - Practical Culture Questionnaire (Stevenson, 2000).	Attitudes towards and commitment to, quality improvement and resistance to change.	Detailed validation approach.	The origin of the items is not clear, or generalizable outside the United Kingdom. It superficially examines the manifestations of culture.
MacKenzie´s Culture Questionnaire – MacKenzie Culture Questionnaire (MacKenzie, 1995).	Employee commitment, attitudes towards innovation, beliefs about innovation, attitudes towards change, conflict resolution style, management style, confidence in leadership, openness and trust, teamwork and cooperation, action orientation, human resource orientation, customer orientation, and organizational direction.	Simple to complete.	The origin of the items is unclear, and scientific properties are unknown.
Survey of Organizational Culture - Organizational Culture Survey (Tucker, Mc Coy& Evans, 1990).	Describes organizational culture in terms of 13 dimensions: customer orientation, employee orientation, stakeholder congruence, mission impact, management maturity/depth, decision making/ autonomy, communication/openness, human scale, incentive/motivation, cooperation versus competition, organizational congruence, performance under pressure, S-theory/T-theory.	Detailed quantitative work, conducted as part of development, has been used in both the public and private sectors.	It has only been used in the United States of America and is mostly used by leaders and executive managers, rather than at all levels of the workforce.

Source: Adapted from Scott et al. (2003).

With the application of these instruments, organizational culture diagnoses are carried out to establish which is the prevailing culture in the organizations. The following measurement instruments to assess organizational culture are mentioned by Pemberton (1995): 1) "The Organizational Culture Assessment Inventory" by Cameron and Quinn (2006) 2) "The Organizational Culture Inventory" by Cooke and Lafferty (1989) and 3) "The Organizational Culture Instrument" by Van der Post, Conning and Smit (1997). As previously mentioned, the present study will allow validating of a measurement instrument that will allow knowing the real and ideal cultures, understanding this relationship is fundamental, since, as it has been stated, from the determination of the gap or existing gap between both cultures, necessary actions will be proposed to close this gap, This is the phase where strategies must be considered to bring the two cultures closer as soon as possible in communication (transmission of the culture), education (improvement of the required competencies), alignment (security in policies, procedures, and systems to achieve the optimal culture), implementation (execution), follow-up of the tasks included in the strategy, as well as the evaluation of the partial and total results achieved. In this context, the generated instrument is based on the organizational culture assessment inventory of Cameron and Quinn (2010), which considers two cultures: current and preferred. The dominant characteristics of the proposed instrument are 1) Achievement of results. 2) Profit consciousness. 3) Staffing. 4) Planning. 5) Control. 6) Coordination. 7) Criticism. 8) Communication. 9) Conflict management and 10) Creativity. With a five-point Likert scale, two categories are generated for both ideal and actual culture. With these characteristics, the data collection instrument measures the actual culture and the ideal approach. In this way, the dominant characteristics are important to give context to the following information:

Achievement of results: emphasizes action taken on important problems.

Profit consciousness: refers to considerations between expenses and profits.

Personal: considers the full, productive, and safe development of the same.

Planning: it is based on administrative concepts and logic, on analysis of specific facts and situations.

Control: It is evaluated and fed back for the maintenance of goals and the search for continuous improvement.

Coordination: describes the work relationships for maximum productive interaction in the different segments of the organization.

Criticism: it is oriented to the necessary help for the progress of the activities.

Communication: is the necessary information that permeates in all directions, oriented, mainly, to the resolution of differences.

Conflict management: it is oriented to the study of the situation where the reasons are to be examined and their negotiation to reach solutions.

Creativity: focuses on people's suggestions to carry out work experiments in innovation and/or creativity.

MAIN FOCUS OF THE CHAPTER

Issues, Controversies, Problems

Skilled labor at all levels is a determining element for the success of organizations. In Mexico, SMEs generally have negative characteristics such as low financing, high failure rates, partners acting as managers, the labor force being satisfied with family members, accounting management without professionals, lack of an administrative and productive structure, lack of skilled labor (essential to create a positive environment in the organizational culture), no level of innovation and training and, finally, dependence on large companies. The sector where SMEs mostly operate is the commercial sector, followed by services and finally manufacturing, which shows that few SMEs operate in this sector due to a lack of technology, financing, and professionals in their workforce (Saavedra and Hernández, 2008). By not having an evaluation and planning in the creation of the SME, it is deduced that it will lack professionals in the workforce. The role of human capital, training, and technology transfer is becoming more widely recognized. This means of technology transfer comes in a variety of forms including, among others, training specifically aimed at technology transfer management (Grosse, 1996), the advice of consultants (Bessant and Rush, 1995), the training of students, with the international training of such students taking prominence (Nataraajan and Chawla, 1994), the exchange or transfer of personnel (Hicks, 1993), and, of course, the informal relationships that occur between the different scientific levels (Bozeman and Papadakis, 1995).

The issue of a relationship between a country's level of education1 and its socioeconomic development has been the subject of many studies. The suspicion is based on the fact that countries with higher social welfare are those with higher levels of education (Lucas 1988; Romer 1986, 1990a, 1990b; Welch 1970). In numerical terms, the correlation between education and economic development is said to be high and positive (Gómez and Sánchez, 2005). Countless studies have also pointed to education as a preponderant component of the economic development of a given country or region (Aghion and Howitt, 1997). Moreover, it has been shown that the so-called intellectual capital, generated through education, is an indispensable factor that enables and favors economic growth (Khurram, Wandschneider, and Wunnava, 2007; Webber, 2002). However, intellectual capital by itself does not create value or generate growth; it needs to be combined, simultaneously, with other factors of production (Moon and Gum, 2006). It has been shown that learning (education process) is positively correlated with the per capita growth rate of countries. However, the process of education somehow involves sacrificing current earnings to obtain a higher level of future earnings. With this premise, Bils and Klenow (2000) showed that economic growth implies education, rather than education implying economic growth.

However, in any modern society, education has become a priority, since it has become a fundamental factor to allow, among many things, its development. This is because education is involved with every one of the components and issues that can be identified; from economic ones, of course, those related to social coexistence and even achieving a successful organizational culture. Therefore, Kostoff et al (2005) assume that the dynamics of both the academic performance of the student population and the proportion of professional personnel in the productive apparatus of a given country or region are indicators of the quantity and quality of the human capital that a country has: This author asserts that education persistently increases the efficiency of the labor force by fostering democracy and that human capital facilitates the absorption of superior technologies from first world countries. Indeed, technological absorption is supposed to be especially important at the secondary and higher education levels. Moreover, education creates better conditions for a good working environment thus improving health and generating social equality (Stijns, 2006; Aghion, Caroli and García-Peñalosa, 1999). Although an increasing number of countries are investing large amounts of money in human resources training, quality has become one of the fundamental concerns of education (Hanushek and Luque, 2003). In this sense, the countries that achieved considerable levels of education in the 20th century are also those that have had a more prominent position in their level of economic development, even in circumstances of scarce endowment of natural resources in proportion to their territory and/or population (Neira Gómez, 2007). This behavior is because the satisfaction of society's expectations and needs about education depends on the quality of its personnel, programs, and students, as well as its infrastructure and academic environment (CONACYT, 2004).

Therefore, and without a doubt, educational quality is currently an important component of human capital when comparing a sample of countries at the international level. However, Guisán and Neira (2001) consider that the variables used as a proxy for human capital in empirical studies are imperfect measures of the educational component since they measure the quantity but not the quality of education, which could weaken the usefulness of international comparisons. This is especially true when quantitative data with very little disaggregation is used. There is strong evidence that the quality of human capital is very important for individual success and nations as a whole. However, it has been far from easy to observe such quality, in some countries, consistently. Consequently, much of the evidence on the determination of this quality has been restricted to the United States of America

(Hanushek and Luque, 2003). It is here that investment in specialized human resources makes sense since innovation, development, and implementation of new technologies rest on these. UNESCO (2012b: 65) concludes, among other things, in one of its reports that the so-called development education currently imposes itself as the convergence point for different types of education focused on different aspects of society (including organizational culture). Therefore, having workers with satisfactory skills and/or competencies is a primary need for the progress and creation of a healthy and successful working environment. Specialized education and its complementary training, with organizational culture, are a clear alternative for workers with visible knowledge in the subject and who also wish to get involved in this sector, even for people who have not had the opportunity to update themselves with more specialized courses. Moreover, human resources who already know about this topic also need continuous and adequate education and training to meet the growing demands of their competencies and work environments (International Labour Organization, 2011).

The main lessons learned summarized by the authors (Wiser et al., 2002: 125-126) on the collaborative participation of the different actors benefited from a successful work environment were: a) Successful fundraising and, b) Consistent messages (i.e., instead of competing, collaborative participation was sought, which strengthened the effectiveness of the message). On the other hand, these authors mention the following challenges of collaborative work: a) The identification of common goals and interests; balancing opinions, objectives, interests, and all those factors immersed in the different actors is a complicated job that must be achieved. For example, some civil society groups may prioritize education in general, while others do not. Consequently, with the different companies involved, there may be a conflict of interest. b) Agreement on education materials: There must be an appropriate balance so as not to have too many revisions in the approval of materials. The members must be educated in professional training as well as the right amount without exceeding or missing some of them and, c) Maintaining the projected objective: significant changes in general understanding and acceptance cannot be achieved in the short term because capital is involved and consumer awareness is a long term process.

SOLUTIONS AND RECOMMENDATIONS

The shortage of qualified personnel and skilled labor can be solved. Young people are the most important sector for the formation of specialized human resources in multiple areas of knowledge (UN, 2005). In turn, the International Labour Organization (2011) recommends the following actions for technicians and skilled manual workers: a) technical and vocational education and training; b) apprenticeships; and

c) providers of innovative technologies. Education is essential to promote the use and development of technologies that produce better manufacturing processes, it is important to mention that education on these issues allows individuals to improve their ability to cope with the basic principle of sustainable development: “meet the needs of the present without compromising the needs of future generations” (United Nations, 1987: 54). Undoubtedly, education is seen as a powerful means of social change, plays a vital role in the development of sustainable growth, creates awareness, trains professionals and scientists who will develop the next generations of technologies. Together, education establishes trust and, effectively, trains in the use of new technologies, trains analysts who design effective policies for industry development, and instructs the people who will provide advice and support to future industry customers. Therefore, and as mentioned above, education is a fundamental factor in building a successful organizational culture.

Thus, this paper takes as input the information from a survey conducted among high school students in the equidistant region of the State of Tlaxcala (Mexico) to find out, among other things, their affinity when choosing a career, some of the implications of this choice and the main causes that lead them to decide to abandon their studies. All this, of course, is to learn about aspects or factors that can influence the construction of an organizational culture. The survey was applied in all the grades of study contemplated in the upper secondary level, to capture the feelings of the population under study and to avoid an evident bias in the collection of information. The questionnaire, previously designed, was applied to the four types of support defined in higher secondary education and located in the geographical area previously defined for the State of Tlaxcala, Mexico: Federal High School, State High School, Autonomous High School, and so-called Private High School (Secretaría de Educación Pública, 2019; Secretaría de Educación Pública, 2018). Following the survey, an interview was conducted with both the owners of a maquiladora company2, located in Tlaxcala (Mexico) and its production process managers.

This interview was conducted personally and consisted of three sections with 10 questions each (the first section dealt with the beginnings of their company, the second section asked them about technological changes and their adoption in their company, and the third section was created to know their opinion about the adoption of specialized human resources in their company and if these have been a preponderant factor for their company to have survived, for more than 50 years, the technological changes previously mentioned in section two of the interview. In other words, the purpose of this interview is to find out, from their perspective, what they consider to have been the main reasons why their family business has remained in the market. In other words, this study focuses on learning more about the problems that this family business has had to overcome in terms of adopting scientific and/ or technological human capital to improve the quality of its production processes.

Moreover, the purpose of this interview was to find out if they consider that the hiring of qualified personnel in science and technology has been preponderant to improve the quality of their production processes and to justify the existence of a successful work environment in an increasingly competitive market segment over time.

Consequently, the results obtained will contribute, to a great extent, to understand the importance of the transfer of science and/or technology, through this specialized human capital, which is indispensable for any Mexican company that today bets on cutting-edge innovation and the creation of a solid organizational culture. We also glimpse the efforts that this family business has had to make for the adoption of specialized personnel, which are trained in the territory that receives an also limited budget from the Federal Government and that will be, in the not too distant future, the lever arm for some companies located in this geographical area of the State of Tlaxcala, Mexico.

In this way, and for the total number of students who were studying in higher secondary education in the State of Tlaxcala (56,570 in public and private modalities), during the period 2017-2018, a significant sample was obtained3 (Pérez, 2017) of 382 students who, in turn, made up the population under study. As already mentioned, the information was collected through a questionnaire, which was applied personally to the student susceptible to being interviewed (this strategy was used to reduce the lack of response from the students interviewed). Based on the four modalities mentioned above, and given that the information was obtained through stratified random sampling with proportional allocation (de León, Pérez & Boza, 2016), we proceeded to carry out a statistical exploration of the results obtained and, with this, to carry out the interpretation of these results. To carry out this interpretation, the data were standardized, that is, a change of scale was made (all the data were captured in an Excel sheet and simultaneously transferred to an ordinal scale). This change of scale had the purpose of detecting those variables that most directly influenced school dropout for students who would opt for a bachelor's degree in the area of science and/or technology. Undoubtedly, knowing the main aspects of school dropout in an area or region makes it possible to justify the level of human resources that have a vocation for science and technology. Based on the latter, it makes sense to ask the following question Does the raw material of companies to improve their production processes, from the point of view of training specialized human resources, justify the survival of a company that has lasted more than 50 years in the manufacturing market? Moreover, how is this raw material, at least in the short term, to respond to the scientific and/or technological needs of companies that have managed to survive these dizzying scientific and technological changes? To identify the most significant variables that justify the dropout of the students defined above, a logit probability model was used (Gujarati & Porter, 2010; Greene, 2012). In this context, the dependent variable for our logit model was the dichotomous response (Yes or

No), of the students interviewed, to question 22a: Do you plan to study a degree that is related to science and technology? Thus, the independent variables were the answers obtained for the remaining 26 questions, with their respective items, that made up the questionnaire.

RESULTS AND DISCUSSION

Of the statistically significant sample, the sex of the respondents was distributed as follows: 56% (214) females, 44% (168) males; the average age, at the beginning of the school cycle, was 16.4 years; the percentage of students attending classes both in the morning and the afternoon was, in both cases, less than 4%; but in no way was this due to their performing paid activities. As for the place of birth of the respondents, 86% (with relative participation of 80% for men and 82% for women) were born in the State of Tlaxcala, Mexico. These results imply that this federative entity educates a considerable number of students born in one of its 60 municipalities (Instituto Nacional de Estadística y Geografía, 2015). Concerning the choice of their current studies, that is, at the time of choosing a career and being accepted for the studies they chose, it was observed that the answers obtained by the students interviewed were more assertive in the case of women than for men (see Figure 1).

In Figure 1, the panorama is surprising in the case of men, since 46.2% of them do not pursue studies related to a profile similar to the one they wanted to study, or their choice was due to inertia because they were not motivated to pursue such studies. Undoubtedly, this leads these students to pursue studies in areas of knowledge that they did not want to study beforehand and, since they are not motivated for the studies they chose, it is more likely that they will not complete those studies. Moreover, this result implies, among other things, that a large number of the human resources who complete their studies, and who in the short term will be employed in the SMEs of some municipalities in the State of Tlaxcala, will be people who are not very motivated with their studies and who, even when they could pursue other studies, will graduate with a profile that they did not want.

The above behavior was related, in turn, to the fact that 58% of all students considered that their performance has been good (with a relative participation of 63% for women and 52% for men). On the other hand, the results of the survey showed students who do not have a vocation for their current academic preparation and the selection of their studies was more on the recommendation of a person or a family member (see Figure 2). These results do not favor the future executives of SMEs and much less the creation of a solid organizational culture, since these companies lack, on the one hand, highly qualified personnel who are continuously innovating to make them highly competitive and, of course, who provide immediate answers to their main problems and, on the other hand, that such personnel is realistic with their achievements. Furthermore, it can be said that the future employees and/or executives of the SMEs located in the geographical area of the State of Tlaxcala (Mexico) will be employees and/or executives who from an early stage of their studies did not feel the vocation to pursue their studies and rather the choice of the same was more for following a tradition, influence or family recommendation than for their vacation.

Figure 1. Distribution by sex for the affinity of the students interviewed at the time of choosing a career
Source: Author's own elaboration.

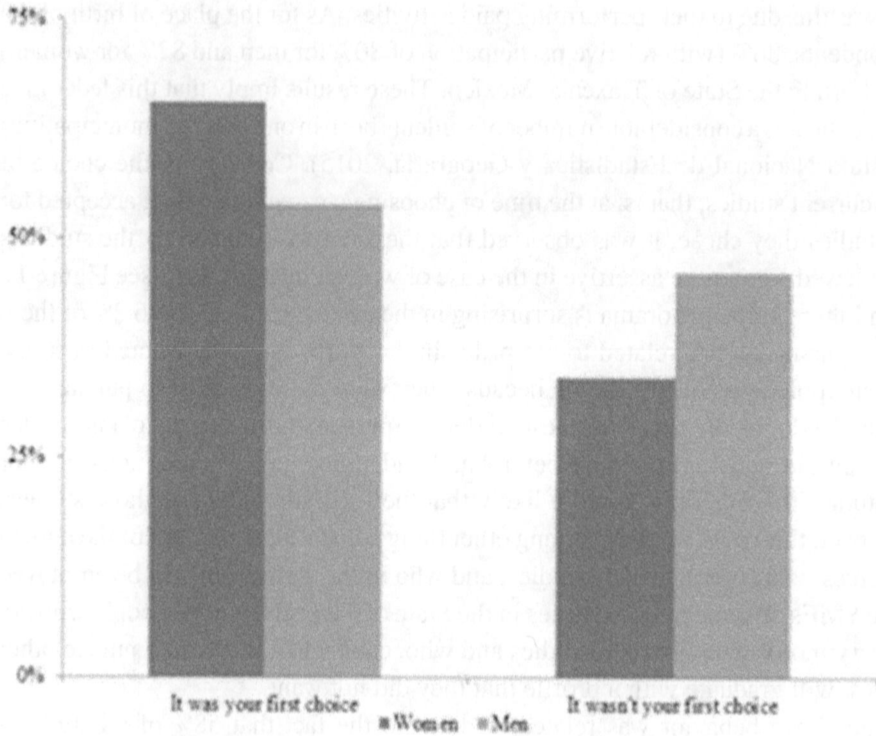

Regarding the question of whether the students interviewed would like to study a degree that is related to a topic related to science and/or technology, the results obtained can be seen in Table 2. In general, it can be seen that only 4 out of 10 students (both women and men) have already thought about pursuing a degree related to science or technology. This result undoubtedly has an impact on the SMEs in the region because they simply lack personnel who are satisfied with their work specialized in science, personnel who carry out technological innovations, and qualified personnel who acquire and transfer new technologies implemented in other countries, which, although they are not developed locally, can be assimilated by the qualified personnel that make up or lead some SMEs in this geographical area of the state of Tlaxcala (Mexico).

Figure 2. Results for the choice of current studies
Source: Author's own elaboration.

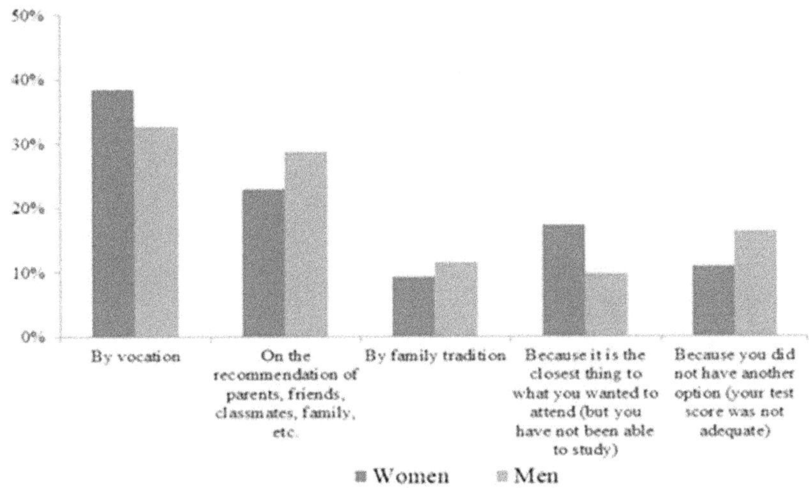

Table 2. Results for the preference of a degree that is related to science and technology

Sex	Yes	No	Unspecified	Total
Women	42.5	51.9	5.6	100.0
Men	43.3	50.2	6.5	100.0
Unspecified	42.3	50.4	7.3	100.0
Total	42.3	50.4	7.3	100.0

Source: Author's own elaboration.

This last result has an impact in the sense that students are already predisposed to face an adverse panorama in their academic vocation and this can undoubtedly increase the decision to drop out of school (see Figure 3). Consequently, and as has been mentioned throughout this paper, these human resources will not facilitate the creation of a solid organizational culture (due to the lack of certain human values), they do not favor technology transfer, which suggests that the innovation developed in SMEs in the Tlaxcala region (Mexico) will be limited. As a result, these companies will be uncompetitive and their lifespan may be considerably affected.

Figure 3. Main reasons why they would abandon their current studies
Source: Author's own elaboration.

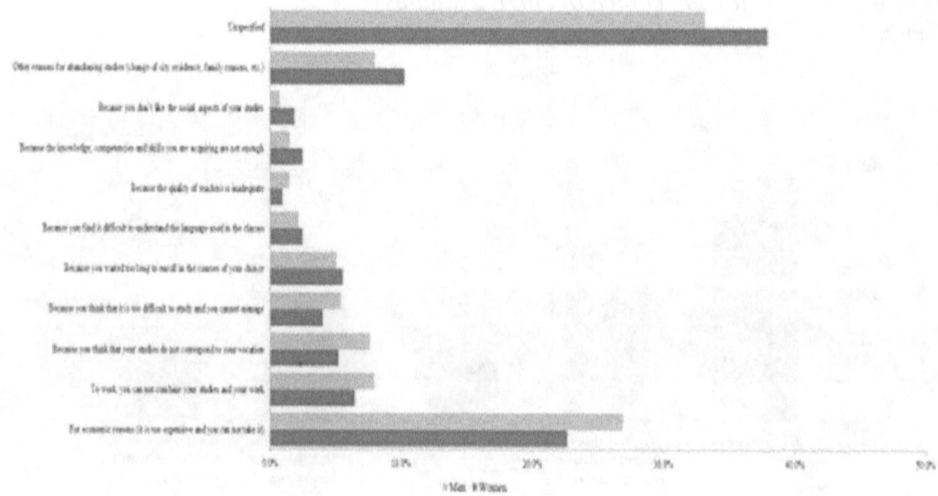

The statistically significant items in the dichotomous logistic model referred to only three questions of the applied questionnaire (see Table 3).

Table 3. Significant variables for the dichotomous logistic model

Variables in the Equation	B	E.T.	Wald Statistics	Degrees of Freedom	Significance	Exp(B)
22b_A(1)	2.122	0.978	4.709	1	0.030	8.351
22b_A(2)	2.305	1.038	4.925	1	0.026	10.020
22b_A(3)	3.623	1.266	8.186	1	0.004	37.448
22b_A(4)	2.296	1.033	4.941	1	0.026	9.938
22c_A(1)	3.259	1.626	4.016	1	0.045	26.021
20F	-0.377	0.156	5.855	1	0.016	0.686
20E	0.314	0.143	4.858	1	0.028	1.369

Source: Author's own elaboration.

In Table 3, the first of these, question 22b, asks the following question: Why would you not study a degree related to science and technology? For this item, four of its five items were significant (22b_A(1): The curricula are very difficult; 22b_A(2): The labor field in the scientific/technological area in Tlaxcala is very bad; 22b_A(3): There is no prestige in the Mexican scientific/technological area and, 22b_A(4): I plan to study another degree that has nothing to do with science/technology). This last result is not accidental, since the instrument for data collection was precisely designed to find out why students in the upper secondary level in Tlaxcala, Mexico would not choose a scientific or technological degree. Likewise, these results are conclusive, because the image of the Mexican scientist, as well as his environment and prestige, is not valued positively by young students, which will undoubtedly lead them to decide to study a degree that is not related to science and technology.

The second statistically significant item, question 22c, was defined as "What do you plan to do when you finish your current studies? In this item, one of the five items turned out to be significant for our study (22C_A(1): Continue my studies, preferably in a public university). Undoubtedly, this is good news for SMEs in Tlaxcala (Mexico), since at the moment there is a clear disposition of the students interviewed to prepare themselves better academically. In the third item, question 20, two of the seven items considered were statistically significant: 20E) You feel worn out by the education you are taking and, 20F) In general, you feel integrated in the cultural and social life of your institution. The significance of these items allows us to appreciate more specific future work to learn about the characteristics of the students considered in this study. In the same way, item 22b revealed that the items that would increase the probability (a betting ratio greater than 1) that the students interviewed would not choose a scientific degree were in the first place because the Mexican scientific/technological area has no prestige (item 22b_A3 and with the highest betting ratio). Secondly, because the labor field of the scientific/technological area in Tlaxcala (Mexico) is very bad (item 22b_A2); thirdly, because they plan to study another degree that has nothing to do with science/technology (item 22b_A4); and finally, because the curricula are very difficult (item 22b_A1).

On the other hand, the interview conducted with the owners of the manufacturing plant and the managers of this plant, located in the State of Tlaxcala (Mexico), allowed us to learn about the importance that specialized human resources have had in all its production processes. In this way, and for the first section of the interview, the owners (who today are still husband and wife) mentioned that when they made the decision to create a manufacturing company it was more out of monetary necessity and that a large part of the family members was part of it (including brothers, cousins, children, nephews, nieces, nephews and currently grandchildren). In other words, all the processes involved in its production were supervised by a family member, and, in turn, all the processes to integrate a garment (design, cutting, tailoring, assembly, packaging, distribution, etc.) were carried out by family members. For many years, more than a decade, the family business was managed and sustained by people who had no specialized studies, no training courses, no marketing experience, no accountant, and no logistics for the delivery of their merchandise (garments under previous design, uniforms for multiple legally established companies, uniforms for multiple legally established companies, etc.), uniforms for multiple legally established companies, uniforms for security companies, school uniforms, among others), did not have a reliable payment system for their employees, did not have a credit system, did not have specialized machinery, did not have personnel (especially women) who had the necessary experience to handle complex sewing machinery, among others.

As time went by, this family-owned maquila company significantly increased the number of employees and, of course, sales increased along with profits. As a result, they purchased a property that they later converted to exclusively house all of their maquila activities. Already in this second decade, some production departments began to take shape and, above all, they started to assign a responsible person, usually a family member, to each of these production departments. However, their production processes were still supervised and executed by poorly qualified personnel and the same conditions, previously mentioned, still prevailed for the family business. The owners of this company explained that it was not until the third decade that they began to see the fruits of their work and effort, since in the previous years a large part of their earnings were destined to support their family, the studies of their children (who grew to 9), the purchase of a means of transportation that was better suited for the delivery of their merchandise, the payment of their workers, the adaptation of the land previously acquired and, above all, the visit and personal attention to new clients.

For the second section of the interview with the owners of the manufacturing company, they agreed that they envisioned at least two very important stages in their family business. The first one was at the beginning of their business because it was at this stage when they lacked everything (both specialized personnel and specialized and modern machines to achieve better quality in their garments). The second stage, at the beginning of the third decade of their business because it was at this stage when they had the opportunity, and economic solvency, to meet the needs they had already identified (such as hiring an accountant, personnel who knew how to operate modern sewing machines, personnel who knew how to repair these machines, advice for payroll, specialized personnel for the design and execution of better logistics in their production processes, among others), but for fear of getting into debt with a financial loan and the lack of advice from a person with financial knowledge, they had not covered them.

The owners also explained that they were aware of the technological changes that were taking place to improve the maquila industry, but that there were also two main reasons why they were unable to adopt these technological changes immediately: first, again, there was a marked limitation of economic capital, since the purchase of new machinery entailed great expense, and second, the lack of specialized personnel who knew how to operate these state-of-the-art machines. They commented that for many years they did not change their sewing machines and that when some of these machines broke down they hired the services of an outside technician to fix them. In addition, they pointed out that their personnel, being largely family members, did not receive any type of training or specialization course, since the information was transmitted verbally from person to person. This type of dynamic had a negative impact on their entire production process, but especially on the economic aspect since the production process was slowed down and logistics, in general, were affected. All of this translated into losses for the family maquila company.

On the other hand, the owners of the family maquila company said that being a rural community where they established their company, a large part of it when they decided to create their company, lacked education, much less could they count people with a Bachelor's degree, let alone a Master's or Doctorate. Undoubtedly, the lack of these specialized human resources had a negative impact on the full development of the companies located in the region mentioned in this study. In this context, the owners commented that even if these types of qualified human resources had existed at that time, they would not have been their first choice to hire them and improve their production processes. This is because the adoption of these human resources would have resulted, in turn, in multiple expenses. In addition, the owners argued that for approximately three decades, all their problems were solved by a family member, which led to considerable savings, which they preferred to use for their employees' New Year's Eve party.

It was not until the third part of the interview that the impact of the training and adoption of specialized human resources by this maquila-oriented family business could be appreciated. That is, in this third part of the interview, the opinions of both the owners of the company and the heads of each production department (there are currently five departments in this family business: raw materials department; cutting and sewing department; maquila department; sales department; and new products department) were already taken into consideration. As was to be expected, the opinions of the employees were not very homogeneous to the opinion of the owners, that is to say, the perspective they had of each other was very palpable and differentiable at this stage of the interview. In the first instance, the owners thought that specialized human resources are indispensable and even necessary, but only for large companies that can pay for their services without any problem. On the other hand, employees felt that it is difficult to be hired in small companies because they are also indifferent to the organizational culture that should prevail in any company. In addition, employees felt that small companies that have their origins in the family are more secretive about hiring new and specialized personnel.

Where there was a consensus between owners and employees was that companies lack highly qualified personnel to improve all their production processes. Both parties agreed that the adoption of new technologies is also indispensable for all those companies that wish to improve the quality of their products and, of course, maximize their profits by increasing production. The owners again emphasized that they were aware of the technological changes but that for a long time, they couldn't assimilate them, mainly due to economic limitations. Regarding the hiring of highly specialized personnel, the owners commented that the absence of such human resources in the region where they established their company led them to hire personnel whose experience was empirical. Employees responded that they preferred to look for a job in large companies, which are located outside the region where the owners established their companies. This is because they believe that these large companies offer more competitive salaries, high benefits, and better opportunities for growth and career development. Undoubtedly, this behavior does not favor the organizational culture of small companies, mainly due to the lack of loyalty and identity to the company among potential employees.

At the time, the owners had to decide to adopt new technologies and hire specialized personnel to increase the quality of all their production processes. Currently, they have also modern machines for the production of their garments, they have personnel (mostly women) to operate these machines, they have hired an accountant, they have better transportation for the transfer of their goods, the infrastructure of their company is continuously maintained and modernized, They have a line of credit in a bank, they have continuous training for all their personnel and, perhaps most importantly, they are using new technologies, such as Augmented Reality, adapted so that all their personnel involved in a maquila process can produce garments more quickly and with higher quality. This adaptation process has not been easy, say both owners and employees, as it has entailed a major change in people's way of thinking, but, above all, of appreciating technological changes and specialized personnel as something good for the company.

On the owners' side, this change in mentality has been in the sense of replacing family members (mainly because they are of legal age, have formed an independent family and their main efforts are oriented towards satisfying the needs of their direct family) with personnel from outside the company. In addition, the owners argued that the dynamics of these technological changes have forced them to hire qualified personnel, i.e., they commented that if it had not been necessary to update some of their production processes, they would not have hired specialized personnel. In other words, the owners specified that they do not consider the existence of their company in the market as a direct result of the adoption of specialized personnel in science or technology. Rather, they consider that the permanence of their company has been the result of hard work by several generations of their family and that the adoption of scientific or technological personnel has been mainly because a family member, even if his or her studies have allowed it, has made the decision to look for better opportunities in another region of the country.

In this context, the employees pointed out that the labor situation in the State of Tlaxcala is complicated and that they have been forced to be hired by small companies even when the economic retribution is not what they expect for a person with their skills and academic knowledge. They also emphasized that they stay in these small companies until they find a better opportunity in a larger company, even if it is located at a great distance from their current home. In addition, they agreed that if they had previously known how difficult it was to get a job in their area of knowledge (generally engineering), they would have opted for another university career with better job opportunities. They also agreed that the permanence of a family-owned maquila company in the market for more than 50 years was not due to the hiring of qualified personnel, but rather to the persistence and economic necessity of the family. Regarding the adoption of new technologies, they said that although they are accessible to understand for the personnel and are also quite low cost, they will take a little longer to be adopted because the employees prefer personal contact to an application that many times they do not know how to use.

FUTURE RESEARCH DIRECTIONS

Today, the world is facing urgent challenges, among them the accelerated depletion of specialized human resources. Decisions made today will undoubtedly have repercussions in the not-too-distant future. In this context, education will play a preponderant role in decision-making and in meeting the needs of the present without compromising those of future generations. There is no doubt that education plays an essential role in the transition to the economies of the so-called first world. Education is a very important mechanism, if not the only one, for changing people's values, attitudes, and behaviors toward so-called sustainable development. Education should not only be directed towards children and young people, on the contrary, it needs to be inclusive of society in both vertical and horizontal directions. Thus, continuity both in education and in the training of highly specialized human resources is becoming a global necessity every day. This is due, among other reasons, to the fact that in today's technical professions, it is essential first, to ensure the adaptation of knowledge as technologies change and second, to professions that are not considered to be technical in nature (e.g. lawyers, administrators, etc.), must urgently acquire the most innovative knowledge, especially to keep up to date.

The imperative need for specialized human resources requires more, but above all better, research (more and better-specialized projects) to demonstrate that highly specialized education is quality education. In other words, the greater the investment in research, the sooner it will be proven that this type of education is, in itself, of quality. Technologies developed in a country or region should not be limited to providing economic opportunities (the development and implementation of projects, construction, and installation of renewable energy technologies entail an incalculable potential for employment). This is because, thanks to the growing, albeit slow, investment in specialized human resources, a wide diversity of markets is now available to generate, within them, numerous employment opportunities, which should be of utmost importance in the public policies of many countries and, above all, of local companies wishing to hire these people to create or strengthen their work environment. Consequently, it is necessary that all stakeholders such as government, business, academia, and society jointly build strategies and desirable scenarios to prevent school dropouts and, at the same time, promote the interest of high school students to study a degree in the scientific and/or technological area, since these should be seen as an attractive option for the professional and economic development of all those who choose to enroll in them. This should not only be seen as a limited benefit for this sector of students, but rather as a strategic starting point for society and the country in its social and economic development within the current knowledge economy.

Therefore, globalization demands, day by day, better-prepared students. Mexico, and in particular its less influential geographical areas (such as the State of Tlaxcala), should not be indifferent to these demands. Thus, future work should be oriented to show first-hand information to know more in-depth about the problems that exist today regarding the formation of scientific and/or technological human capital working in local companies in all the Mexican states. Undoubtedly, these results will contribute, to a great extent, to know and understand more aspects of the creation or consolidation of the organizational culture that these specialized human resources can generate in these local companies, which can help to justify the success or permanence of these local companies that, without a doubt, are a lever arm in both the local and national economy of Mexico. Of course, these studies will also provide a glimpse of the local public policy efforts being undertaken for the training and adoption of scientists and/or technologists by companies located in each geographic area of Mexico.

CONCLUSION

SMEs play an important role in every economy, as they contribute to both the generation of wealth and the creation of jobs in a region or country. Education in Mexico, and particularly in the State of Tlaxcala, presents important challenges for the training of human resources specialized in science and technology. The present work shows a panorama that reveals, on the one hand, the disinterest that prevails in the population under study to carry out studies in the scientific-technological area and, on the other hand, the adoption of this specialized human capital in an adverse environment for some companies in the State of Tlaxcala. This circle of dependence does not allow for the creation of an organizational culture that transcends to other regions. Although the organizational culture of the family business presented in this paper is perfectly defined, the constant adaptation to modern times forced it to open its doors to new people and, consequently, to new ways of thinking and working. This, with the only premise of its sole owners: to continue in an increasingly competitive market.

About the human resources interviewed, it was found that they are not assertive when choosing a degree they wish to study (this generally happens more in men). That is, the academic profiles chosen by these students are on the advice of third parties, which will lead to a decrease in the effectiveness of the selected academic career and, consequently, there is a high probability that they will not finish it because they will lack the motivation they should have had from the first moment they chose the area of their professional studies. Once the students selected a career in an unreflective manner, knowing that when they finish their studies they will work in something that does not completely satisfy them, it was detected that these students find it difficult to adapt to the learning system (especially the men), so, without a doubt, these students will reflect little motivation during their studies and, subsequently, they will be human resources that do not have the entrepreneurial spirit that the companies in the region need to be more competitive and strengthen their culture. Consequently, these human resources will not reflect the human values that are needed in a company where these values are transmitted from generation to generation.

Public universities in Mexico are the main trainers of specialized human resources that will be hired by companies, even at the international level. However, the human resources interviewed argued that they will not study a degree related to science or technology because they consider their curricula to be very difficult. The main consequence of this result is that SMEs in the State of Tlaxcala, which are in the first instance the ones that will hire graduates of these degrees, will be forced to hire people with little disposition to perform their work. That is to say, these graduates will not be innovative, competitive, and qualified to perform their tasks, which should respond to the problems of each company that wishes to have entrepreneurial employees to create, assimilate or transmit new technology and, of course, strengthen the culture promoted by the company.

Among the most worrying aspects is the fact that there is a clear lack of motivation on the part of students to pursue this type of study, in addition to providing elements that help to characterize the context that shapes this problem and that gives rise to the necessary actions to help mitigate this adverse environment. All these results justify, in turn, the low innovation indicators attributed to Mexico and could serve as a basis for the authorities to take the necessary actions to guide students before and during their professional studies. Consequently, it is necessary for all stakeholders such as government, business, academia, and society to jointly build strategies and desirable scenarios to avoid school dropouts and, at the same time, promote the interest of high school students to first, pursue a scientific-technological degree, since these should be seen as an attractive option for the professional and economic development of all those who choose to enroll in them, and second, to generate specialized human resources with motivation and commitment to strengthening the organizational culture of the company where they will be hired.

This should not only be seen as a benefit limited to this sector of students, but rather as a strategic starting point for society and the country in its social and economic development within the current knowledge economy. This would undoubtedly favor Mexican SMEs, since dependence on foreign technologies would be reduced and, consequently, sources of better-paid jobs would be created for people with a high specialization in science or technology. The opinion of the owners of the family business dedicated to the maquila justifies the absence of these specialized human resources since they are not hired because they can be replaced by a family member or less qualified personnel, but who can solve their immediate needs. In addition, the use of new technologies does not justify the permanence of this company in an increasingly competitive market segment. This is because the purchase or updating of their machinery always implied a considerable expense, which they never considered as an investment, rather they assumed it as an obligatory expense. All these factors showed the specialized human resources, and those to be hired, as people who "did not fit in" with the customs of the business family and, consequently, were seen as "arrogant and presumptuous" by the other workers who did not have a specialized education. Undoubtedly, all these drawbacks did not allow the creation of a solid organizational culture.

On the other hand, employees with specialized studies, and those responsible for the current departments of the family business, agreed that they are employed in small companies while they find better job opportunities. In other words, a sense of commitment on the part of these workers to the owners of the company was not appreciated, mainly due to the few benefits they see in working in a local company with these characteristics. The dynamic that exists between employers and employees is undoubtedly complex, but it does not favor the strengthening of their organizational culture. The present work can be taken into account to show an edge of this complexity: on the one hand, companies lack specialized human resources that are committed to their main objectives to be more competitive and, on the other hand, these human resources require a workspace where they can develop all their intellectual capacities and help them to have a more promising future. This paradox should be the starting point for all those involved (government, entrepreneurs, students, and society) to initiate a program with multiple viable strategies that allow, in turn, to generate specialized human resources with better job opportunities in the long term and companies that dare and have the perspective of hiring qualified personnel (who not only come to them for a temporary job but who are involved, committed and strengthen their organizational culture), and do not see it as an expense, to improve all their production processes always to be more competitive.

REFERENCES

Acosta Guzmán, J. A. (2015). La innovación empresarial y la cultura organizacional. *3C Empresa, 4*(3), 160-174. Retrieved from https://dialnet.unirioja.es/servlet/articulo?codigo=5165298

Aghion, P., Caroli, E., & García-Peñalosa, C. (1999). Inequality and economic growth: The perspective of the new growth theories. *Journal of Economic Literature, 37*(4), 1615–1660. doi:10.1257/jel.37.4.1615

Aghion, P., & Howitt, P. W. (1997). *Endogenous growth theory*. MIT Press.

Araújo, C., & Teixeira, A. (2014). Determinants of International Technology Transfer: An Empirical Analysis of the Enterprise Europe Network. *Journal of Technology Management & Innovation, 9*(3), 120–134. doi:10.4067/S0718-27242014000300009

Barro, R. (1991). Economic growth in a cross-section of countries. *The Quarterly Journal of Economics, 106*(2), 407–443. doi:10.2307/2937943

Barro, R. (1997). *Determinants of Economic Growth. A cross-country empirical study*. MIT Press.

Barro, R., & Beckerg, G. (1989). Fertility Choice in a Model of Economic Growth. *Econometrica, 57*(2), 481–501. doi:10.2307/1912563

Bessant, J., & Rush, H. (1995). Building bridges for innovation: The role of consultants in technology transfer. *Research Policy*, *24*(1), 97–115. doi:10.1016/0048-7333(93)00751-E

Bils, M., & Klenow, P. (2000). Does schooling cause growth? *The American Economic Review*, *90*(5), 1160–1183. doi:10.1257/aer.90.5.1160

Bowen, E., Lloyd, S., & Thomas, S. (2004). Changing Cultural Attitudes towards Graduates in SMEs to Stimulate Regional Innovation. *Industry and Higher Education*, *18*(6), 385–390. doi:10.5367/0000000042683575

Bozeman, B., & Papadakis, M. (1995). Company interactions with federal laboratories: What they do and why they do it. *The Journal of Technology Transfer*, *20*(3-4), 64–74. doi:10.1007/BF02280349

Calderón, H. G., & Serna, G. H. M. (2009). Relaciones entre recursos humanos y cultura organizacional. un estudio empírico. *Acta Colombiana de Psicologia*, *12*(2), 97–114. https://www.redalyc.org/pdf/798/79815640010.pdf

Cambridge University Press. (2023). https://dictionary.cambridge.org/es/diccionario/ingles/ultimate

Cameron, K. S., & Quinn, R. E. (2006). Diagnosing and changing organizational culture: based on the competing values framework. Jossey-Bass.

Cameron, K. S., & Quinn, R. E. (2010). Diagnosing and changing organizational culture: based on the competing values framework. Jossey-Bass.

Carrillo, J. (2007). Maquiladoras en México: ¿Evolución o agotamiento? *Revista Comercio Exterior, 57*(8), 668-681. Retrieved from http://revistas.bancomext.gob.mx/rce/magazines/106/5/Carrillo.pdf

Castelblanco, J., & Robledo, J. (2014). Relación entre el PIB y algunos indicadores de Ciencia y Tecnología: Colombia vs. Corea del Sur. *Revista Escenarios: Empresa y territorio, 3*, 79-99. https://repositorio.esumer.edu.co/jspui/bitstream/esumer/326/2/Esumer_relacion.pdf

CONACYT. (2004). *Informe General del Estado de la Ciencia y la Tecnología (IGECYT), México*. Retrieved from https://www.siicyt.gob.mx/index.php/transparencia/informes-conacyt/informe-general-del-estado-de-la-ciencia-tecnologia-e-innovacion/informe-general-2004

Cooke, R., & Lafferty, J. (1989). Organizational Culture Inventory (OCI). Human Synergistics.

de León, L. J., Pérez, R. J. V., & Boza, C. J. (2016). *Introducción a las Técnicas de Muestreo*. Ediciones Pirámide.

Denison, D. (1996). What is the difference between organizational culture and organizational climate? A native's point of view on a decade of paradigm wars. *Academy of Management Review*, *21*(3), 619–654. doi:10.2307/258997

Dextras-Gauthier, J. (2014). *Culture organisationnelle et santé mentale au travail. Université de Montréal*. Philosophiae. Faculté des Études Supérieures et Postdoctorales. Retrieved from https://papyrus.bib.umontreal.ca/xmlui/handle/1866/12019

Edwards, A. (2013). El diagnóstico de la cultura organizacional o las culturas de la cultura. *Global Media Journal México, 6*(11), 67-81. https://gmjmexico.uanl.mx/index.php/GMJ_EI/article/view/79/78

García, L., Hernández, R., Vargas, B., & Cuevas, H. (2012). Diagnóstico de la cultura organizacional en universidades tecnológicas bajo el Modelo de Valores en Competencia. *Estudios en Ciencias Sociales y Administrativas. Universidad de Celaya, 2*, 9-29. Retrieved from https://www.researchgate.net/profile/Hector-Cuevas-Vargas/publication/282353614_Diagnostico_de_la_cultura_organizacional_en_universidades_tecnologicas_bajo_el_Modelo_de_Valores_en_Competencia/links/560d7ac308ae6cf68153f578/Diagnostico-de-la-cultura-organizacional-en-universidades-tecnologicas-bajo-el-Modelo-de-Valores-en-Competencia.pdf

Gómez, C., & Sánchez, J. (2005). HR's strategic role within MNCs: Helping build social capital in Latin America. *International Journal of Human Resource Management*, *16*(12), 2189–2200. doi:10.1080/09585190500358596

Greene, H. W. (2012). *Econometric Analysis*. Pearson.

Grosse, R. (1996). International technology transfer in services. *Journal of International Business Studies*, *27*(4), 781–800. doi:10.1057/palgrave.jibs.8490153

Guberman, N., Fournier, D., Belleau, J., Beeman, J., & Gervais, L. (1994). Des questions sur la culture organisationnelle des organismes communautaires. *Nouvelles Pratiques Sociales*, *7*(1), 45–62. doi:10.7202/301251ar

Guisán, M., & Neira, I. (2001). Capital humano y capital físico en la OCDE, su importancia en el crecimiento económico en el período 1965-95. *Estudios Económicos de Desarrollo Internacional, 1*, 1-13. Retrieved from https://www.usc.gal/economet/reviews/eedi123.pdf

Gujarati, D., & Porter, D. (2010). *Econometría (Quinta edición)*. McGraw Hill.

Hanushek, E. A., & Luque, J. A. (2003). Efficiency and equity in schools around the world. *Economics of Education Review, 22*(5), 481–502. doi:10.1016/S0272-7757(03)00038-4

Hernández, R., Fernández, C., & Baptista, M. P. (2010). *Metodología de la Investigación*. Mc. Graw Hill.

Hicks, D. (1993). University-industry research links in Japan. *Policy Sciences, 26*(4), 361–395. https://www.jstor.org/stable/4532299. doi:10.1007/BF00999478

Instituto Nacional de Estadística y Geografía. (2015). *Encuesta Intercensal 2015.* Recuperado de https://www.inegi.org.mx/programas/intercensal/2015

International Labour Organization. (2011). *Skills and Occupational Needs in Renewable Energy*. Geneva: European Commission. Retrieved from https://www.ilo.org/wcmsp5/groups/public/---ed_emp/---ifp_skills/documents/publication/wcms_166823.pdf

Keogh, W., & Galloway, L. (2004). Teaching enterprise in vocational disciplines: Reflecting on positive experience. *Management Decision, 42*(3/4), 531–541. doi:10.1108/00251740410519001

Khurram, J., Wandschneider, K., & Wunnava, P. V. (2007). The effect of political regimes and technology on economic growth. *Applied Economics, 39*(11), 1425–1432. doi:10.1080/00036840500447906

Kostoff, R. J., Antonio del Río, J., Cortés, H. D., Smith, C., Smith, A., Wagner, C., Leydesdorff, L., Karypis, G., Malpohl, G., & Tshiteya, R. (2005). The structure and infrastructure of Mexico's science and technology. *Technological Forecasting and Social Change, 72*(7), 798–814. doi:10.1016/j.techfore.2005.02.001

Kotter, J., & Heskett, J. (1992). *Corporate culture and performance*. Free Press.

Lima-Cruz, C. M., Fleith de Medeiros, J., Carvalho-Tatim, D., & Mara-Meurer, A. (2013). Interfaces entre cultura organizacional e comunicação organizacional: um estudo multicasos em universidades. *Análise A Revista Acadêmica da FACE, Porto Alegre, 24*(1), 92-103. Retrieved from https://revistaseletronicas.pucrs.br/ojs/index.php/face/article/view/18340

Lucas, R. Jr. (1988). On the mechanics of economic development. *Journal of Monetary Economics, 22*(1), 3–42. doi:10.1016/0304-3932(88)90168-7

Mankiw, N. G., Romer, D., & Weil, D. N. (1992). A contribution to the empirics of economic growth. *The Quarterly Journal of Economics, 107*(2), 407–437. doi:10.2307/2118477

Marcondes-Leite, B., & Cristiane de Oliveira, H. (2014). *Rotatividade de Pessoal, a partir do problema de cultura e clima organizacional, Faculdade de Pindamonhangaba*. Retrieved from https://www.educaedu-brasil.com/centros/faculdade-de-pindamonhangaba--fapi-uni2843

Martín, X., Segredo, A., & Perdomo, I. (2013). Capital humano, gestión académica y desarrollo organizacional. *Educación Médica Superior*, *27*(3), 288–295. http://scielo.sld.cu/pdf/ems/v27n3/ems14313.pdf

Martínez, M. A. (2010). Relaciones entre cultura y desempeño organizacional en una muestra de empresas colombianas: reflexiones sobre la utilización del modelo de Denison. *Cuadernos de Administración, 23*(40), 163-190.

Moon, Y. J., & Kym, H. G. (2006). A Model for the Value of Intellectual Capital. *Canadian Journal of Administrative Sciences*, *23*(3), 253–269. doi:10.1111/j.1936-4490.2006.tb00630.x

Nataraajan, R., & Chawla, S. K. (1994). Random transfer of technology: An unexplored phenomenon. *The Journal of Technology Transfer*, *19*(1), 27–32. doi:10.1007/BF02373668

National Economic Council. (2011). *A strategy for American innovation: securing our economic growth and prosperity*. Council of Economic Advisers, and Office of Science and Technology Policy. Retrieved from https://obamawhitehouse.archives.gov/sites/default/files/uploads/InnovationStrategy.pdf

Nazarian, A., Atkinson, P., & Foroudi, P. (2017). Influence of national culture and balanced organizational culture on the hotel industry's performance. *International Journal of Hospitality Management*, *63*, 22–32. doi:10.1016/j.ijhm.2017.01.003

Neira Gómez, I. (2007). Capital humano y desarrollo económico mundial: Modelos econométricos y perspectivas. *Estudios Económicos de Desarrollo Internacional,* 7(2), 53-80. Retrieved from https://www.redalyc.org/pdf/165/16570203.pdf

ONU. (2005). *La juventud y los objetivos de desarrollo del milenio. Desafíos y Oportunidades para su Implementación*. Reporte Final del Grupo de Trabajo Ad Hoc para la Juventud y los ODM's, Centro de Información de las Naciones Unidas (CINU). Retrieved from https://www.unicef.org/venezuela/media/961/file/La%20juventud%20y%20los%20objetivos%20de%20desarrollo%20del%20milenio.pdf

Pemberton, C. (1995). Organizational Culture and Equalities Work. In J. Shaw & D. Perrons (Eds.), *Making Equal Opportunities* (pp. 108–123). Open University Press.

Pérez, C. (2017). *Muestreo estadístico a través de ejemplos*. Garceta Grupo Editorial.

Robbins, P., & Coulter, M. (2005). *Management* (8th ed.). Pearson Prentice Hall.

Romer, P. (1986). Increasing returns and long run growth. *Journal of Political Economy, 94*(5), 1002–1037. doi:10.1086/261420

Romer, P. (1990a). ¿Are non convexities important for understanding growth? *The American Economic Review, 80*(2), 97–103. https://www.jstor.org/stable/2006550

Romer, P. (1990b). Capital, labour, and productivity. In *Brookings Papers on Economic Activity.* Brookings Institution Press. Retrieved from https://www.brookings.edu/wp-content/uploads/1990/01/1990_bpeamicro_romer.pdf

Rubio, A., & Aragón, A. (2002). Factores explicativos del éxito competitivo. Un estudio empírico en la PYME. *Cuadernos de Gestión, 2*(1), 49–63. https://ojs.ehu.eus/index.php/CG/article/view/19218

Saavedra, M., & Hernández, Y. (2008). Caracterización e importancia de las MIPYMES en Latinoamérica: Un estudio comparativo. *Actualidad Contable, 17*, 122-134. Retrieved from https://www.redalyc.org/pdf/257/25711784011.pdf

Sala-I-Martin, X. (2009). The Global Competitiveness Index: Measuring the Productive Potential of Nations. *World Economic Forum.* Retrieved from https://relooney.com/NS3040/0_New_3044.pdf

Scott, R. (2005). Organizaciones. Características duraderas y cambiantes. *Gestión y Política Pública, 3*, 439–463. https://www.redalyc.org/articulo.oa?id=13314302

Scott, T., Mannion, R., Davies, H., & Marshall, M. (2003). The quantitative measurement of the organizational culture in health care. A view of an available instruments (Methods). *Health Services Research, 38*(3), 923–946. doi:10.1111/1475-6773.00154 PMID:12822919

Secretaría de Educación Pública. (2018). *Sistema Educativo de los Estados Unidos Mexicanos.* Principales cifras ciclo escolar 2017-2018. Recuperado de https://www.planeacion.sep.gob.mx/Doc/estadistica_e_indicadores/principales_cifras/principales_cifras_2017_2018_bolsillo.pdf

Secretaría de Educación Pública. (2019). *Principales Cifras del Sistema Educativo Nacional 2018-2019*. Recuperado de https://www.planeacion.sep.gob.mx/Doc/estadistica_e_indicadores/principales_cifras/principales_cifras_2018_2019_bolsillo.pdf

Serrate, A., Portuondo, A., Sánchez, N., & Suarez, R. (2014). Evaluación de la cultura organizacional y su incidencia en la efectividad grupal. *Ingeniería Industrial, 35*(1), 2-12. Retrieved from http://scielo.sld.cu/pdf/rii/v35n1/rii02114.pdf

Stijns, J.-P. (2006). Natural Resource Abundance and Human Capital Accumulation. *World Development, 34*(6), 1060–1083. doi:10.1016/j.worlddev.2005.11.005

Syeda-Masooda, M., Oakey, R., & Kippling, M. (1999). Utilisation of science and technology graduates by the small and medium-sized enterprise sector. *International Journal of Entrepreneurial Behaviour & Research, 5*(3), 126–143. doi:10.1108/13552559910284083

Torre, F. (2014). Contribución de la Ciencia e Ingeniería en el desarrollo económico. *The Twelfth Latin American and Caribbean Conference for Engineering and Technology.* Retrieved from https://laccei.org/LACCEI2014-Guayaquil/RefereedPapers/RP080.pdf

UNESCO. (2012b). *Shaping the Education of Tomorrow: 2012 Report on the UN Decade of Education for Sustainable Development, Abridged.* Retrieved from https://sustainabledevelopment.un.org/content/documents/919unesco1.pdf

United Nations. (1987). *Report of the World Commission on Environment and Development: Our Common Future.* Retrieved from https://www.are.admin.ch/are/en/home/media/publications/sustainable-development/brundtland-report.html

Van der Post, W. Z., de Coning, T. J., & Smit, E. M. (1997). An instrument to measure organizational culture. *South African Journal of Business Management, 28*(4), 147–168. doi:10.4102ajbm.v28i4.800

Webber, D. J. (2002). Policies to stimulate growth: Should we invest in health or education? *Applied Economics, 34*(13), 1633–1643. doi:10.1080/00036840110115109

Welch, F. (1970). Education in production. *Journal of Political Economy, 78*(1), 35–59. doi:10.1086/259599

Wiser, R. (2002). *Innovation, renewable energy, and state investment: Case studies of leading clean energy funds.* Lawrence Berkeley National Laboratory. Retrieved from https://eta-publications.lbl.gov/sites/default/files/report-lbnl-51493.pdf

Wu, J. Y. (2008). A General Behavior Model and New Definitions of Organizational Cultures. *Journal of Socio-Economics, 37*(6), 2535–2545. doi:10.1016/j.socec.2007.10.002

ENDNOTES

1. Of note are the works of Barro (1997, 1991), Barro and Beckerg (1989) and Mankiw et al (1992), who used schooling rates and found a positive and significant contribution of human capital to output growth.
2. The company manufactures uniforms for several transnational companies. It has been in business for 55 years and has 70 employees on its payroll. However, for reasons of confidentiality and security of the families who own the company, we cannot provide detailed information about this manufacturing company.
3. The sample was calculated with a 5% margin of error, 95% confidence, and 50% homogeneity. In addition, the technique used was stratified random sampling with proportional allocation.

Chapter 2
Institutional Policymaking and Its Implications in the Analysis of Institutional Change

José G. Vargas-Hernandez
Tecnológico Superior de Jalisco, Mexico

Omar C. Vargas-González
https://orcid.org/0000-0002-6089-956X
Tecnológico Nacional de México, Cuidad Guzmán, Mexico

ABSTRACT

This study has the purpose of analyzing the implications of institutional policymaking in the analysis of institutional change. The analysis departs from the assumption that the analysis of institutional policymaking is a framework to design and implement institutional change. The method used is the meta cognitive-analytic-descriptive based on the conceptual-theoretical and empirical review of the literature on these issues. It is concluded that the analysis of institutional change must be supported by a framework of a policymaking development.

DOI: 10.4018/978-1-6684-6567-7.ch002

INTRODUCTION

This research stream contributes to study the characteristics a wide range of institutions and its influence. Lack of incentives in transdisciplinary and interdisciplinary research, shortage of academic and training in multimethod qualitative and quantitative research and mono-disciplinary review research are some of the obstacles that arise in academic and scientific research institutions (Dedeurwaerdere, 2013). A set of institutional hurdles and barriers have been identified to overcome in the development of institutional sustainability science research practice in non-oriented and industry oriented research (Wiek, et al 2011).

Lack of institutional sustainability mechanisms for research partnerships and training capacities development with different stakeholders, communities, and academic and scientific institutions (Van der Leeuw, 2012). The institutional barriers and challenges have variations and modalities for strategic sustainability research constructed on temporary and ad hoc basis.

Institution is used differently reflecting the diversity of disciplinary backgrounds. Characteristics of the institutional heterogeneity is a critical link between the institutions and firm behavior. At multiple levels of analysis, institutional intersectionality operationalization addresses the complexity of the barriers to equity and the ways to design inequity, which may be critical in some kinds of institutions which have more reflexivity about knowledge and learning intensive such as the academic, scientific, technological and innovation institutions as long as they remain hegemonically inequitable (Harding, 1986, 1991; Collins, 1990; Foucault, 1978). Institutions cannot be transferred as technologies can.

The state innovation institutions have their mandates in public policy increasingly interacting in line between private and public institutions (Hounkonnou et al., 2012). Public policies in formal institutions encourage policy continuity because they face difficulties to change past decisions based on set policy paths that have already institutionalized actor and policies which necessitates higher costs and heroic efforts to make any change (Pierson, 2000). Policy reform analysis on the degree of public control varies considerably because of different political systems with diverse institutional structures in each one fostering different coalitions of interests among the actors (Immergut, 1992; Wilsford, 1994). Public officials play a critical role in advancing the institutional transformation and change agendas which inspire and enable institutions to act for social justice and equality The Commonwealth Secretariat, 2016; Staab, & Waylen, 2020).

To achieve the purpose of this study, to analyze the implications of institutional policymaking in the analysis of institutional change, the analysis begins with a brief analytical description of institutions. The study continues analyzing the institutional change followed by the institutional policymaking. Finally, some conclusion remarks are offered.

INSTITUTIONS

Institutions are the set of rules shaping collective action distinguishing between repeated and non-repeated collective actions such as the case of revolutions and wars (North, 1990a). An institution, according to Commons is the collective action in restraining, liberate and expand individual actions (Commons, 1934/1961). Politics is considered as a series of collective action dilemmas with outcomes determined by the strategic interactions among the political actors, due to the absent of institutional arrangements to encourage cooperation (Hall & Taylor 1996). Institutions are a relevant factor in sustainable capacity building, innovation and technology management and technological promotion during the dissemination process.

Capacity development of public leadership across the different public sectors contributes at the systematic level to visualize and activate institutional transformation and change required. Each group is struggling to build institutions unaware of the institutional knowledge required to succeed (Ostrom, 2005, 1990; Bromley & Anderson (2012). Institutional learning perspective occurs with individuals receiving knowledge and training into a specific institutional and policy approaches (Pierson, 2000; Rose, 1990).

Extensive acquisition and passing down knowledge and training from peers to individuals in institutions make confident policymaking to stand above any other institutional alternative. Institutional audits provides information to examine perceptions and conceptualizations for the effective creation and transmission of knowledge and preventing from communication gaps (Boughey, 2009). Judgements are attached to categories of institutions based on unidimensional institutional self-conceptions. Institutional quantitative analysis has limits to represent the reality dimension of people (Mohr & Bogdanov, 2013).

Institutions are at the core of regimes but do not constitute by themselves a regime formed by institutions operating in combined infrastructures, individual behaviors, networks of actors, etc. Networks are more fluid developing over time into an institutional structure. Policymaking implementation process of the network structure is not a bilateral relationship between the government institutions and others (Gornitzka, Kyvik & Stensaker 2005).

Predictions of actor's behaviors based on institutional structural characteristics is problematic because they need to be scrutinized since their preferences shape institutional outcomes. Institutional building and disruption, interactions between and within formal and informal institutions are issues of concern for developing countries (Estrin & Prevezer, 2011, Grzymala-Busse, 2010, Slater, 2010). Institutions have crucial roles in formal functions aimed to create opportunities (Roling et al., 2012).

Management research care about the challenges of global society. The building blocks of motivation are littered around the societal landscape (Meyer & Rowan, 1977). Independent professionals become involved in business entrepreneurship activities through the participation in management by objectives (Covaleski, Dirsmith, Heian, & Samuel, 1998). Policy entrepreneurship seeks opportunities in an equilibrium model including local factors such as institutional complexity and size, policy responses, etc. (McLaughlin, 1987). These sources cannot be used interchangeable because the inconsistency of the theoretical frameworks.

Aligned complexity can adopt blended hybrid structures accommodating demands and profiting from compatibilities (Raynard, 2016). The transaction costs are related to interdependencies affecting the choices of others and emerging conflict (Knight, 1992). Social change and institutional transformation need the support of leadership beyond equal representation embracing the potential for equal genders to become change agents to challenge injustices by transformative policies and programs (Munive et al. 2023). Policies are institutions as they constitute rules implemented, legitimated, and enforced by institutional agents and actors on behalf of the society (Streeck & Thelen 2005).

INSTITUTIONAL CHANGE

Changing institutional policies is often difficult because institutions tend to be sticky and the protection of institutional actors to the existing model (Cerna, 2013; Greener, 2002, Levi, 1997). Social conflict has a positive dimension derived from the ability to improve existing institutions (Hirschman, 1982). Institutional change is mediated by conflict and rule enforcement or through bargaining process. A typology developed for institutional change formalize institutional rules to be enforced upon a third party (Streeck & Thelen 2005). The layering type of institutional change and transformation levels involves a set of elements in amendments, additions, revisions, etc. set in motion dynamics system over time (Streeck & Thelen, 2005). The multiple layers of policy-making implementation are composed of complex institutional, state, federal, regional, state, local, etc. (Gornitzka, Kogan and Amaral 2005).

Resource-based perspective argues that resources and demands to elaborate products are valuable and difficult to copy giving the success to firms (Hitt et al., 2016). Characteristics of the firm heterogeneity is a critical link between the institutions and firm behavior. Resources are also related to the institutional habitus and the capability of institutions to support activities and influencing others (Bourdieu, 1977). Resources management adopted at the community level provide insights on institutional arrangements (Abernethy et al. 2014).

The use of institutional administrative arrangements and knowledge about policies in one place can be replicated in other place and time (Dolowitz & Marsh, 1996). These alternative institutional arrangements should promote natural resources sustainable management and economic growth and development performance although the results have been poor and, in some cases, opposite to the intended (Squires, & Qi, 2017). There is a positive link between the French occupation in Germany, economic growth, and urbanization (Acemoglu *et al.* 2011).

Institutional capacities need to be developed aimed to tailor solutions addressing specific characteristics. Engagement and development of human resources is a parameter for institutional re-creation. Institutional climate is varied in relation to mentoring and by equity compositions (Fox & Fonesca, 2006). Unintended outcomes are recaptured to strengthen the counter-intuitive standards (Slager et al. 2012)

The policy venues are institutional locations to make authoritative decisions on issues and mobilize different constituencies (Baumgartner & Jones 1991). Locations offer different opportunities to access natural resources and strategic assets, low costs, skilled labor, access to markets and strategic assets in some regions than in others. Local actors may give different treatment to foreignness of companies (Mezias, 2002). Marginal actors are defined as the ones having inadequate resources, less power and being peripheral actors including overlapping with separate marginality in power and group identity (Martí & Mair, 2009).

Shift from personal and individual power to institutional power moves the emphasis away into the community, focusing more on enhancing their leadership role, developing their capacity to collaborate, and enabling them to co-create integrated policies aimed to systematic realization of institutional social changes and transformations (Munive, Donville & Darmstadt, 2023).

Intersectional approach refers to institutional oppression in multiple sites and processes while attending individuals in disadvantaged structural locations (Davis, 2008; Cho et al., 2013).

Affections have marginal considerations, and the affective institutional dynamics may obstruct the institutional work undertaken by individuals to create, maintain and disrupt institutions (DiMaggio, 1988; Oliver, 1991; Lawrence & Suddaby, 2006; Clemens & Cook, 1999; Seo & Creed, 2002; Powell & Colyvas, 2007). Emerging pressures and exogenous criticisms are external strategically used for marginalized individuals to discredit existing and supportive policies and influential allies who are outside the institution and to strength legitimacy and influence (Mahoney & Thelen, 2010; Thelen, 2003).

The revolution notion is related to the concepts of institutions and institutional change, from the assumption that revolution emerges from an institutional vacuum into an institutional innovation. Revolution is not an appropriated means for institutional change because the free-rider problem shuns the masses from bringing it but used by elites to deal among themselves and with the ruler. Revolutions can be considered as positive institutional change to generate sovereignty, economic efficiency, secure economic efficiency.

The elite revolution is a revolution without a revolution. Elite revolutions maintain the old institutional forms while adding gradually added content. The elites have a role on evolution of institutional change to identify changes in the revolution leading to secure property rights (North, 1981, North *et al.* 2009; North *et al.* 2013; North & Weingast (1989) a declaration criticized by Hodgson (2017) who adopts a legal institutional approach stating that the absence of property rights is rather different than feudal property rights. The evolutionary approach of Darwing inspired Veblen (1899/1994) to underlie variation, inheritance, and modified selection of the fittest to institutional change.

The elite revolutions such as the British revolution of 1689 resulting on a bargaining process are the source of institutional innovation and instigate institutional transformation and changes, although they exclude the masses because the free riding problem leading to institutional innovation comes from ruling class (North,1981, 1990a, b, and North *et al.* 2009). The French revolution was not an elite revolution as the Britain one. Aristocracy was attached to feudal order unfolding a political crisis motivated by a monarchy that was financial powerlessness and unable to reform due to privileges of the aristocracy (Soboul, 1982). The radicalism of the French revolution transformed institutions and created new ones (Boix, 2003).

Feudal institutions expressed the existing rules were attacked and destroyed under peasant violence falling in the scream and not the voice galvanizing the revolutionary measures (Blanning, 1986). Reforms from feudal institutions within the aristocracy are close to people more sensitive to liberal ideas. Aristocracy was attached to feudal order unfolding a political crisis motivated by a monarchy.

Elites are the driving force of institutional transformation and change since they can resolve the free-rider problem. An intra-elite revolution and conflict can assess the institutional change streaming from above and compromise in diverse types of secure property rights (North & Weingast, 1989).

The presence or absence of secure property rights for wealth holders (North & Weingast, 1989; Hodgson, 2017) followed from a revolution in the property rights of labor underlined by Locke (Commons, 1934; Broda, 2020). Institutional changes after the revolution of 1688 confirmed the autonomy of property rights and recognized the permanent right of subordinate classes in the participation of shaping the royal will.

Upheavals from below undermine fundamental institution regimes, whereas other revolutions are more limited in questioning renovating institutions. Mass revolutions has as characteristics to attack older institutions to originate new institutions for national sovereignty in a modern bureaucratic administration and not only a populist movement to save order with new forms of power who have degenerated into centralized bureaucratic states (Furet, 1980/2006; Goldstone, 2009; Brown, 2013; Jones, 2006). A Mexican political party, the Party of the Institutionalized Revolution or PRI, held uninterruptedly power in the country for more than 71 years (1929-2000) leading to a revolution that is considered institutionalized (Chavance, 2012).

Revolution is a repeated collective action considered as a form of institution in which institutional relationships replace social relationships. Revolution is a collective action defined as scream from existing rules and voicing new rules questioning the established order but not an institution or replacing it with a new one, ushering a period of institutional vacuum and contributing to the creation of new institutions on the property rights and the state. Revolution is a singular unpredictable and irreducible event in any type of institutions although there are institutions of political parties that are relevant.

The revolution against any political system demonstrates the fundamental institutional change considered changes in politics and ideology, property ownership, and the coordination mechanisms (Kornai, 1991). Revolution develops in an institutional vacuum in a state lacking authority and anarchy. The emerging new rules are not strong to rule and govern activities prevailing an institutional vacuum with the insufficient power to enforce collective actions (Veblen, 1899/1994). An institutional vacuum ensues people to perceive themselves as the legitimate sovereign power to create new institutions than reject the ruling power.

Revolution is a repeated collective action. The free rider problem explains the state stability because the rulers are motivated to initiate and maintain institutional innovation hindering the collective action of masses (North, 1981). The stability of political regimes is enlightened by the impossibility of concerted revolutionary action (Buchanan, 1979). A revolution against the existing rules causes institutional innovation by introducing new rules to improve economic efficiency as the result of the scream when discontent cannot be voiced.

Institutional innovation is a process that results from positive revolutions conceived on the Schumpeterian terms of creative destruction by replacing new institutions (Schumpeter, 1951). Creative destruction is an incremental innovation process (Schumpeter, 1951) including gradual and revolutionary innovation dimensions more oriented towards product innovation rather than institutional dimension.

Intersectional approaches to inequalities contributes to underrepresented and disadvantaged groups calling for institutional strategies to increase representation (Carbado et al., 2013). Mechanisms to challenge the dominant imaginaries galvanize shifts in institutional orders. Images and narratives galvanize visceral commitments to protect human rights affecting laden stories that may undermine human right institutions in ubiquitous ticking time bomb scenarios (Celermajer, 2019).

Western modernity is approaching a sense of disenchantment with the loss of the sacred in a spiritual crisis marked by the breakdown of trust in state and corporate actors (Sherwin, 2019). Exhaustion is the process that happens working in an institution that undermines external preconditions resulting in the erosion of resources leading to gradual breakdown and collapse (Streeck & Thelen 2005). Resistant displayed by public protest and other real and fictional different characters as citizens to occupy an emotional space to transform political institutions. The institutional critique emerged with the participatory arts movement formed by artists that step outside the established institutions (Stephens, 2019, 2016; Bishop, 2012; Jackson, 2011).

An institutional model is needed to obtain technology and information as well as serve the needs of innovation in end users. Institutional systems can be compared in their differences through interpretive models in political and institutional dynamics which may contribute to increase economic growth and distributions, for instance on the varieties of capitalism (Acemoglu & Robinson, 2015, Piketty, 2014). Political cultivation promotes change (Streeck & Thelen 2005). Policy – feedback processes focused on the analysis of institutional decision-makers in collusion with civil society actors provide a limited approach to analyzing multilateral agencies, depending on their coalition partnership. Civil society pressure on multilateral agencies has a questionable influence. Multinational agencies lobby the reform of governing actors on their behalf, the media, and the NGOs.

INSTITUTIONAL POLICY MAKING

Institutional layering influences multilateral agencies with reform actors and internal resistance to reform bureaucracy through the creation and preexisting committees. Feedback process occurs with the policies and institutions creation leading to civil societal and political coalitions able to sustain themselves (Skocpol, 1995 & Pierson, 2004). Some multilateral agencies can be compared to each other in their similar path dependent challenges as institutional legitimacy. Changes in leadership of multilateral agencies with interests, bold ideas and supportive governing boards may provide to at some extent with autonomy and political resources to pursues institutional and policy changes.

For example, the Bank initially provide loans in economic reconstruction has pressures to increase assistance to help nations to combat poverty Kapur & Lewis, 1997; Philips, 2009). Civil societal and political coalitions safeguard institutional and policy preferences which are perceived as inefficient, costly, and as needing reform. Except for some global institutions policy making and sustainability processes are dependent on the support from civil society actors. Future research must explore the institutional power and influence in multinational agencies through the combination of political support and governing boards (Kapur, Lewis, & Webb,1997; Philips, 2009; Wade, 2001)

Multilateral and international institutions face challenges of institutional legitimacy despite the technical and financial resources to perform their duties. International institutions tend to become path dependent with external inducements encouraging change although some of them are breaking away by pursuing institutional change by establishing institutional capacity (Nay, 2012; UNAIDS, N.d.). Institutional changes occur as a shift from rules with short-term goals into active innovation actors and groups, with rules mutually agreed upon, controlled behaviors and long-term goals in a well-performing local and regional innovation systems.

Institutional change and transformation processes as part of development has the objective to internalize productivity increasing resource utilization, simultaneously creating new balance. Trust between the innovation actors in the network lead to encourage among them to actively participate in institutional changes affecting the performance. Institutional conversion explains the multinational agencies breaking away the path dependent tendency to change policy mandates from focusing and lending for economic restructuring to fund to social welfare policies.

Corporate capitalism institutions exercising corporate control are not characterized as state or market dominated. Government and market are the dual power present during all phases of an economic transition. Financial capital has an institutional role in economic activities to feature prominently in this analysis to distinguish between financial systems based on institutional patterns of ownership and corporate finances using typological elements incorporating other institutions such as legal systems, etc., aiming to capture the similarities, differences and complementarities to systematically cohere (Lopez-de-Silanes *et al.*, 1998 ; Hall and Soskice, 2001 ; Roe, 2003).

Global flows of capital portfolios influence the foreign institutional investors. Corporate governance indicators are critical related to internal decision making processes in business strategies to meet the institutional investors. Institutional investors pressure for financial returns emanating from economies. Increasing return is a challenge emerging from individuals investing in financial and technical resources into the institution while making costly to shift to other institution knowing the inefficiencies associated with the existing institution (Pierson, 2000; Arthur,1989;

David, 1985). Institutional pressures may tend to come from local institutional investments that strengthened by the management of large accumulations of pensions assets become powerful corporate shareholders.

Control of government over financial institutions in allocation of credit is a tool to influence evolution of economy. Specialized financial institutions and banks after being concentrated by the state, are the most important issuers in the bond markets used in their management of their businesses (Icard & Drumetz, 1994). State bureaucratic control is diluted and dictated by financial markets and demands of institutional investors influencing global corporations, a shift that is in tune with capitalism. Non-state-owned enterprises development with significant institutional sensitivity is more influenced by financing constraints, fiscal and taxation policies.

The institutional collaborative activities related to the position in networks are related to competence and autonomy in situations where the collaboration and diffusion component are embedded with other institutions in international networks to extract some benefits from global research flows (Gök et al., 2016). The relationship between the government and research and development institutions built by equipping institutions with the needed facilities to get involved as intermediary institutions to have access to innovations and to disseminate technologies in top-down programs leading to underutilized technologies (Wijayanti, et al. 2016). Intermediary institutions have a relevant role in bringing innovations closer to the end users for their benefit.

The intermediary institutions of local innovation systems must be active in serving the community needs and aspirations, identifying problems and finding solutions in technological innovation. In this sense, intermediary institutions must actively coordinate relevant agencies with duties to assist and provide training if needed to end innovation users.

Research and innovation institutions can perform dual role having significant degree of agency to set its own research agenda and contribute to policymaking. Research and innovation institutions actively participating in policymaking may stimulate competition while facing recent problems and persistent challenges. Institutions are an element of innovation systems in managing the occurring interactions between innovation actors and within other existing elements.

Institutions in innovation systems have functions of uncertainty reduction, conflict resolution, incentives provision for learning and participation and efficient and effective management of resources (Johnson, 2001). The innovation system derives from focus group discussions involving government official actors, intermediary institutions, and end innovation users. Government officials must develop different accountability tools to promote institutional change and transformation to examine the degree in which institutional strategies, policies, and programs must be integrated in their work.

The intermediary institutions are the innovation disseminators in the local innovation systems who manage the links between the innovators and the end users at the community. These intermediary research and development institutions, however, are not managed properly causing instead of solving problems. Research and development provide innovation to end users and communities through intermediaries that bridge the interactions needed to make work the systems among the actors, benefit them in the community. Innovation system is a set of market and non-market institutions which affects the direction and speed of innovation and technology development (OECD, 1999). The institutional elements of an innovation system synergize the process of diffusion and adoption of technology and strengthens the local and regional innovation systems.

Technological and institutional innovation synergy drives the implementation of innovation strategies in industries (Murmann, 2003; Pelikan, 2003). Institutional and technological innovation can develop a synergy to transform manufacturing industries (Zhao, Li & Sun, 2019). Institutional transformation of innovation system actors requires changes in attitude, behaviors, and mindsets. Institutional transformation and change involving compromise of institutional actors to exploit ambiguities to promote the type of change (Streeck & Thelen 2005). Changing institutions requires strategic brokers to facilitate the interactions and formation of configurations of innovation actors (Hounkonnou et al., 2012).

Marketing institutional innovation can coordinate the manufacturing and services development (Guo, 2019). Development of service industry is highly dependent sensitive on institution-intensive due to their trust and heterogeneous attributes. Servitization of manufacturing industries has effects on institutional supply is conducive to adjustments. Wang & Xiong, 2020; Peng & Heath, 1996).

State initiated moves to create and develop national research and innovation systems and their funding mechanisms from public and private university research systems (Crow & Bozeman, 1998). Institutional agency supports the research and innovation agenda-setting, with independence in choosing the research themes in vertical governance structures and contributes to design policymaking and implementing. The emerging adaptive governance processes is linked to institutional change (Olsson, Gunderson, Carpenter, Ryan, Lebel et al. 2006). Technological and institutional change dynamics unfolds at various levels and time scales.

The institutional change processes among innovation actors in local innovation systems are characterized by the elements of institution as the intermediaries in the sector for dissemination and diffusion, innovation providers as the research and innovation center and the innovation users in the community. The innovation system is a network of institutions interacting among them to provide, modify and diffuse technology (Audretsch, & Link, 2012; Muller, 2009). The elements of the local innovation institutions are the emergence and legal basis of the institution.

Institutions for governance are sticky (Hooghe & Marks 2003). An analysis of multi-level governance examines the diffusion of decision making to overlapping informal policy networks (Ansell, 2000, Kohler-Koch & Eising 1999). The policy networks model provides the policy process to make predictions of actors expecting to behave under institutional arrangements (Dowding, 1995). The organic shift in governance framed by institutional change remains a self-organized and transient collaboration without governance authority and legitimacy (Chaffin & Gunderson, 2016; Rijke, Farrelly, Brown, Zevenbergen, 2013; Cosens, 2013). Spatial centrality among institutional markers can contribute to regional decentralization of research institutions in the national research and innovation system (Motoyama et al., 2014, Tang & Shapira, 2011).

Dominant research institutions receive large budgets and supervision from the state in some countries over the research agenda to conduct fundamental and advanced research separated from the industrial research conducted in private institutes and universities (Graham, 1998). Dominant institutions in innovation and research systems differ in shifting strategic priorities and the level of engagement in the institutional re-interpretation agenda leading to reconfigurations in policymaking and reinforcement of centrality (Jackson, 2005).

The introduction and implementation of institutional reforms in developing economies through transition processes aimed to transform chronical dysfunctional economies resolving the emerging conflicts, creating new institutions to fill the vacuum to meet the expectations with alternative institutional arrangements. Analysis of concepts and propositions of institutional economy explain persistence of conflicts in institutional reforms implicitly introduced to resolve them. Some developing economies are struggling to find the balance between the external pressures, new technology developments and increasing economic growth (Bell & Feng, 2007, Gabriele, 2002).

Developing economies dealing with institutional inertia have challenges of creating and shaping new institutions and transforming existing institutions (Chen, 2008; Amable, 2000). Benchmark in institutional schemas of emerging economies seek to improve performance in institutional systems (Rip & van der Meulen, 1996). Remaking institutional systems often requires political will for significant changes to long-standing institutions (Mehta, 2013). The performance of intermediary institution connecting government institutions and end users of innovation requires information and knowledge. The reporting obligations of accountability for institutions in the government approach goes beyond the quantitative data performance in core functions pointing to institutional barriers.

The national and local development is an outcome that depends primarily on higher education systems (Sarkar, 2020). Transformative quality in higher education is a measure of access-quality and inclusiveness-excellence divide in a dichotomous high education system investigated through a front-line faculty perspective. The scale to measure transformative quality in a dichotomous high education system tends to balance the conflicts between inclusive access and inclusiveness with quality and excellence. Agency measures the level of institutional independence and dependence of institutions.

Policy making must promise a reasonable solution to decision making on the actions which have to be perceived as effective and legitimate with constituents to resonate with the prevailing public sentiments (Campbell, 2004). Institutional de-legitimacy occurs in individuals within institutions seeking to discredit their leadership by their shortcomings and failures in achieving policy objectives.

CONCLUSION

The purpose of the study analyzes the implications of institutional policymaking in the analysis of institutional change departing from the assumption that the analysis of institutional policymaking is a framework to design and implement institutional change. The study concludes that the analysis of institutional change must be supported by a framework of a policymaking development.

Path dependent patterns of institutions inhibit and constraint international interdisciplinary linkages of institutional collaboration. Multilateral agencies are breaking away from the path dependency inefficiencies of institutional legitimacy. Scientific, technological, and academic institutions may maintain conventional institutional power and the intersectional perspective to equity leading to rethink social science knowledge.

Institutional change and policy change are different concepts although both have some overlapping instances. Institutional actors play a relevant role in policy reform. Conflict and revolution are sources of economic and political efficiency in institutional change. Conflict is not reduced to an economic transaction but has a role in changing the institutional rules of the game in redistributing and destroying resources. The institutional innovation patterns are radically different when comparing elite and mass revolutions.

Strategic research for institutional sustainability transformation and reform of research funding mechanisms to become effective must be supported at the same time by the capacity building for research training and research at academic and scientific institutions. The development of sustainability science poses some major institutional barriers which need to be overcome by a proposed framework to address the challenges though a gradual institutional change process which enables to analyze the reforms and transformation of organizational research for sustainability research.

Organizing institutional sustainability research in the long term address the issues of career and training rewards, networking, and capacity building for stakeholder partnerships. Organization academic and research institutions require the institutional transformation of exiting research curricula, incentives, and evaluation structures, which contrasts more with institutional labor division that with institutional nature of scientific research. Full-fledged institutional research programs for sustainability distinguish between the modalities for organizing institutionalized gradual change.

The institutional capacity building measures must create and developed in research funding at the level of academic and research institutions and networking. The strategic research for institutional sustainability transformation and reforms become effective if they are supported by academic and training activities of higher education. At the strategic research level and networking, institutional changes require capacity building for the support of leadership in science and policy management in academic and scientific institutions to set a frontier for sustainability.

Transdisciplinary research development for institutional sustainability research must involve stakeholders in partnerships aimed to social transformation processes. Institutional barriers for the development of institutional sustainability science can be overcome through an organizational reform of scientific research. Institutional rewards for action oriented research are not well represented in long-term academic research projects and capacity building for participatory relationships engagement in transformative institutional change through transdisciplinary research efforts towards sustainability science. Gradual change can be implemented through incremental institutional transformation approach.

Best practices and methodologies for institutional sustainability research between the involved institutions in transdisciplinary research collaborations in synergy for consortia of institutions and supported for hybrid academic and non-academic competence. Synergy for institutional consortia to build cross-institutional methodological competences on institutional sustainability research based on ethical expertise combined with natural and social sciences and stakeholder expertise. Hybrid academic and non-academic competences support available sustainable research methodologies developed by research institutions and stakeholder organizations to produce knowledge.

REFERENCES

Abernethy, K. E., Bodin, T., Olsson, P., Hilly, Z., & Schwarz, A. (2014). Two steps forward, two steps back: The role of innovation in transforming towards community-based marine resource management in Solomon Islands. *Global Environmental Change*, *28*(1), 309–321. doi:10.1016/j.gloenvcha.2014.07.008

Acemoglu, D., Cantoni, D., Johnson, S., & Robinson, J. (2011). The Consequences of Radical Reform: The French Revolution A Theory of Political Transitions. *The American Economic Review*, *101*(7), 3286–3307. doi:10.1257/aer.101.7.3286

Acemoglu, D., & Robinson, J. (2015). The rise and fall of general laws of capitalism J. *Economic Perspectives*, *29*(1), 3–28. doi:10.1257/jep.29.1.3

Amable, B. (2000). Institutional complementarity and diversity of social systems of innovation and production. *Review of International Political Economy*, *7*(4), 645–687. doi:10.1080/096922900750034572

Ansell, C. (2000). The networked polity: Regional development in Western Europe. *Governance: An International Journal of Policy, Administration and Institutions*, *12*(2), 303–333. doi:10.1111/0952-1895.00136

Arthur, B. (1989). Competing technologies, increasing returns, and lock-in by historical events. *Economic Journal (London)*, *1989*(99), 116–131. doi:10.2307/2234208

Audretsch, B. D., & Link, N. A. (2012, February). Entrepeneurship and innovation: Public policy frameworks. *The Journal of Technology Transfer*, *37*(1), 1–17. doi:10.100710961-011-9240-9

Baumgartner, F., & Jones, B. (1991). Agenda dynamics and policy sub-systems. *The Journal of Politics*, *53*(4), 1044–1074. doi:10.2307/2131866

Bell, S., & Feng, H. (2007). Made in China: IT infrastructure policy and the politics of trade opening in post-WTO China. *Review of International Political Economy*, *14*(1), 49–76. doi:10.1080/09692290601081343

Bishop, C. (2012). *Artificial Hells: Participatory Art and the Politics of Spectatorship*. Verso. Print

Blanning, T. C. (1986). *The origins of the French revolutionary wars*. Longman Group Limited.

Boix, C. (2003). *Democracy and Redistribution*. Cambridge University Press. doi:10.1017/CBO9780511804960

Boughey, C. (2009). *A meta-analysis of teaching and learning at five research-intensive South African universities*. Research Commissioned by the Higher Education Quality Committee. Unpublished.

Bourdieu, P. (1977). *Outline of a Theory of Practice*. Cambridge University Press. doi:10.1017/CBO9780511812507

Broda, P. (2020). Institutions, economy and politics: The debate between Commons and North. *European Journal of the History of Economic Thought, 22*(October). Advance online publication. doi:10.1080/09672567.2020.1837197

Bromley, D. W., & Anderson, G. (2012). *Vulnerable People, Vulnerable States: Redefining the Development Challenge*. Routledge. doi:10.4324/9780203113325

Brown, H. (2013). The new security state. In P. McPhee (Ed.), *A companion to the French Revolution* (pp. 343–358). Blackwell Publishing Ltd.

Buchanan, J. M. (1979). Natural and artifactual man. In The Collected Works of James M. Buchanan, Volume 1: The Logical Foundations of Constitutional Liberty. Indianapolis: Liberty Fund, Inc.

Carbado, D. W., Crenshaw, K. W., Mays, V. M., & Tomlinson, B. (2013). Intersectonality: Mapping the movements of a theory. *Du Bois Review, 10*, 303–312. doi:10.1017/S1742058X13000349 PMID:25285150

Celermajer, D. (2019). The Tick-Tick-Ticking Time Bomb and Erosion of Human Rights Institutions. *Angelaki, 24*(4), 87–102. doi:10.1080/0969725X.2019.1635829

Cerna, L. (2013). *The Nature of Policy Change and Implementation: A Review of Different Theoretical Approaches*. OECD.

Chaffin, B. C., & Gunderson, L. H. (2016). Emergence, institutionalization, and renewal: Rhythms of adaptive governance in complex social-ecological systems. *Journal of Environmental Management, 165*, 81–87. doi:10.1016/j.jenvman.2015.09.003 PMID:26426283

Chavance, B. (2012). John Commons's organizational theory of institutions: A discussion. *Journal of Institutional Economics, 8*(1), 27–47. doi:10.1017/S1744137411000336

Chen, L. (2008). Institutional inertia, adjustment, and change: Japan as a case of a coordinated market economy. *Review of International Political Economy, 15*(3), 460–479. doi:10.1080/09692290801931404

Cho, S., Crenshaw, K. W., & McCall, L. (Eds.). (2013). Toward a field of intersectionality studies: theory, applications, and praxis. Theory Signs, 38, 785–810. doi:10.1086/669608

Clemens, E. S., & Cook, J. M. (1999). Politics and Institutionalism: Explaining Durability and Change. *Annual Review of Sociology, 25*(1), 441–466. doi:10.1146/annurev.soc.25.1.441

Collins, P. H. (1990). *2000. Black Feminist Thought: Knowledge, Consciousness, and the Politics of Empowerment*. Routledge.

Commons, J. R. (1934/1961). *Institutional Economics. Its Place in Political Economy* (Vols. 1–2). The University of Wisconsin Press.

Cosens, B. (2013). Legitimacy, adaptation, and resilience in ecosystem management. *Ecology and Society*, *18*(1), 3. doi:10.5751/ES-05093-180103

Covaleski, M. A., Dirsmith, M. W., Heian, J. B., & Samuel, S. (1998). The calculated and the avowed: Techniques of discipline and struggles over identity in Big Six public accounting firms. *Administrative Science Quarterly*, *43*(2), 293–327. doi:10.2307/2393854

Crow, M., & Bozeman, B. (1998). *Limited by Design: R & D Laboratories in the U.S. National Innovation System*. Columbia University Press.

David, P. (1985). Clio and the economics of QWERTY. *The American Economic Review*, *1985*(7), 332–337.

Davis, K. (2008). Intersectionality as buzzword: A sociology of science perspective on what makes a feminist theory successful. *Feminist Theory*, *9*(1), 67–85. doi:10.1177/1464700108086364

Dedeurwaerdere, T. (2013). Transdisciplinary Sustainability Science at Higher Education Institutions: Science Policy Tools for Incremental Institutional Change. *Sustainability*, *5*(9), 3783–3801. doi:10.3390u5093783

DiMaggio, P. J. (1988). Interest and Agency in Institutional Theory. In L. G. Zucker (Ed.), *Institutional Patterns and Organizations: Culture and Environment* (pp. 3–22). Ballinger.

Dolowitz, D. P., & Marsh, D. (1996). Who Learns What from Whom? A Review of the Policy Transfer Literature. *Political Studies*, *44*(2), 343–357. doi:10.1111/j.1467-9248.1996.tb00334.x

Dowding, K. (1995). Model or metaphor? A critical review of the policy network approach. *Political Studies*, *43*(1), 136–158. doi:10.1111/j.1467-9248.1995.tb01705.x

Estrin, S., & Prevezer, M. (2011). The role of informal institutions in corporate governance: Brazil, Russia, India, and China compared. *Asia Pacific Journal of Management*, *28*(1), 41–67. doi:10.100710490-010-9229-1

Foucault, M. (1978). *The History of Sexuality* (Vol. 1). Vantage Books, Random House.

Fox, M. F., & Fonesca, C. (2006). Gender and mentoring of faculty in science and engineering: Individual and organisational factors. *International Journal of Learning and Change*, *1*(4), 460–483. doi:10.1504/IJLC.2006.013912

Furet, F. (1980/2006). The French Revolution Revisited. In G. Kates (Ed.), *The French Revolution, recent Debates and New Controversies* (2nd ed., pp. 53–567). Routledge.

Gabriele, A. (2002). S&T policies and technical progress in China's industry. *Review of International Political Economy*, *9*(2), 333–373. doi:10.1080/09692290110126137

Gök, A., Karaulova, M., & Shapira, P. (2016). Dynamics of Transition in Core-Periphery Structures in Global Research System. Presented at the *EU-SPRI Conference, Lund*, Sweden.

Goldstone, J. (2009). Rethinking Revolutions: Integrating Origins, Processes, and Outcomes. *Comparative Studies of South Asia, Africa and the Middle East*, *29*(1), 18–32. doi:10.1215/1089201X-2008-040

Gornitzka, A., Kyvik, S., & Stensaker, B. (2005). Implementation analysis in higher education. In A. Gornitzka, M. Kogan, & A. Amaral (Eds.), *Reform and change in higher education: analyzing policy implementation* (pp. 35–56). Springer. doi:10.1007/1-4020-3411-3_3

Graham, L. R. (2010). *What Have We Learned About Science and Technology from the Russian Experience?* Stanford University Press.

Greener, I. (2002). Understanding NHS reform: The policy-transfer, social learning and path-dependency perspectives. *Governance: An International Journal of Policy, Administration and Institutions*, *15*(2), 161–183. doi:10.1111/1468-0491.00184

Grzymala-Busse, A. (2010). The best laid plans: The impact of informal rules on formal institutions in transitional regimes. *Studies in Comparative International Development*, *45*(3), 311–333. doi:10.100712116-010-9071-y

Guo, C. (2019). *Synergy mechanism and empirical research of manufacturing and producer services in China from the perspective of Global Value Chain* [Ph.D. Thesis]. Shanghai Academy of Social Sciences.

Hall, P., & Soskice, D. (2001). *Varieties of Capitalism: The Institutional Foundations of Comparative Advantage*. Oxford University Press. doi:10.1093/0199247757.001.0001

Hall, P., & Taylor, R. (1996). Political science and the three new institutionalisms. *Political Studies*, *44*(5), 936–957. doi:10.1111/j.1467-9248.1996.tb00343.x

Harding, S. G. (1986). *The Science Question in Feminism*. Cornell University Press.

Harding, S. G. (1991). *Whose Science? Whose knowledge? Thinking From Women's Lives*. Cornell University Press.

Hirschman, A. (1982). *Shifting Involvements, Private Interest and Public Action*. Princeton University Press.

Hitt, M. A., Xu, K., & Carnes, C. M. (2016). Resource based theory in operations management research. *J. Operat. Manag.*, *41*, 77–94. doi:.2015.11.002 doi:10.1016/j.jom

Hodgson, G. (2017). 1688 and all that: Property rights, the Glorious Revolution, and the rise of British capitalism. *Journal of Institutional and Theoretical Economics*, *13*(1), 79–107. doi:10.1017/S1744137416000266

Hooghe, L., & Marks, G. (2003). Unraveling the central state, but how? Types of multi-level governance. *The American Political Science Review*, *97*(2), 233–243.

Hounkonnou, D., Kossou, D., Kuyper, T. W., Leeuwis, C., Nederlof, S., Roling, N., Dawson, O. S., Traore, M., & Huis, V. A. (2012). An innovation systems approach to institutional change: Smallholder development in West Africa. *Agricultural Systems*, *108*, 74–83. doi:10.1016/j.agsy.2012.01.007

Icard, E., & Drumetz, F. (1994). Développement des Marchés de Titres et Financement de l'Économie Française. Bulletin de la Banque de France, 6.

Immergut, E. (1992). *Health Politics: Interests and Institution in Western Europe*. Academic Press.

Jackson, G. (2005). Contested boundaries: ambiguity and creativity in the evolution of German codetermination. In Beyond Continuity: Institutional Change in Advanced Political Economies. Oxford University Press.

Johnson, A. (2001). *Functions in innovation system approaches*. Retrieved June 26, 2015, from https://www.druid.dk/uploads/tx_picturedb/ds2001-205.pdf

Jones, C. (2006). Bourgeois revolution revivified: 1789 and social change. In G. Kates (Ed.), *The French Revolution, recent Debates and New Controversies* (2nd ed., pp. 87–112). Routledge.

Kapur, D., & Lewis, P. (1997). *Webb R: The World Bank: Its First Half Century*. Brookings Institution Press.

Knight, J. (1992). *Institutions and Social Conflict*. Cambridge University Press. doi:10.1017/CBO9780511528170

Kohler-Koch, B., & Eising, R. (Eds.). (1999). The transformation of governance in the European Union. Routledge.

Kornai J. (1991). *The Soviet Union's Road to a free economy, comments of an outside observer.* Tanner Lecture (part II), delivered at Leningrad University.

Lawrence, T. B., & Suddaby, R. (2006). Institutions and institutional work. In *Sage Handbook of organization studies* (2nd ed., pp. 215-254). Sage. https://www.researchgate.net/publication/242437344_Institutions_and_institutional_w ork/link/550aa6900cf290bdc10fdad3/download

Levi, M. (1997). A model, a method, and a map: rational choice in comparative and historical analysis. In M. Lichbach & A. Zuckerman (Eds.), *Comparative Politics: Rationality, Culture, and Structure* (pp. 19–41). Cambridge University Press.

Lopez-de-Silanes, F., La Porta, R., & Shleifer, A. (1998). Law and Finance. *Journal of Political Economy*, *106*(6), 1113–1155. doi:10.1086/250042

Mahoney, J. & Thelen. (Eds.). (2010). *Explaining Institutional Change*. New York: Cambridge University Press.

Martí, I., & Mair, J. (2009). Bringing change into the lives of the poor: Entrepreneurship outside traditional boundaries. In T. Lawrence, R. Suddaby & B. Leca (Eds.), Institutional work: Actors and agency in institutional studies of organizations (pp. 92–119). Cambridge University Press.

McLaughlin, M. W. (1987). Learning from experience: Lessons from policy implementation. *Educational Evaluation and Policy Analysis*, *9*(2), 171–178. doi:10.3102/01623737009002171

Mehta, J. (2013). Why American education fails and how lessons from abroad could improve it. *Foreign Affairs*, *92*(3), 72–79.

Meyer, J., & Rowan, B. (1977). Institutionalized organizations: Formal structure as myth and ceremony. *American Journal of Sociology*, *83*(2), 340–363. doi:10.1086/226550

Mezias, J. (2002). Identifying liabilities of foreignness and strategies to minimize their effects: The case of labor lawsuit judgments in the United States. *Strategic Management Journal*, *23*(3), 229–244. doi:10.1002mj.220

Mohr, J. W., & Bogdanov, P. (2013, December). Introduction—Topic models: What they are and why they matter. *Poetics*, *41*(6), 545–569. doi:10.1016/j.poetic.2013.10.001

Motoyama, Y., Cao, C., & Appelbaum, R. (2014). Observing regional divergence of Chinese nanotechnology centers. *Technological Forecasting and Social Change, 81*, 11–21. doi:10.1016/j.techfore.2013.02.013

Muller, E. (2009). *Innovation system and policies.* Retrieved June 26, 2015, from: http://www. evoreg.eu/doc/files/lete/200912.Emmanuel_Muller_Innovation _systems _and_ policies.pdf

Munive, A., Donville, J. & Darmstadt, G. L. (2023). Public leadership for gender equality: A framework and capacity development approach for gender transformative policy change. *eClinicalMedicine, 56*, 101798. doi:10.1016/j.eclinm.2022.0179

Murmann, J. P. (2003). *Knowledge and competitive advantage: The co-evolution of firms, technology, and national institutions.* Cambridge University Press. doi:10.1017/CBO9780511510953

Nay, O. (2012). What drives reforms in international organizations? External pressure and bureaucratic entrepreneurs in the UN response to AIDS. *Governance: An International Journal of Policy, Administration and Institutions, 2012*(24), 71–88.

North, D. (1981). *Structure and change in economic history.* W.W. Norton and Company.

North, D. (1990a). *Institutions, Institutional Change and Economic Performance.* Cambridge University Press. doi:10.1017/CBO9780511808678

North, D. (1990b). A Transaction Cost Theory of Politics. *Journal of Theoretical Politics, 2*(4), 355–367. doi:10.1177/0951692890002004001

North, D., Qallis, J., & Weingast, B. (2009). *Violence and social orders: A conceptual framework for interpreting recorded human history.* Cambridge University Press. doi:10.1017/CBO9780511575839

North, D., Wallis, J., Webb, S., & Weingast, B. (Eds.). (2013). In the Shadow of Violence, Politics, Economics, and the Problems of Development. Cambridge University Press.

North, D. C. & Weingast, B. R. (1989). Constitutions and Commitment: The Evolution of Institutions Governing Public Choice in Seventeenth Century England. *The Journal of Economic History, 49*(4), 803-832.

OECD. (1999). *Managing national innovation system.* Organization for Economic & Cooperation Development.

Oliver, C. (1991). Strategic Responses to Institutional Processes. *Academy of Management Review*, *16*(1), 145–179. doi:10.2307/258610

Olsson, P., Gunderson, L. H., Carpenter, S. R., Ryan, P., Lebel, L., Folke, C., & Holling, C. S. (2006). Shooting the rapids: Navigating transitions to adaptive governance of social-ecological systems. *Ecology and Society*, *11*(1), 18. doi:10.5751/ES-01595-110118

Ostrom, E. (1990). *Governing the Commons: The Evolution of Institutions for Collective Action*. Cambridge University Press. doi:10.1017/CBO9780511807763

Ostrom, E. (2005). *Understanding Institutional Diversity*. Princeton University Press.

Pelikan, P. (2003). Bringing institutions into evolutionary economics: Another view with links to changes in physical and social technologies. *Journal of Evolutionary Economics*, *13*(3), 237–258. doi:10.100700191-003-0157-9

Peng, M. W., & Heath, P. S. (1996). The growth of the firm in planned economies in transition: Institutions, organizations, and strategic choice. *Academy of Management Review*, *21*(2), 492–528. doi:10.2307/258670

Philips, D. (2009). *Reforming the World Bank: Twenty Years of Trial – and Error*. Cambridge University Press. doi:10.1017/CBO9780511814327

Pierson, P. (2004). *Politics in Time: History, Institutions, and Social Analysis*. Princeton University Press. doi:10.1515/9781400841080

Pierson, P. (2000). *Increasing returns, path dependence, and the study of politics*. Academic Press.

Piketty, T. (2014). *Capital in the Twenty-First Century*. Harvard University Press. doi:10.4159/9780674369542

Powell, W. W., & Colyvas, J. A. (2007). *Microfoundations of Institutional Theory*. Academic Press.

Raynard, M. (2016). Deconstructing complexity: Configurations of institutional complexity and structural hybridity. *Strategic Organization*, *14*(4), 310–335. doi:10.1177/1476127016634639

Rijke, J., Farrelly, M., Brown, R., & Zevenbergen, C. (2013). Configuring transformative governance to enhance resilient urban water systems. *Environmental Science & Policy*, *25*, 62–72. doi:10.1016/j.envsci.2012.09.012

Rip, A., & van der Meulen, J. R. (1996). The post-modern research system. *Science & Public Policy*, *23*, 343–352.

Roe, M. (2003). *Political Determinants of Corporate Governance*. Oxford Oxford University Press.

Roling, N., Hounkonnou, D., Kossou, D., Kuyper, T.W., Nederlof, S., Dawson, O. S., Traoré, M., & Huis, A. V. (2012). Diagnosing the scope for innovation: Linking smallholder practices and institutional context Introduction to the special issue. *Wageningen Journal of Life Science*, *60-63*, 1-6. .njas.2012.06.004 doi:10.1016/j

Rose, R. (1990). Inheritance before choice in public policy. *Journal of Theoretical Politics*, *1990*(2), 263–291. doi:10.1177/0951692890002003002

Sarkar, S. (2020). The idea of a university in India. *Economic and Political Weekly*, *55*(14).

Schumpeter, J. A. (1951). *Capitalism, Socialism, and Democracy*. George Allen & Unwin.

Seo, M. G., & Creed, W. E. D. (2002). Institutional Contradictions, Praxis, and Institutional Change: A Dialectical Perspective. *Academy of Management Review*, *27*(2), 222–247. doi:10.2307/4134353

Sherwin, R. J. (2019). Character is a Sacred Bond: Reflections on Sovereignty, Grace, and Resistance. *Angelaki*, *24*(4), 70–86. doi:10.1080/0969725X.2019.1635828

Skocpol, T. (1995). *Protecting Soldiers and Mothers: The Political Origins of Social Policy in the United States*. Harvard University Press. doi:10.2307/j.ctvjz81v6

Slager, R., Gond, J.-P., & Moon, J. (2012). Standardization as institutional work: The regulatory power of a responsible investment standard. *Organization Studies*, *33*(5–6), 763–790. doi:10.1177/0170840612443628

Slater, A. (2010). Altering authoritarianism: institutional complexity and autocratic agency in Indonesia. In Explaining Institutional Change. Cambridge University Press.

Soboul, A. (1982). *La Révolution française*. Gallimard, Tel.

Squires, V. R., & Qi, L. (2017). *Sustainable Land Management in Greater Central Asia: An Integrated and Regional Perspective*. Routledge. doi:10.9774/gleaf.9781315679396

Staab, S., & Waylen, G. (2020). Institutional change in constrained circumstances: Gender, resistance, and critical actors in the Chilean executive. *Latin American Politics and Society*, *62*(4), 50–74. doi:10.1017/lap.2020.15

Stephens, A. C. (2016). The affective atmospheres of nationalism. *Cultural Geographies*, *23*(2), 181-198. doi:10.1177/1474474015569994

Stephens, A. C. (2019). National Atmospheres and the 'Brexit' Revolt." *Society and Space*. societyandspace.org/2016/08/23/national-atmospheres-and-the-brexit-revolt-angharad-closs-stephens/

Streeck, W., & Thelen, K. (2005). Introduction: institutional change in advanced political economies. In *Beyond Continuity: Institutional Change in Advanced Political Economies* (pp. 1–39). Oxford University Press.

Tang, L., & Shapira, P. (2011). Regional development and interregional collaboration in the growth of nanotechnology research in China. *Scientometrics*, *86*(2), 299–315. doi:10.100711192-010-0274-9

The Commonwealth Secretariat. (2016). *Advancing gender equality: case studies from across Commonwealth*. The Commonwealth Secretariat. https://www.oecd-ilibrary.org/content/publication/9781848599451-en

Thelen, K. (2003). How Institutions Evolve. In J. Mahoney & D. Rueschemeyer (Eds.), *Comparative Historical Analysis in the Social Sciences* (pp. 208–234). Cambridge University Press. doi:10.1017/CBO9780511803963.007

UNAIDS. (n.d.). *Technical Support Facilities*. UNAIDS Press.

Van der Leeuw, S., Wiek, A., Harlow, J., & Buizer, J. (2012). How much time do we have? Urgency and rhetoric in sustainability science. *Sustainability Science*, *7*(S1), 115–120. doi:10.100711625-011-0153-1

Veblen T. (1899/1994). *The Theory of the Leisure Class: An Economic Study in the Evolution of Institutions*. Macmillan.

Wade, R. (2001). Showdown at the World Bank. *New Left Review*, *2001*(7), 124–137.

Wang, W., & Xiong, J. (2020). Research on institutional supply effect in innovation development of manufacturing industry. *Technoeconomics & Management Research.*, *2020*(5), 117–121.

Wiek, A., Withycombe, L., & Redman, C. L. (2011). Key competencies in sustainability: A reference framework for academic program development. *Sustainability Science*, *6*(2), 203–218. doi:10.100711625-011-0132-6

Wijayanti, F., Dyah, S., Saparita, R., & Abbas, A. (2016). Institutional Transformation of Local Innovation Systems in Farmer Community of Belu, East Nusa Tenggara. *Journal of STI Policy and Management*, *1*(2), 137–151. doi:10.14203/STIPM.2016.51

Wilsford, D. (1994). Path dependency, or why history makes it difficult but not impossible to reform health care systems in a big way. *Journal of Public Policy*, *14*(3), 251–283. doi:10.1017/S0143814X00007285

Zhao, Y., Li, Y., & Sun, X. (2019). The realizing mechanism of the synergy between technological innovation and institutional innovation to drive the evolution of a manufacturing enterprise: A longitudinal grounded analysis of guangming furniture. *Journal of Management Case Studies*, *12*(2), 188–180.

Chapter 3
Organisational Philosophy and Culture:
Human Capital as Pivot, Women as Fulcrum

Catherine Hayes
https://orcid.org/0000-0003-3870-2668
University of Sunderland, UK

ABSTRACT

This chapter considers the ongoing issues faced in relation to gender discrimination and change in relation to global recovery from the COVID-19 pandemic. A theoretical approach is adopted to consider the agency women are afforded within the context of leadership generally and change management, specifically. These debates are contextualised within global higher education and examined through theoretical lenses of influence, such as neoliberalism, which have impacted so much on the context specificity of change management in higher education and the cultures within which it has influenced so greatly. The recent global COVID-19 pandemic is used as a vehicle by which to drive thinking around concepts, which have had such an impact on women during this time, such as emotional labour, systemic equity, and structural inequality. The chapter concludes with a consideration of organisational structures and the agency that this has afforded women both historically and within the leadership challenges they currently face.

DOI: 10.4018/978-1-6684-6567-7.ch003

INTRODUCTION

"Equality is leaving the door open for anyone who has the means to approach it; equity is ensuring there is a pathway to that door for those who need it." ~– Caroline Belden (2021)

The impact of the COVID-19 pandemic has ensured not only that humanity has dealt with a sudden and harsh reminder of its own position relative to the risks man lives with on an everyday basis, but also the opportunities to initiate and manage change that these bring, specifically for women in business (Peters et al, 2020). The existential crisis facing Higher Education Institutions as a direct consequence of 2020 has served as a lens through which other facets of ambiguity and contingency also influence meta-thinking concerning their strategic governance and operationalisation of policies in practice (Pellegrini et al, 2020). Facing ethical dilemmas, institutional leaders also must grapple with compounding intraneous and extraneous variables which exacerbate the current crisis situations HEIs now face (Rapanta et al, 2020).

Whereas the majority of HEIs across the globe work within specific methodological and management methodologies, the capacity for flexible adaptation, creativity, and innovation in crisis, arguably manifests more commonly amongst women leaders than their male counterparts (El-Besomey, 2020). The gender balance and diversity that women bring to executive leadership positions during times of crisis provides a correspondingly more diversified epistemic standpoint through which crises can be considered (Aldrich and Lotito, 2020). These often subtle but diverse differences in knowledge positionality serve to be more transformative than transactional and as such are often more contextually and situationally relevant to immediately pressing issues, offering a wider lens through which to present, frame and articulate considered solutions (Martinez-Leon et al, 2020). Crises impact upon the theoretical underpinnings of the institutional rationales, designs, and operations of these contexts – within HEI and in parallel fields of praxis, where women have been witnessed at executive leadership levels, coping better and more appropriately than their male peers, almost as if facing a hypothetical wartime battle (Benziman, 2020; Maas et al, 2020).

The malalignment of the theoretical framework of HEI relative to the disciplinary perspectives of education has long been annotated as an issue for address (Barnett, 1990), however this was framed at a particularly politically volatile time as a means of highlighting larger ethical issues of concern, rather than crisis as an independent concept (Jandrić et al, 2020). The most recent challenge, presented by COVID-19, is to ensure that pedagogic practice across HEIs can adapt to new teaching and assessment methodologies, whilst at the same time ensuring an optimal quality and student experience for those joining academic programmes of study at HEIs (Rapanta et al, 2020) These experiences will potentially form the foundational bedrock which will ultimately underpin their future careers, lives and capacity for wider civic societal contributions.

Media reports that women in leadership roles have greatly outperformed men in the strategic management of the implications of COVID-19 globally, have become an everyday source of interest and intrigue. The positive lauding of female prime ministers, presidents and politicians has also been counterbalanced by accounts from women with more standard positions on career trajectories, for whom home working, home schooling and the attempted continuance of everyday norms amidst a global pandemic are, by their very nature, far more routine and mundane prospects (Whitty-Collins, 2020). On an even more negative and resonant note, the media have reported on the increased incidence and prevalence rates of domestic violence crimes committed against women, which further detail the challenges that some women (and their children) in 21st Century society also face (Wenham, Smith and Morgan, 2020).

The scope and parameters of this chapter do not permit a consideration of all issues that all women face, rather this chapter provides an insight into the agentic roles of women leaders in global crises, which have ensured their credibility and dependability in times of greatest challenge to the context of Higher Education (HE) leadership across the world. A collective insight into the roles of women leaders within the COVID-19 pandemic has featured widely in the international press, where multi-agency perspectives on their actions and reactions have been largely positive (Trent, 2020). Belying this media frenzy, however lies a far deeper debate in just how representative these women leaders are of those working within diverse HE leadership contexts and settings and indeed how far transferable their situational skills of leadership actually are (Henley and Roy, 2020).

The individual positionality of all women is equally important to those who operate as strategic heads of state and whose lives are largely characterised by the privilege of hierarchical positions and the status accompanying them (Bright, Acosta and Parker, 2020; Inman, 2020)). This chapter aims to provide an insight into the existing evidence base of how women leaders in Higher Education during a global pandemic, such as COVID-19, cope in reality. Not only does this illuminate the reality of concepts such as emotional labour, mental health and wellbeing and authenticity, it also serves to delineate the personhood of women from the professional roles they occupy across our global societies, within the situational specificity of Higher Education (Tshivhase, 2020).

In its entirety, this chapter also serves to deconstruct the characteristic and agentic qualities of women leaders amidst global crises, which are also reflected in the traits of women managing in more recognisable and relatable leadership roles in the context of Higher Education leadership (Thomas, 2020). The core acknowledgements that on a global level the impact of crises inevitably leads to a disproportionate impact on women, a lack of prioritisation of global impetus to address levels of gender inequality and the embedded role of gender equity in relation to human progression and development on a macro level is apparent (Power, 2020; WHO, 2020). This global perspective illuminates the inequalities that women educators face and the impact that this has on the broader scope of professional development through educational impact (Barba and Iraizoz, 2020). Whilst situational specificity is significant in terms of the context of HE leadership, the universality of human experience underpinning them remains the connecting thread, which enables the deconstruction of meaning making in applied educational leadership experiences.

PROACTIVE APPROACHES IN CRISIS MANAGEMENT

Crisis management of any variety necessitates a proactive response, rooted in complex ambiguity, which is non-conventional and is underpinned by active application of cognition, metacognition, and epistemic cognition to practice. In terms of temporal issues, response times can necessitate an immediacy of thinking and correspondingly rapid response, all of which may have potentially long-term consequences, necessitating leaders to be both accountable and responsible for their actions. Parallel to this lies Mezirow's (2009) Perspective Transformation Theory, posited by Mezirow, in relation to transformative learning as,

The epistemology of how adults learn to reason for themselves - advance and assess reasons for making a judgement - rather than act on the assimilated beliefs, values, feelings and judgements of others.

In terms of overall cognitive processing in the contexts of crisis, how gender is of direct relevance is rooted in the increased capacity women have, relative to men, to think flexibly, adaptably and with compassion (Villiers, 2019). This is not to denigrate the gender attributable skill sets of male employees across HEIs but to acknowledge that how people problem solve and react can often have its basis in concepts which are adjuncts to, rather than facets of gender. Whereas men are geared towards objective problem solving in binary 'black and white' fashions as opposed to the capacity to think in shades of grey, which women more clearly demonstrate, what is clear, is that situation and context are the pivotal deciding variables in terms of the need for immediacy of action (Cahdriyana, et al, 2019). These problematic frames of reference, described by Mezirow in the context of education, serve to explain how humans monitor their problem-solving capacities, once engaged in contexts and settings of complex ambiguity, where contingency planning comes to the fore (Mezirow, 2009).

UNEXPECTED, COMPLEX AND DISRUPTIVE AMBIGUITY

Within the context of complex and disruptive ambiguity in crisis, the capacity for both critical reflection and critical reflexivity are paramount. Self-awareness features highly as one of the core aspects of being able to undertake either optimally and effective action, since how responsive behaviours may be viewed by others, and the interrelationship of this with the alternative perspective of others can be indicators of potential success in crisis management. Illuminating this awareness enables a further conceptual consideration of the gender delineation occurring naturally because of the agentic qualities and attributes of women in the context of crisis management. What is pivotal in these incidences is the capacity for and subsequent integration of tacit knowledge to practice, which stems from not only an extant evidence base but also experiential learning and wisdom, rather than any certainty or concretisation of new knowledge (Dewey, 1933). It is this which is transformational rather than transactional in terms of application and use in leadership praxis and aligns directly with the traditional gender traits of women and men in executive leadership positions, respectively. Through the advancement of the body of work in cognitive psychology at the turn of the 21st century, and the understanding of epistemic assumptions, models such as 'the reflective judgement model' posited by King and Kitchener (2004) (see Table 1 overleaf) lend themselves to adapted application in relation to gender delineation. Whilst all of these are evidence based on the extant literature, the issues of situational specificity and context are pivotal in any consideration of complex ambiguity in crisis, not least because of the relative certainty of knowledge within them.

CONTEMPLATING WHETHER REFLEXIVITY CAN BE INFLUENCED BY GENDER

Axiologically identifiably fixed and typically white male, middle-aged, middle-class mindsets have shaped the society within which corporate leadership operates, with global Higher Education Institutions being no exception. The perspectives these fixed mindsets are rooted in, stems not only from professional bias, but the constraints of cultures which seek to categorise, label and define men and women in relation to biology rather than their capacity to function as leaders, where gender

Table 1. A gender delineation adaptation of the King and Kitchener (2004) reflective judgement model

Thinking Stage	Potential Impact on Gender-Based Agentic Qualities
Stage 1 ***Pre-reflective***	Knowledge is absolute and concrete, no reason to ask why, I believe only what I have seen and thus know it to be true-single category belief system – exposure to diversity of thinking.
Stage 2 ***Pre-reflective***	Knowledge is absolutely certain but not readily available to everyone, the right person in authority needs to be sought– some people hold right beliefs and some people hold wrong beliefs - similar to Perry's dualism observed or taught by an authority figure.
Stage 3 ***Pre-reflective***	Knowledge is assumed to be absolutely certain or temporarily uncertain and believe that absolute truth will be manifest in concrete data sometime in the future. Implicitly they maintain that ultimately all problems have solutions.
Stage 4 ***Quasi-reflective***	Knowledge is no longer certain, there is always a layer of ambiguity, limitations of the knower are acknowledged and without certainty knowledge cannot be validated. Well-structured problems such as arithmetic can be described completely, and ill-structured problems are afforded legitimacy at this stage.
Stage 5 ***Quasi-reflective***	Knowledge is contextual and subjective, interpretations are different, so knowledge is different.
Stage 6 ***Reflective***	Knowing is uncertain and knowledge must be understood in relation to the context from which it was derived. Knowledge is constructed through evaluation, comparing knowledge and opinions across contexts, an initial basis for forming judgement/solutions to ill-structured problems.
Stage 7 ***Reflective***	Knowing is uncertain and subject to interpretation and epistemically justifiable claims can be made about the best solution to the problem. Knowledge as an outcome and a process of evaluation. Re-evaluation, new methods of inquiry, or new perspectives become available over time.

is and ought to be regarded as matterless. What is evident is that the characteristic agentic qualities of both genders differ but what is equally clear is that these have been socially constructed over the course of lifetimes and it is a change in the fixed mindset of modern society that is gradually enabling recognition and acknowledgement of this. Sadly, whilst the COVID-19 pandemic may increase access to educational opportunities and potentially widen participation, the economic effects will have a greater negative impact, restricting even basic access to educational opportunity. In May 2020 the World Bank estimated that 60 million people at risk of being pushed into extreme poverty worldwide as a result of Covid; erasing all progress made to alleviate poverty over the past 3 years. This will likely adversely impact upon women.

Tversky & Kahneman (1974) provided some of the first insights into how judgements under uncertainty, which primarily rely on three heuristics are made. The first, is the probability or likelihood of something, the second is the plausibility of it occurring at all and finally the capacity to develop dual process thinking. Considering all three in the context of the COVID-19 pandemic, has necessitated an instinctual and emotional response, which fits into Tversky and Kahneman's definitive System

1 thinking, whereas System 2 tends to engage logic and systematic thinking. The agentic qualities of women and men, although attributable to societal construction correspond with these Systems of duality. What enables coping in crisis situations, is not actually an innate capacity to cope, but the recognition and address of complex ambiguity. Where the agentic qualities of women are an advantage here, is that they have a tendency for relationality and transformation as opposed to the functionalism and transactional approaches traditionally adopted by men.

BRIEF SUMMARY OF EVIDENCE FROM THE EXTANT LITERATURE

Using Bronfenbrenner's Ecological Systems as a theoretical lens through which to view globally published literature to date is useful. It provides a means of relating to macro, meso and micro levels of infrastructure which directly impact upon the policy level, institutional level, and individual levels in which gender continues to influence and matter.

MACRO (POLICY LEVEL)

Gender-Based Admonishment of Women has had a global impact on the capacity for women to mobilise their active contribution to the workplace and frame an identity within it. Within and between culturally diverse geographical regions across the world, this has had a significant impact on the potential of women to also begin to address the ongoing existence of physical and emotional violence against them. Globally, in tandem with this there are huge grass roots implementation gaps in policy, which would empower women to establish their own professional identities and career trajectories. Having policy commitment could potentially revolutionise these cultures and provide a mechanism of making gendered differences everyone's moral responsibility. Because of traditionalist approaches to gendered leadership there has also been a prioritisation of men in leadership roles, particularly across Asia and Africa, with the exception of female dominated professions such as nursing and childcare. Sociocultural perspective lenses frame backgrounds and serve as significant constraints to women who wish to follow an academic career trajectory across these continents. The appropriateness of women's work was often positioned within gendered roles of care and nurture, which is reflective of this workforce today. To increase women's representation, this ought to be addressed. Alongside this the intersectionality of structural inequalities within social class, caste, religion, ethnic origin and language remain key issues.

MESO (INSTITUTIONAL LEVEL IMPLEMENTATION)

Across strategic studies of the gendered workplace the core enablers for women have been identified as approaches to internationalisation, courses of study and learning in leadership which have been tailored and designed specifically for women's only strategic development planning. Often, organisational culture is rooted to an endemic patriarchal culture, which is reflective of wider societal and communal expectation. This can lead to issues of gender discrimination and incorporate both conscious and unconscious bias and even violence in some international Higher Education Institutions. There is a cultural hesitancy of women in countries across Africa and Asia to challenge issues of opportunities for promotion and leadership opportunity. Often there is no consistency in terms of the processes of academic promotion within and between Higher Educational Institutions, which often leads to an inevitability of gender bias within paternalistic societies. One exception to the contextual opportunity for women to progress, is within single sex organisations, where women are afforded the opportunity of leadership positions. However these positions are often denigrated in terms credibility in relation to the equivalent roles of their male counterparts.

MICRO (LEVEL OF INDIVIDUAL IMPACT)

At an individual level, across multiple global societies and communities, women still experience active gender discrimination in the context of work based practice. This two tier system of regard has led to an increasing subculture of women who feel unworthy of promotion and an aspirational sense of value and as a consequence never apply for leadership roles or positions. This has the negative impact of further consolidating male dominated workplaces. Whilst family circumstances can practically constrain the level of input women can have in the Higher Education workplace due to the cultural expectation that women will be primary caregivers for their children, it remains pivotal that if women are to succeed in the workplace that they have a degree of support in their endeavours so that career progression can even be contemplated.

GENDERED LEADERSHIP IN HIGHER EDUCATION

Despite HEI's making formal recognition of barriers to women reaching senior management positions across their organisational hierarchies, their executives have done relatively little to address issues of structure and agency in relation to antiquated practices that perpetuate these identified inequities (O'Connor, 2020). The situational and contextual backdrops which influence these inequities globally are, of course, largely defined, as outlined previously, by subcultures and contexts at macro, micro and meso levels – the ecological perspectives of where change has been lost in translation in an effort to quite often tokenistically address gender inequity in the workplace are often clearly tangible (Grimson and Grimson, 2019). However authentic approaches to tackling the provision of opportunities for women are rooted too, in wider societal actions and agencies which women respond to prior to and in the early development of establishing a professional identity. The perpetuation of an underrepresentation of women in senior management positions within the labour market generally, and the higher education senior leadership market specifically, is an issue for address. The commonality of issues surrounding women in HEI leadership positions within and between diverse countries, is widely reported as something which transcends cultural barriers and contextual specificities. What unites the relative framing and positioning of these roles is the inflexibility of organisational infrastructures to accommodate diversity beyond feminist tokenism, which contributes directly to a lack of accessibility to leadership roles for women. This is a historical legacy characterised predominantly by dated approaches to the integration of women into the labour market at executive leadership levels (O'Connor, 2019). Remuneration levels are all too often aligned with this inequity and what is evident is that whereas globally most institutions are making moves to close the gender pay gap, they are doing relatively little to change the infrastructure and support for potential women leaders, which impacts on the degree of opportunity afforded to them during their career trajectories (Heymann et al, 2019; Taylor et al, 2017). These career trajectories, by virtue of biological function, are still inevitably interrupted by maternity leave and caring responsibilities to a larger extent than the careers of their male counterparts. Equality and diversity initiatives at national levels in the UK, now ensure that many organisations are designated the status of equal opportunities employers, which have seen the rise of initiatives such as the Athena Swann mark emblazoned across HEI provider websites, reflecting their articulated capacity to advocate and support equal opportunities in the workplace. Whether this impacts authentically on these wider issues of structures and agency is something only longer-term evaluation will reveal.

Whilst equality proofing quality initiatives serve well in the identification of the impact of policies which have unintentionally negative impacts on women in practice, one key challenge is being able to identify and filter out the factors underpinning them. In the context of wider professional practice measures these can potentially serve to identify unintended policy impacts but serve neither to identify mechanisms to monitor or reverse the ongoing masculinisation of HEI provision. It ought to be expected that those countries which implement these policy initiatives (e.g., UK,

New Zealand, Australia and Sweden) have a greater degree of success in their levels of equal opportunity for women in HEIs but the published research evidence actually points to countries such as Turkey, Portugal and Cyprus having better success rates despite having no formal nationally applied gender based equality initiatives in formal operation (Tanova et al, 2008; Reay, 2004).

THE COMMODIFICATION OF HIGHER EDUCATION AND WOMENS' LEADERSHIP

Neoliberalism has had an extraordinary impact on the structure and agency of HEIs, with the commodification of education necessitating a new wave of managerialism which has been equally entrenched with misogyny as an integral part of the realms of traditional academia (Meyers, 2013). Characterised by a culture of often toxic masculinity, the tangible and lasting impact, which actively disadvantages women leaders, is well reported in the existing published evidence base surrounding this issue (Canaan and Shumar, 2008). On a global level, this impact varies in relation to the extent of the emergence of managerialism in HEIs, where female academic presence is predominant in humanities and those disciplines perceived as 'soft' in comparison to their overtly male led empirical science disciplines. The interrelationship with poor opportunities for external research funding across these female dominated academic disciplines has provided a now historically visible delineation between the genders, with the motivational climate for progression being negatively affected since there is little to no opportunity for the development and integration of creativity and imagination (Bagilhole, 2019).

This has not only had an impact at a disciplinary level for women, it also directly impacts on their future likelihood of being able to gain full professorships, a pathway which is often necessary to gain an academic senior management position in reputable and credible HEIs. Since the relative number of women operating at professorial level is significantly different across countries, and particularly in countries such as Ireland, which has the least proportion of women employed at either professorial or associate professorial levels, then it is also still evident that these women have least opportunity for promotion to executive roles in HEIs (Bailes and Guthery, 2020). As an adjunct to these statistics, is the fact that women also are far more likely to shoulder additional responsibilities in relation to caring for children, elderly relatives. This, alongside having to continually make a stand against the gender stereotyping which characterises 21st Century HEI workplaces paints a picture, which to some women leaders can be perceived as overwhelming and not worth the additional effort needed to challenge them. By continually instilling and reinforcing this culture into the contexts and settings of where women work in academia, these women often also begin to recognise that the gate keeping which prevents their progression in organisations, also ensures that their perception of a career trajectory at professorial level and consequently in executive management is fundamentally illusory to them (ibid, 2008).

To move beyond the tokenism that characterises male hegemony in HEIs globally, a key issue for address is the minimal representation of women within senior management positions. The challenges faced by women who do venture into these positions often serves to further highlight the extent of male domination at senior management level that exists within these HEIs. This tokenism has also ensured that women are not in positions where they can actively challenge either toxic masculinity or the supplementary structure and agency that prevail in today's HEI workplaces and which continue to resonate in the context of HEI women leadership (Wheaton and Kezar, 2019).

DRIVERS OF GENDER EQUITY AND EQUALITY IN HIGHER EDUCATION

The longevity of male dominance in particular disciplinary subjects such as mathematics, science and engineering has done little to positively enhance the quality and duration of HEI women leaders' career trajectories. An evidence-based insight into this reveals a clear deficit of female professors across these disciplines, which bears witness to the corresponding longevity and history of education locally, nationally, and globally. One of the first steps to deconstructing this inequality is, as the STEM initiative in the UK has focused upon, to encourage equity and new awareness of careers available in traditionally male dominated professions via the consideration of the concept of 'signature pedagogies' (Shulman, 2005; Fitzgerald, 2020). Where gendered organisational culture and processes are evident in favour with male employees, it is apparent from the literature that, conformity is also more widely valued than attributes of creativity, and, as a by-product, innovation. This has been both historically and contemporaneously apparent in the body of literature available but amidst crisis with the advent of the COVID-19 pandemic, has never been more relevant. In HEIs which have demonstrably lower levels of women at senior executive levels across their organisations, this brings into question the purist epistemic assumptions which are clearly non diverse and non-aspirational in terms of equality, diversity and therefore creativity. The exponential reach afforded by a clear capacity for a diverse workforce, not merely constructed of ideological representation, but one of operationalised knowledge and skill, is immeasurable and has been clearly evidenced by the progression of parallel fields of practice. As an active consequence of these dilemmas which have pervaded organisations for the best part of half a century, issues of gatekeeping, the impact of gendered cultures and infrastructures policies and initiatives are at last beginning to feature mechanisms of moving forward positively but they also indicate the extreme way to go that organisation must correct these systemic imbalances. What is clear is that if central policy does not change to reflect these needs, the governments, which also reflect an imbalance in the representation of women in executive roles, will persist in influencing the macro levels of society at which meso and micro levels are then by default poised to remain indefinitely.

DISPELLING TRADITION AND THE PERPETUATION OF STEREOTYPICAL THINKING

Research has been conducted which conclusively identifies that senior managers of HEI organisations believe or hold assumptions that women, from a signature pedagogy perspective, are far more likely to work in the context of disciplines such as the social sciences, arts and humanities - those often termed 'soft subjects' or those which are responsible in health and medical care in the remit of 'caring' such as nursing (Dilnot, 2018; Henderson et al, 2018). They also perceived those empirical sciences due to the cultural necessity of maintaining the status quo of daily operations would potentially be interrupted by career breaks and the accommodation of caring responsibilities. In contrast to this perspective though, remains the fact that women's choice of study during school and university years also demonstrates that relatively few young women wish to study subjects such as science, technology, engineering and mathematics and as the current initiatives in UK educational settings indicate, this has become an identified area for redress in terms of changing the misconceptions that girls have about academic study in the post-compulsory sector (Lannelli and Duta, 2018). At a macro level, the labour market dictates the value of subject disciplines by leaders of global societies, where the representation of women leadership is also comparatively low. Reflective of this, is the fact that a corresponding hierarchy of subjects and disciplines exist, which is positively reinforced by the masculine perspectives driving their need. Because of this, fewer women follow maths, technology and sciences in preferences to the arts, humanities and social sciences. Aligned with the capacity for maximal earning capacity in the labour market are the opportunities to work in disciplines of these empirical studies, hence widening the gap between men and women in the potential to gain highly paid roles. Again, the redress of this balance would serve to close the gender income gap which characterises global economies. Research also highlights that those disciplines with which women more readily engage, also contribute widely to the development of the skill sets which men are known to lack. Gender segregation in the early stages of student learning at school can be regarded as a key cause of the gender gap, both economically and in terms of leadership opportunity that women experience throughout their academic careers. Where these are of greatest concern is in relation to the concepts of citizenship, which HEIs often claim to incorporate as an integral part of their organisational strength across global communities. Within this context, diversity and equality are two issues upon which capacity for citizenship and capacity for active civic reach, can hinge.

WOMEN AND POLITICS

The delineating features of women who have dominated as successful political leaders, both historically and contemporaneously, can be aligned with the agentic qualities associated with the concept of stereotypical gender stereotyping. In European contexts, two of the most typical examples are Baroness Margaret Thatcher and Angela Merkel. What these distinguished women reveal, upon analysis is a capacity for both the transactional autocratic style characterised by professional positionality and a task-oriented approach, usually associated with male hegemony alongside an equally desirable skill set which is linked not only with strategic success but also social justice in a truly transformative sense. The transformative leadership usually associated with successful female leadership echoes and reinforces the theoretical perspectives of Mezirow. This capacity for remaining person centred alongside the strength and resilience associated with making decisions which are not always palatable for a wider collective benefit remains at the heart of realising that organisational factors such as gender comparison, situation, context, and hierarchy are all important moderators of leadership style in practice. All these agentic qualities are still confounded with the concept of gender.

The active delineation of leadership from management is important. It was perhaps best operationally defined for the context of HEIs by Gardner (1995), when he defined it, accounting for both task and relationship dimensionality, as

'The ability to influence, either directly or indirectly, the behaviour, thoughts, and actions of a significant number of individuals'

Since temporality, situation and context are inherently dynamic and altered at any given point, it can be stated that there is no such thing as definably perfect leadership. It is optimal leadership and not management which is the greatest determinant of organisational success. This was a key mechanism for solving both public and private sector challenges, often many of which are politically underpinned in the context of HEI settings.

In times of societal crisis, the words of Fitzgerald (2003) resonate harshly in the culture and climate of today's HEI organisations, when the assertion 'Conceptualisations of leadership without full account of both gender and ethnicity are futile'. Recent impacting factors on how we consider all leaders, not merely based on their gender, add an extra dimension to how best crisis ought to be managed and how long held assumptions and pre-suppositions can be actively challenged in practice.

Critical to this is the capacity for self-reflection and the desire to implement critical reflexivity at the heart of crisis environments. Mezirow's now seminal work on transformative learning can be seen as the keystone that enables all people to be seen as more than simply a collection of qualifications and experience, towards knowing people who know themselves. This is arguably one of the few mechanisms of being able to claim true and authentic approaches to the leadership and management of self, alongside organisations and institutions whose infrastructures serve to permeate wider society as an integral part of their civic contribution to society.

THE CONSIDERATION OF DEFICIT MODELS

Within longstanding published literature it is well established that the skills that leading in the context of HEIs entails are not actually gendered at all (Burke and Crozier, 2014). More recently it has been recognised that these skills are centred around the capacity and capability for endurance in relation to hard work, strategic vision, evidence of reputational impact in research, the courage to manage in the context of taking measured risk and the resilience and integrity to operationalise what is necessary for success (Meletiadou, 2022). From an axiological standpoint, it is more often the case that the value placed upon what women leaders do, stems from the value of the disciplinary perspectives from which they emerge, rather than any overt judgement surrounding gender (Jamali et al, 2022). Within the context of male senior management there are far more likely to be male academics from traditionally masculine subjects such as science and engineering, whereas, due to the historical legacies and patterns of humanities and caring professions, women are far less likely to have worked with and alongside them (Bauer and Taylor, 2022).

New public governance of organisations has meant that a strategic revamp of most of the organisational structuring has taken place across HEIs globally, however whilst these have shifted things predominantly towards a consumer led market perspective, the impact on the gendered leadership in HEIs has arguably been only vaguely considered. Therefore, these axiological standpoints are often little more than tokenism in relation to the practical application of values based strategic vision to practice. Arguably the best starting point for axiological underpinnings to be addressed, lies at the heart of organisational structures and cultures, which enable the authentic agency of women to flourish and to be genuinely valued (Tiwary and Gupta, 2022). Since core values lie at the credibility of every HEI across the globe, these remain ongoing areas for address and further research.

Women leaders are far more likely to express a capacity for collective and relationship behavioural approaches in practice, than male leaders, who are more likely to adopt purely transactional leadership strategies and operationalise these in practice. Because of this approach, women are often deemed to be less effective since their capacity to deal with complex ambiguity often entails detailed critical thinking as opposed to the binary decision making associated with transactional approaches (O'Connor et al, 2022). This is wholly dependent on the situational specificity of organisational contexts, which ultimately provides a platform for leadership execution and the ethos evident within it, in relation to differing leadership styles and approaches (Ruben, Mahon and Shapiro, 2022).

ORGANISATIONAL INFRASTRUCTURES AND IMPACT ON GENDERED AGENCY

The formal administration structures of HEIs have altered little in a century. Still featuring a pyramidal structure where women notoriously occupy the bottom rung of the organisational hierarchy, remains a typical profile for the majority of global HEIs. In European and American HEIs, initiatives aimed specifically at addressing gender equity in education, are thriving, which aim to provide transformational leadership opportunities and development for women. These provide bespoke training, education, and progression pathways for those who wish to further their academic career trajectories but are limited in availability and opportunity to access them is often lacking in equity of opportunity. The central issue of capacity for women leaders in HEIs is not actually the number of women in HEIs across the globe but rather the positions they occupy, which tend to be traditionally clustered at the bottom of the organisational hierarchy with minimal degrees of representation at higher levels, As a consequence, women rarely progress to the level of Dean, but do occupy their subordinate positions as Associate Deans, Directors or Pro Vice Chancellors, rather than linchpin positions at the top. This is a source of blocking women's access to powerful positions and thus exerting a vision for the next generation of female leaders. Perhaps the greatest danger in this dynamic is the sheer invisibility of organisational and gender-based bias, which serves to block female progression. As a key aspect of social justice and equity in action, as both process and goal this is a fundamental area for address across the globe where untapped potential and the provision of opportunity warrant redress (McNair, Bensimon, and Malcom-Piqueux, 2020; Okoli et al, 2020).

Men are far more likely to attribute the underrepresentation or lack of women in executive level positions to the breaks they necessarily take in relation to family caring responsibilities, career interruptions due to pregnancy and their comparative and relative lack of research impact in HEI praxis. In contrast women's perceptions of the same experience are littered with reports of actively overt and covertly demonstrated workplace discrimination, fuelled by the basis of their gender. Unlike the successes of Merkel and Thatcher in a political setting, where transformative learning is valued, the opposite has been found to be largely true in the context of HEI settings, where the higher women climb within the organisational hierarchy, the more they assume the character traits represented by male leaders, where they become deliberately and overly transactional (Allen and Flood, 2018). As a direct consequence of this, they progressively develop the same perspectives, that recruitment on the basis of gender is something that ought to be tokenistic rather than something actually addressed in HEI professional practice. These deficit models are potentially damaging, but even more so where this is often unintentionally reinforced by members of their own gender because of the cultural normalisation of gender stereotyping (Teelken and Deem, 2013). Göransson, et al (2008) stated that gendered organisational cultures are in turn linked to gendered knowledge, which means the naturally occurring agentic qualities with which women are wired to lead, are often masked by the bureaucracy and culture of organisations, rather than anything else. Therefore, the hegemonic and often toxic masculinity which drives organisations pervades into the wider cultural climate and becomes entrenched and difficult to address. At the heart of addressing these issues is the nature of recruitment and the nature of actively retaining women through to the point where they have visibly recognisable opportunities to apply for promotion or at least seek a career trajectory reflective of their capacity and capability. This is apparent across many professional disciplines out with the context of Higher Education (Hayes and Graham 2020; Bellini et al, 2019). The nature of women's participation is also an issue, since they need the basis of equity and inclusivity to participate on an equal footing with their male counterparts. Those pragmatic issues which serve as barriers to this, are often found in the institutional operational policies within which all staff are required to work, regardless of academic or professional discipline (Cardel et al, 2020).

ACTIVE PARTICIPATION VERSUS VISIBILITY OF GENDER IDENTITY IN EDUCATION

The agentic qualities that women do bring to the context of executive leadership within the context of HEIs are based around their capacity for creativity and as a direct consequence the bridge to innovation that this secures (Lipton, 2015). They are also widely reported as enhancing capacity for effective communication and an authentic approach to dealing with both the professional and personal needs of others.

Perhaps dwelling overly on long held debates of both the metaphorical glass ceiling and glass escalator ought to be diminished by the consideration of women, who whilst largely atypical of female representativeness across HEIs, provide important lessons surrounding the agentic qualities which have underpinned their success (Arriaga, Stanley and Lindsey, 2020).

Presenting these women as exemplars, however runs two distinct risks which have important implications for professional practice (Jameson, 2019). Firstly, the situations and contexts within which all women operate as leaders are largely unique and therefore the opportunity to emulate success is limited and secondly, women who are unable to transfer approaches into the context of their own workplace have an increased potential to perceive they will fail. Actually, in relation to the concept of failure, there are far wider independent variables and contextual issues at play, which correspondingly align with the far wider cultural challenges of organisational norms (Benslimane and Moustaghfir, 2020). One of the most insightful set of perspectives are those presented by Syed (2019) whose perspectives on the need for accuracy rather than creativity in the progressive development of change on major world issues such as feminism. His debate that during COVID-19 some leaders have demonstrated a clear capacity to pivot between leadership styles via the integration of both diverse views and binary decision making processes. Reconciling the perceived tension that arises when seeking to increase diversity within established meritocracies remains a pivotal debate in any consideration of women and their opportunities to use innate agency within crisis. Doubtless this will prevail, although the pandemic has provided a forum for the illumination of not just exceptional women from the higher echelons of society but all those coping in more everyday settings of the home, the office and beyond.

CONCLUSION

This chapter has explored the fundamental impact of how gendered leadership in Higher Education Institutions can shape culture, context, and the civic progression of women's roles across professional contexts. It is possible to see from this work that the global political implications of gendered workplace discrimination remain a key challenge, particularly across Asia in countries such as Afghanistan, Pakistan, India, Sri Lanka and Bangladesh. If monitored at all records and statistics of women in Higher Education Institutions are rarely recorded, other than in relation to student numbers. Specific focus in Western culture has led to an emphasis on the development of capacity within the disciplines of Science and Technology, with gender becoming almost a tokenistic addition to key considerations of curriculum quality rather than equal opportunities for women, which can be offered through, for example Universal Design for Learning, which ensures equity of opportunity as well as equality. The sociocultural power which men provide across the globe, means from an international perspective women are still very much regarded as domestic commodities, who ought never to have authority over men.

The chapter has also provided a theoretical insight into how the gender balance and diversity that women bring to leadership positions can strategically influence recovery from crisis, such as the global pandemic. It has been possible to consider how traditional signature pedagogies and disciplinary perspectives can often serve to stereotype and create assumptions about the need for leadership styles which are traditionalist, outmoded and lacking in creativity. The agentic roles occupied by women, as outlined in the chapter enable the illumination of workplace issues such as emotional labour and mental health to highlight core issues in the professional context of Higher Education Institutes. The proactivity that global responses to crisis necessitate have ensured that the universality of human experience, is now an integral part of not only the dynamic management of crisis but also recovery from it. Gender delineation and theoretical consideration of how crisis impacts on the agentic qualities of leadership in crisis has been a fundamental part of considering how best to address progressive thinking in the context of future progression in educational leadership in this chapter, within which capacity for critical reflexivity is essential. It is here that the relational capacity of women and their ability to undertake processes of metacognition which not only impact on functional responses but the potential impact of them, can be considered. Creativity and innovation that stems from unlocked diversity of thought will be sorely needed to address both the educational delivery challenges presented by the COVID-19 and adaptations necessary to deal with its long-lasting economic impact. The ongoing challenge for women, is to engage these as opportunities to be grappled with, as opposed to avoiding them for any perceived lack of confidence, knowledge and skill which has arisen from the projection of wrong assumption and traditionally male dominated organisational cultures and climates.

REFERENCES

Aldrich, A. S., & Lotito, N. J. (2020). Pandemic Performance: Women Leaders in the Covid-19 Crisis. *Politics & Gender*, *16*(4), 1–9. doi:10.1017/S1743923X20000549

Allen, T. G., & Flood, C. T. (2018). The Experiences of Women in Higher Education: Who Knew There Wasn't a Sisterhood? *Leadership and Research in Education, 4*, 10–27.

Arriaga, T. T., Stanley, S. L., & Lindsey, D. B. (2020). *Leading While Female: A Culturally Proficient Response for Gender Equity*. Corwin.

Bagilhole, B. (2019). Against the odds: Women academics' research opportunities. In *Gender, teaching and research in higher education* (pp. 46–56). Routledge. doi:10.4324/9781315254548-5

Bailes, L. P., & Guthery, S. (2020). Held Down and Held Back: Systematically Delayed Principal Promotions by Race and Gender. *AERA Open, 6*(2). doi:10.1177/2332858420929298

Barba, I., & Iraizoz, B. (2020). Effect of the Great Crisis on Sectoral Female Employment in Europe: A Structural Decomposition Analysis. *Economies, 8*(3), 64. doi:10.3390/economies8030064

Barnett, R. (1990). *The idea of higher education*. McGraw-Hill Education.

Bauer, N. M., & Taylor, T. (2022). Selling them short? Differences in news coverage of female and male candidate qualifications. *Political Research Quarterly*.

Bellini, M. I., Graham, Y., Hayes, C., Zakeri, R., Parks, R., & Papalois, V. (2019). A woman's place is in theatre: Women's perceptions and experiences of working in surgery from the Association of Surgeons of Great Britain and Ireland women in surgery working group. *BMJ Open, 9*(1), e024349. doi:10.1136/bmjopen-2018-024349 PMID:30617103

Benslimane, M., & Moustaghfir, K. (2020). Career development practices and gender equity in higher education. *International Journal of Management Education, 14*(2), 183–211.

Benziman, Y. (2020). "Winning" the "battle" and "beating" the COVID-19 "enemy": Leaders' use of war frames to define the pandemic. *Peace and Conflict, 26*(3), 247–256. doi:10.1037/pac0000494

Bright, A., Acosta, S., & Parker, B. (2020). Humility Matters: Interrogating Our Positionality, Power, and Privilege Through Collaboration. In Handbook of Research on Diversity and Social Justice in Higher Education (pp. 19-40). IGI Global.

Burke, P. J., & Crozier, G. (2014). Higher education pedagogies: Gendered formations, mis/recognition and emotion. *Journal of Research in Gender Studies, 4*(2), 52.

Cahdriyana, R. A., Richardo, R., Fahmi, S., & Setyawan, F. (2019, March). Pseudo-thinking process in solving logic problem. *Journal of Physics: Conference Series, 1188*(1), 012090. doi:10.1088/1742-6596/1188/1/012090

Canaan, J. E., & Shumar, W. (Eds.). (2008). *Structure and agency in the neoliberal university* (Vol. 15). Routledge. doi:10.4324/9780203927687

Cardel, M. I., Dhurandhar, E., Yarar-Fisher, C., Foster, M., Hidalgo, B., McClure, L. A., ... Willig, A. L. (2020). Turning chutes into ladders for women faculty: A review and roadmap for equity in academia. *Journal of Women's Health, 29*(5), 721–733. doi:10.1089/jwh.2019.8027 PMID:32043918

Dewey, J. (1933). *How We Think A Restatement of the Relation of Reflective Thinking to the Educative Process*. Heath & Co Publishers.

Dilnot, C. (2018). The relationship between A-level subject choice and league table score of university attended: The 'facilitating', the 'less suitable', and the counter-intuitive. *Oxford Review of Education, 44*(1), 118–137. doi:10.1080/03054985.2018.1409976

El-Besomey, D. A. M. (2020). The Contemporary Vision of Universal Strategic Planning for Facing (COVID-19) Crisis in the Field of Higher Education Via Virtual Learning-Training. *European Journal of Education, 3*(2), 151–164. doi:10.26417/869dvb85y

Fitzgerald, T. (2020). Mapping the terrain of leadership: Gender and leadership in higher education. *Irish Educational Studies, 39*(2), 1–12. doi:10.1080/03323315.2020.1729222

Gardner, H. (1995). *Leading Minds*. Harper Collins.

Göransson, K. E., Ehnfors, M., Fonteyn, M. E., & Ehrenberg, A. (2008). Thinking strategies used by Registered Nurses during emergency department triage. *Journal of Advanced Nursing, 61*(2), 163–172. doi:10.1111/j.1365-2648.2007.04473.x PMID:18186908

Grimson, J., & Grimson, W. (2019). Eliminating gender inequality in engineering, industry, and academia. In *The Engineering-Business Nexus* (pp. 315–339). Springer. doi:10.1007/978-3-319-99636-3_15

Hayes, C., & Graham, Y. N. (2020). Prophylaxis in Action:# MeToo for Women of Medical and Surgical Disciplines. In Gender Equity in the Medical Profession (pp. 270-279). IGI Global.

Henderson, M., Sullivan, A., Anders, J., & Moulton, V. (2018). Social class, gender and ethnic differences in subjects taken at age 14. *Curriculum Journal, 29*(3), 298–318. doi:10.1080/09585176.2017.1406810

Henley, J., & Roy, E. A. (2020). Are female leaders more successful at managing the coronavirus crisis. *Guardian.* https://www. theguardian. com/world/2020/apr/25/why-do-female-leadersseem-to-be-more-successful-at-managing-the-coronavirus-crisis

Heymann, J., Levy, J. K., Bose, B., Ríos-Salas, V., Mekonen, Y., Swaminathan, H., ... Darmstadt, G. L. (2019). Improving health with programmatic, legal, and policy approaches to reduce gender inequality and change restrictive gender norms. *Lancet, 393*(10190), 2522–2534. doi:10.1016/S0140-6736(19)30656-7 PMID:31155271

Inman, A. G. (2020). Culture and Positionality: Academy and Mentorship. *Women & Therapy, 43*(1-2), 112–124. doi:10.1080/02703149.2019.1684678

Jamali, A., Bhutto, A., Khaskhely, M., & Sethar, W. (2022). Impact of leadership styles on faculty performance: Moderating role of organizational culture in higher education. *Management Science Letters, 12*(1), 1–20. doi:10.5267/j.msl.2021.8.005

Jameson, J. (Ed.). (2019). *International perspectives on leadership in higher education: Critical thinking for global challenges*. Routledge. doi:10.4324/9781315122410

Jandrić, P., Hayes, D., Truelove, I., Levinson, P., Mayo, P., Ryberg, T., ... Jackson, L. (2020). Teaching in the Age of Covid-19. *Postdigital Science and Education*, 1-162.

King, P. M., & Kitchener, K. S. (2004). Reflective judgment: Theory and research on the development of epistemic assumptions through adulthood. *Educational Psychologist, 39*(1), 5–18. doi:10.120715326985ep3901_2

Lannelli, C., & Duta, A. (2018). Inequalities in school leavers' labour market outcomes: Do school subject choices matter? *Oxford Review of Education, 44*(1), 56–74. doi:10.1080/03054985.2018.1409970

Lipton, B. (2015). A New" ERA" of Women and Leadership: The Gendered Impact of Quality Assurance in Australian Higher Education. *Australian Universities Review, 57*(2), 60–70.

Maas, B., Grogan, K. E., Chirango, Y., Harris, N., Liévano-Latorre, L. F., McGuire, K. L., ... Primack, R. B. (2020). Academic leaders must support inclusive scientific communities during COVID-19. *Nature Ecology & Evolution, 4*(8), 1–2. doi:10.103841559-020-1233-3 PMID:32493950

McNair, T. B., Bensimon, E. M., & Malcom-Piqueux, L. (2020). *From equity talk to equity walk: Expanding practitioner knowledge for racial justice in higher education*. John Wiley & Sons. doi:10.1002/9781119428725

Meletiadou, E. (2022). The lived experiences of female educational leaders in higher education in the UK: Academic resilience and gender. In *Handbook of Research on Practices for Advancing Diversity and Inclusion in Higher Education* (pp. 1–19). IGI Global. doi:10.4018/978-1-7998-9628-9.ch001

Meyers, M. (2013). The war on academic women: Reflections on post-feminism in the neoliberal academy. *The Journal of Communication Inquiry*, *37*(4), 274–283. doi:10.1177/0196859913505619

Mezirow, J. (2009). Transformative learning theory. In J. Mezirow & E. W. Taylor (Eds.), *Transformative Learning in Practise: Insights from Community, 39 Workplace, and Higher Education* (pp. 18–32). Jossey Bass.

Milovanović, A., Kostić, M., Zorić, A., Đorđević, A., Pešić, M., Bugarski, J., Todorović, D., Sokolović, N., & Josifovski, A. (2020). Transferring COVID-19 Challenges into Learning Potentials: Online Workshops in Architectural Education. *Sustainability*, *12*(17), 7024. doi:10.3390u12177024

O'Connor, P. (2019). Gender imbalance in senior positions in higher education: What is the problem? What can be done? *Policy Reviews in Higher Education*, *3*(1), 28–50. doi:10.1080/23322969.2018.1552084

O'Connor, P. (2020). Creating gendered change in Irish higher education: Is managerial leadership up to the task? *Irish Educational Studies*, *39*(2), 139–155. doi:10.1080/03323315.2019.1697951

O'Connor, P. J., Jimmieson, N. L., Bergin, A. J., Wiewiora, A., & McColl, L. (2022). Leader tolerance of ambiguity: Implications for follower performance outcomes in high and low ambiguous work situations. *The Journal of Applied Behavioral Science*, *58*(1), 65–96. doi:10.1177/00218863211053676

Okoli, G. N., Moore, T. A., Thomas, S. L., & Allen, T. T. (2020). Minority Women in Educational Leadership. *Handbook on Promoting Social Justice in Education*, 1711-1727.

Pellegrini, M., Uskov, V., & Casalino, N. (2020). Reimagining and Re-Designing the Post-COVID-19 Higher Education Organizations to Address New Challenges and Responses for Safe and Effective Teaching Activities. Law and Economics Yearly Review Journal, 9(part 1), 219-248.

Peters, M. A., Rizvi, F., McCulloch, G., Gibbs, P., Gorur, R., Hong, M., ... Quay, J. (2020). Reimagining the new pedagogical possibilities for universities post-Covid-19: An EPAT Collective Project. *Educational Philosophy and Theory*, 1–44.

Power, K. (2020). The COVID-19 pandemic has increased the care burden of women and families. *Sustainability: Science. Practice and Policy*, *16*(1), 67–73.

Rapanta, C., Botturi, L., Goodyear, P., Guàrdia, L., & Koole, M. (2020). Online university teaching during and after the Covid-19 crisis: Refocusing teacher presence and learning activity. *Postdigital Science and Education*, 1-23.

Reay, D. (2004, January). Cultural capitalists and academic habitus: Classed and gendered labour in UK higher education. *Women's Studies International Forum*, *27*(1), 31–39. doi:10.1016/j.wsif.2003.12.006

Ruben, B., Mahon, G., & Shapiro, K. (2022). Academic Leader Selection, Development, Evaluation, and Recognition: Four Critical Higher Education Challenges. In International Perspectives on Leadership in Higher Education (Vol. 15, pp. 115-138). Emerald Publishing Limited.

Shulman, L. S. (2005). Signature pedagogies in the professions. *Daedalus*, *134*(3), 52–59. doi:10.1162/0011526054622015

Syed, M. (2019). Rebel Ideas: The power of diverse thinking. Hachette UK.

Tanova, C., Karatas-Özkan, M., & Inal, G. (2008). The process of choosing a management career: Evaluation of gender and contextual dynamics in a comparative study of six countries: Hungary, Israel, North Cyprus, Turkey, UK and the USA. *Career Development International*, *13*(4), 291–305. doi:10.1108/13620430810880790

Taylor, L. L., Beck, M. I., Lahey, J. N., & Froyd, J. E. (2017). Reducing inequality in higher education: The link between faculty empowerment and climate and retention. *Innovative Higher Education*, *42*(5-6), 391–405. doi:10.100710755-017-9391-1

Teelken, C., & Deem, R. (2013). All are equal, but some are more equal than others: Managerialism and gender equality in higher education in comparative perspective. *Comparative Education*, *49*(4), 520–535. doi:10.1080/03050068.2013.807642

Thomas, S. (2020). Women in Higher Education Administration Leadership and the Role of Institutional Support. In *Accessibility and Diversity in the 21st Century University* (pp. 234–249). IGI Global. doi:10.4018/978-1-7998-2783-2.ch012

Tiwary, A. R., & Gupta, T. (2022). Stereotypical Barriers Affecting Women Aspiring High-ranking Leadership Role in Higher Education. In *Role of Leaders in Managing Higher Education* (Vol. 48, pp. 99–116). Emerald Publishing Limited. doi:10.1108/S2055-364120220000048007

Trent, R. J. (2020). *Women's Perspectives on the Role of Organizational Culture in Their Career Advancement to Leadership Positions: A Generic Inquiry* [Doctoral dissertation]. Capella University.

Tshivhase, M. (2020). Personhood: Implications for Moral Status and Uniqueness of Women. Handbook of African Philosophy of Difference, 347-360.

Tversky, A., & Kahneman, D. (1974). Judgment under uncertainty: Heuristics and biases. *Science, 185*(4157), 1124-1131.

Villiers, C. (2019). Boardroom Culture: An Argument for Compassionate Leadership. *European Business Law Review, 30*(2), 253–278. doi:10.54648/EULR2019012

Wenham, C., Smith, J., & Morgan, R. (2020). COVID-19: The gendered impacts of the outbreak. *Lancet, 395*(10227), 846–848. doi:10.1016/S0140-6736(20)30526-2 PMID:32151325

Wheaton, M. M., & Kezar, A. (2019). Interlocking systems of oppression: Women navigating higher education leadership. In *Challenges and opportunities for women in higher education leadership* (pp. 61–83). IGI Global. doi:10.4018/978-1-5225-7056-1.ch005

Whitty-Collins, G. (2020). *Why Men Win at Work:...and How to Make Inequality History*. Luath Press Ltd.

World Health Organization. (2020). COVID-19 and violence against women: what the health sector/system can do, 7 April 2020 (No. WHO/SRH/20.04). World Health Organization.

ADDITIONAL READING

Aldossari, M., Chaudhry, S., Tatli, A., & Seierstad, C. (2023). Catch-22: Token women trying to reconcile impossible contradictions between organisational and societal expectations. *Work, Employment and Society, 37*(1), 39–57. doi:10.1177/09500170211035940

Ansar, A. (2023). Bangladeshi women migrants amidst the COVID-19 pandemic: Revisiting globalization, dependency and gendered precarity in South–South labour migration. *Global Networks*, *23*(1), 31–44. doi:10.1111/glob.12368 PMID:35599743

Cronshaw, S., Stokes, P., & McCulloch, A. (2022). Online communities of practice and doctoral study: Working women with children resisting perpetual peripherality. *Journal of Further and Higher Education*, *46*(7), 959–971. doi:10.1080/0309877X.2021.2023734

Fine, C., & Sojo, V. (2019). Women's value: Beyond the business case for diversity and inclusion. *Lancet*, *393*(10171), 515–516. doi:10.1016/S0140-6736(19)30165-5 PMID:30739677

Mate, S. E., McDonald, M., & Do, T. (2019). The barriers and enablers to career and leadership development: An exploration of women's stories in two work cultures. *The International Journal of Organizational Analysis*, *27*(4), 857–874. doi:10.1108/IJOA-07-2018-1475

Merma-Molina, G., Urrea-Solano, M., Baena-Morales, S., & Gavilán-Martín, D. (2022). The satisfactions, contributions, and opportunities of women academics in the framework of sustainable leadership: A case study. *Sustainability*, *14*(14), 8937. doi:10.3390u14148937

Mousa, M., Boyle, J., Skouteris, H., Mullins, A. K., Currie, G., Riach, K., & Teede, H. J. (2021). Advancing women in healthcare leadership: A systematic review and meta-synthesis of multi-sector evidence on organisational interventions. *EClinicalMedicine*, *39*, 101084. doi:10.1016/j.eclinm.2021.101084 PMID:34430838

Pervin, N., Mokhtar, M., & Haque, N. Z. (2023). A Conceptual Study of Urban Spaces in Bangladesh: Exploring Patriarchy From a Feminist Perspective. In *Urban Poetics and Politics in Contemporary South Asia and the Middle East* (pp. 240–268). IGI Global. doi:10.4018/978-1-6684-6650-6.ch012

Sougou, N. M., Ndiaye, O., Nabil, F., Folayan, M. O., Sarr, S. C., Mbaye, E. M., & Martínez-Pérez, G. Z. (2022). Barriers of West African women scientists in their research and academic careers: A qualitative research. *PLoS One*, *17*(3), e0265413. doi:10.1371/journal.pone.0265413 PMID:35353842

Wilkinson, J., & Male, T. (2023). Perceptions of women senior leaders in the UK Higher Education during the COVID-19 pandemic. *Educational Management Administration & Leadership*. doi:10.1177/17411432221150079

KEY TERMS AND DEFINITIONS

Crisis: A time of intense difficulty or danger, when the immediacy of decision making, and strategic leadership is paramount.

Critical Reflection: A process of identifying, questioning, and assessing our deeply held assumptions.

Critical Reflexivity: The capacity to see one's own perspective and assumptions and understand how one's perspective, assumptions and identity are socially constructed through critical reflection.

Emotional Labour: The management of emotional response in order to present the outward image of control and reassurance in order to continue interaction with other people in a certain way while doing a job in stressful circumstances.

Inequality: Inequality in this chapter refers to the phenomenon of unequal and/ or unjust distribution of resources and opportunities among members of a given society, in this instance female leaders.

Neoliberalism: Neoliberalism is a political philosophical term used to signify the political reappearance of 19th-century ideas associated with free-market capitalism, and in this chapter refers to the commodification of global Higher Education provision.

Positionality: Refers to the social and political context that creates your identity in terms of race, class, gender, sexuality, and ability status.

Signature Pedagogy: Refers to the forms or styles of teaching and instruction that are common to specific disciplines, areas of study, or professions and as such can unintentionally define and constrain them.

Chapter 4
Development and Validation of the Scale of Intergenerational Conflict in Organizations

María de Lourdes Elena García Vargas
https://orcid.org/0000-0002-1724-4744
Universidad Autónoma del Estado de Hidalgo, Mexico

Maria Teresa De la Garza
Universidad Tecnológica de Celaya, Mexico

Gerardo Reyes Ruiz
https://orcid.org/0000-0003-0212-2952
Center for Superior Naval Studies (CESNAV), Mexico

ABSTRACT

The study validates a scale that allows the exploration of intergenerational conflict in organizations. To validate the questionnaire, the descriptive statistics of the sample are obtained, Cronbach's alpha and Pearson's correlations between variables are calculated, an exploratory factor analysis is performed with the SPSS software. A first-order confirmatory factor analysis is performed with the AMOS software, and the Dillon-Goldstein rho (or composite reliability) is calculated to verify the internal consistency of the indicators for each latent variable. The result is that all the acceptance criteria have been met, the Rho de Dillon-Goldstein is acceptable, the first factor (opening of the generation gap) is 0.85, and the second factor (limitations for intergenerational work) is 0.78, so the model obtained the required validation quality.

DOI: 10.4018/978-1-6684-6567-7.ch004

INTRODUCTION

The importance of this study lies in detecting this degree of conflict intergenerational through a measurement instrument. Once the state of the art has been reviewed, no instrument was found to reveal the degree of intergenerational conflict and now the opening of the generational gap forces companies to establish strategies so that different generations can live together with fewer problems when carrying out work and therefore expect an improvement in business results. Furthermore, organizations need to be more skillful and proactive in formulating growth and sustainability strategies based on a talent management that considers the various trends and conflicts between generations, which that draws attention to this issue is the growing generational diversity that exists in all the contexts and the consequences that this attracts, due to the increase of people of more advanced age worldwide, so that this phenomenon today reaches greater relevance and significance, this justifies the investigation, so the objective of the study is to validate a scale that allows exploring the intergenerational conflict in organizations under factors of opening of the generational gap and limitations for intergenerational work. The application of the proposed psychometric instrument allows anticipating challenges in employees from multiple generations in the workplace that may arise from differences in perceptions of right or wrong between members of various generational cohorts and their potential consequences. The sample was obtained from workers from the State of Mexico and Mexico City in 5%, Hidalgo 16%, Nuevo León 26%, Guanajuato 47% and other states 6%.

BACKGROUND

The term generation is associated with a group of people who share characteristics that identify or differentiate it from other descendants. This process depends on various aspects, including the influence of the historical moment and the events experienced, the environment geographical, territorial, values and the cultural-educational period experienced. These contexts condition the profile, character and personality of a generation through a process of synergy that allows it to contribute to its community, which is known as imprinting generational (Gutierrez and Herráiz, 2009). Since 2005 Gelleard and Higgs conceptualize generations as a "set of dispositions that generate and structure individual practices that emerge and are defined by the forces operating within a particular generational field (time frame)'' (p. 70). This approach suggests that generations should not be considered as fixed forms and recognizes that conditions can change the dynamics of relationships within and between groups generations over time. They point out that certain aspects of modernity, such as the greater economic prosperity among the elderly, greater control over economic resources among the retirees, increased access to technology, and common lifestyles through age have reduced typical generational differences.

Leccardi and Feixa (2011) mention three historical moments in the development of the concept of generation: a) The world wars, when the philosophical bases on succession and generational coexistence were founded; b) The 1960s, when the work focused on generational conflict, c) The 1990s, with the emergence of the networked society, with the expertise of young people in digital technology compared to previous generations.

The Baby Boomer generation can historically be characterized as the generation born in the era of American world preference, which followed World War II World Wide and lasted until the early 1960s (Tulgan, 1996). They grew during a healthy and prosperous economy (Jones et al., 2018) the characteristics of this generation are individualistic, free spirited, oriented to social causes. The Babies Boomer known as cohort #2 (born 1955 to 1964), have as key characteristics be less optimistic, are distrustful of the government, present a general cynicism, (Schuman and Scott 1989; Meredith and Schewe, 1994; Noble and Schewe, 2003), they value the international career, they prefer the extra benefits such as checks, nursery, gym, prioritize family and friends, prefer to help others, like their autonomy and interdependence (Generation and Talent Observatory [OGT], 2020).

Growing up in an era of economic prosperity, this generation became believers' employment for life, are loyal to the company, prefer to pay union dues to earn respect and receive seniority (Elsdon & Lyer, 1999). It follows that Baby Boomers are more resistant to change, less adept with technology (Paul & Townsend, 1993; Taylor & Walker, 1994). Productivity of Baby Boomers has been shown to compare favorably with other age groups due to their experience, organizational commitment, stability and less rotation, these characteristics are considered as real advantages over the high mobility of younger generations (Appelbaum et al., 2005).

McEvoy and Cascio (1989) argue that generation X fears the stereotypes that belong as being less honest, less trustworthy, career fatalistic, and somewhat lacking in respect for authority. Such perceptions can lead to an organizational climate of hostility in the organization. Hill (2002) argues that Baby Boomers have formed a generation of employees, known as generation X who do not share the commitment of their competent parents, but rather have emphasized participation and the development of esteem. O´Bannon (2001) asserts that the philosophy, instilled by Baby Boomer parents, has not prepared generation X for the real-world approach, this generation does not show the same organizational loyalty; rather, they highly value working for themselves, capitalizing job opportunities elsewhere. Members of this generation are financially less successful than their parents, they grow up with an unstable economy (Jones et al., 2018). The Generation X cohort (born from 1965 to 1976) manifested a social malaise, they come from single-parent families, as key characteristics they seek security emotional, be independent, prefer informality, like entrepreneurship (Schuman and Scott, 1989; Meredith and Schewe, 1994). Noble and Schewe (2003) found that success, professional and personal fulfillment in this generation is linked to individuals who they seek immediate gratification and tangible outward signs of success.

Among the values of generation X can be considered teamwork, the collaboration, their quality of life and the development of human relations are highly entrepreneurs and innovators in their work. Estimate their performance within the organization and they look for the benefits that it offers them, such as checks, nurseries, pensions, in addition to the internal training programs, their priorities are related to the family, autonomy and personal growth (OGT, 2020). The balance between work and personal life is very important, they seek to establish themselves in organizations that invest in their professional development, they change jobs frequently and are not afraid authority like other generations (Twenge, 2010; Lester et al., 2012; Jones et al., 2018; Heyns et al., 2019).

Due to work style and belief systems, Generation Y also known as other denominations such as Millennials. Millennial Generation, digital natives and Generation MT, consider themselves fundamentally different from any other group of young people (O'Reilly and Vella-Zarb, 2000). The generation born in the eighties witnessed memorable events such as the rise of the internet, 9/11 attacks, cultural diversity, wars in Iraq. Its characteristics are the search for physical security, patriotism, manifested with greater fears, accepts change, likes knowledge (Schuman & Scott, 1989; Meredith and Schewe, 1994; Noble & Schewe, 2003) are much more likely than their parents to drop out school and take study time to do non-degree work or to travel for a couple of years, are more willing than their parents to delay buying a house, marry or have children. This generation values the benefits of the company where they work, their business projection and a good social reputation, their priorities are focused on the family, in growing professionally and being interdependent (OGT, 2020). These clear differences in values and perspectives of generational work groups have arranged challenges for HR managers, force planning employment and succession. Manage the expectations of the different generational groups in the workplace have forced HR departments to design spaced sets of motivators to optimize the performance of each group (Appelbaum et al., 2005).

Generational Diversity and Its Implications

Between people, intergenerational relationships are complex and can be extremely positive or extremely negative. The benefits of positive solidarity between generations appear frequently in the literature (Lee et al.) but also customarily in publications focusing on aging as a chance for negative consequences or conflictive relationships between the generations (Seedesman, 2017). It is difficult to separate solidarity from conflict. In a way, when solidarity fails or is absent, there is the possibility of conflict. The idea of solidarity/conflict implies that exchanges between generations can be imbalanced (Vandenkendelaere, 2013) for different reasons. First, generational exchanges are not only determined by individuals but mediated by the state and the market (Tobio, 2010). The distribution between who pays taxes, buys services, and gives or receives time or care is a function of many different factors, some of them established as state obligations of market rules. Over time economic and financial factors also have an influence on the number of resources available to different generations.

In organizations, socio cognitive conflicts are often tasking related meaning that co-workers hold different opinions about which tasks and how these tasks should be done. Applied to generations in organizations, members of different generations could have divergent understandings about the organization's mission, values and strategies. Moreover, as a result of different socialization and educational backgrounds, we expect that generations could have different communication and/or work styles (Bontekoning, 2007) or different problem-solving approaches, providing a source of task conflicts. Undoubtedly, the introduction of modern communication and information technology determined generational differences. Younger generations grew up with these new technologies, giving them a head start to develop and apply computer skills in the work context compared with older workers.

Organizations look to utilize a wider array of skills and knowledge by focusing on diversity and Inclusion, this has paved the way to create a more heterogeneous workforce, however, this diversity also increases the variables for conflicts. An overarching cause of conflict in this new heterogeneous workforce is generational conflict. Various social, political, and economic developments have shaped how people from different eras are inclined to think, feel, and act. Thereby changing their working behavior and values (Tortorella et al., 2019), an organization with a generationally diverse workforce must embrace and value each generation and look to capitalize on their strength. While also recognizing the generational diversities that help create a dynamic, rich, engaging and fulfilling work environment where everyone feels valued and supported by their peers (André, 2018).

Harris (2015) defined generation conflict as: "Differences in communication preferences (the use of technology vs. face-to-face meeting), work values/attitudes (a work-centric perspective vs. a balanced perspective), career aspirations (opportunities for advancement vs. the desire to make a difference), and power/influence among generations." Each generation has unique characteristics that define them, it is from these characteristics that friction is created thus, leading to conflict in the workplace. That being said, there is research that indicates generational conflict is overstated.

With generational conflict having such a wide scope, there are multiple reasons why an individual may react in a certain way, it is also possible that reasons behind certain behaviors and actions might be confused with one another (Rudolph et al., 2020), even with contrasting opinions it is still important to investigate the impact and prevalence of generational conflict. What researchers learn today will not only be beneficial for current generations in the work force but, new generations as well.

Farr et al. (1998) argued that organizational politics are frequently directed not to encourage older employees to participate in training activities and development to update or acquire knowledge and skills in a flexible environment. An examples of flexible work options are tolerance in job scheduling work and the amount of time spent at work including time employment alternatives partial and half-year schedules, shared work and teleworking.

Hutchings (2006) argued that the mobility of younger workers increases and employers in slowly growing, aging industrialized nations are eager for talent. To retain these workers, Cetron and Davies (2003) argue that organizations must provide challenging work and opportunities for advancement and generational training and identify the importance of resource interventions human resources to achieve and manage interaction between groups in order to create an environment of positive and rewarding work.

Due to declining fertility and mortality rates, the rapid increase in elderly population has been a global phenomenon in recent years, the rise of older adults still working and subsequent cohorts entering the labor force and the age diversity are becoming important management issues in organizations. Research by Ali and Kulik (2014) found that age diversity is associated with poor organizational performance and intergroup conflict that may be attributable to intergenerational conflict as the underlying antecedent of these relationships.

From the perspective of social identity, intergenerational conflict is the result of processes based on social categorization related to belonging to age groups. A Second Prominent Theoretical Perspective in the Area of Age Diversity Research It is the attraction-selection-attrition (ASA) paradigm. The ASA theory predicts that individuals will They are attracted to work groups based on their perceptions of similarity to them. When this perception of similarity is violated, employees feel uncomfortable and less integrated into the work group and may ultimately withdraw from it (Schneider, 1987).

From the ASA perspective, intergenerational conflict is a function of age difference that an individual can find in work groups and can be manifested in behaviors Specifics such as rotation. Intergenerational conflict can be expected to be evident in the workplace, particularly in recent years has become increasingly common, which requires more frequent and formal interactions between employees. The values Generational differences may be evident in work styles, communication styles, and information revealed in conversations about personal matters. The interactions within and between teams expose individuals to different norms and values with people of different generations.

Deal et al. (2010) found that differences between generations, such as the use of technology, are simply due to personal and individual discrepancies between workers and not as members of generational cohort. They argued that adaptations should not be made for different generations such as training or communication, and employees they should be treated as individuals without regard to generational-cohort membership. Without However, according to studies on social stigma (Crocker & Major, 1989), the attitudes of setback at the hands of older workers can be seen as coping responses to the age-related stigma. In fact, like race and gender, age is an important criterion for classifying human beings and can be used as a basis for prejudices and discrimination (Allison, 1998). The process of systematic stereotyping and discrimination against people because they are older has been called "ageism" (Butler, 1987).

Numerous studies have shown that older workers are perceived as less competent and less motivated than their younger colleagues (Chiu et al., 2001; Hummert, 1999). Being an "older worker" means being a member of a stigmatized group in the workplace. The work, and the negative social identity associated with that group can lead to some older workers to face the threat to their social being and leave the labor force to avoid the stigma dealing with stress-related stigma. In fact, people stigmatized often perceive stigma as a stressor and are aware of their possible negative effects (Miller and Major, 1998). In particular, Steele and Aronson, (1995) conducted studies that revealed the deleterious effects of negative stereotypes on the performance of people stigmatized based on their ethnicity.

In older adults, the idea of improving the position of the teacher as a bearer and transmitter of moral norms from a position of power from the line of the transfer and verticality and even, with some suspicions of manipulation. Young express greater awareness towards particular situations of older adults, their state physical, family life, etc., but considered holders of extemporaneous positions or schematized that do not correspond to the experiences of current youth (Hernandez, 2011).

Defenders of the generational theory have argued that this life experience Shared drives collective assumptions and values that translate into attitudes, beliefs. common sense and a cohesive sense of group identity. It is important to note that the "differences generations" are cause for concern in the design and implementation of various policies and practices in the workplace and business strategies must be aligned to manage differences effectively (Blythe, et al., 2008; Cennamo & Gardner, 2008; Kowske et al. 2010).

Institutions shape the lives of their workers through interrelated domains of family, education, and work at various points of the life stage that lead to a common set of expectations and behaviors of people belonging to different ages and generations (Mayer and Tuma, 1990). To understand generations, it is important to consider relevant institutions, social welfare policies (Mayer and Schoepflin, 1989), cultural norms associated with appropriate age classifications and expectations of "youth", "adulthood", "middle age" and "old age" (Cameron, 1969; Hagestad, 1990; Kohli, 1994; Lawrence, 1996; Marini, 1984). Thus, various social institutions exert control over behavior through socialization, or with social sanctions, so that norms associated with various age groups are institutionalized and taken for granted.

The specific intergenerational practices examined by Charness and Czaja (2006) such as training and developing opportunities for older workers and flexible working options are very important. Providing access to training is one way the organization communicates value and contribution to an older worker (Patrickson and Hartmann, 1995). Farr et al. (1998) argued that organizational policies were frequently aimed at not encouraging older employees to participate in training and development activities to update or acquire knowledge and skills in a flexible environment. Examples of flexible work options include tolerance in work scheduling and the amount of time spent at work including part-time employment alternatives and half-year schedules, job sharing and telecommuting. Hutchings (2006) argued that the mobility of workers is older due to declining fertility and mortality rates, the rapid increase in the population of older adults has been a global phenomenon in recent years, the rise of older adults still working and subsequent cohorts entering the workforce and 10 age diversity are becoming major management issues in organizations. Research by Ali and Kulik (2014) found that age diversity is associated with poor organizational performance and intergroup conflict that may be attributable to intergenerational conflict as the underlying antecedent of these relationships.

Research around generational conflicts at the workplace is done for the past, but events that shape the generational characteristics and circumstances that may cause potential intergenerational conflicts are chronological. Donkin's book, The Future of Work, placed Millennials as one of the most influential factors shaping the future of work, largely due to their significant size in the workplace and some unique attributes that typify their behaviours (Donkin, 2014). However, the oldest Millennials turned 39 years old in 2020, and many of this generation are now first-line supervisors or becoming mid-level managers (Gabrielova & Buchko, 2021). Gen Z, the generation after Millennials, is just entering the workforce. Although Gen Z and Millennials display similarities, Gen Zs bring their own unique behaviours into organizations (Iorgulescu, 2016).These behaviours, again just like those of the Millennials, will be shaping the future of work with even greater effectiveness, as this youngest workgroup is expected to make up 27% of the global workforce by

2025, outnumbering the Millennials (Stahl, 2021). Since Millennials may become the managers of those Gen Zs at the more entry level, their differences could potentially cause intergenerational conflicts in the area of management and leadership (Gabrielova & Buchko, 2021).

Work-from-home and Work-from-anywhere, are among the trends that companies are embracing (Choudhury, 2021). As the world cautiously envisaged returning to the office, resistance appeared in younger generations; the majority of the opponents are millennials. Nonetheless, Gen-Xers, which currently represent more than 50% of the leadership positions, believe that technologies like Zoom do not build trust and admiration which are among the key elements of networking (Dishman, 2021). These factors must be kept in mind as new generations enter the workforce. The issue of generational conflict is not fixed and changes with time. As one generation retires another enters the workforce. Researchers must continue to investigate the changing landscape so managers and organizations can better resolve these conflicts.

METHOD

For the construction of the questionnaire, 10 Mexican HR specialists were consulted of manufacturing, service and trade companies. In the interviews, the experts validated the questionnaire and their suggestions were incorporated, generating 17 items. It is important to mention that of the 17 items generated, only 14 remained because after performing a factor analysis confirmatory and exploratory some items (7,8 and 13) did not cover the requirements to be considered within the final instrument.

The sample to validate the questionnaire consisted of 525 workers, it was explained to the participants that the information is for research purposes only, therefore their answers they are confidential. The information was collected from August 2019 to December 2019 with support of master's students as part of their academic work where the following is requested: a) Work experience. 35% of the sample have less than 4 years of experience, 29% have between 4 and a half and ten years, 19% are between 11 and 20 years old and finally, 16% are older 20 years old. b) Years working in the current job. 54% are less than 3 years old, 22% have between 4 and 9 years and finally, 24% have more than 10 years in their current job. c) The size of the company where the interviewees work. Of less than 50 employees 44%, from 50 to 100 employees 23%, between 100 and 500 employees 14% and more than 500, 19%. d) Gender. 40% are women and 60% are men. e) Degree of studies: Primary 7%, secondary 12%, high school 42%, undergraduate 28% and postgraduate 11%. e) date of birth: between 1946 to 1964 6%, of 1965 to 1982 21%, from 1983 to 2001 71% and after 2002 2%. g) Origin of the sample. State of Mexico and Mexico City 5%, Hidalgo 16%, Nuevo León 26%. Guanajuato 47% and other states 6%. 37% of the workers were from the manufacturing sector, 25% from services, 16% commerce, 12% belong to the government sector and 10% are educational personnel. Once the questionnaire was developed, the necessary statistical procedures were carried out to test reliability and validity.

To validate the questionnaire, the following steps were followed: 1) An analysis was carried out exploratory factorial with SPSS V24 software. 2) A confirmatory factor analysis was performed of first order with the AMOS V24 software and 3) the Dillon-Goldstein rho (or the composite reliability) that can be used to check the internal consistency of the indicators for each latent variable.

Exploratory Factor Analysis

As a first step to validate the questionnaire, an exploratory factor analysis was performed. The objective of this multivariate method is to reduce the number of variables to a common factor. For To determine the adequacy of the exploratory factor analysis test, the measure of Kaiser, Meyer, Olkin (KMO) sampling adequacy that tests whether the partial correlations between the variables are very small. Allows you to compare the magnitude of the coefficients of observed correlation with the magnitude of the partial correlation coefficients. the statistician KMO is between 0 and 1. Small values indicate that factor analysis is not adequate. In this case, the values obtained in the KMO test are close to one, and the test was also calculated of Barlett's sphericity (Table 1). The test contrasts the null hypothesis stating that the matrix correlation is an identity matrix, in which case there would be no significant correlations between the variables and the factorial model would not be relevant. In this matter, the significance value of the test is 0.00, which represents that the variables are highly correlated for provide a basis for factor analysis (Mohamed et al., 2013). As a result of the analysis exploratory factorial analysis, it was concluded that the items could be grouped into two factors.

Figure 1.

Parámetro estadístico		Resultado
Kaiser-Meyer-Olkin (adecuación de la muestra)		0.854
Bartlett's sphericity test	Aprox. Chi-Square Grados de libertad p	2356.86 91 0.00

To complement the exploratory factor analysis, the eigenvalues, the load of the items, the percentage of variance explained and the communality of the items. This study was based on the varimax rotation analysis to evaluate the structure of the 14 items of the questionnaire. The Note in Table 2 that the eigenvalues of each factor must be greater than 1 since it is the generally accepted criteria. If the eigenvalue is less than 1, it implies that the factor should not considered. The variance explained by the first factor is 28.6% and that of the second factor is 20.3%, which totals 49.9%. In other words, the questionnaire explains 49.9% of the variance and the remaining 50.1% is explained by other factors. Communalities represent the relationship between variables and the rest of them before the rotation. If they are less than 0.30, they should not be accepted or should be subsequently analyzed with confirmatory factor analysis (Mohamed et al 2013). Finally, all factor loadings are greater than 0.40 which measures how they contribute to the group or factor of the that form part of.

Figure 2.

Note. The items are grouped into two factors. The first has been called "Opening in the generation gap" or factor A and the second, "Limitations for intergenerational work" or factor B. These grouping factors were defined based on the concepts implicit in the designed questions. Items 1, 7, 8, 11, 13 and 14 are possible candidates for not contributing to explain the factors because the values of their communalities are less than 0.40. Without However, through confirmatory factor analysis, it will be identified if the items contribute or not inside factor.

Item	Factor load 1st.	2nd.	communalities
	0.621		.393
1	0.775		.611
2	0.738		.563
3	0.771		.648
4		0.718	.518
5	0.751		.570
6	0.598		.392
7	0.439		.272
8		0.804	.651
9		0.808	.659
10	0.508		.379
11		0..686	.493
12		0.563	.321
13 14	0.598		0.380
eigenvalues	4.27	2.56	
explained variance	28.6	20.31	

Confirmatory Factor Analysis

In the second phase of the analysis to test the validity of the model, an analysis was performed First-order confirmatory factorial (AFC) through the structural equation model using the AMOS V.24 software (Figure 1). CFA allow you to compare whether the data is consistent with the theory (Sánchez-Sandoval and Verdugo, 2016). The maximum method likelihood represents an improvement from exploratory factor analysis performed in SPSS and provides more accurate results. As can be see, items 7, 8 and 13 were removed from the analysis as they did not present the desired significance. It´s observes that for all the items, the values presented in the final analysis meet the criteria established for this technique.

Once the first order AFC was carried out, the goodness of fit was evaluated determining the corresponding statistics as shown in Table 3. The chi square statistic (ÿ2), root mean square error of approximation (RMSEA), goodness index comparative fit (CFI) and the Tucker-Lewis index (TLI). These parameters of goodness of adjustment are generally used when an SEM model is presented (Vargas, 2019) so it is observing that the acceptance criteria are met for the model to have the required quality. Cronbach's Alpha for the instrument is 0.80 taking items 5, 9, 10 and 12 as negative since the measurement scale is inverted (R). The Dillon-Goldstein Rho is acceptable. The first factor it is good in 0.85 and in the case of the second factor it is 0.78.

Once the statistical requirements are covered, the results show that it is possible to identify factors that determine the existence of intergenerational conflict. Factor A "Opening in the generation gap" that includes the questions 1) I support the idea of involving collaborators of any age in a company, 2) I accept that colleagues outside my age range will teach me new processes or correct me, 3) I support gender diversity in my organization, 4) I recognize the initiative of my peers regardless of age, 6) I agree to renew processes and using more and more technology at work, 11) I manage to adapt well to the demands of my immediate boss and 14) I collaborate in projects that involve employees from various age ranges, are integrated into a single factor that identifies how the worker is willing to adapt to new positions of other generations.

The second factor, "Limitations for intergenerational work" or factor B, is made up of the items 5) I have conflicts when dealing with peers outside my age range, 9) I have problems arguing my ideas in a debate with classmates of another age, 10) It is difficult communicate my ideas to colleagues of any age and 12) I relate only to workers of my age.

Figure 3.

Note. In the model you can see the number of items and their standardized load for the contribution to factor.

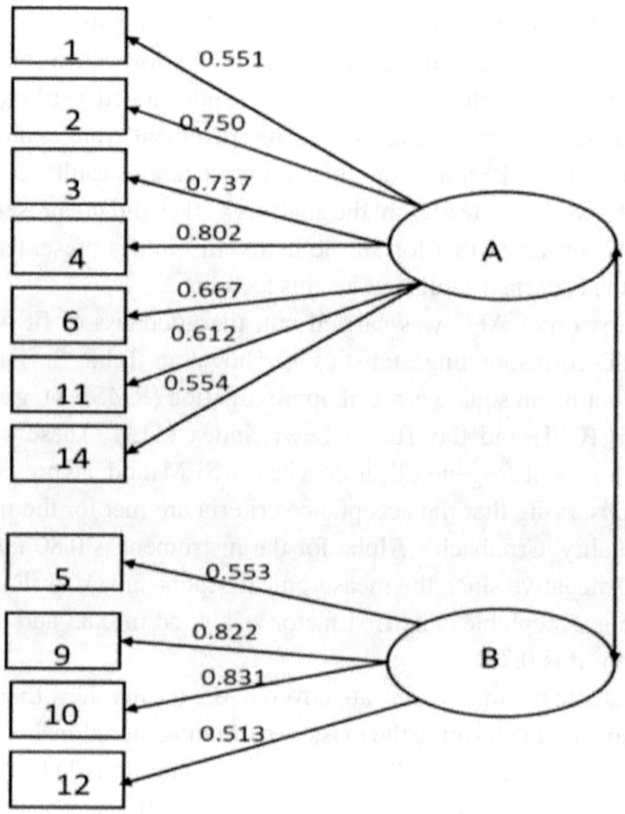

Figure 4.

	First Order CFA	Acceptance requirements
2	79.16 gl= 40 p= 0.000	P<= 0.05
RMSEA	0.043	RMSEAÿ0.08
IFC	0.980	>0.90
TLI	0.972	>0.90

CONCLUSION

There are strengths in a generationally diverse workforce but, there can also be conflict caused by the same diversity. Organizations and managers must have strategies to resolve these inevitable conflicts. Research shows that a generational conflict can be caused by many different variables. There is no one strategy or model that best resolves these conflicts, to solve generational conflicts, one should understand the root of conflict first and then look at the generational characteristics that lead to the conflict.

We need healthy environments to carry out our work; for that reason, the entrepreneurs, have the responsibility of identifying intergenerational conflicts and counting with professionals who can do it or advise on its approach. The validated instrument shows that it is possible to identify factors that determine the existence of intergenerational conflict presented as factor A "opening of the generation gap" and factor B "limitations for generational work" and highlight that the "differences generations" should be of concern in the design and implementation of various workplace policies and practices (Blythe, et al., 2008; Cennamo & Gardner, 2008; Kowske et al., 2010), so it is necessary to generate aligned strategies to manage differences effectively. The instrument is able to determine why young workers and older people are divided into separate subgroups and have generational limitations and thus discuss and locate possible causes of intergenerational conflict.

Knowledge of factor A "opening of the generation gap" is relevant for the organizations that have employees of various ages and that are characterized by a clear division between younger and older workers, because forcing them to be recategorized as a common group can produce intergroup bias when perceiving a threat to their identities distinctive.

In the same way, the understanding of factor B "limitations for work Generational" is useful for organizations that have workers who are constrained by generational characteristics. Employers are encouraged to contact and cooperate intergroup as an effective approach to build a work environment that facilitates respect and positive interaction in a situation of equality, in addition to generating cooperation sustained by a non-competitive work environment, as well as fostering helpful, fair and accepting attitudes.

Applying the measurement instrument allows to examine and understand problems related to conflicts between generations since the conflict generates an impact organization, has negative consequences for both productivity and the health of the workers and of course for the organizational climate. By timely detecting an intergenerational conflict through the instrument validated, the company can design or develop protocols on intergenerational conflict in organizations to be really effective, mediate when there is a situation of manifest conflict and the parties are willing to reach agreements, empower the parties' people to reduce the negative impacts of this and build comprehensive management plans intergenerational conflicts.

The study is limited by the origin of the sample since it was not homogeneous: State of Mexico and Mexico City 5%, Hidalgo 16%, Nuevo León 26%. Guanajuato 47% and other states 6%. A convenience sample was used, without However, the results were consistent. The instrument should be considered as part of an effort to examine the process socio-cognitive of intergenerational relationships that provides a new direction of research into intergenerational conflict.

REFERENCES

Ali, M., & Kulik, C. (2014). Matching age and gender diversity: A linear and curvilinear prediction test competitive. *Journal of Business Ethics, 125*, 497–512. doi:10.100710551-013-1930-9

Allison, K. (1998). Membership in the social category of stressed and oppressed. In J. Swim & C. Stangor (Eds.), *Prejudice: The Target Perspective, 145-170.* Academic Press. doi:10.1016/B978-012679130-3/50042-9

André, S. (2018). Embracing generational diversity: Reducing and managing workplace conflict. *ORNAC Journal, 36*(4), 13–13.

Appelbaum, S., Serena, M., & Shapiro, B. (2005). Generation X and the Boomers: An analysis of realities and myths. *Management Research News, 28*(1), 1–33. doi:10.1108/01409170510784751

Blythe, J., Baumann, A., Zeytinoglu, I., Denton, M., Akhtar-Danesh, N., Davies, S., & Kolotylo, C. (2008). Nursing generations in the contemporary workplace. *Public Personnel Management, 37*(2), 137–159. doi:10.1177/009102600803700201

Bontekoning, A. C. (2007). *Generations in organizations* [Generaties in Organisaties. Een onderzoek naar generatieverschillen en de effecten daarvan op de ontwikkeling van organisaties] [Doctoral thesis]. University of Tilburg.

Butler, R. (1987). *Ageism: The enclyclopedia of Aging*. Springer.

Cameron, P. (1969). Age parameters of young, middle-aged, and elderly adults. *Journal of Gerontology, 24*(2), 201–202. doi:10.1093/geronj/24.2.201 PMID:5789257

Cennamo, L., & Gardner, D. (2008). Generational differences in work values, outcomes, and person organization values. *Journal of Managerial Psychology, 23*(8), 891–906. doi:10.1108/02683940810904385

Cetron, M., & Davies, O. (2003). Trends that shape the future: Technological, labor, management and institutional trends. *The Futurist, 37*(2), 30–43.

Charness, N., & Czaja, S. J. (2006). *Training Older Workers: What We Know and What We Don't Know. # 2006-22*. AARP.

Chiu, W., Chan, A., Snape, E., & Redman, T. (2001). Age stereotypes and discrimination attitudes towards older workers: An east-west comparison. *Human Relations, 54*, 629–661. doi:10.1177/0018726701545004

Choudhury, P. (2021). Our work-from-anywhere future. *Harvard Business Review*. Retrieved November 30, 2021, from https://hbr.org/2020/11/our-work-from-anywhere-future

Deal, J., Altman, D., & Rogelberg, S. (2010). Millennials at work: What we know and what we need to do. *Journal of Business and Psychology*, *25*(2), 191–199. doi:10.100710869-010-9177-2

Dishman, L. (2021). *This is how each generation is feeling about returning to the office*. Fast Company. Retrieved December 1, 2021, from https://www.fastcompany.com/90673558/this-is-howeach-generation-is-feeling-about-returning-to-the-office

Donkin, R. (2014). *Future of work*. Palgrave Macmillan.

Elsdon, R., & Lyer, S. (1999). Creating Value and Improving Retention Through Employee Development: The Sun Microsystems Experience. *Human Resources Planning, 22*(2), 39-40.

Farr, J., Tesluk, P., & Klein, S. (1998). Organizational structure of the workplace and the older worker. In Impact of work on older adults (Vol. 19, pp. 143-206). Springer.

Gabrielova, K., & Buchko, A. A. (2021). Here comes generation Z: Millennials as managers. *Business Horizons*, *64*(4), 489–499. doi:10.1016/j.bushor.2021.02.013

Gelleard, C., & Higgs, P. (2005). *Aging contexts: cohort class and community*. Polity Press.

Gutiérrez, M., & Herráiz, G. (2009). Intergenerational Grandparents School Program. *Espai Social, Revista del Colegio Oficial d'Educadores i Eeducadors Socials de la Comunitat Valenciana, 9*, 41-44.

Harris, M. C. (2015). *Exploring different generations: A phenomenological study on conflict management in the workplace* (Order No. 3722198). Available from ABI/INFORM Collection; ProQuest Central; ProQuest Dissertations & Theses Global. (1728126657)

Hernandez, D. (2011). *Young people and intergenerational dialogue in community transformation and social*. Center for Psychological and Sociological Research.

Heyns, E., Eldermire, E., & Howard, H. (2019). Unsubstantiated Conclusions: A Scoping Review on Generational Differences of Leadership in Academic Libraries. *Journal of Academic Librarianship*, *45*(5), 102054. doi:10.1016/j.acalib.2019.102054

Hummert, M. (1999). A social cognitive perspective on age stereotypes. In *Social Cognition and Aging (pp. 175-196).* Academic Press. doi:10.1016/B978-012345260-3/50009-4

Hutchings, K. (2006). *Diversity and HRD.* Pearson.

Iorgulescu, M. C. (2016). Generation Z and its perception of work. *CrossCultural Management Journal, 18*(1), 47–54.

Jones, J., Murray, S., & Tapp, S. (2018). Generational Differences in the Workplace. *Journal of Business Diversity, 18*(2), 88–97.

Kohli, M. (1994). Work and retirement: a comparative perspective. In Age and structural retardation. Wiley.

Kowske, B., Rasch, R., & Wiley, J. (2010). Millennials' (lack of) attitude problem: An empirical examination of generational effects on work attitudes. *Journal of Business and Psychology, 25*(2), 265–279. doi:10.100710869-010-9171-8

Lawrence, B. (1996). Organization Age Standards: Why is it so hard to know one when you see one? *The Gerontologist, 36*(2), 209–220. doi:10.1093/geront/36.2.209 PMID:8920090

Leccardi & Feixa. (2011). The concept of generation in theories on youth. *Last Decade, 34*, 11-32.

Lester, S., Standifer, R., Schultz, N., Windsor, J., & Gerhardt, M. (2012). Actual Versus. Perceived Generational Differences at Work: An Empirical Examination. *Journal of Leadership & Organizational Studies, 19*(3), 341–354. doi:10.1177/1548051812442747

Marini, M. (1984). Age and sequence norms in the transition to adulthood. *Social Forces, 63*(1), 229–244. doi:10.2307/2578867

Mayer, K., & Schoepflin, U. (1989). The state and course of life. *Sociology Annual Review,* 187-209.

Mayer & Tuma. (1990). *Life history analysis in life course research (Comp). University of Wisconsin.* Press.

McEvoy, G., & Cascio, W. (1989). Employee and job performance. *Journal of Applied Psychology,* 11.

Miller, C., & Major, B. (1998). Dealing with stigma and prejudice. In Prejudice: The Target Perspective (pp. 243-272). Academic Press.

Mohamed, Collier, Sutton, Davern, & Leech. (2013). Enhancing the business value of business intelligence: the role of knowledge sharing and assimilation. *Journal of Information Systems, 27*(2), 87–105. doi:10.2308/isys-50563

Noble, S., & Schewe, C. (2003). Cohort segmentation: An exploration of its validity. *Journal of Business Research, 56*(12), 979–987. doi:10.1016/S0148-2963(02)00268-0

O'Reilly, B., & Vella-Zarb, K. (2000). *Meet the Future. The Sociological Outlook: A text with readings* (7th ed.). Collegiate Publishing Group.

OGT. (2020). *Management of intergenerational teams.* Obtained from Generation and Talent Observatory: https://observatoriorh.com/revista/31/la-gesti-6-n-de equipos-intergeneracionales-veteranos-boomers-xers-y-nets

Patrickson, M., & Hartmann, L. (1995). Australia's aging population: Implications for human resource management. *International Journal of Manpower, 15*(5), 34–46. doi:10.1108/01437729510095935

Rudolph, C. W., Rauvola, R. S., Costanza, D. P., & Zacher, H. (2021). Generations and generational differences: Debunking myths in organizational science and practice and paving new paths forward. *Journal of Business and Psychology, 36*(6), 945–967. doi:10.100710869-020-09715-2 PMID:32901173

Sanchez-Sandoval, Y., & Verdugo, L. (2016). Development and validation of the Future Expectations Scale in Adolescence (EEFA). *Anales de Psicologia/ Annals of Psychology, 32*(2), 545-554.

Schewe, G. (1994). Successful innovation management: An integrative perspective. *Journal of Engineering and Technology Management, 11*(1), 25–53. doi:10.1016/0923-4748(94)90023-X

Schneider, B. (1987). The people make the place. *Personnel Psychology, 40*(3), 437–453. doi:10.1111/j.1744-6570.1987.tb00609.x

Schuman, H., & Scott, J. (1989). Generations and collective memories. *American Sociological Review, 54*(3), 359–381. doi:10.2307/2095611

Seedsman, T. (2017). Building a humane society for older people: Compassionate policy making for integration, participation positive ageing within a framework of intergenerational solidarity. *J Intergender Relationsh., 15*(3), 204–220. doi:10.1080/15350770.2017.1329582

Stahl, A. (2021, May 10). How gen-Z is bringing a fresh perspective to the world of work. *Forbes*. Retrieved November 30, 2021, from https://www.forbes.com/sites/ashleystahl/2021/05/04/how-gen-z-isbringing-a-fresh-perspective-to-the-world-of-work/

Steele, C., & Aronson, J. (1995). Stereotype threat and intellectual test performance of African Americans. *Journal of Personality and Social Psychology*, *69*(5), 789–811. doi:10.1037/0022-3514.69.5.797 PMID:7473032

Taylor, P., & Walker, A. (1994). The aging workforce: Employer attitudes toward old people. *Work, Employment and Society*, *8*(4), 569–591. doi:10.1177/095001709484005

Tobío, C. (2010). Demographic change, intergenerational solidarity, and social policy. *J Intergener Relationsh.*, *8*(4), 431–433. doi:10.1080/15350770.2010.521098

Tortorella, G., Nascimento, D., Caiado, R., Arrieta Posada, J. G., & Sawhney, R. (2019). How do different generations contribute to the development of a learning organization in companies undergoing a lean production implementation? *The Learning Organization*, *27*(2), 101–115. doi:10.1108/TLO-02-2019-0035

Tulgan, B. (1996). *Managing Generation X: How to Bring Out the Best in Young Talent.* Oxford: Capstone.

Twenge, J. (2010). A review of the empirical evidence on generational differences in work attitudes. *Journal of Business and Psychology*, *25*(2), 201–210.

Urick, M., Hollensbe, E., Masterson, S., & Lyons, S. (2017). Understanding and managing intergenerational conflict: An examination of influences and strategies. *Work, Aging and Retirement*, *3*(2), 166–185.

Vandenkendelaere, T. (2013). Intergenerational solidarity: A two-way street that needs new paving. *Eur View.*, *12*, 235-242.

APPENDIX: QUESTIONNAIRE DEVELOPMENT

Once the categories proposed by Urick et al. (2017) researchers associated with the project wrote the questions related to the intergenerational conflict. These were reviewed and validated by 10 Mexican HR managers who collaborated with the project through interviews. The managers worked in manufacturing, service and trade. The interviews were made personally in the period from June to July 2019 a discussion was held with different HR managers from 10 different companies to build a quantitative questionnaire that would allow knowing if there are conflicts intergenerational in organizations.

Questionnaire Items

______ I support the idea of involving employees of any age in a company.
______ I accept that colleagues outside my age range teach me new processes or correct me
______ I support gender diversity in my organization.
______ I recognize the initiative of my peers regardless of age.
______ I have conflicts when dealing with peers outside my age range.
______ I agree to renew processes and use more and more technology at work.
______ I support the use of social media at work.
______ I consider it a challenge to work with cutting-edge technology.
______ I have trouble arguing my ideas in a debate with colleagues from another age.
______ It is difficult to communicate my ideas to peers of any age eleven.
______ I manage to adapt well to the demands of my immediate boss.
______ I associate only with workers my age.
______ I prefer to work individually rather than support a team.
______ I collaborate on projects that involve employees of various age ranges.
______ I have a strong commitment to social responsibility.
______ I have a strong commitment to the environment.
______ I actively participate in different social roles (volunteer work, club, associations, etc)

Chapter 5
Institutional Change and Institutionalization

José G. Vargas-Hernandez
Tecnológico Superior de Jalisco, Mexico

Omar C. Vargas-González
https://orcid.org/0000-0002-6089-956X
Tecnológico Nacional de México, Ciudad Guzmán, Mexico

ABSTRACT

This study has the purpose to analyze the implications between institutional change and institutionalization. It departs from the assumption that some institutional change theories provide through different framework perspectives to explain and analyze the different strengths and challenges of the institutionalization processes. The methods used are the meta-cognitive analytical descriptive based on the conceptual, theoretical, and analytical literature review. As it had been assumed, the study concludes in that institutional change theoretical frameworks lead to provide the intellectual tools to describe, explain, and analyze the strengths and challenges posed by the institutionalization processes.

DOI: 10.4018/978-1-6684-6567-7.ch005

INTRODUCTION

The emergence of new institutional fields such as institutional change is relevant in development of institutional theory (Lawrence & Phillips, 2004). Individuals as well as organizations are somewhat reflexive and creative in understanding the pressures for institutional change to construct the relationship between the professional and managerial logic (Bévort & Suddaby, 2016). Institutional theory for praxis and institutional change has some institutional contradictions (Seo & Creed, 2002)

Research on institutional theory used institutional work as the theory of institutional change exploring action in institutions. Institutional research on institutions is dependent on the formation and core on enthusiastic identification to analyze institutional change enable to grasp the extent of captured people by institutional arrangements (Friedland, 2013). The development of an institutional integrative research framework emphasizes the multilevel nature and external institutional change in evolutive human resource management. The use of mixed methods and qualitative analysis to study institutional changes in institutional work show the ambivalence (Wallenburg et al. 2016). The dependent variable determines the institutional change.

Research on strong and long lasting institutions with rigid structure and enforcement are akin to institutionalization of work such as bureaucracies (Goodstein & Velamuri, 2009; Xiao & Klarin, 2019). Institutionalization is potentially contradictory process that produce actors and institutional strategies aimed to subvert the system (DiMaggio (1988, 1991). Institutionalization processes create their own opponents and losers among the stakeholders with new grievances pushing them to contest or accept the relationship of dominance by the winners and periphery of losers claiming for new forms and ideas, persisting on resources, transposing logics and forming partnerships and coalitions with other partners (Clemens, 1997; Leblebici et al., 1991; Morrill, 2005).

Academic and research institutions moving consistently towards appraisal systems in sustainability provide a holistic assessment encompassing academic and scientific programs based on institutionalization of sustainability research communities and networks, experiential learning in sustainability projects and collaboration with external stakeholders (Brousseau, Dedeurwaerdere & Siebenhüner, 2012). A direction for research on institutional change is to connect emotional competence to institutional complexity and pluralism (Greenwood et al., 2011; Smets & Jarzabkowski, 2013; Kraatz & Block, 2008).

The study concentrates firstly on the institutional change theoretical framework leading to the institutional processes in the second part. Finally, it offers some concluding remarks.

INSTITUTIONAL CHANGE

Institutional change is the process of creating new institutions, replacing, and adjusting existing ones to changing social and bio-physical conditions (Zikos, 2020). The analysis of the conditions of change institutions are facilitated by the institutionalism theoretical framework aimed to explain institutional change (Campbell, 2004, 1998). Institutional change grounds on new institutions or adapting the existent ones to respond to crisis, although is questionable its legitimization, which in turn may legitimize the emergence of rules contradicting the institutions of crisis response (Vatn, 2005; Vatn, 2015b).

Institutional change theories depart from the assumption that change is designed or spontaneous and questions the institutional status quo changes through different perspectives, that it is initiated by top or bottom of the hierarchy having different strengths and challenges (Zikos & Thiel, 2013). Institutionalism is a relevant theoretical framework in political analysis of contested ideas to examine the politics in institutional change to create protective spaces for innovation networks.

Earlier institutionalist theories focused on institutions fundamentally stable and path dependent recognizing the incremental institutional change, which is more gradual endogenous institutional change with internal institutional actors (Unruh, 2000; Streeck and Thelen, 2005; Battilana et al., 2009). Historical institutionalism and policy-process framework promote radical changes termed as windows of opportunity (Kingdon, [1984], 2011), critical junctures and punctuated equilibriums (Baumgartner & Jones [1993] 2009). Political actors and political dynamics play different roles in dominant policymaking process frameworks of historical institutionalism to ensure policy stability and change outcomes as the result of social structures, government mechanism and groups of interests (Pierson, 2004; Moe, 2015).

Institutional change is relevant on the lead to the emergence of new organizational fields in the development of institutional theory (Lawrence and Phillips, 2004). In institutional theory, praxis and institutional change are related to the institutional contradictions (Seo & Creed, 2002). The types of institutional change are related to the political context, the institutional characterization and institutional entrepreneurship are analyzed by the institutionalism theory framework proposed by Mahoney & Thelen (2010). Research on institutional change and reforms occurring within transformative contexts has produced fragmentary knowledge dealing with resources and addressing dynamic interrelationships between actors, natural systems, and decisions. The institutional change processes from the micro to the macro processes shape the changes in the new institutional order (Bitektine & Haack, 2015).

The institutional change theoretical framework proposed by Mahoney and Thelen (2010) offers an analytical tool about the role of agency of actors and testable explanations on the modes of change in socio-technical transitions deployed in discourses and narratives to create protective spaces, although as a theory of institutional change has deficiencies in the analysis.

The institutional change nature depends on the degree to which discretional institutional actors may interpret and enforce institutional rules in situations where there is a gap between formal rules and enforcement leading to discretional institutional change (Mahoney and Thelen, 2010).

An institutionalism theoretical framework to analyze specific gradual forms of institutional change that occur in instruments and goals is proposed by Kern & Howlett (2009). The gradual institutional change theory of Mahoney and Thelen (2010) and the hypotheses on the conditions of ideas influencing the institutional change of Campbell (2004) are joint to elaborate a powerful institutional analysis framework.

Institutional change may take the form of layering rather than displacement, in contexts drawing on the notion of veto points, the institutional actors have veto possibilities to resist both internal and external pressures for change displacing the existing institutional rules and goals (Mahoney & Thelen, 2010; Tsebelis, 2002). Institutional change modes layering are associated with the different types of change agents labelled as subversives who working on their own, behind the scenes and in shadows, rather than creating coalitions with other institutional incumbents and challenger, seek institutional change in which they are located without breaking the institutional rules, tending to bide their time and encouraging of new rules on top of the existing ones (Mahoney & Thelen, 2010).

The implementation of institutional rules is a way to have more control in the modes and forms of institutional change associated with different types of change agents. The possibilities of institutional change make relevant the rules organized in multiple layers including the operational rules to regularize activities, to change the collective choice rules need collective efforts and time horizon and constitutional choice rules are more difficult to change (Ostrom, 1992; Baerlein, Kasymov & Zikos, 2015).

Layering tends to associate institutional agents seeking to change locations of institutions in pursuing the goals by not breaking the institutional rules. Institutional agents are labeled subversives because they tend to bide their time and encouraging the new rules on top of existing ones. These institutional agents tend to work on their own, behind the scenes and in shadows instead of forming coalitions of change with institutional incumbents and challengers. (Mahoney and Thelen, 2010).

An integrative institutional approach introduce the value of equality through corporate social responsibility activities (Karam & Jamali, 2013) by depriving the moral basis of the institution to initiate institutional change toward equality. Institutional change motivated by the engagement of mobilized people experiencing changes of self-sense in roles of actor and dissatisfaction with the focal institutional conditions (Hochschild, 2016). Phenomenology of the life of people grounds the self-concept leading to novel explanations of institutionalization, institutional change, and de-institutionalization (Patriotta & Lanzara, 2006).

Institutional change at a phenomenological level breaks down with experience of social reality (Kennedy & Fiss, 2013). The formation of new institutions based on experiences, beliefs and perceptions of reality is followed by institutional change, as pro-social behavior in response to unexpected developments is discouraged by weak institutions that hamper mutual confidence (Dasgupta, P. (2005).

Endogenous institutional change involves programs that may be possible for institutional changes to put forward institutional programs. Institutional change programs need to be developed to analyze privilege, power, causes and effects of systemic and institutional racism (Banks & McGee Banks, 2004). Feminist institutionalism analyses institutions with an emphasis on the concept of power exercised to perpetuate or disrupt broader gendered and raced power relations and social scale rules that impede or support institutional change (Chappell & Waylen; Kenny, 2007; Mackay, Kenny, & Chappell, 2010; Krook and Mackay, 2010).

The organizational identity responses to institutional complexity environment leads to institutional changes (Kodeih & Greenwood, 2014). Institutional change is motivated by emotions linked to social identities as part of an institutional order (Emirbayer & Goldberg, 2005). Institutional change analyzes empirically why people internalize institutional ethos and the emotional competence of the person leads to processes and questions arising at institutional level.

Discussions on institutional theory sustains that the institutional identities face demands that not always are expressed in isomorphic behaviors but recognizes actors with their internal organizational structures and capacities as elements generating variability in response to institutional pressures aimed to generate institutional change escaping the immersed agent paradox. A theory of institutional change should address the issue that change agents deploying broad discursive concepts and narrative to create protective spaces in socio-technical transitions although the theory deployed is undetermined.

Discursive and structural theoretical approaches to incremental institutional change are consistent with evidence although change actors' characterizations and the policy paradigms are not flexible raising the question about how theorize politics in the sustainability transitions analysis (Lockwood, 2016). Institutional change and policy making are related to the engaged vision of actors for the future desired state of things, implying the market structures emergence with multiplicity of meanings of concepts on scarcity and access over resources articulated in different groups (Fischhendler, 2015).

The term institutional work (IW) has originated and defined as the purposive individual and organizational actions aimed at creating, maintaining, and disrupting institutions. The conceptual and theoretical sources come from the institutional theory, the institutional change, and the role of agency (Lawrence & Suddaby, 2006). The different actions in the institutional field generates diverse behaviors guided by the diversity of interests leading to institutional changes (Battilana et al., 2009; Thornton et al., 2012). Given interests of institutional change are at interest formation and at odds with institutions. Institutional work does not value institutional change and its impacts as different in institutional entrepreneurship and institutional training.

Institutional logics is an evolving field with more theoretical opportunities in structured areas to give more delimitation and clarity of identities in response to institutional complexity and other emerging fields in categorization and hybridization of institutional change. In the concept of institutional changes is a connection between institutional logics and other strategy elements leading to changes in legitimacy forms and change of organizational access to resources (Bitektine & Haack, 2015; Meyer & Rowan, 1977). The normative ideas, discourses and narratives falling in the same category are the frames used by advocacy groups and policy elites for decision making in institutional change and to legitimate changes to target constituents (Campbell, 2004, 1998) Ideas are more relevant for institutional change under uncertainty conditions of crisis (Campbell, 2004).

The causal mechanisms impose institutional change to release the market forces and achieve di-embeddedness of the economy, turn of land, resources and people into fictitious commodities and transform the interactions between economic, social, and ecological systems as the responses to growing crises (Ide, 2015). Institutional change is an occurring process of transition from a centralized economy towards a free market economy. Economic crises influence institutional change and using notions of modernity and ideology modify the negotiations and bargaining power between agents used to maintain or change institutions (Haller & Merten, 2008). The post euro crisis in Mediterranean Europe has presented the same processes (Zikos & Hagedorn, 2017).

Lockwood (2016) adopts the institutionalism theoretical framework for the analysis of institutional change in neo-institutionalism theory. Institutional change and the linked elements are related to empirical research on institutional logics focusing the change at institutional levels not reflecting the micro level technologies (Cloutier & Langley, 2013). Institutional change is intrinsic to institutional logics in relation to neo-institutionalism (Thornton & Occasio, 2008; Thornton et al., 2012).

Institutional change focuses on theorization in motivating change to engage actors in new practices (Greenwood et al. 2002). Through various institutional logics acting differently in composition and intensity, the impact of individual actions acting on institutional change can be analyzed under the assumption of the institutional complexity. Institutional logics explains the emergence of new practices and their dissemination, institutional changes, variations in organizational behavior in institutional fields (Edman, 2016; Greenwood et al., 2010; Lee & Lounsbury, 2015).

Institutional logics influences all types of innovations and institutional change (Battilana & Casciaro, 2012; Malsch & Gendron, 2013). Network nature as a regulated monopoly is the evolution locus of creating protective spaces for innovation is the politics of institutional change related to regulatory institutions. Creation of protective spaces for network innovation is concerned with the institutional change in regulatory regimes sustained by institutionalist theory in political analysis to explain institutional change leading to the incremental creation of new protective spaces for research, development and innovation in networks (Peters, 2012). The relationship between strategy and institutional logics in dialogue with the Resource Based View (RBV) are aligned with choice of creation identities in the hybridization between institutional logics and institutional change leading to enhance legitimacy.

Innovations generated by the action of institutional entrepreneurs are institutional changes that can be disruptive innovations as the result of institutional changes. Entrepreneurship institutional represents an institutional change in which actors contest, deconstructs and give new meanings to beliefs, identities and practices sustained by an institutional logic dominant (Battilana et al., 2009; Leca & Naccache, 2006; Martí, 2017). The concept of institutional entrepreneur can influence institutional change (DiMaggio, 1988). Institutional entrepreneurship actions performed by individuals, groups, and organizations as social actors that results in social practices, some of which become institutions through institutional changes leading to creation, development, and maintenance.

Other institutional practices focus on agents as institutional entrepreneurs enacting institutional change (Battilana, Leca, & Boxenbaum, 2009). Accreditation agencies are under pressures from the various actors led by institutional entrepreneurship contributing to representativeness may led to institutional changes.

Institutional change induces and resolves conflict. Institutional change is in the interest of economic efficiency, or redistributes income (Bromley, 1989). Institutional contradictions result in rational recognition of the fit between the institutional arrangements and the interests of persons with not emotional detachment and disinvestment from the institutional arrangements may be likely to become institutional change agents (Voronov & Vince, 2012). Several attempts have been made to rectify problems of dysfunctional institutions in a persistent pattern aimed to enforce institutional change, support institutional buildings and institutional reforms by national and international organizations.

Polycentric governance, institutional change and institutional conflict focusing on the management of natural resources are interrelated phenomena under empirical research (Lubell, Mewhirter, Berardo, 2020; Favero, Gatto, Deutsch, Pettenella, 2016; Carlisle, & Gruby, 2019). Polycentric governance or not and self-organization and community-based management focusing on institutional performance rather than institutional change processes. Instead, it created new conflicts, ignited, and fueled the suppressed ones leading to question if these conflicts are related to institutional change processes.

Institutional research on conflict from a pluralistic perspective assumes that conflict in institutional transformative change is a contextual factor in which institutional processes are framed and take place for non-cooperative strategies adopted by the agents, actors and stakeholders influencing the institutional changes.

Conflicts over natural resources management are neither under the governance of a coherent institutional theoretical framework nor by the strict disciplinary boundaries but grounded on a multitude of etymological assumptions and disciplinary conceptions concerning the interrelationships, links and connections between institutional change and conflicts. Institutional economy has rarely touched the concept of transformation to enhance the institutional change underlying emerging conflicts (Blyth et al. 2011). Economic orthodoxy explores institutional change to transform relationships between humans and nature related to resource conflicts, but it is unable to explain institutional change.

Borders between countries create discontinuities in socio-economic and ecological and geographic spaces leading to abrupt institutional changes in regulations, laws, culture, etc. (Beugelsdijk & Mudambi, 2013). Institutional distance captures the dynamic context reflecting the institutional changes across the international borders among the countries. A contextual analysis of the institutional sphere questions the institutional dynamic interdependence, the mobilization of people for institutional change, their experience and engagement to change their self-sense in situations of dissatisfaction with other conditions (Hochschild, 2016).

Technology innovation disrupts education and provides shortcuts for institutional change. The interactions between the different institutional digital logics and actors demonstrates the institutional changes and processes from organizational fields two. To organizational fields four.

INSTITUTIONALIZATION

Institutions have a cyclical nature and institutional change which questions the sequential approach to institutionalization (Kostova & Roth, 2002). The institutionalization process adapts the organizations to their environment searching for survival and legitimacy. However, adoption and implementation of change processes not always is necessarily institutionalization.

Among the different institutional theory perspectives are the sociological neo institutional strand, the institutional pressure, coercive and normative order, institutionalization and legitimacy, institutional entrepreneurship, rational choice, etc. The rational-choice approaches to implement the institutional theory change poses some challenges including uncertainty and the lack of institutionalization across different areas in the implementation networks, the active multilateral implementation management to reduce uncertainty and lack of institutionalization in the network context (O'Toole, 1995). Some analysis uses institutional theory without identifying it but other expressions such as institutionalization, isomorphism, legitimacy, normative pressure, coercive and normalization, conformity, mimetic, etc.

The old institutionalism is defined as the institutionalization process linked to the need for survival, social recognition, and the organizational adaptation to the interests of the exiting environment (Selznick, 1996). Sociological neo institutionalism assumes that the institutionalization of an organization incorporates rationalized procedures predominant in society, assuring survival and legitimacy (Meyer & Rowan, 1977). Research centered on sociological neo institutional strand is more used than the rational choice proposed by North (1990) changing the institutionalization and legitimacy processes to the market.

Institutionalized organizations analysis focuses on complex relations between values, norms, preferences, etc., in the context of adopting or resisting the institutionalization of organizational context of digitalization processes. Plural contexts slow the shared understanding development leading to prevent the diffusion needed for the occurrence of institutionalization. Multiple institutional logics affect institutional alignment that may hinder and block the institutionalization of transformative changes.

The different institutional mechanisms suggests that institutionalization produces resource scarcities, exhaustion, accumulating costs, and conflicts of interest undermining the institutional (Greif, 1998; Leblebici et al., 1991; North and Weingast, 1989; Peltzman, 1989).

Institutionalization of new rules and practices are subject to policymaking changes in horizontal and vertical structures and mechanisms of the state, as confirmed by the perspectives of historical and sociological institutionalism.

Institutionalization of transformative policies across sectors in public sphere requires of a leadership to challenge injustices (Hackler, 2022; Zeinali, Muraya, Govender, Molyneux, & Morgan, 2019; Thomson, 2020). Formal institutional regulative structures are established to the institutionalization, although the corporate social responsibility does not provide insights into how is accomplished. The analysis of institutional regulative aspects of responsible organizational practices is limited in the institutionalization of practices.

The cognitive legitimacy of corporate social responsibility enhances institutionalization (Höllerer, 2013). The institutional normative approach is meaningful to the interactions between business and society, such as the corporate social responsibility involving the actors driven by specific values that have influence on the institutionalization of organizations described as infusion with values (Selznick, 1996). Societies are organized power networks escaping from institutionalization meaning that the institutionalization is not a driving force of human society to generate networks of intensive and extensive power relations and direct relation to goal attainment leading to non-institutionalized social relationships such as revolutions and wars play a role in the institutional emergence and evolution (Mann, 1986),

By the end of the first decade of this Century, institutionalization entered the administrative state bureaucracy logic as the indicators of performance driven by accountability for their promises as the political, intellectual, and moral reduction of institutions to be measured and demonstrated in terms of equity (Lange, 2020). To establish an institutional sustainability in industry oriented research program, require an incremental institutional transformation and change approach based on the capacity building and a gradual social learning and institutionalization process is needed for sustainability science aimed to face the existing institutional and epistemological barriers.

The efforts of institutional reform to overcome the current barriers in institutional sustainability can contribute to the long-term institutionalization initiatives at national, regional, and local levels of governments and stakeholders in partnership collaborations and networking among public sector, academia and industry. Sustainability science requires the institutional reform on evaluation procedures and long-term institutionalization to support the transition towards interdisciplinary and transdisciplinary new modes for institutional research funding in research and academic institutions.

Institutional work may demonstrate failed repairs that might lead to the institutionalization of misconduct of institutional entrepreneurship with subtle consequences because institutional work explicit performance might self-destruct (Herepath & Kitchener, 2016; Harmon, 2019). The organizational fields can be reconfigured with the institutionalization of new practices giving support to the development of an institutional, entrepreneurship theoretical framework supporting the establishment of institutions (Mahoney and Thelen, 2010).

Phenomenology-based life and self-concept may have an explanation of institutionalization, de-institutionalization, and institutional change processes (Patriotta & Lanzara, 2006). Any revolution has the de-institutionalization and re-institutionalization processes. Creative destruction implies the de-institutionalization and re-institutionalization processes determined by the economic conditions for redistributive policies and the interaction between new powerholders without economic power, and economically strong property-holders with political power. The re-institutionalization and restoration phase arises after the mass revolutions consolidates the new institutions considering that expropriation and use of brutal force does not establish and egalitarian society. Restorations do not reproduce the past but adopts new institutional order.

Iinstitutional entrepreneurship characterized as institutional work has a weak theoretical foundation to analyze de-institutionalization and re-institutionalization processes (Jacometti, 2013; Lago, 2018). A platform provided to aggregate institutional work to use theoretical and empirical setting to combine the institutional and actor types, considering the strong or weak level of institutionalization in the spectrum view (Zucker, 1977). Actor specific norms are placed at the center of an institutional perspective stating that institutionalization occurs in habitualized actions of actors (Berger & Luckmann, 1966). Institutionalization occurs in a typification of habitual actions by different types of actors. The de-institutionalization is followed by re-institutionalization.

The institutionalization of war including the internal class wars and the external revolutionary wars originated by authoritarian methods creates a permanent war economy. A theoretical framework on revolution is the source of institutional innovation processes characterized by de-institutionalization and re-institutionalization. The revolutionary situation in the unity phase begins with the de-institutionalization process leading to the differentiation entailing the polarization among moderated and revolutionary forces with the selection and domination phase in which institutions are born. The mass revolutions theoretical framework examines the de-institutionalization and re-institutionalization processes.

The de-institutionalization phase marks the collapse or state of standstill in coordination and regulation of social relationships. In the phase of de-institutionalization process, the power networks multiply but there are not hegemonic political tendencies in the opposition De-institutionalization process is an analytical and empirical phase of revolution changes developed before the overthrow of an old regime (Goldstone, 2009). The institutionalization requires selective adaptation and domination with the emergence of new institutions determined by the survival of the fittest (Goldstone 2009).

The source and trajectory of fundamental institutional change caused by contestation to exogenous shocks and disruptions and leading to deinstitutionalization, re-institutionalization, and the institutional consolidation under a new organizational logic of forms (Crouch & Farrell, 2004; Ingram & Clay, 2000; Orren & Skorownek, 1994). An institutional rupture between the old and new institutions carries out institutional innovation in the form of Schumpeterian technological change shunning institutional vacuum in which there is not leaps leading to continuous coevolution process of de-institutionalization and re-institutionalization. The new institutions are generated as the result of survival struggle in the long term requiring economic support but may be economically inefficient.

Restoration or re-institutionalization secures a sustainable political and economic order by compromising the economically fittest social groups and the politico-military. The interactions between the economic and politico-military powers determines re-institutionalization in an emerging new institutional order sustained by the adaptive selection leading to survival, variation and inheritance of newly created institutions may contain some old contents. The re-institutionalization process implies the economic interest's consolidation reshaping the ruling political and military elites' orientation.

The re-institutionalization and restorations began with the end of the Montagne Convention after which new institutions gradually ensured consolidation producing a positive economic and institutional impact on the partial destruction of feudal institutions and nobility leading to the demarcation between sovereignty and property. The emerging new institutions such as the civil code, questioning the aristocratic privileges, equality before the law, etc. were exported and impose in other nations producing positive externalities.

Building on the work of Polanyi (1951), Blyth (2002) argues that the double movement is not a robust institutional change theory but a plausible heuristic that needs to be reconceptualize (Blyth, 2002). According to Blyth (2002), the economic interests and institutions can be remodeled through institutional change based on assumptions that in economic crisis the ideas are uncertainty reducing mechanisms and weapons to guarantee the institutional stability prevailing the collective action in the struggle over institutional change. After institutions are delegitimized, the new ideas are the institutional blueprints in institutional crafting, although some existing institutions in transformative contexts are not delegitimized.

Path dependence institutionalism leads to the sequences punctuated equilibria for fundamental and incremental change that unfolds exogenous shocks, crises, deinstitutionalization, settlements, diffusion, rise and re-institutionalization of a new institutional systems. However, other institutionalism paths lead to institutional equilibria, fundamental and incremental change that begins endogenously and develop and internal sequence of failures accumulating controversies and costs, the transposition of new institutional forms and models in dynamic combination of change conditions.

Transition theory linked with institutional and regulatory theories lead to identify institutional change mechanism and their use in institutionalization of institutional and organizational radical innovation.

The conceptualization of transitions triggers research to apply an institutional perspective to analyze socio-technical systems aimed to transform in regional and urban contexts, taken for granted the deinstitutionalization of regime structures, and the strategic institutionalization based on competing rationality in collective institutional activities (Frantzeskaki et al., 2017; Strambach & Pflitsch, 2020; Kungl & Geels, 2018; Rosenbloom & Rinscheid, 2020; Binz et al., 2016a; Fuenfschilling and Truffer, 2016). Institutionalization processes involve agency and propose some possibilities of deinstitutionalization (Oliver, 1991, 1992). The re-institutionalization process coordinated by actors who are usually institutional entrepreneurs reconfiguring power initiated with the deinstitutionalization of practices (Battilana et al., 2009).

Transitions are conceptualized as a de-institutionalization taken for granted field logic drawing on core values, materials, elements, and technologies. The complex de-institutionalization dynamics transforming the socio-economic sectors connect the transition studies with neo institutional theory and organizational studies (Fuenfschilling, 2019; Runhaar et al., 2020). Institutional complexity and hybridization issues may deal with communication, rhetoric, convergent and divergent changes within the institutional logics field affecting the power relations, the re-institutionalization process and deinstitutionalization assuming new practices of logic (Kim, Shin, Oh, & Jeong, 2007).

The institutional logics and social movements research perspectives have led to the processes of institutionalization and deinstitutionalization to become more prone for contestation (Thornton et al., 2012; Davis, McAdam, Scott, & Zald,2005; Weber, Heinze, & DeSoucey, 2008; Weber et al., 2009). Institutionalization of accreditation promotes normalization of practices, but unfortunately not necessarily the best practices (Romero, 2008).

The Scandinavian institutionalism framework analyzes the drives of different national policies and internal pressures for the institutionalization of a dual digitalization through strategic documents translating organizational narratives for the study of complex organizational concepts from functionalism and structuralist organizational theories.

From an institutional theory perspective leading to institutionalization of digital advancements and progress becomes relevant in competitive organizational fields environments. The digitalization of organizational structures, processes and practices in organizations requires the deconstruction processes of emergence ad adoption to analyze the institutionalization processes and developments of organizations and organizational fields. Drawing on critical realism, Bygstad, Øvrelid, Ludvigsen, & Dæhlen (2021) analyze the institutionalization of the dual digitalization merging coordination of teaching and communication.

Adaptive governance is an emergent issue in developed contexts while institutionalization of adaptive governance is remaining elusive (Chaffin, Gosnell, & Cosens, 2014; Schultz, Folke; Osterblom, & Olsson, 2015; Cosens, Gunderson, Chaffin, 2014).

Space creation for the emergence and institutionalization of adaptive governance requires of processes and some factors such as informal network formation, nested leadership, polycentric governance, public participation, social learning, experimentation, etc., in such a way that coproduction of knowledge, learning, and knowledge dissemination are elements of the emerging adaptive governance and institutionalization processes within the governance structures (Huitema, Mostert, Egas, Moellenkamp, Pahl-Wostl, & Yalcin, 2009; Wyborn, 2015; Chaffin, Gunderson, 2016;

CONCLUSION

The purpose of this study is to explain and analyze the implications between institutional change and institutionalization, departing from the assumption that some institutional change theories provide through different framework perspectives to explain and analyze the different strengths and challenges of the institutionalization processes. As it is assumed, the study concludes in that institutional change theoretical frameworks lead to provide the intellectual tools to describe, explain and analyze the strengths and challenges posed by the institutionalization processes.

The analysis bridges the research gap in institutional change with the findings from and propositions from different institutional settings and disciplines enables a holistic perspective.

Institutionalization process of an emerging adaptive governance in social norms, rules, policies, procedures at the local socio-ecological systems lead to resource conflicts in degraded system state. Policy making in sustainability science in academia and research institutions must manage the institutionalization process. Institutional sustainability science has the challenge to remove barriers addressing incremental institutional change based on a process of gradual institutionalization of existing initiatives to consolidate efforts for far-reaching institutional change.

Political, social and functional in nature pressures for de-institutionalization interpreted in meanings and contested by organizational actors and stakeholders not always lead to the breakdown of institutional norms.

Future research raises the possibilities of institutional complexity hybridization including the definition of limits related to institutional changes (Greenwood et al. 2011). A research direction on branches of person-institutions fusion may occur enabling people to envision the institutional change needed. Also, future research on institutional stability and institutional change must be conducted.

REFERENCES

Baerlein, T., Kasymov, U., & Zikos, D. (2015). Self-Governance and Sustainable Common Pool Resource Management in Kyrgyzstan. *Sustainability*, *7*(1), 496–521. doi:10.3390u7010496

Banks, J. A., & McGee Banks, C. A. (2004). *Handbook of research on multicultural education* (2nd ed.). Jossey-Bass.

Battilana, J., & Casciaro, T. (2012). Change agents, networks, and institutions: A contingency theory of organizational change. *Academy of Management Journal*, *55*(2), 381–398. doi:10.5465/amj.2009.0891

Battilana, J., & D'Aunno, T. (2009). Institutional work and the paradox of embedded agency. In T. B. Lawrence, R. Suddaby, & B. Leca (Eds.), *Institutional work: Actors and agency in institutional studies of organizations* (p. 3158). Cambridge University Press. doi:10.1017/CBO9780511596605.002

Battilana, J., & D'Aunno, T. (2009). Institutional work and the paradox of embedded agency. In T. B. Lawrence, R. Suddaby, & B. Leca (Eds.), *Institutional work: Actors and agency in institutional studies of organizations* (p. 3158). Cambridge University Press. doi:10.1017/CBO9780511596605.002

Battilana, J., Leca, B., & Boxenbaum, E. (2009). How actors change institutions: Towards a theory of institutional entrepreneurship. *The Academy of Management Annals*, *3*(1), 65–107. doi:10.5465/19416520903053598

Baumgartner, F. R., & Jones, B. D. (2009). *Agendas and Instability in American Poli-tics* (2nd ed.). University of Chicago Press. (Original work published 1993)

Berger, P., & Luckmann, T. (1966). *The social construction of reality: A treatise in the sociology of knowledge*. Anchor Books.

Beugelsdijk, S., & Mudambi, R. (2013). MNEs as border-crossing multi-location enterprises: The role of discontinuities in geographic space. *Journal of International Business Studies*, *44*(5), 413–426. doi:10.1057/jibs.2013.23

Bévort, F., & Suddaby, R. (2016). Scripting professional identities: How individuals make sense of contradictory institutional logics. *Journal of Professions and Organization*, *3*(1), 17–38. doi:10.1093/jpo/jov007

Binz, C., Harris-Lovett, S., Kiparsky, M., Sedlak, D. L., & Truffer, B. (2016). The thorny road to technology legitimation-institutional work for potable water reuse in california. *Technological Forecasting and Social Change*, *103*(February), 249–263. doi:10.1016/j.techfore.2015.10.005

Bitektine, A., & Haack, P. (2015). The "macro" and the "micro" of legitimacy: Toward a multilevel theory of the legitimacy process. *Academy of Management Review*, *40*(1), 49–75. doi:10.5465/amr.2013.0318

Blyth, M. (2002). *Great Transformations: Economic Ideas and Institutional Change in the Twentieth Century*. Cambridge University Press. doi:10.1017/CBO9781139087230

Blyth, M., Hodgson, G. M., Lewis, O., & Steinmo, S. (2011). Introduction to the Special Issue on the Evolution of Institutions. *Journal of Institutional Economics*, *7*(3), 299–315. doi:10.1017/S1744137411000270

Bromley, D. W. (1989). Institutional Change and Economic Efficiency. *Journal of Economic Issues*, *23*(3), 735–759. doi:10.1080/00213624.1989.11504936

Brousseau, E., Dedeurwaerdere, T., & Siebenhüner, B. (2012). *Reflexive Governance for Global Public Goods*. MIT Press. doi:10.7551/mitpress/9780262017244.001.0001

Bygstad, B., Øvrelid, E., Ludvigsen, S., & Dæhlen, M. (2021). Dual Digitalisation – a Framework for Digital Transformation of Higher Education NOS-HS Workshop 1, 30-31 March 2021 - Understanding digital transformations of teaching and learning in Nordic higher education and beyond. University of Agder (Norway), Aarhus University (Denmark) and KTH Royal Institute of Technology (Sweden).

Campbell, J. L. (1998). Institutional analysis and the role of ideas in political economy. *Theory and Society*, *27*(3), 377–409. doi:10.1023/A:1006871114987

Campbell, J. L. (2004). *Institutional Change and Globalization*. Princeton University Press. doi:10.1515/9780691216348

Carlisle, K., & Gruby, R. L. (2019). Polycentric systems of governance: A theoretical model for the commons. *Policy Studies Journal: the Journal of the Policy Studies Organization*, *47*(4), 927–952. doi:10.1111/psj.12212

Chaffin, B. C., Gosnell, H., & Cosens, B. A. (2014). A decade of adaptive governance scholarship: Synthesis and future directions. *Ecology and Society*, *19*(3), 56. doi:10.5751/ES-06824-190356

Chaffin, B. C., & Gunderson, L. H. (2016). Emergence, institutionalization, and renewal: Rhythms of adaptive governance in complex social-ecological systems. *Journal of Environmental Management*, *165*, 81–87. doi:10.1016/j.jenvman.2015.09.003 PMID:26426283

Chappell, L., & Waylen, G. (2013). Gender and the Hidden Life of Institutions. *Public Administration*, *91*(3), 599–615. doi:10.1111/j.1467-9299.2012.02104.x

Clemens, E. (1997). *The People's Lobby: Organizational Innovation and the Rise of Interest Group Politics in the United States*. University of Chicago Press.

Cloutier, C., & Langley, A. (2013). The Logic of Institutional Logics: Insights From French Pragmatist Sociology. *Journal of Management Inquiry*, *22*(4), 360–380. doi:10.1177/1056492612469057

Cosens, B. A., Gunderson, L. H., & Chaffin, B. C. (2014). The adaptive water governance project: Assessing law, resilience and governance in regional socio-ecological water systems facing a changing climate. Ida. *Law Rev. Nat. Resour. Environ. Law Ed*, *51*, 1–28.

Crouch, C., & Farrell, H. (2004). Breaking the path of institutional development? Alternatives to the new determinism. *Rationality and Society*, *16*(1), 5–43. doi:10.1177/1043463104039874

Dasgupta, P. (2005). The Economics of Social Capital. *The Economic Record*, *81*(s1), 2–21. doi:10.1111/j.1475-4932.2005.00245.x

Davis, G. F., McAdam, D., Scott, W. R., & Zald, M. N. (Eds.). (2005). *Social movements and organization theory*. Cambridge University Press. doi:10.1017/CBO9780511791000

DiMaggio, P. (1988). Interest and agency in institutional theor y. In L. Zucker (Ed.), *Research on institutional patterns: Environment and culture* (pp. 3–21). Ballinger Publishing Co.

DiMaggio, P. (1988). Interest and agency in institutional theory. In L. Zucker (Ed.), *Institutional Patterns and Organizations: Culture and Environment: 3–22*. Ballinger.

DiMaggio, P. (1991). Constructing an organizational field as a professional Project: U.S. art museums, 1920–1940. In P. DiMaggio & W. Powell (Eds.), *The New Institutionalism in Organizational Analysis: 267–292*. University of Chicago Press.

Edman, J. (2016). Cultivating Foreignness: How Organizations Maintain and Leverage Minority Identities. *Journal of Management Studies, 53*(1), 55–88. doi:10.1111/joms.12129

Emirbayer, M., & Goldberg, C. A. (2005). Pragmatism, Bourdieu, and collective emotions in contentious politics. *Theory and Society, 34*(5-6), 469–518. doi:10.100711186-005-1619-x

Favero, M., Gatto, P., Deutsch, N., & Pettenella, D. (2016). Conflict or synergy? Understanding interaction between municipalities and village commons (regole) in polycentric governance of mountain areas in the Veneto Region, Italy. *The International Journal of the Commons, 10*(2), 821–853. doi:10.18352/ijc.470

Fischhendler, I. (2015). The securitization of water discourse: Theoretical foundations and research gaps. Int. Environ. Agreem. *Politics Law Econ, 2015*(15), 245–2.

Frantzeskaki, N., Broto, V. C., Coenen, L., & Loorbach, D. (2017). *Urban Sustainability Transitions* (1st ed.). Routledge. doi:10.4324/9781315228389

Friedland, R. (2013). Review: The institutional logics perspective: An innovative approach to culture, structure, and process. *M@n@gement, 15*(5), 583-595.

Fuenfschilling, L. (2019). *An Institutional perspective on sustainability transitions Handbook of Sustainable Innovation*. Edward Elgar Publishing. https://www.elgaronline.com/view/edcoll/9781788112567/9781788112567.00020.xml

Fuenfschilling, L., & Truffer, B. (2014). The structuration of socio-technical regimes-conceptual foundations from institutional theory. *Research Policy, 43*(4), 772–791. doi:10.1016/j.respol.2013.10.010

Goldstone, J. (2009). Rethinking Revolutions: Integrating Origins, Processes, and Outcomes. *Comparative Studies of South Asia, Africa and the Middle East, 29*(1), 18–32. doi:10.1215/1089201X-2008-040

Goodstein, J. D., & Velamuri, S. R. (2009). States, power, legitimacy, and maintaining institutional control: The battle for private sector telecommunication services in Zimbabwe. *Organization Studies, 30*(5), 489–508. doi:10.1177/0170840609104395

Greenwood, R., Diaz, A. M., Li, S. X., & Lorente, J. C. (2010). The Multiplicity of Institutional Logics and the Heterogeneity of Organizational Responses. *Organization Science, 21*(2), 521–539. doi:10.1287/orsc.1090.0453

Greenwood, R., Raynard, M., Kodeih, F., Micelotta, E. R., & Lounsbury, M. (2011). Institutional complexity and organizational responses. *The Academy of Management Annals, 5*(1), 317–371. doi:10.5465/19416520.2011.590299

Greenwood, R., Suddaby, R., & Hinings, C. R. (2002). Theorizing Change: The Role of Professional Associations in the Transformation of Institutionalized Fields. *Academy of Management Journal, 45*(1), 58–80. doi:10.2307/3069285

Greif, A. (1998). Self-enforcing political systems and economic growth: Late medieval Genoa. In R. Bates, A. Greif, M. Levi, J. L. Rosenthal, & B. Weingast (Eds.), *Analytical Narratives: 23–63*. Princeton University Press. doi:10.2139srn.49207

Hackler, N. (2022). Managing masculinity in public organizations. Handbook on gender and public administration. doi:10.4337/9781789904734.00014

Haller, T., & Merten, S. (2008). "We are Zambians—Don't tell us how to fish!" institutional change, power relations and conflicts in the Kafue flats fisheries in Zambia. *Human Ecology, 36*(5), 699–715. doi:10.100710745-008-9191-4

Harmon, D. J. (2019). When the Fed speaks: Arguments, emotions, and the microfoundations of institutions. *Administrative Science Quarterly, 64*(3), 542–575. doi:10.1177/0001839218777475

Herepath, A., & Kitchener, M. (2016). When small bandages fail: The field-level repair of severe and protracted institutional breaches. *Organization Studies, 37*(8), 1113–1139. doi:10.1177/0170840615622065

Hochschild, A. R. (2016). *Strangers in Their Own Land: Anger and Mourning on the American Right*. The New Press.

Höllerer, M. A. (2013). From taken-for-granted to explicit commitment: The rise of CSR in a corporatist country. *Journal of Management Studies, 50*(4), 573–606. doi:10.1111/joms.12029

Huitema, M., & Egas, M. (2009). Adaptive water governance: Assessing the institutional prescriptions of adaptive (co-) management from a governance perspective and defining a research agenda. *Ecology and Society, 14*(1), 26. doi:10.5751/ES-02827-140126

Ide, T. (2015). Why Do Conflicts Over Scarce Renewable Resources Turn Violent? A qualitative comparative analysis. *Global Environmental Change, 2015*(33), 61–70. doi:10.1016/j.gloenvcha.2015.04.008

Ingram, P., & Clay, K. (2000). The choice-within-constraints new institutionalism and implications for sociology. *Annual Review of Sociology, 26*(1), 525–546. doi:10.1146/annurev.soc.26.1.525

Jacometti, M. (2013). *Institutional Work na conformação do conhecimento difundido em redes interorganizacionais: estudo de APLs no Estado do Paraná*. Tese (Doutorado em Administração). Universidade Federal do Paraná, PR, 2013. Diponível em: https://acervodigital.ufpr.br/handle/1884/34682

Karam, C. M., & Jamali, D. (2013). Gendering CSR in the Arab Middle East: An institutional perspective. *Business Ethics Quarterly*, *23*(1), 31–68. doi:10.5840/beq20132312

Kennedy, M. T., & Fiss, P. C. (2013). An ontological turn in categories research: From standards of legitimacy to evidence of actuality. *Journal of Management Studies*, *50*(6), 1138–1154. doi:10.1111/joms.12031

Kenny, M. (2007). Gender, Institutions and Power: A Critical Review. *Politics*, *27*(2), 91–100. doi:10.1111/j.1467-9256.2007.00284.x

Kern, F., & Howlett, M. (2009). Implementing transition management as policy reforms: A case study of the Dutch energy sector. *Policy Sciences*, *42*(4), 391–408. doi:10.100711077-009-9099-x

Kim, T.-Y., Shin, D., Oh, H., & Jeong, Y.-C. (2007). Inside the Iron Cage: Organizational Political Dynamics and Institutional Changes in Presidential Selection Systems in Korean Universities, 1985–2002. *Administrative Science Quarterly*, *52*(2), 286–323. doi:10.2189/asqu.52.2.286

Kingdon, J. W. (2011). *Agendas, Alternatives, and Public Policies*. Little, Brown. (Original work published 1984)

Kodeih, F., & Greenwood, R. (2014). Responding to Institutional Complexity: The Role of Identity. *Organization Studies*, *35*(1), 7–39. doi:10.1177/0170840613495333

Kostova, T., & Roth, K. (2002). Adoption of an organizational practice by subsidiaries of multinational corporations: Institutional and relational effects. *Academy of Management Journal*, *45*(1), 215–233. doi:10.2307/3069293

Kraatz, M. S., & Block, E. (2008). Organizational implications of institutional pluralism. In R. Greenwood, C. Oliver, K. Sahlin-Andersson, & R. Suddaby (Eds.), *The Sage handbook of organizational institutionalism*. Sage. doi:10.4135/9781849200387.n10

Krook, M. L., & Mackay, L. (2010). *Gender, Politics, and Institutions: Towards a Feminist Institutionalism*. Palgrave Macmillan.

Kungl, G., & Geels, F. G. (2018). Sequence and alignment of external pressures in industry destabilisation: Understanding the downfall of incumbent utilities in the German energy transition (1998–2015). *Environmental Innovation and Societal Transitions, 26*(March), 78–100. doi:10.1016/j.eist.2017.05.003

Lago, E. C. (2020). *Wandembruck. Trabalho institucional na implementação do roteiro turístico Sentidos do Campo no Estado do Paraná* (Dissertação Mestrado em Administração). Universidade Tecnológica Federal do Paraná, Curitiba, PR, 2018. Disponível em: http://repositorio.utfpr.edu.br/jspui/handle/1/3890

Lange, L. (2020). Transformation Revisited Twenty Years of Higher Education Policy in South Africa In: Transforming Universities in South Africa. African Higher Education: Developments and Perspectives, 6. doi:10.1163/9789004437043_003

Lawrence, T., & Suddaby, R. (2006). Institutions and institutional work. In S. Clegg, C. Hardy, T. Lawrence & W. Nord (Eds.), Sage handbook of organization studies (2nd ed. pp. 215–254). Sage. doi:10.4135/9781848608030.n7

Lawrence, T. B., & Phillips, N. (2004). From Moby Dick to Free Willy: Macro-cultural discourse and institutional entrepreneurship in emerging institutional fields. *Organization, 11*(5), 689–711. doi:10.1177/1350508404046457

Leblebici, H., Salancik, G., Copay, A., & King, T. (1991). Institutional change and the transformation of interorganizational fields: An organizational history of the U.S. broadcasting industry. *Administrative Science Quarterly, 36*(3), 333–363. doi:10.2307/2393200

Leca, B., & Naccache, P. (2006). A Critical Realist Approach to Institutional Entrepreneurship. *Organization, 13*(5), 627–651. doi:10.1177/1350508406067007

Lee, M.-D. P., & Lounsbury, M. (2015). Filtering Institutional Logics: Community Logic Variation and Differential Responses to the Institutional Complexity of Toxic Waste. *Organization Science, 26*(3), 847–866. doi:10.1287/orsc.2014.0959

Lockwood, M. (2016). Creating protective space for innovation in electricity distribution networks in Great Britain: The politics of institutional change. *Environmental Innovation and Societal Transitions, 18*, 111-127. https://www.sciencedirect.com/science/article/pii/S2210422415000453 doi:10.1016/j.eist.2015.05.007

Lubell, M., Mewhirter, J., & Berardo, R. (2020). The Origins of Conflict in Polycentric Governance Systems. *Public Administration Review, 80*(2), 222–233. doi:10.1111/puar.13159

Mackay, F., Kenny, M., & Chappell, L. (2010). New Institutionalism through a Gender Lens: Towards a Feminist Institutionalism? *International Political Science Review*, *31*(5), 573–588. doi:10.1177/0192512110388788

Mahoney, J., & Thelen, K. (2010). A theory of gradual institutional change. In J. Mahoney & K. Thelen (Eds.), *Explaining institutional change: ambiguity, agency, and power* (pp. 1–37). Cambridge University Press.

Malsch, B., & Gendron, Y. (2013). Re-theorizing change: Institutional experimentation and the struggle for domination in the field of public accounting. *Journal of Management Studies*, *50*(5), 870–899. doi:10.1111/joms.12006

Mann, M. (1986). *The Sources of Social Power, A history of power from the beginning to A.D. 1760* (Vol. I). Cambridge University Press.

Martí, G. (2017). New Concepts for New Dynamics: Generating Theory for the Study of Religious Innovation and Social Change. *Journal for the Scientific Study of Religion*, *56*(1), 6–18. doi:10.1111/jssr.12325

Meyer, J. W., & Rowan, B. (1977). Institutionalized organizations: Formal structure as myth and ceremony. *American Journal of Sociology*, *83*(2), 340–363. doi:10.1086/226550

Moe, T. (2015). Vested interests and political institutions. *Political Science Quarterly*, *130*(2), 277–318. doi:10.1002/polq.12321

Morrill, C. (2005). Institutional change and interstitial emergence: The growth of alternative dispute resolution in American law, 1965–1995. In W. Powell & D. Jones (Eds.), *How Institutions Change*. University of Chicago Press.

North, D. C. (1990). *Institutions, Institutional Change and Economic Performance*. Cambridge University Press. doi:10.1017/CBO9780511808678

North, D. C. & Weingast, B. R. (1989). Constitutions and Commitment: The Evolution of Institutions Governing Public Choice in Seventeenth-Century England. *The Journal of Economic History*, *49*(4), 803-832.

O'Toole, L. Jr. (1995). Rational choice and policy implementation: Implications for interorganizational network management. *American Review of Public Administration*, *25*(1), 43–57. doi:10.1177/027507409502500103

Oliver, C. (1991). Strategic responses to institutional processes. *Academy of Management Review*, *16*(1), 145–179. doi:10.2307/258610

Oliver, C. (1992). The antecedents of deinstitutionalization. *Organization Studies, 13*(4), 563–588. doi:10.1177/017084069201300403

Orren, K., & Skowronek, S. (1994). Beyond the iconography of order: Notes for a 'New Institutionalism. In L. Dodd & C. Jilson (Eds.), *The Dynamics of American Politics*. Westview.

Ostrom, E. (1992). *Crafting Institutions for Self-Governing Irrigation Systems*. ICS Press.

Patriotta, G., & Lanzara, G. F. (2006). Identity, institutions, and new work roles: The case of a green field automotive factory. *The American Behavioral Scientist, 49*(7), 987–999. doi:10.1177/0002764205285180

Peltzman, S. (1989). The economic theory of regulation after a decade of deregulation. In *Brookings Papers: Microeconomics* (pp. 1–41). Brookings Institution. doi:10.2307/2534719

Peters, B. G. (2012). *Institutional Theory in Political Science* (3rd ed.). Continuum. doi:10.5040/9781501397813

Pierson, P. (2004). *Politics in Time: History, Institutions and Social Analysis*. Princeton University Press. doi:10.1515/9781400841080

Polanyi, M. (1951). *The Logic of Liberty. Reflections and Rejoinders*. University of Chicago Press.

Romero, E. J. (2008). AACSB accreditation: Addressing faculty concerns. *Academy of Management Learning & Education, 7*(2), 245–255. doi:10.5465/amle.2008.32712622

Rosenbloom, D., & Rinscheid, A. (2020). Deliberate decline: An emerging frontier for the study and practice of decarbonization. *Wiley Interdisciplinary Reviews: Climate Change, 11*(6), e669. doi:10.1002/wcc.669

Runhaar, H., Fünfschilling, L., Dasselaar, A. P. V., Moors, E. H. M., Temmink, R., & Hekkert, M. (2020). Endogenous regime change: Lessons from transition pathways in dutch dairy farming. *Environmental Innovation and Societal Transitions, 36*(September), 137–150. doi:10.1016/j.eist.2020.06.001

Schultz, L., Folke, C., Österblom, H., & Olsson, P. (2015). Adaptive governance, ecosystem management, and natural capital. *Proceedings of the National Academy of Sciences of the United States of America, 112*(24), 7369–7374. doi:10.1073/pnas.1406493112 PMID:26082542

Selznick, P. (1996). Institucionalism 'old' and 'new'. *Administrative Science Quarterly*, *41*(2), 270–277. doi:10.2307/2393719

Seo, M. G., & Creed, W. D. (2002). Institutional contradictions, praxis, and institutional change: A dialectical perspective. *Academy of Management Review*, *27*(2), 222–247. doi:10.2307/4134353

Smets, M., & Jarzabkowski, P. (2013). Reconstructing institutional complexity in practice: A relational model of institutional work and complexity. *Human Relations*, *66*(10), 12791309. doi:10.1177/0018726712471407

Strambach, S., & Pflitsch, G. (2020). Transition topology: Capturing institutional dynamics in regional development paths to sustainability. *Research Policy*, *49*(7), 104006. Advance online publication. doi:10.1016/j.respol.2020.104006

Streeck, W., & Thelen, K. (2005). Introduction: institutional change in advanced political economies. In W. Streeck & K. Thelen (Eds.), *Beyond Continuity: Institutional Change in Advanced Political Economies* (pp. 1–39). Oxford University Press.

Thomson, K. (2020). By the light of the corona (virus): Revealing hegemonic masculinity and the double bind for men in responding to crises. *Health Sociology Review*, *29*(2), 149–157. doi:10.1080/14461242.2020.1784773 PMID:33411649

Thornton, P. H., & Ocasio, W. (2008). Institutional Logics. In R. Greenwood, C. Oliver, K. Sahlin, & R. Suddaby (Eds.), *The SAGE Handbook of Organizational Institutionalism* (pp. 99–129). Sage Publications Ltd. doi:10.4135/9781849200387.n4

Thornton, P. H., Ocasio, W., & Lounsbury, M. (2012). *The institutional logics perspective: A new approach to culture, structure and process*. Oxford University Press. doi:10.1093/acprof:oso/9780199601936.001.0001

Tsebelis, G. (2002). *Veto Players: How Political Institutions Work*. Princeton University Press. doi:10.1515/9781400831456

Unruh, G. (2000). Understanding carbon lock-in. *Energy Policy*, *28*(12), 817–830. doi:10.1016/S0301-4215(00)00070-7

Vatn, A. (2005). Rationality, Institutions and Environmental Policy. *Ecological Economics*, *55*(2), 203–217. doi:10.1016/j.ecolecon.2004.12.001

Vatn, A. (2015b). *Environmental Governance: Institutions, Policies and Actions*. Edward Elgar.

Voronov, M., & Vince, R. (2012). Integrating emotions into the analysis of institutional work. *Academy of Management Review*, *37*, 58–81.

Wallenburg, I., Hopmans, C. J., Buljac-Samardzic, M., den Hoed, P. T., & IJzermans, J. N. M. (2016). Repairing reforms and transforming professional practices: A mixed-methods analysis of surgical training reform. *Journal of Professions and Organization*, *3*(1), 86–102. doi:10.1093/jpo/jov012

Weber, K., Heinze, K., & DeSoucey, M. (2008). Forage for thought: Mobilizing codes in the movement for grass-fed meat and dairy products. *Administrative Science Quarterly*, *53*(3), 529567. doi:10.2189/asqu.53.3.529

Weber, K., Rao, H., & Thomas, L. G. (2009). From streets to suites: How the anti-biotech movement affected German pharmaceutical firms. *American Sociological Review*, *74*(2), 106127. doi:10.1177/000312240907400106

Wyborn, C. (2015). Co-productive governance: A relational framework for adaptive governance. *Global Environmental Change*, *30*, 56–67. doi:10.1016/j.gloenvcha.2014.10.009

Xiao, Q., & Klarin, A. (2019). Subordinate actors' institutional maintenance in response to coercive reforms. *Journal of Management Inquiry*, *30*(1), 24–39. doi:10.1177/1056492619868027

Zeinali, Z., Muraya, K., Govender, V., Molyneux, S., & Morgan, R. (2019). Intersectionality and global health leadership: Parity is not enough. *Human Resources for Health*, *17*(1), 29. doi:10.118612960-019-0367-3 PMID:31029139

Zikos, D. (2020). Revisiting the Role of Institutions in Transformative Contexts: Institutional Change and Conflicts. *Sustainability*, *12*(21), 9036. doi:10.3390u12219036

Zikos, D., & Hagedorn, K. (2017). Competition for Water Resources from the European Perspective. In J. R. Ziolkowska & J. M. Peterson (Eds.), *Competition for Water Resources: Experiences and Management Approaches in the US and Europe* (pp. 19–35). Elsevier. doi:10.1016/B978-0-12-803237-4.00002-1

Zikos, D., & Thiel, A. (2013). Action Research's Potential to Foster Institutional Change for Urban Water Management. *Water (Basel)*, *5*(2), 356–378. doi:10.3390/w5020356

Zucker, L. (1977). The role of institutionalization in cultural persistence. *American Sociological Review*, *42*(5), 726–743. doi:10.2307/2094862

Chapter 6
Organizational Change Models in Practice:
The Case of Michelin Group

Umut Uyan
https://orcid.org/0000-0002-8466-2903
Munzur University, Turkey

ABSTRACT

In a competitive business environment, it is vital that firms consider implementing techniques to cope with constant change to remain competitive and survive. Most change initiatives, however, suffer from several difficulties and are often hampered by resistance, primarily caused by fear of adopting new practices or concern about competence. As a result, such initiatives could result in unintended consequences. In fact, they might result in irreversible situations, impairing the dynamics of an organization. Michelin Shanghai underwent an organizational change initiative to enhance its competitiveness. The initiative resulted in significant improvements in the company's productivity and profitability as well as increased employee satisfaction. The main objective of the study is to understand the organizational change dynamics of Michelin Shanghai Co. The chapter also attempts to evaluate challenges encountered during the process and critically analyze the leadership approaches that were applied by Mr. Ballarin (plant manager of Michelin Co.) based on related theories.

DOI: 10.4018/978-1-6684-6567-7.ch006

INTRODUCTION

The ability to cope with constant change is crucial for firms to compete with their rivals and thrive in a challenging business environment (Jamali, 2005; Eriksson-Zetterquist, Lindberg & Styhre, 2009). However, most change initiatives involve various challenges and are often met with resistance (Al-Alawi et al., 2019), resulting from fear of adopting new practices or concerns about acquiring new competencies (Kanter, 2012; Johannessen, 2021). In addition, implementing change simultaneously in different levels such as individual, team and organizational level can make the process incredibly complicated (Pettigrew, Woodman & Cameron, 2001). Therefore, many initiatives have a potential to end up in an unintended consequence, in fact, it may create irreversible situations, which may impair current organizations' dynamics. A well-managed change process, on the other hand, may play a crucial role in forming a new flourishing organizational culture.

Previous studies suggest different determinants for a successful change route. Yet, most of them emphasize the significance of communication and participation as a common ground (Erwin & Garman, 2010; Chiang, 2010; Rogiest, Segers & van Witteloostuijn, 2015; Men, Neill & Yue, 2020). The reason is that codifying change techniques with regard to the involvement of all sides may encourage entire parties and create a considerable synergy that is required for organizational change initiatives.

The manufacturing plant of Michelin in China, one of the world-renowned tire brand, would have to undergo an organizational change initiative by the end of the 2000s. Despite many challenges such as working under different organizational values, which is triggered by joint-venture, Michelin Shanghai Co. successfully managed to change through unrevealing problems and effective dissemination strategy. After looking at Michelin's organizational environment (both internal & external), this paper attempt to evaluate challenges the company encountered during the initiative and try to critically analyze the leadership approaches that were applied by Mr. Ballarin (plant manager of Michelin Co.) in the light of related theories.

RESEARCH METHODOLOGY

This study employs a case study design to investigate the organizational change models in practice at Michelin, a global tire manufacturer. The company was selected as the case study organization, because of its history of successful organizational change initiatives. The study will examine the change models through the change initiative occurred at Michelin Shanghai manufacturing plant. The data for this study is collected by analyzing the range of quality research and online collections.

In addition, company documents related to the change initiatives, such as project plans and progress reports, were reviewed.

The study is a promising one as it illustrates organizational change models through a real change initiative, including the challenges encountered, the strategies used to overcome these challenges, and the factors that contributed to the success or failure of the initiatives. Despite several limitations, such as the potential for bias in the selection of the case and the limited generalizability of the findings to other contexts (Yin, 1994, p. 9), the case study approach will allow for a detailed examination of the phenomenon in its real-life context, providing insights that can inform future organizational change initiatives in other contexts (Yin, 1994, p. 13).

ORGANIZATIONAL ENVIRONMENT

Change initiatives cannot be considered independently of an organization's internal or external environment, as these can facilitate or hinder the process of change (Sune & Gibb, 2015). Therefore, organizations should consider these factors in order to guide their change strategy effectively. Michelin is one of the major players in the highly competitive tire industry along with more than 70 manufacturing plants across the world. The French-based company is the world's oldest company and operating more than 170 different areas with 112,300 employees in order to become the market leader. Generally, the company has a recognizable brand image across the world with its icon (Bibendum). Michelin, however, faced many challenges related to the organizational environment when it entered the Chinese market through a joint venture with a state-owned enterprise.

External Factors

One of the most significant external determinants that could have influenced Michelin's change process is fierce competition in the industry. In those years, there were four main rivals in the tire sector; Bridgestone, Goodyear, Continental, and Michelin and they are all set their business in China to gain cost efficiency and reach one of the widest markets across the world. Thus, the company was struggling to protect and raise their market share over time. Another problematic area is adaptation and usage of new technology that could have jeopardized the possible change practice. Although the company adopted new manufacturing process along with other major players, the usage of technology in Michelin was sub-optimal and the maintenance of machines was not done properly. High rejection rate, poor quality production and unstable daily production rate can be given as relevant illustrations of the technological problem. Environmental issues can be addressed as a last external factor. Michelin had many deserted tire dump outside the company and this could have affected the firm in terms of either being in charge of environmental degradation or a source of demotivation for their employees

Internal Factors

Despite the presence of many possible internal determinants, it can be stated that there are two major internal motives that might have strongly influenced possible change processes, organization culture and leadership style (Hansen, 2018). Michelin Shanghai organizational culture had not actually aided the future conversion initiative since Mr. Ballarin began to manage the company. The joint venture between Michelin and a former state-owned enterprise triggered a huge internal motivation and trust problem. Before the joint venture occurred, management practices were totally different from the current alliance and therefore workers confused about what Michelin expected from them. In addition, it might be suggested that there was a leadership problem before Ballarin. When something went wrong in the plant, it was hard to find a liable person who takes the responsibility. A lack of efficiency in Michelin Shanghai's tracking system also contributed to this situation. Working conditions must be dealt as another crucial internal factor. In case of Michelin, the company had an unfavorable working area, which has a negative impact on current employees. Another decisive factor that may have influenced the organization's change process was the perception of being unemployed. Over 2000 employees were sacked from the firm; many undesirable social reactions appeared within the workers and this situation damage emotional connection between employees and their superiors. Those factors mostly mentioned above will be discussed in the next section as challenges that company must have tackled in order to complete its alteration process successfully.

CHALLENGES

Michelin Shanghai had to tackle many difficulties, but the major problem was the presence of psychological contract with the former state-owned organization. Principally, regardless of their performance, they had never perceived that they would be sacked from the organization when they were working on behalf of the state-owned enterprise; in fact, they had better reward and welfare system in the former organization. However, shortly after joint venture occurred, a significant number of employees were fired and reward system became worse than before. This situation generated a huge trauma in terms of trust between especially blue-collar workers and management level in the way of job security. Another important problem appeared in motivation techniques that had been applied by the company. Lack of affirmation and praise affected employees' instinct motivation negatively and low-level motivation might have ended up with poor performance. Meanwhile, apart from intrinsic motivation problems in Michelin, the company did not utilize extrinsic motivation factors, including a fair reward system and welfare benefits. In addition, highly demanding goal setting was almost unachievable for workers. The absence of these two motivation factors simultaneously could have diminished workers' loyalty to Michelin.

Working under more than one different organization culture often generates conflict in terms of a clash between previous management practices and the new one. When Ballarin took control of the company, initially he observed a confusion that is triggered by diverse management routines. Labors had dilemmas in terms of leave old practices (role culture) behind and internalize the new organization culture (person culture) (Harrison, 1972 cited in Green, 2007). In order to dispel communication barriers and make workers' expectations more clear, this confusion needed to be addressed. Another enormous difficulty appeared in Michelin is cultural differences which is mostly triggered by the diversity of cultural background and also language variety. The main problem that arises around this issue was due to previous management practices. They did not did not embrace all these diversities. Therefore, employees did not perceive that management team effort to do something for them. Moreover, some foreigner managers did not respect their Chinese colleagues and did not trust their competencies. Some strong evidence suggests that a small group of people without actual participation managed the company. Recent evidence suggests that 'the intense negative emotions experienced by employees are at the heart of employees' low commitment to change' (Kiefer, 2005 cited in Seo et al., 2012). Thus, lack of trust and absence of participation became a course of action within the plant that could have constrained the change initiatives in terms of both individual and group.

The last crucial factor that must be emphasized as a huge challenge for Michelin is workplace condition. The general atmosphere of the plant was unpleasant and depressing which could have inhibited the change process within the organization. There were many useless machines located somewhere in the plant and the design of the offices was too small and old-fashioned. Furthermore, outside the firm was full of deserted tire dumps. Hence, it can be suggested that under these physical conditions encouraging employees to change might be pointless.

CHANGE PROCESS

Changing an existing organizational culture is often more challenging than implementing a new one. An explanation is that workers in new organizations are fairly open to learning and accepting the culture of a new organization (Sims, 2000). On the contrary, attempting to change an existing corporate culture that consists of both individual and group behavioral transformations is difficult and time-consuming. In the case of Michelin, Ballarin had to face many difficulties in terms of changing both individual and group behaviours. In terms of team level change in Michelin, Lewin's change model might be used, as a worthwhile tool in order to understand firms' transformation process. Lewin's change suggests a cycle that contains three main steps; unfreezing, changing and refreezing. Ballarin applied several small conversions such as planting trees and renovating old-fashioned offices in order to make employees motivated to the change (unfreezing).

After a while, he carried out many organizational changes such as establishing PSMT and communication department, refining human resources and environmental amendments (changing). In order to make these changes sustainable, he set regular meetings for different departments and provided some training programs for BULs in order to implement their interpersonal skills (refreezing). Yet, the secret that was underlying this successful change process is communication and participation. Correspondingly, Quirke's communication model can be clearly seen from the Michelin case. 'At the bottom of the communication escalator the focus is on the distribution of information, one-way, to a passive audience. Towards the middle, the balance shifts to greater dialogue and face-to face communication. At the top end of the escalator the focus is more on management willingness to listen and do less talking' (Quirke, 1995, p. 92 cited in Hewitt, 2006). As shown in Figure 1, Ballarin successfully applied Quirke's communication escalator during the process.

Mr. Ballarin not only created new internal communication channels for Michelin but also, he strongly committed to encouraging people to change in an effective way. Since the plant was suffering from degeneration, he created a sense of urgency rather than planning change process and he began with changing small and easy things. For instance, planting trees and flowers outside the plant and repainting the walls of the factory. These small attempts culminated positive reactions of employees' right after perception of recognition by the managers. After that, in order to connect with his employees, he took advantages of using lunch times and 'unification days' as a field of capturing their ideas. Once he created awareness, then he attempted to build an enabling conditions for change process along with removing the barriers that were likely to generate resistance to change. Establishing the communication department, implementing reward system and empowering front-line managers can be given as good examples of providing enabling context for the change process. For the next step, He aimed to make these achievements sustain and make sure all employees internalize the new organizational culture. Therefore, he set regular meetings that required for participation of various levels of employees. Cotter's 8-step model was exemplified successfully by Mr. Ballarin that can be seen from Table 1.

Figure 1. Quirke's 'The Escalator of Communication' theory adapted to Michelin Shanghai

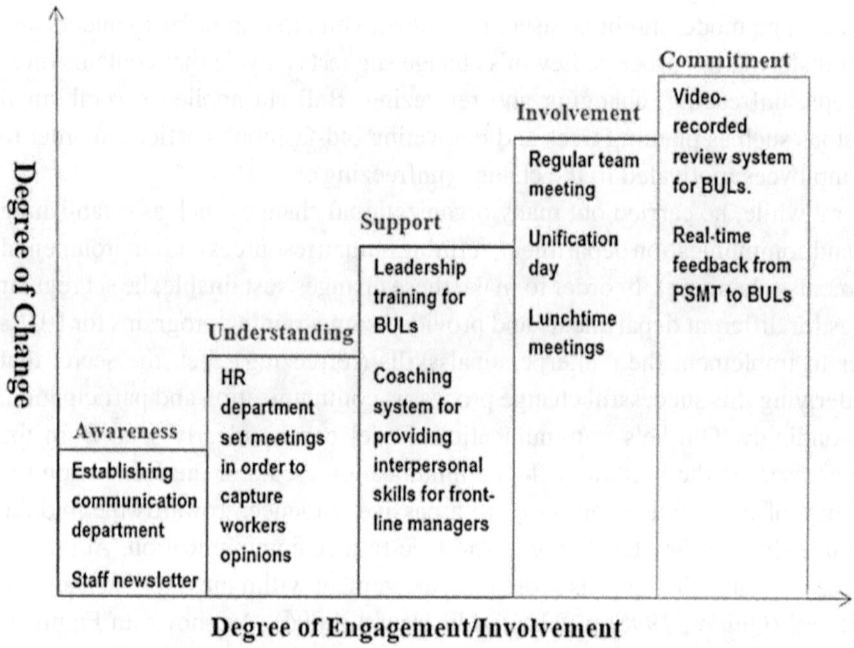

Note. From Managing Change: A critical perspective, p.154 by Hughes M. 2014, 2nd edn. CIPD: London

The perception of organizational change can vary; it could be seen either as positive and welcome or as something to be feared (Antonacopoulou & Gabriel, 2001). However, every change processes have various emotional phases which is addressed in Kubler and Ross change curve study. Although it is hard to indicate all phases of this curve in Michelin Shanghai case, this curve is essential for particularly team leaders in terms of monitoring and interpreting dissimilar emotional responses through different phases of a particular change and recognizing different managerial approaches for each these stages (Goodman and Loh, 2011). Dilts introduce another team-level change theory, which is called logical levels of change. 'Dilts draw a natural hierarchy and indicates where change is required in the team to assist its effectiveness in the wider organization' (Goodman and Loh, 2011). In order to create more sustainable change in Michelin, Ballarin mostly concentrated on higher levels (mostly invisible) in the pyramid such as values, identity and purposes that are shown in Figure 2. It can be also stated that the Michelin's organizational change driven by mostly internal factors and this process required both voluntarism and determinism. The problems that were stressed above determined the change process along with Ballarin's managerial choices and practices.

Table 1. Cotter's 8-step theory adapted to Michelin Changhai Co.

Create	Build	Form	Enlist	Enable	Generate	Sustain	Institute
Sense of urgency	**Guiding**	**Strategic vision & initiatives coalition**	**Communicating vision**	**removing barriers**	**Short- term wins**	**Acceleration**	**Change**
Major problems are observed, defined and discussed by Mr. Ballarin and his team.	Plant senior management team (PSMT) and Business Unit Leaders (BUL) were formed in order help employees to change their mind-set.	Mr. Ballarin and PSMT created a plant vision, which focuses on emotional connection with employees. They also considered cultural aspects in order to connect with workers.	'Communication department' was established in order to enhance internal communication. Besides, lunchtime and 'unification day' were used for communication with employees.	Business units' leaders are defined and formed as independent in order to solve accountability issue. Along with 'Coaching System' these leaders become better in communication with their subordinates. Mr. Ballarin also revised the incentive system, which contains unachievable targets.	Management team set a good behaviour policy, which aimed to decrease motivation problems that are triggered by lack of affirmation and praise. They set some rewards for good behaviours.	Ballarin creates a community that were regularly gathered in order to improve frontline manager's competencies about personal development and internal communication.	Productivity, customer satisfaction, machine utilization and the performance of factory overall increased in consequences of the well-managed change process.

LEADERSHIP STYLE

Leadership style might play a vital role in the succession of a change process especially in organizations where to suffer from moral and ethical issues. In terms of Michelin, Ballarin's role in this change process was tackling with plenty of challenges in order to lift up the plant's industrial performance. When Michelin was suffering from many problems, Ballarin applied paternalistic and democratic style of leadership rather than authoritarian, in order to reinstate lack of trust. However, the question arises whether these two approaches are appropriate in manufacturing industry especially in China. Employees might have ignored these new managerial practices due to previous behaviours that are inherited from state

Figure 2. Dilts' 'Logical Levels of Change' adapted to Michelin Shanghai

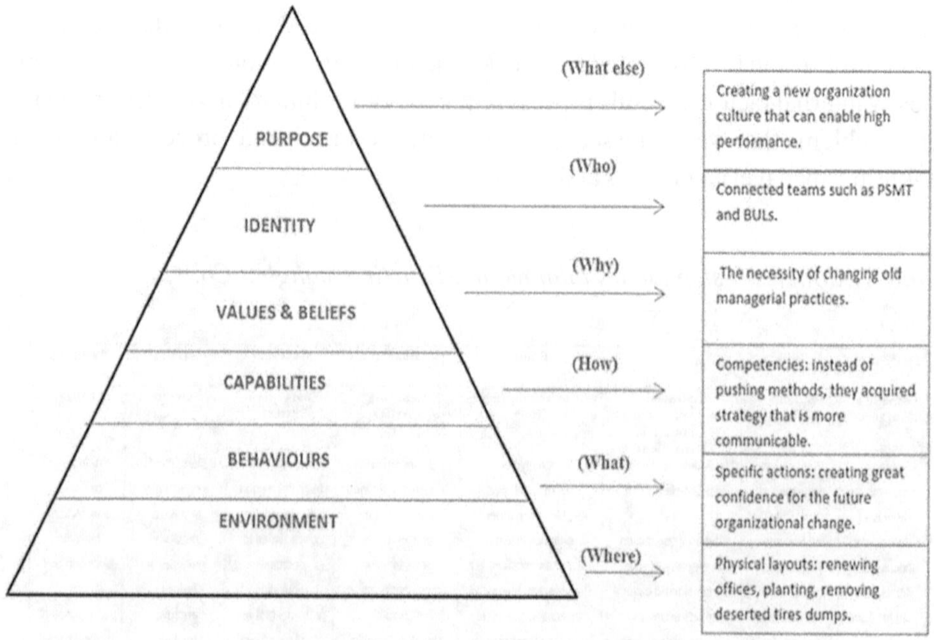

Note. From *Organizational Change: A critical challenge for team effectiveness* by Goodman and Loh (2011).

owned enterprise. On the other hand, Ballarin's leadership style can be specified as a visionary according to (Goleman, 2000). To enhance Michelin's organizational practices, Ballarin has established a vision and mobilizes employees to accomplish it. In order to do this, he gave them self-confidence with several empowerments and he improved internal communication channels during the process. Nevertheless, Goleman (2000) stressed that visionary leadership works best when change require new vision and for Michelin case coercive or affiliative leadership style might have been more appropriate according to Goleman's chart. For the reason that, coercive and affiliate leadership styles work best where the organizations in a crisis and have some motivation problems as it happened in Michelin.

In most cases, different organizational changes have different characteristics in terms of the balance between control and freedom (Popescu & Popa, 2012). Tannenbaum Schmidt Continuum model highlights range of management styles (democratic - autocratic) which can be appropriate for different situations (Mullins, 2007). For Michelin, lack of trust and morale problems leads Ballarin to acquire approach that is more democratic and welcomed non-managers' input. In order to remove barriers, he empowered PSMTs in terms of giving instructions to BULs and rather than pushing his method, he emphasized the importance of delegation. The main problem with applying democratic style of leadership in this sort of plants might be consuming more time than as it must be. Moreover, this style could also constraint standardization that was considered as the biggest challenge in front of industrial performance. However, Ballarin successfully managed this process along with using two different strategies at the same time.

SOLUTION AND RECOMMENDATIONS

The organizational change that occurred at Michelin Shanghai involved the implementation of a new production system, which aimed to improve efficiency and reduce costs. The change was confronted with resistance from employees, who were used to the old system and felt that their jobs were at risk. To address the resistance, Michelin Shanghai took several steps, such as involving employees in the change process, providing training and support, and communicating the benefits of the new system. These steps helped to mitigate the resistance and enable a successful implementation of the new system.

Based on the case study, several critical issues must be addressed for organizations that are planning to implement organizational change: *Involve employees in the change process:* This can help to build buy-in and reduce resistance (Van Dam, Oreg & Schyns, 2008; Cummings & Worley, 2014, p.27). Employees can provide valuable insights and suggestions that can improve the change process. *Provide training and support:* Change can be difficult, especially if it involves new technology or processes. Providing support can help employees to feel more comfortable and confident with the new system (Meyer et al., 2007). *Communicate the reciprocal benefits:* It is important to communicate the benefits of the change to employees (Aladwani, 2001). This can help to motivate and inspire them to embrace the change. *Address resistance:* Resistance is a natural part of the change process. It is important to address it proactively and provide solutions that can help to mitigate it (Mathews & Linski, 2016). *Monitor and evaluate:* It is important to monitor and evaluate the change process to determine its effectiveness. This can help to identify areas for improvement and ensure that the change is achieving its intended goals.

FUTURE RESEARCH DIRECTIONS

One possible direction for future research is to examine the long-term effects of the organizational change that occurred in Michelin Shanghai. This could include assessing the sustainability of the changes and their impact on the company's performance over time. Another potential area for future research is to investigate how cultural differences between France and China affected the change process, and how the company adapted to these differences. This could include exploring the challenges and opportunities that arose during the change process and how they were addressed. A third possible direction for future research is to examine the impact of the organizational change on employee attitudes and engagement. This could involve assessing how employees perceived the change, how it affected their job satisfaction, and how it influenced their commitment to the company. Finally, future research could focus on analyzing the change management strategies employed by Michelin Shanghai and their effectiveness. This could include evaluating the role of leadership, communication, and stakeholder involvement in the change process, and identifying best practices for managing organizational change in multinational companies.

CONCLUSION

This paper has given an account of Michelin change process that contains several internal and external difficulties. Before Mr. Ballarin took control of the company, Michelin Shanghai had been suffering many issues such as lack of trust, absence of participation, lack of affirmation and praise, motivation problems, poor physical conditions and so on. The most obvious finding to emerge from this study is that in spite of forcing people to change, Mr. Ballarin inspired his employees and convinced them to positive consequences of this change process. Besides, he removed the lack of trust between workers and managers, which was the biggest barrier in front of the change process. Although it is tough to manage cultural differences in a multinational organization, he made an emotional connection with his employees and attempted to create a superior organizational culture that encompasses all diversities. In addition, he established teams and assist them with several pieces of trainings that can encourage further change processes.

Another achievement that must be stressed in this paper is creating a flourishing new corporate culture and increasing the plants performance simultaneously. The poor industrial performance of the company might have put extra pressure on the change initiative and might have prevented it. However, Ballarin focused on these two significant issues at the same time in order to reduce possible pressures that might have triggered by board of director of the firm. Ballarin did not change the Michelin organizational culture, rather he generated an enabling context to people change their behaviours without any enforcement. However, inadequate information about post-Ballarin period limits whether this change process was transferred and distributed in the wider organization for future.

Overall, Michelin Shanghai's organizational change initiatives have been successful in achieving their desired outcomes. The company's proactive approach to addressing its organizational environment has resulted in a more efficient and effective work atmosphere. Additionally, by prioritizing employee satisfaction, Michelin Shanghai has been able to maintain a motivated and productive workforce. Overall, the success of these initiatives highlights the importance of considering both the organizational environment and employee satisfaction when implementing change in a company. Michelin Shanghai serves as a positive example of how a company can navigate change successfully by prioritizing its employees and organizational environment.

REFERENCES

Al-Alawi, A. I., Abdulmohsen, M., Al-Malki, F. M., & Mehrotra, A. (2019). Investigating the barriers to change management in public sector educational institutions. *International Journal of Educational Management, 33*(1), 112–148. doi:10.1108/IJEM-03-2018-0115

Aladwani, A. M. (2001). Change management strategies for successful ERP implementation. *Business Process Management Journal, 7*(3), 266–275. doi:10.1108/14637150110392764

Antonacopoulou, E. P., & Gabriel, Y. (2001). Emotion, learning and organizational change: Towards an integration of psychoanalytic and other perspectives. *Journal of Organizational Change Management, 14*(5), 435–451. doi:10.1108/EUM0000000005874

Chiang, C. F. (2010). Perceived organizational change in the hotel industry: An implication of change schema. *International Journal of Hospitality Management, 29*(1), 157–167. doi:10.1016/j.ijhm.2009.08.002

Cummings, T. G., & Worley, C. G. (2014). *Organization development and change*. Cengage Learning.

Eriksson-Zetterquist, U., Lindberg, K., & Styhre, A. (2009). When the good times are over: Professionals encountering new technology. *Human Relations, 62*(8), 1145–1170. doi:10.1177/0018726709334879

Erwin, D. G., & Garman, A. N. (2010). Resistance to organizational change: Linking research and practice. *Leadership and Organization Development Journal, 31*(1), 39–56. doi:10.1108/01437731011010371

Goleman, D. (2017). *Leadership that gets results (Harvard business review classics)*. Harvard Business Press.

Goodman, E., & Loh, L. (2011). Organizational change: A critical challenge for team effectiveness. *Business Information Review*, *28*(4), 242–250. doi:10.1177/0266382111427087

Green, M. (2007). *Change management masterclass: A step-by-step guide to successful change management*. Kogan Page Publishers.

Hansen, M. (2018). *Cultivating change: The relationship between organizational culture, leadership style and communication style with organizational change* [Doctoral dissertation]. Marquette University.

Hewitt, P. (2006). Electronic mail and internal communication: A three-factor model. *Corporate Communications*, *11*(1), 78–92. doi:10.1108/13563280610643570

Hughes, M. (2014). *Managing change: A critical perspective* (2nd ed.). CIPD.

Jamali, D. (2005). Changing management paradigms: Implications for educational institutions. *Journal of Management Development*, *24*(2), 104–115. doi:10.1108/02621710510579473

Johannessen, J. A. (2021). How can we reduce resistance to changes within organisations? In *Continuous Change and Communication in Knowledge Management* (pp. 57–73). Emerald Publishing Limited. doi:10.1108/978-1-80117-033-820211003

Kanter, R. M. (2012). Ten reasons people resist change. *Harvard Business Review*, 74.

Kotter, J. (2014). *The 8-step process for leading change*. The Kotter International Home Page. Retrieved July 20, 2023, from https://www.kotterinc.com/methodology/8-steps/

Mathews, B., & Linski, C. M. (2016). Shifting the paradigm: Reevaluating resistance to organizational change. *Journal of Organizational Change Management*, *29*(6), 963–972. doi:10.1108/JOCM-03-2016-0058

Men, L. R., Neill, M., & Yue, C. A. (2020). Examining the effects of symmetrical internal communication and employee engagement on organizational change outcomes. *The Public Relations Journal*, *13*(4), 1–19.

Meyer, J. P., Srinivas, E. S., Lal, J. B., & Topolnytsky, L. (2007). Employee commitment and support for an organizational change: Test of the three-component model in two cultures. *Journal of Occupational and Organizational Psychology*, *80*(2), 185–211. doi:10.1348/096317906X118685

Mullins, L. J. (2007). *Management and organisational behaviour*. Pearson education.

Pettigrew, A. M., Woodman, R. W., & Cameron, K. S. (2001). Studying organizational change and development: Challenges for future research. *Academy of Management Journal, 44*(4), 697–713. doi:10.2307/3069411

Popescu, D. I., & Popa, I. (2012). Managing Organizational Change and Innovation: IV. Success Factors in Change and Innovation. *Calitatea, 13*(130), 99.

Rogiest, S., Segers, J., & van Witteloostuijn, A. (2015). Climate, communication and participation impacting commitment to change. *Journal of Organizational Change Management, 28*(6), 1094–1106. doi:10.1108/JOCM-06-2015-0101

Seo, M. G., Taylor, M. S., Hill, N. S., Zhang, X., Tesluk, P. E., & Lorinkova, N. M. (2012). The role of affect and leadership during organizational change. *Personnel Psychology, 65*(1), 121–165. doi:10.1111/j.1744-6570.2011.01240.x

Sims, R. R. (2000). Changing an organization's culture under new leadership. *Journal of Business Ethics, 25*(1), 65–78. doi:10.1023/A:1006093713658

Sune, A., & Gibb, J. (2015). Dynamic capabilities as patterns of organizational change: An empirical study on transforming a firm's resource base. *Journal of Organizational Change Management, 28*(2), 213–231. doi:10.1108/JOCM-01-2015-0019

Van Dam, K., Oreg, S., & Schyns, B. (2008). Daily work contexts and resistance to organisational change: The role of leader–member exchange, development climate, and change process characteristics. *Applied Psychology, 57*(2), 313–334. doi:10.1111/j.1464-0597.2007.00311.x

Yin, R. K. (1994). *Case Study Research Design and Methods* (2nd ed.). Sage Publication.

Chapter 7
Power Structure as a Guide to Organizational Culture:
OC Strategies for Adapting to Change

K. S. S. Kanhaiya
https://orcid.org/0000-0001-9117-1654
Steel Authority of India Limited, India

ABSTRACT

Organizational culture is a crucial element for the success of any organization. It encompasses shared beliefs, values, attitudes, and assumptions that influence how members perceive and respond to situations. Power structure affects the organizational culture significantly, including how employees behave, communicate, and collaborate. This chapter explores the advantages and disadvantages of different power structures, their relationship with organizational culture, and their impact on organizational adaptability to change. Organizational culture strategies are essential for adapting to change. Providing an overview of different types of strategies, their advantages, and disadvantages, the chapter emphasizes the importance of aligning power structures with organizational culture strategies. A case study is also included, and the chapter highlights the significance of understanding the power structure's influence on organizational culture strategies and the importance of an aligned approach. The chapter concludes by suggesting future research directions in the field.

DOI: 10.4018/978-1-6684-6567-7.ch007

INTRODUCTION

Organizational culture refers to the shared values, beliefs, attitudes, customs, and behaviors that characterize an organization. It is the collective identity of the organization and shapes the way its members interact with one another, as well as with external stakeholders such as customers and suppliers. A strong organizational culture can lead to increased employee engagement, better performance, and a more positive workplace environment.

Power structures refer to the formal and informal systems of authority, control, and decision-making within an organization. They define who holds power and how that power is exercised. Power structures can be hierarchical, with decision-making power concentrated at the top, or they can be decentralized, with decision-making power distributed more broadly across the organization.

However, the constantly evolving business environment makes it crucial to ensure that the organizational culture is adaptable to change. We will explore the relationship between power structures and organizational culture, with a specific focus on organizational culture strategies for adapting to change; as power structures can potentially guide organizational culture and the strategies that organizations can use to adapt to change.

POWER STRUCTURE AND ORGANIZATIONAL CULTURE

Understanding Power Structure

Power structure in the organizational context refers to the distribution and exercise of power within an organization. Power structure determines the distribution of authority among individuals and groups within an organization. The power structure of an organization is the system of relationships among individuals and groups that determines who has the power to make decisions and how those decisions are made (Kanter, 1977). Power can be defined as the ability to influence the behaviour of others. Power is the ability of one actor to influence the behaviour of another actor (French & Raven, 1959). Authority is the legitimate right to exercise power. Power structure is the distribution of power and authority within an organization (Kanter, 1977) and is the pattern of control and influence among individuals and groups in an organization (Pfeffer, 1981). It involves understanding the formal and informal relationships, hierarchies, and mechanisms through which power is wielded and decision-making is influenced. Power can manifest in various forms, such as legitimate authority, control over resources, expertise, or personal influence. Analyzing the power structure helps identify who holds power, how it is acquired, and how it is used to shape organizational dynamics.

Power structure is the system by which resources are allocated and decisions are made (Mintzberg, 1979). It is the pattern of control and influence among individuals and groups within an organization (Pfeffer, 1981). Power structure can be formal or informal. Formal power structure is based on the organization's hierarchy, while informal power structure is based on the relationships between individuals and groups within the organization.

Power structure can have a significant impact on an organization's performance. A well-functioning power structure can help to ensure that decision making and resource allocation are done efficiently. A power structure that is characterized by trust and cooperation can lead to increased productivity and innovation. However, a dysfunctional power structure characterized by a lack of trust and cooperation can lead to conflict, inefficiency, corruption and even failure.

Power structure is a system of relationships between individuals or groups within an organization that determines who has the ability to influence others. It is often conceptualized as a hierarchy, with some individuals or groups having more power than others. There are a number of factors that can influence the power structure of an organization. These include the organization's size, industry, and culture. The organization's history and the individual characteristics of its leaders can also play a role. The different factors that can influence power structure in an organization include:

- Formal authority: This is the power that is derived from an individual's position in the organization's hierarchy. For example, a CEO has more formal authority than a manager.
- Expertise: This is the power that is derived from an individual's knowledge or skills. For example, a technical expert may have more power in the matters of his or her expertise than a non-expert.
- Networks: This is the power that is derived from an individual's connections to other people within and outside of the organization. For example, an individual with a strong network of contacts with influential persons may have more power than an individual with a weak network.
- Resources: This is the power that is derived from an individual's control over resources, such as money, information, or technology. For example, a manager who controls a budget may have more power than a manager who does not.

The power structure of an organization is a complex and dynamic system that is constantly evolving (Mintzberg, 1979; Dahl, 1957). However, changing power structure of an organization can be a difficult and time-consuming process. It is important to have a clear understanding of the current power structure before attempting to change it. It is also important to have the support of key stakeholders, such as the organization's leaders and employees.

Power structure is an important concept to understand for anyone who works in an organization. By understanding the power structure, one can not only understand how decisions are made and resources are allocated but also appreciate how their own actions can affect the power structure.

Understanding Organizational Culture

When seen in the context of society, culture is the way of life defined as a community value system that characterizes values shared and accepted in one understanding with different backgrounds of members of the organization and is used as the basis for the rules of behaviour within the organization (lndajang et al., 2021). Some define Organizational culture as a set of shared values and beliefs that interact with individuals, as well as an organizational structure and control system, to create behavioral norms (Berthon, 1993; Schiefele & Schaffiier, 2015) while others have defined culture as a set of fundamental assumptions that have been established or created in order to discover new methods of integrating that have worked effectively (Edgar, 1996; Elsbach & Stigliani, 2018). Thus, culture is defined as the shared values, beliefs, assumptions, and patterns of behavior that define the organization, and a high-performing culture can lead to a competitive advantage for a company (Denison, 2012) and, organizational culture is the group's desire to act according to the expectations and manifestations of life in achieving the values espoused by the organization.

There are several determinants of organizational culture, including the following:

Leadership: The behaviour and actions of leaders play a significant role in shaping organizational culture. Leaders set the tone for the organization and their values and beliefs can heavily influence the values and beliefs of the employees.

History: An organization's history, including its founding principles, mission statement, and past successes and failures, can shape its culture and influence how employees perceive the organization.

Industry: The industry in which an organization operates can also impact its culture. For example, a highly competitive industry may foster a culture of competitiveness and individualism, while a more collaborative industry may promote teamwork and cooperation.

Geographical Location: The cultural values and norms of the geographical region where an organization is located can also influence its organizational culture.

Importance of Organizational Culture

The presence of organizational culture is significant because it is taught to new members as an excellent way to think about, perceive, and be engaged in the organization's issues (Wardhani & Gulo, 2017). Research result has concluded that organizational culture is crucial in encouraging the improvement of innovative work behaviour (Baharuddin et al., 2019; Sembiring et al., 2020). Organizational culture plays a critical role in shaping employee behavior, attitudes, and performance, which ultimately impacts the success of the organization. Here are some of the key reasons why organizational culture is important:

Employee Engagement: A positive organizational culture can lead to increased employee engagement and commitment to the organization, which can result in higher levels of productivity and retention.

Performance: Organizational culture can also impact employee performance by setting expectations for behavior, communication, and work ethic.

Reputation: Organizational culture can also influence the reputation of the organization. A positive culture can lead to a strong reputation for the organization, which can attract top talent and customers.

Innovation: A culture that values innovation and creativity can foster an environment that encourages employees to generate new ideas and solutions.

In summary, organizational culture is the collective identity of an organization and is shaped by various determinants such as leadership, history, industry, and geographical location. A strong organizational culture is essential for employee engagement, performance, reputation, and innovation, and can contribute significantly to the success of the organization.

Influence of Power Structures on Organizational Culture

Power structures have a significant influence on organizational culture, as they shape the way power and authority are distributed and exercised within the organization. Here are some ways that power structures can impact organizational culture:

Centralization vs. Decentralization: The degree of centralization or decentralization of decision-making power can impact the culture of the organization. A highly centralized power structure may lead to a culture of hierarchy and obedience, while a more decentralized structure may foster a culture of collaboration and empowerment.

Leadership Style: The leadership style of those in power in the organization can shape its culture. Authoritarian leaders who exercise strict control over their subordinates may create a culture of fear and compliance, while more democratic leaders who encourage participation and collaboration may create a culture of trust and engagement.

Perceived Fairness: The perception of fairness in the distribution of power and decision-making can impact the culture of the organization. If employees perceive that power is concentrated in the hands of a few, or that decisions are made unfairly, it can create a culture of resentment and distrust.

Resistance to Change: Power structures can also impact an organization's ability to adapt and change. If power is highly concentrated at the top, it may be more difficult to implement changes, as those with power may be resistant to giving it up.

Thus, power structures within an organization have a significant influence on organizational culture. The degree of centralization or decentralization of decision-making power, leadership style, perceived fairness, and resistance to change are just a few ways that power structures can impact the culture of an organization. Understanding and managing power structures is therefore essential for creating a positive and effective organizational culture.

Types of Power Structure

According to Cameron and Quinn's Competing Values Framework, there are three primary types of power structures: hierarchical, flat, and matrix. Each of these power structures has distinct characteristics and can impact organizational culture in different ways.

Hierarchical Power Structure

A hierarchical power structure is a traditional, top-down approach to organizational structure where decision-making power is concentrated at the top of the organization, with managers and executives making decisions and delegating tasks to lower-level employees. The hierarchical culture is a control-oriented culture. The control orientation comes from the need for stability and control over the environment and resources (Cameron and Quinn, 2011).

Hierarchical power structures can create a culture of obedience and compliance, where employees follow instructions from their superiors without question. This type of power structure may be most effective in stable environments where efficiency and consistency are paramount. However, it can also stifle innovation and creativity, as employees may feel discouraged from taking risks or suggesting new ideas.

Flat Power Structure

A flat power structure, also known as a decentralized structure, is characterized by a more equal distribution of decision-making power across the organization. The collaborative culture emphasizes teamwork, participation, and communication. ...The flat structure is an appropriate structural design when the culture emphasizes teamwork and empowerment (Cameron and Quinn, 2011).

In a flat power structure, employees may have more autonomy and be encouraged to take ownership of their work. This type of power structure can foster a culture of innovation and creativity, as employees are more likely to feel empowered to suggest new ideas and take risks. However, it can also lead to ambiguity and confusion, as decision-making may be less centralized and more difficult to track.

Matrix Power Structure

A matrix power structure combines elements of both hierarchical and flat structures. In a matrix structure, employees are organized into teams or projects based on their expertise or skills, and decision-making power is shared between team leaders and functional managers. Culture of the matrix organization is flexible. The matrix structure requires a culture that is responsive, adaptable, and quick to change. The primary value of the matrix culture is adaptability (Cameron and Quinn, 2011).

Matrix structures can promote collaboration and innovation, as employees are organized into cross-functional teams and encouraged to work together to achieve common goals. However, they can also create conflict and confusion, as employees may have to report to multiple managers and navigate complex decision-making processes.

We can see that the type of power structure within an organization can significantly impact its culture. Hierarchical structures may promote stability and control, while flat structures may encourage innovation and collaboration and matrix structures may offer a balance between the two. Organizations should carefully consider the pros and cons of each structure and select the one that best aligns with their goals and values.

Advantages and Disadvantages of Different Power Structures

Now, let us briefly enumerate the pros and cons of each of the above noted types of power structure prevalent in organizations.

Hierarchical Power Structures

Advantages.

- Clear authority and reporting lines: Hierarchical power structures provide clear lines of authority and reporting, which can promote efficiency, accountability, and decision-making clarity.
- Centralized decision-making: A hierarchical structure allows for centralized decision-making, enabling quick and decisive actions when needed.
- Clearly defined roles and responsibilities: Roles and responsibilities are typically well-defined in hierarchical structures, which can help with task clarity and performance expectations.

Disadvantages.

- Lack of flexibility and adaptability: Hierarchical power structures can be rigid and slow to respond to change or adapt to new circumstances, making it challenging to navigate a dynamic environment.
- Limited employee autonomy: Employees may have limited autonomy and decision-making authority, leading to reduced creativity, motivation, and job satisfaction.
- Potential for communication barriers: The hierarchical structure can create communication gaps, delays, or distortion as information flows through multiple layers of management.

Flat Power Structures

Advantages.

- Increased employee empowerment: Flat power structures provide opportunities for increased employee involvement in decision-making processes, fostering a sense of empowerment, ownership, and engagement.
- Quick decision-making: With fewer layers of management, decisions can be made more quickly and with greater agility.
- Enhanced communication and collaboration: Flat structures promote open communication, information sharing, and collaboration among employees, fostering teamwork and innovation.

Disadvantages.

- Potential for role ambiguity: In flat power structures, there may be less clarity regarding roles, responsibilities, and reporting lines, leading to confusion and potential conflicts.
- Overreliance on individual expertise: Flat structures may place excessive reliance on individual expertise, potentially overlooking broader organizational perspectives or the benefits of diverse input.
- Risk of decision-making overload: With more employees involved in decision-making, there is a risk of decision-making overload, resulting in delays or decreased decision quality.

Matrix Power Structures

Advantages.

- Cross-functional collaboration: Such structure promotes collaboration and coordination across different departments or teams, facilitating the pooling of diverse expertise and resources.
- Flexibility and adaptability: Matrix structures can be adaptable to changing project or market demands, allowing organizations to quickly form or dissolve teams as needed.
- Enhanced skill development: Employees in this structure often have opportunities to work on diverse projects or with various teams, fostering skill development and knowledge sharing.

Disadvantages.

- Complexity and potential for conflict: Matrix structures introduce additional complexity and potential for conflicts arising from dual reporting lines, competing priorities, and resource allocation challenges.
- Role ambiguity and blurred authority: Employees may experience role ambiguity and uncertainty due to reporting to multiple supervisors or dealing with conflicting instructions or expectations.
- Increased coordination and communication demands: Matrix structures require effective coordination and communication to ensure alignment, which can be demanding and time-consuming.

It is essential to note that these advantages and disadvantages are general and can vary depending on the specific organizational context, industry and implementation of the structure. Organizations also adopt a combination of these structures to fit their needs and circumstances.

ORGANIZATIONAL CULTURE STRATEGIES FOR ADAPTING TO CHANGE

Understanding Organizational Culture Strategies

Organizational culture strategies refer to deliberate and planned interventional approaches taken by organizations to actively manage, shape and transform their culture to ensure it supports desired outcomes, employee engagement, and organizational effectiveness.

These strategies encompass initiatives aimed at shaping and managing the shared values, beliefs, and behaviors within the organization to align with its goals. By proactively managing and nurturing culture, organizations can foster a positive work environment to align values, behaviors, and norms with organizational goals and enhance employee engagement, satisfaction and performance to adapt to change effectively.

Importance of Organizational Culture Strategies can be appreciated by pondering over the following:

- Organizational Culture strategies help to align organizational culture with strategic objectives, ensuring that values, norms, and behaviours support the desired outcomes and direction of the organization.
- Effective culture strategies promote employee engagement, job satisfaction, and commitment by creating a positive and supportive work environment that values employees and their contributions.
- A strong and positive organizational culture can attract top talent and contribute to employee retention, as individuals are more likely to remain in organizations with a culture that aligns with their values and fosters their growth.
- Culture strategies enable organizations to adapt and thrive in the face of change by creating a culture that embraces innovation, agility, and continuous learning, and by reducing resistance to change.
- Cultivating a collaborative and inclusive culture through strategies promotes effective teamwork, knowledge sharing, and cooperation among employees, leading to improved productivity and performance.

Types of Organizational Culture Strategies

Organizational culture strategies can be broadly classified into two categories: people-oriented and outcome-oriented strategies (Denison, 2012) while there is another classification as preservation, adaptation and transformation strategies (Cameron and Quinn, 2011). It needs to be noted that Denison published his classification first in 1990 while of Cameron and Quinn first published their work in 1999. Each of these strategies has distinct characteristics and can impact organizational culture in different ways.

People-Oriented and Culture Outcome-Oriented Strategies

A people-oriented culture strategy emphasizes the well-being of employees and focuses on creating a supportive and inclusive work environment. A people-oriented culture strategy values participation, empowerment, and human development (Schein, 2010).

An outcome-oriented culture strategy prioritizes achieving specific goals and objectives. This type of strategy values achievement, competitiveness, and goal accomplishment (Schein, 2010).

It is evident that both people-oriented and outcome-oriented culture strategies address the two extremes of the continuum - people and outcome orientation and represent two fundamental but opposite human needs. One need is for people to feel supported, cared for, and respected, while the other need is to achieve, to be successful, and to win (Schein, 2010). Organizations should carefully consider their goals and values and select the strategy that best aligns with their needs. A balance between both strategies may be the most effective approach for creating a positive and productive organizational culture.

Preservation Strategy

The preservation strategy focusses on maintaining and upholding the existing organizational culture. It aims to reinforce and sustain the current cultural values, beliefs, and practices within the organization. This strategy is typically employed when the current culture is strong, aligned with the organization's objectives, and seen as a source of competitive advantage. The preservation strategy emphasizes stability, continuity, and the perpetuation of the status quo.

Organizations adopting a preservation strategy often prioritize a) Cultural Reinforcement by promoting and reinforcing the existing cultural norms, values, and behaviours through various means, such as leadership messaging, recognition programs, and performance evaluations; b) Socialization and On boarding by socializing new employees into the existing culture through mentorship programs, orientation sessions and cultural immersion activities for assimilation of the cultural values and norms; c) Selective Hiring and Retention by emphasising selection and retention of individuals whose values and behaviours align with the existing culture, reinforcing cultural continuity and coherence and d) Symbolic actions, such as rituals, ceremonies, and symbols, to celebrate and perpetuate the existing culture, fostering a sense of identity, belonging, and shared purpose.

Adaptation Strategy

This strategy involves modifying and adjusting the organizational culture in response to external or internal changes recognizing the need to align the culture with evolving environmental demands, market conditions, and organizational goals. The adaptation strategy emphasizes flexibility, learning, and responsiveness to change.

Organizations adopting an adaptation strategy employ the approaches like a) Cultural Assessment and Diagnosis to identify gaps between the existing culture and the desired culture and thus pinpoint areas that require adaptation and change; b) Cultural Training and Development programmes such as workshops, coaching, and mentoring to enhance employees' skills, knowledge, and behaviours that align with the desired culture; c) Change Management processes to facilitate cultural adaptation by communicating the need for change, involving employees in the change process, and providing support during the transition; and d) Encouraging Innovation and Risk-Taking by fostering a culture of continuous improvement that promotes innovation, experimentation, and calculated risk-taking to adapt to changing market dynamics.

Transformation Strategy

The transformation strategy entails a comprehensive change to the existing organizational culture. This strategy is pursued when the current culture is perceived as a hindrance to achieving organizational goals, addressing significant challenges or embracing new opportunities. The transformation strategy emphasizes radical change, often driven by visionary leaders who seek to reshape the organization's culture.

Organizations adopting a transformation strategy often focus on a) Visionary Transformational leaders who articulate vision for the desired culture, communicate it effectively and inspire employees to embrace the change journey; b) Systematic Culture Redesign by revisiting organizational policies, procedures, and systems in line with desired cultural changes, redefining core values, norms, and behaviours that align with the new vision; c) Employee Empowerment and Involvement at all levels in the transformation process, encouraging their active participation, soliciting their input, and empowering them to contribute to shaping the new culture; and d) Employing Effective Communication through meetings, newsletters, and interactive forums to ensure clarity and transparency regarding the reasons for cultural transformation, the progress made, and the expected outcomes.

Advantages and Disadvantages of Different Organizational Culture Strategies

Now we should examine the advantages and disadvantages of each of these types of organizational culture strategies one by one.

People-Oriented Culture Strategy

Advantages. This type of strategy can foster a positive work environment and enhance employee satisfaction and engagement. When employees feel supported and valued, they may be more likely to stay with the organization and be motivated to perform at their best. Additionally, a people-oriented culture strategy may lead to increased collaboration and teamwork, as employees are encouraged to share their ideas and opinions.

Disadvantages. Focusing too much on employee well-being may lead to a lack of focus on achieving organizational goals. Additionally, it may be difficult to balance the needs and desires of individual employees with the needs of the organization as a whole.

Outcome-Oriented Culture Strategy

Advantages. Such culture strategy may help organizations to achieve their goals more efficiently and effectively. By focusing on results, employees may be more motivated to work hard and achieve their objectives. Additionally, an outcome-oriented culture strategy may lead to a clearer sense of purpose and direction for the organization.

Disadvantages. An outcome-oriented culture strategy may create a high-pressure work environment that leads to burnout and turnover. Additionally, focusing too much on achieving outcomes may lead to a lack of attention to employee well-being and satisfaction.

Preservation Strategy

Advantages. The advantages include the following:

- Stability and Continuity: Preservation strategies help maintain stability and continuity within the organization by reinforcing existing cultural norms and practices.
- Cultural Cohesion: By preserving the existing culture, organizations can foster a sense of shared values and identity among employees, enhancing cohesion and teamwork.
- Organizational Identity: Preservation strategies reinforce the organization's unique identity and brand, which can contribute to customer loyalty and stakeholder trust.

Disadvantages. Similarly, the advantages include the following:

- Resistance to Change: An overemphasis on preservation may lead to resistance to change, hindering organizational adaptation and innovation.
- Lack of Flexibility: Overemphasis on maintaining the status quo may limit the organization's ability to respond effectively to changing market conditions or emerging opportunities.
- Cultural Inertia: Preservation strategies can perpetuate outdated or dysfunctional cultural elements that no longer align with organizational goals or evolving external demands.

Adaptation Strategy

Advantages. The advantages of this strategy include the following:

- Flexibility and Agility: These strategies enable organizations to respond to changing market dynamics and environmental demands, enhancing their ability to navigate uncertainty.
- Learning and Growth: Promoting a culture of continuous learning in this strategy fosters employee development, innovation, and the acquisition of new skills and knowledge.
- Improved Performance: Aligning the culture with evolving organizational goals and market conditions can lead to improved performance, productivity, and competitiveness.

Disadvantages. The disadvantages may be enumerated as below.

- Disruption and Resistance: Cultural adaptation can be met with resistance and scepticism from employees who may be attached to the existing culture, impeding the change process.
- Lack of Cultural Continuity: Excessive adaptation may erode the organization's unique cultural elements, potentially diluting its identity and distinctiveness.
- Strategic Alignment Challenges: Balancing the need for cultural adaptation with the organization's core values and strategic direction can be complex and require careful management.

Transformation Strategy

Advantages. The following advantages are significant:

- Innovation and Breakthrough Thinking: Transformation strategies encourage radical thinking, innovation, and the exploration of new possibilities, fostering a culture of creativity and breakthrough ideas.
- Addressing Deep-Seated Issues: Transformation efforts can address underlying cultural issues that may be impeding organizational effectiveness, such as silo mentalities or resistance to change.
- Renewed Organizational Energy: Cultural transformation can inject new energy, enthusiasm, and commitment into the organization, revitalizing employee engagement and motivation.

Disadvantages: At the same time, the following disadvantages must be borne in mind while evaluating the selection of appropriate strategy:

- Resistance and Uncertainty: Cultural transformation is often met with resistance and uncertainty, as employees may feel a loss of familiarity, leading to potential productivity disruptions.
- Lengthy and Challenging Process: Transforming the culture requires significant time, effort, and resources. Sustaining commitment and overcoming obstacles throughout the transformation journey can be demanding.
- Leadership Alignment: Transformation strategies heavily rely on strong and consistent leadership alignment and support. In the absence of such alignment, cultural transformation efforts may falter or fail.

It's important to note that the advantages and disadvantages depend upon the specific organizational context, industry, and the effective implementation of each strategy. As such, organizations often adopt a combination of these strategies or tailor them to their unique needs and circumstances.

ALIGNING POWER STRUCTURES WITH ORGANIZATIONAL CULTURE STRATEGIES

Alignment of power structures with organizational culture strategies refers to the degree to which the formal and informal distribution of power and authority within an organization is consistent with its culture strategies. Power structures influence how culture is perceived and enacted within organization (Van Maanen, 2012). Therefore, it is crucial to align power structures with organizational culture strategies to promote effective performance and ensure that the culture is being implemented as intended.

Importance of Aligning Power Structures with Organizational Culture Strategies

Organizational structures and practices have been so that the distribution of power has become a key element in culture. The importance of aligning power structures with organizational culture strategies lies in the fact that leadership is critical to shaping and building a culture. Leaders must be able to articulate the organization's mission, values, and goals and create a culture that supports them (Van Maanen, 2012). The key reasons why aligning power structures with organizational culture strategies is important include the following.

- Consistency and coherence: When power structures and culture are aligned, there is consistency in how decisions are made and implemented. This consistency creates a coherent and unified approach to achieving organizational goals and reducing ambiguity.
- Employee empowerment: Aligning power structures with culture empowers employees by giving them a voice in decision-making processes. It encourages a participative and inclusive work environment where employees feel valued and motivated to contribute.

- Cultural reinforcement: Power structures can influence and shape organizational culture. By aligning power structures with desired cultural values, leaders can reinforce and promote the desired behaviours, norms, and beliefs within the organization. This helps in building a strong and positive organizational culture.
- Adaptability and innovation: An aligned power structure and culture enable organizations to be more adaptable and innovative. When employees feel empowered to take risks, experiment, and challenge the status quo, it fosters a culture of innovation and continuous improvement. This adaptability is crucial in today's rapidly changing business environment.

Advantages and Disadvantages of Aligned Power Structures and Organizational Culture Strategies

When power structures are aligned with organizational culture strategies, it can have several advantages, including:

- Improved performance: An aligned power structure can help to foster a culture that promotes high performance, accountability, and goal achievement (Van Maanen, 2012).
- Enhanced employee engagement: An aligned power structure can help to create a sense of trust and fairness among employees, leading to increased engagement and commitment.
- Better decision-making: An aligned power structure can help to ensure that decisions are made in line with the organization's culture and values, promoting ethical behaviour and integrity.

However, there are also some potential disadvantages of aligning power structures with organizational culture strategies, including:

- Resistance to change: If an organization has an established power structure that is not aligned with the desired culture, there may be resistance to change.
- Limited diversity of perspectives: An aligned power structure may lead to a homogenization of perspectives, which can limit creativity and innovation.
- Inflexibility: An aligned power structure may limit an organization's ability to adapt to changing circumstances and respond to new challenges.

Ways to Align Power Structures With Organizational Culture Strategies

Now we will briefly discuss some of the possible ways to align power structures with organizational culture strategies, although every organization has to examine their own unique circumstances and the advantages as well as disadvantages of the possible approaches before selection of the most appropriate one.

- Clearly define and communicate organizational values: Start by clearly defining the core values and desired cultural attributes of the organization. Communicate these values to all employees and ensure they understand how these values should guide their behaviour and decision-making.
- Assess and adapt power structures: Evaluate the existing power structures within the organization and identify any misalignments with the desired culture. Consider making changes to the hierarchy, decision-making processes, and authority distribution to promote transparency, collaboration, and employee empowerment.
- Develop leadership capabilities: Invest in developing leadership capabilities at all levels of the organization. Leaders should be trained to embody and promote the desired culture, and they should have the skills to effectively empower and engage employees.
- Foster open communication and feedback channels: Establish open channels of communication throughout the organization to encourage feedback, suggestions, and ideas from employees. This includes regular town hall meetings, surveys, suggestion boxes, and other mechanisms that facilitate two-way communication between leaders and employees.
- Recognize and reward cultural alignment: Create recognition and reward systems that reinforce the desired cultural behaviors. Recognize and celebrate individuals and teams who exemplify the desired values and contribute to a positive organizational culture.
- Lead by example: Leaders should serve as role models for the desired culture and consistently demonstrate the values they expect from others. When leaders embody the desired culture, it sets the tone for the rest of the organization.
- Regular readjustments: Aligning power structures with organizational culture strategies is an ongoing process till stabilisation in line with the environmental demands. Regular evaluation, feedback and adaptation are essential to ensure that the alignment remains strong and relevant as the organization evolves.

ILLUSTRATIVE CASE STUDY (2013)

One published case study that could be appropriate for illustrating how one company successfully aligned power structures with organizational culture strategies is "How Cisco Systems Manages Strategic Alliances for Innovation and Growth" reported by George C. Ormiston and David W. DeLong in the Harvard Business Review in 2013.

The Company, Their Structure and Organizational Culture Strategy

Cisco Systems is a multinational technology company that designs, manufactures, and sells networking equipment. It specializes in networking hardware, software, and telecommunications equipment. Founded in 1984, Cisco has grown into one of the largest and most successful technology companies in the world.

Strategic alliances are a key part of Cisco's growth strategy, but they're also inherently risky. Poorly managed alliances can lead to misunderstandings, intellectual-property disputes, and conflicts with partners (Ormiston & DeLong, 2013). To support this, Cisco has implemented a rigorous alliance management process that ensures alignment between partners and helps to mitigate risks.

Rather than adopt the command-and-control mentality that characterized the old guard, Cisco developed a collaborative approach to power that mirrored the company's emphasis on building relationships and capturing collective intelligence (Ormiston & DeLong, 2013). The company has a decentralized highly matrixed organizational structure, where employees are organized both functionally and geographically, allowing for effective collaboration and decision-making. The power structure allows for cross-functional collaboration and decision-making where multiple stakeholders are involved.

The company's organizational culture strategy is based on a set of core values, including a focus on customer satisfaction, teamwork, and innovation. The company has a strong culture of innovation, where employees are encouraged to take risks and pursue new ideas.

Advantages and Disadvantages of Their Power Structure and Organizational Culture Strategy

Advantages of Cisco's power structure and organizational culture strategy include increased collaboration and innovation, improved decision-making, and a strong focus on customer needs. The collaborative power structure at Cisco allows for effective decision-making and helps to build strong relationships with partners. The company's culture of innovation also enables it to stay ahead of competitors and develop new products and services.

However, there are also potential disadvantages, such as increased complexity and potential for conflict in decision-making. The highly matrixed structure can sometimes lead to confusion and slow decision-making. Additionally, the focus on strategic alliances can pose risks, such as potential conflicts with partners or the loss of intellectual property.

Lessons From the Case Study

The case study highlights the importance of aligning power structures with organizational culture strategies in order to drive innovation and growth. It also emphasizes the importance of effective communication, cross-functional collaboration, and a strong focus on customer needs.

The case study highlights the importance of effective alliance management in supporting a company's growth strategy. Cisco's alliance management process helps to ensure that partnerships are aligned with the company's overall objectives and that potential risks are identified and mitigated. The case study also underscores the importance of a collaborative power structure and a culture of innovation in supporting strategic initiatives.

CONCLUSION

Summary of the Chapter

Organizational culture needs to adapt to the prevailing business environment so as to remain a vital determinant for success of a company. We have seen that power structures can guide organizational culture and the organizational culture strategies for adapting to change have to focus on the former.

Aligning power structures with organizational culture strategies is crucial for the smooth functioning and long-term success of an organization. When power structures and culture are in alignment, it promotes a positive work environment, increases employee engagement and productivity, and fosters a sense of shared values and goals. It also helps in building trust among employees and leaders, leading to better decision-making processes and overall organizational performance.

The insights into the interrelation of power structures and organizational culture gained by the readers should equip them to effectively determine their strategies for adapting to change.

Future Research Directions

Scholars may like to consider the following suggestions for future research directions in the field.

- Investigate the impact of power structures on different types of organizational cultures during change: Researchers can explore how hierarchical, flat, and matrix power structures affect the implementation of people-oriented and outcome-oriented organizational culture strategies during times of change. This research can help organizations choose the right power structure and culture strategy for a particular change initiative.
- Examine the role of leadership in aligning power structures with organizational culture: Researchers can explore how leaders can facilitate the alignment of power structures with organizational culture strategies to drive successful change. This research can help organizations understand how leadership behaviors and actions impact the power structure and culture alignment during change.
- Explore the impact of cultural diversity on power structure and organizational culture alignment: Researchers can investigate how cultural diversity impacts power structures and organizational culture alignment. This research can help organizations understand how to design power structures and culture strategies that are sensitive to cultural diversity and inclusive of diverse perspectives during change.
- Investigate the impact of technology on power structure and organizational culture alignment: Researchers can explore how technological advancements impact power structures and organizational culture alignment. This research can help organizations understand how to design power structures and culture strategies that leverage technology to drive successful change initiatives.
- Study the impact of external environmental factors on power structure and organizational culture alignment: Researchers can investigate how external factors, such as economic, social, and political conditions, impact power structure and organizational culture alignment. This research can help organizations understand how to design power structures and culture strategies that adapt to changes in the external environment.

REFERENCES

Baharuddin, M. F., Masrek, M. N., & Shuhidan, S. M. (2019). Innovative Work Behaviour of School Teachers: a Conceptual Framework. *International E-Journal of Advances in Education*, S(14), 213-221. 10.1876B/ijaedu.593851

Berthon, P. (1993). Psychological Type And Corporate Culture: Relationship And Dynamics. *Omega*, *21*(3), 329–344. doi:10.1016/0305-0483(93)90090-8

Cameron, K. S., & Quinn, R. E. (2011). *Diagnosing and changing organizational culture: Based on the competing values framework*. John Wiley & Sons. doi:10.1002/9780470661628

Dahl, R. A. (1957). The concept of power. *Behavioral Science*, *2*(3), 201-215. doi:10.1002/bs.3830020303

Denison, D. R. (2012). *Corporate culture and organizational effectiveness*. John Wiley & Sons. doi:10.1002/9781119205472

Edgar, H. S. (1996). Three Cultures of Management: The Keyto Organizational Learning. *Sloan Management Review*, *38*(1), 9. http://cmapspublic.ihmc.us/rid=1255442538593_81326613_21696/Three cultures of management schein.pdf

Elsbach, K. D., & Stigliani, I. (2018). Design thinking and organizational culture: A review and framework for future research. *Journal of Management*, *44*(6), 2274–2306. doi:10.1177/0149206317744252

French, J. R. P., Jr., & Raven, B. (1959). The bases of social power. In D. Cartwright (Ed.), Studies in social power (pp. 150-167). Ann Arbor, MI: University of Michigan Press.

Indajang, K., Halim, F., & Sudirman, A. (2021). The Effectiveness of Teacher Performance in Terms of the Aspects of Principal Leadership, Organizational Culture, and Teacher Competence. *Proceedings of the 2nd Annual Conference on Blended Learning, Educational Technology and Innovation (ACBLETI 2020), 560*, 402-408. https://www.atlantis-press.com/article/125957871.pdf

Kanter, R. M. (1977). *Men and women of the corporation*. Basic Books.

Mintzberg, H. (1979). *The structuring of organizations*. Prentice Hall.

Ormiston, G. C., & DeLong, D. W. (2013). How Cisco Systems manages strategic alliances for innovation and growth. *Harvard Business Review*, *91*(3), 1–9. doi:10.2139srn.2229271

Pfeffer, J. (1981). *Power in organizations*. Pitman.

Schein, E. H. (2010). *Organizational culture and leadership* (Vol. 2). John Wiley & Sons. doi:10.1002/9781119212043

Schiefele, U., & Schaffner, E. (2015). Teacher interests, mastery goals, and self-efficacy as predictors of instructional practices and student motivation. *Contemporary Educational Psychology*, *42*, 159–171. doi:10.1016/j.cedpsych.2015.06.005

Van Maanen, J. (2012). *Organizations in action: Social science bases of administrative theory*. Transaction Publishers. doi:10.4324/9781315006252

KEY TERMS AND DEFINITIONS

Adaptation Strategy: An adaptation strategy involves adjusting and modifying the organizational culture to respond to changes in the external environment or internal dynamics. It emphasizes flexibility, innovation, and agility, encouraging the organization to adapt its cultural elements, structures, and processes to remain relevant and competitive.

Culture Outcome-Oriented Strategy: A culture outcome-oriented strategy places a strong emphasis on the desired outcomes and results of the organizational culture. It involves defining specific cultural attributes, values, and behaviors that align with strategic goals and measuring and assessing the impact of the culture on organizational performance and effectiveness.

Flat Power Structure: A flat power structure, also known as a horizontal power structure, is a system in which power and decision-making are decentralized and distributed across different levels and positions within an organization. It promotes collaboration, autonomy, and open communication, reducing hierarchical layers and promoting a more egalitarian approach to power.

Hierarchical Power Structure: A hierarchical power structure is a system in which power and authority are concentrated at the top of the organizational pyramid, with a clear chain of command and decision-making flowing from higher-level positions to lower-level positions. This structure emphasizes control, accountability, and vertical communication.

Matrix Power Structure: A matrix power structure is a hybrid organizational design that combines elements of both functional and project-based structures. It involves multiple lines of authority and allows employees to work across different teams or projects, often reporting to both functional managers and project managers. This structure facilitates cross-functional collaboration and flexibility.

Organizational Culture: Organizational culture refers to the shared values, beliefs, assumptions, norms, and behaviors that define the social and psychological environment within an organization. It encompasses the collective mindset, attitudes, and practices that shape how members interact, make decisions, and perceive their work.

Organizational Culture Strategy: Organizational culture strategy refers to the deliberate alignment of an organization's culture with its strategic goals and objectives. It involves cultivating a culture that supports and enhances the desired strategic direction, values, and behaviors, thus creating a strong and coherent organizational identity.

People-Oriented Strategy: A people-oriented strategy emphasizes the importance of human resources and focuses on developing and empowering employees. It involves creating a supportive work environment, fostering employee engagement and motivation, promoting teamwork and collaboration, and investing in the growth and well-being of individuals.

Power Structure: Power structure refers to the distribution and arrangement of power within an organization or a social system. It represents the formal and informal relationships, hierarchies, and mechanisms through which authority, influence, and decision-making are exercised and shared among individuals or groups.

Preservation Strategy: A preservation strategy aims to maintain and sustain the existing organizational culture, values, and practices over time. It focuses on preserving core cultural elements that are deemed valuable, fostering continuity and resisting significant changes or disruptions that may threaten the established culture.

Strategy: Strategy refers to a set of planned actions and decisions formulated to achieve specific goals or objectives in a competitive or uncertain environment. It involves analyzing the internal and external factors, determining the direction, allocating resources, and making choices to position an organization for success.

Transformation Strategy: A transformation strategy involves a significant and comprehensive change in the organizational culture, often driven by a need to address major challenges or seize new opportunities. It requires redefining core values, beliefs, and behaviors, reshaping structures and processes, and guiding the organization through a fundamental cultural shift.

Chapter 8
Conflict Management in Organisations of Emerging Economies:
A Literature Review and Future Research Agenda

Nirma Sadamali Jayawardena
O.P. Jindal Global University, India

Darshana Jayawardena
National School of Business Management, Sri Lanka

ABSTRACT

The purpose of this chapter is to provide an overview on conflict management strategies within the emerging economies via a detailed literature review. The study of organisational conflicts in emerging economies is a very rare research topic. This study was able to identify four major gaps in this area. Firstly, the topic organisational conflict research focuses more on organizational behaviour and occupational psychology research with less consideration on human resource management. Secondly, a majority of these studies has been conducted in Western and European countries with less focusing on the Asian context and emerging economies. Thirdly, few studies used the mixed research methodology to investigate the scenarios which provides more accurate findings. Fourthly, few studies analysed perspectives of both employees and employers since the majority of the existing studies used the perspective of either employee or the employer.

DOI: 10.4018/978-1-6684-6567-7.ch008

INTRODUCTION

A cooperative alliance, as well as its coexistence as a cooperative competition within an alliance, is characterized by mutual trust and conflict. To clarify the interaction between conflict and trust, conflict and trust have often been treated as unidimensional variables. It is an unavoidable truth that organizational conflict is an unavoidable fact that has functional and dysfunctional effects on an organization (Odetunde, 2013). Effective conflict management is a must to survive in the long run and to establish a quality leadership. Therefore, the importance of research studies on the organisational conflict management vary depending on the industry type and diversity of the cultures in the organisation (Song, Xie, & Dyer, 2000). Proper conflict handling behaviour within the organisations enables the employees to solve their problems and issues effectively and efficiently (Mohr & Spekman, 1994). Rahim and Bonoma (1979) mentioned that most of the organisational conflicts research can be seen in the psychology and philosophy area. It is evident that in recent literature this concept is becoming increasingly common in the human resource management field.

Organisational conflict is an unavoidable practical concept which has functional and dysfunctional effects towards an organisation (Odetunde, 2013). Effective conflict management is a must to survive in the long run and to establish a quality leadership. Therefore, the importance of research studies on the organisational conflict management vary depending on the industry type and diversity of the cultures in the organisation (Song, Xie, & Dyer, 2000). Proper conflict handling behaviour within the organisations enables the employees to solve their problems and issues effectively and efficiently (Mohr & Spekman, 1994). Rahim and Bonoma (1979) mentioned that most of the organisational conflicts research can be seen in the psychology and philosophy area. It is evident that in recent literature this concept is becoming increasingly common in the human resource management field.

Emerging markets are typified by industrialization and quick economic expansion, according to Rugman and Collinson (2009). There are currently more than forty emerging markets worldwide, including nations like China, Brazil, and India. Emerging markets have recovered from the recent economic downturn considerably more swiftly than many Western nations, and they are already a significant market for many businesses (Custance et al., 2012). Conflict resolution in workplaces that are part of multinational corporations (MNEs) typically takes place inside organisational structures that have been imported from the West. When multinational corporations (MNCs) operate in developing economies, there is a possibility of a gap between the conflict management procedures used by the MNC and the preferences of the local workforce. We developed a comprehensive review for 'leveraging' indigenous knowledge by drawing on literature from the fields of management, anthropology, and international development, as well as authors' experience as participant observers in the industrial sector in Sri Lanka.

Figure 1. Pyramid analogy of the study
Note: *The pyramid analogy of the study represents the breakdown of a generic research idea of: "organisational conflict management in both developed and developing nations" to a more granular level: "conflict management in emerging economies"*

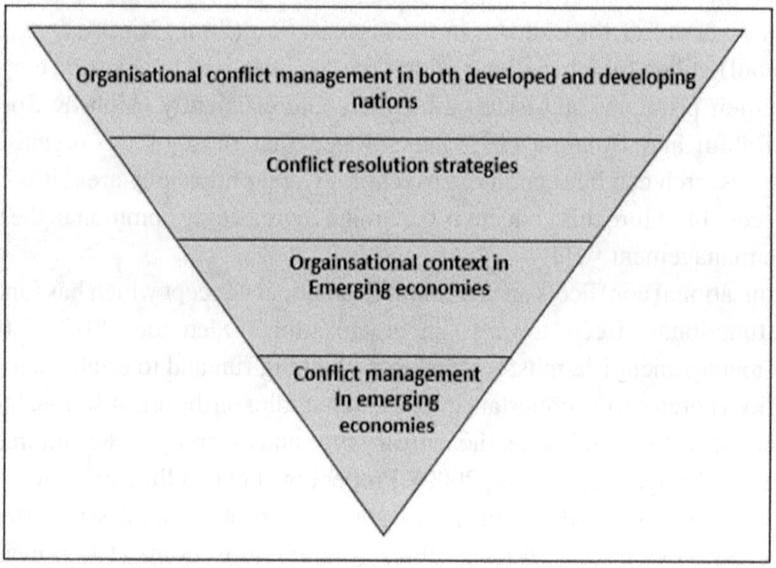

LITERATURE REVIEW

This study includes an extensive literature review using thirty (30) research articles. This section covers various scholarly studies on organisational conflict about the developed and developing economies. The structure of this literature review can be represented by way of an upside-down triangle as presented in Figure 1.

As per the above Figure 1, we started our review though searching the broader view of organisational conflict management aspect in both developing and developed nations. Next, we expanded the search to find the conflict resolution strategies. Thirdly, we searched for organisational context in emerging economies. Finally, we limited the entire literature review towards discussing about the conflict management in emerging economies.

Organisational Conflict Management in Both Developed and Developing Countries

Organisational conflicts are a common aspect in the psychology and philosophy research (Rahim & Bonoma, 1979). There are various ways to define the concept of conflict management. According to Stephen McKenna and Julia Richardson (1995) conflict management in the organizational world reflects the power structures of the individuals within organizational and societal levels. Even though conflicts are functional within the organizational level, mostly organizational conflicts still fall within the "conflict resolution," reduction, or minimization realm (Stephen McKenna & Julia Richardson, 1995; Rahim & Bonoma, 1979). For many societies and organisations, the harmony and consensus are both prevalent and positive. However, societies and organizations often experience conflicts in their day-to-day lives which is the reality (Stephen McKenna & Julia Richardson, 1995). Therefore, organizational conflicts are an increasingly popular topic with the rapid development of technology, competition, and the increasing stress levels due to the high amount of workload and unsuccessful work-life balance. According to Opatha (2010) work life means "life that is related to a person's employment" therefore there is a link between the work life towards their families and personnel life.

Rahim and Bonoma (1979) mentioned that conflicts as an interactive process which happens due to the incompatibility between the individuals, organisations, groups, or any other social entity. Conflicts are of multidimensional and one dimension of conflict enhances the effectiveness whereas other will hinders consensus and commitment between group members (F. J. Medina, Munduate, Dorado, Martínez, & Guerra, 2005). Jehn (1995) introduced the two types of conflicts as task confiict and relationship confiict. In the task confiict there is a disagreement among group members or individuals on the content of their decisions, differences on viewpoints, and opinions. For example, the distribution of resources, company policies and procedures interpretation of facts. Moreover, relationship confiict denoted the perception of interpersonal incompatibility, annoyance, and animosity among people. Such examples are disagreements on values, personal norms, and personal taste (Jehn, 1995).

Conflict Resolution Strategies

The emphasis is away from resolution of conflict, to management of conflict and conflict may originate at a number of intra- and inter-personal levels in the organization (Rahim & Bonoma, 1979). Moreover, research on the organisational conflicts are of two types as (1) Some researchers have attempted to measure the amount of conflict experienced by the organizational participants and to explore the sources of such conflict (2) Others have attempted to relate the various conflict-handling styles of the organizational participants and their effects on quality of solutions to problems or attainment of social objectives. Conversely, these two methods are not integrated in improving the quality of the management of organisational conflicts (Rahim & Bonoma, 1979). In most human resource management research, the ability to resolve conflicts in a more successful way is an important skill which involves with two subskills: Those two subskills are named as cognitive and behavioural skills.

It is vital to have knowledgeable managers who knows how to resolves conflicts by understanding the situation effectively (Stephen McKenna & Julia Richardson, 1995). Previous researchers identified general ways in which individuals deal with conflict situations. Firstly, individual responds to conflict by ceasing to react and secondly it is the suppression which is the individual ability to deal with the conflict as nothing wrong has happened. The compromise nature of individual results in maintaining the relationship, win/lose which is that the person turns into physically violent, win/win where the individuals seek differences and solutions together. Thomas and Kilmann developed a model by indicating that all reactions to conflict stem from two general urges. Those are assertive behaviour, which is that the desire to satisfy personal concerns and non-assertive behaviour which is the desire to satisfy the concerns of others (Stephen McKenna & Julia Richardson, 1995). However, with the development of Blake and Mouton's (1964) "Managerial Grid", dual concern theory, several self-report five-style conflict resolution instruments been developed to examine conflict in organisations as Rahim's Organisational Conflict Inventory II (Holt & DeVore, 2005).

Organisational Context and Conflict Management in Emerging Economies

The economy in emerging economies are often segregated as multinational corporations, private and public sector organisations. The organisational infrastructure and resources influence organisational experience of most individuals. Most of the times the emerging economics may face a bureaucratic leadership style (Boakye-Sarpong, 1998). It is explicit that conflicts are inevitable by nature and the characteristics and behaviours of each parties influence the conflicts to take place (Kasim Randeree & Faramawy, 2011). The Islamic approach to conflict management is based on the major principles in the Islam religion such as equality, freedom, and affirmative critical and goal oriented thinking (Kasim Randeree, 2008). In Islamic countries there is an adaptive method of thinking which allows individuals to use several techniques in handling the conflicts (Abdalla, 2000).

When considering the Chinese viewpoint, there is a profound moral justice and proper conduct due to Confucianism (Hau-siu Chow & Ding, 2002). This helps to maintain the harmony among the human beings. The most recommended way to solve problems are the collective approaches rather than the individualistic approach (Hau-siu Chow & Ding, 2002). According to Tang and Kirkbride (1986) the Chinese management prefer more non-confrontational approaches in conflict management than the Western counterparts. Therefore, Chinese executives behave in an avoiding and compromising manner while British workers use a highly competitive approach (Hau-siu Chow & Ding, 2002). In Chinese context the harmony, norms, context long term perspectives and obedience contributes towards conflict management approaches. A study on comparison of Indian and Chinese conflict handling behaviour by Ndubisi (2011) mentioned that compromising conflict handling on trust and commitment is moderated by culture and significantly higher among Chinese employees compared to the Indians. Moreover, Van de Vliert, Nauta, Giebels, and Janssen (1999) argued that suitability of the conflict management style depends on the situational realities and conflict handling is mentioned as the supplier's ability to minimize the negative consequences of manifest and potential conflicts.

Summary of the Key Literature

Main objective of this study is to identify research gaps in organisational conflict management in emerging economies. Desk research method was adopted to achieve the main research objective of this study using secondary data sources. Four different databases were used to access the research articles including Sage, Google Scholar, Scopus, and ProQuest. Additionally, researcher used other published books to achieve the research objective of the study. The below Table 1 presents the summary of the key studies which focused on the organisational conflict management in emerging economies.

Table 1. Summarises the studies on organisational conflict management

	Authors	Findings
01	Song et al., (2000)	A cross-cultural conceptual model was developed and tested regarding the antecedents and consequences of marketing managers' conflict-handling behaviours during the new product development process. The hypotheses tested in 968 companies including Japan, China, Hong Kong, United States, and United Kingdom. The results indicated the varying role of conflict management among diverse cultures
02	Ndubisi, (2011)	There is a direct relationship between trust and commitment when integrating conflict handling, accommodating conflict handling, and compromising conflict handling. There is a greater influence of compromise strategy on trust and commitment among Chinese service providers than among Indians

continues on following page

Table 1. Continued

	Authors	Findings
03	Stephen McKenna and Julia Richardson, (1995)	These findings are based on a survey of Singapore managers and future managers in the public and private sectors. The survey indicated that conflict management requires an understanding of concepts such as power, needs, assertiveness, personal styles, leadership styles, and influencing styles
04	Zapf, (1999)	There are many possible causes of bullying in the workplace, including the social system, the perpetrator, and the victim. There is evidence that one-sided explanations of the causes of mobbing are unlikely to be appropriate, and that many cases are characterized by multi-causality, which is a regular finding in conflict handling studies
05	Cerni et al., (2012)	According to the cognitive-experiential self-theory (CEST), 426 undergraduate students' conflict-handling styles influenced the relationship between rational and experiential systems. Both integrating and compromising conflict-handling styles were positively influenced by the rational system, experiential system, and constructive thinking. In contrast, the experiential system and constructive thinking had a positive relationship with the obliging conflict-handling style. Conflict-avoiding style was negatively correlated with rational system and constructive thinking
06	Chow and Ding, (2002)	The findings indicated a significant relationship between the stage of moral development and the use of integrating conflict handling approaches among Hong Kong and Chinese undergraduate students. Moral reasoning and conflict resolution styles were influenced by the Chinese culture
07	Tang and Kirkbride, (1986)	This study examines the orientations towards conflict and preferred conflict management styles of Chinese managers in Hong Kong. In order to develop contingent conflict handling skills among Chinese managers in Hong Kong, two central problems of attitude change and learning styles were identified.
08	Medina et al., (2002)	According to the results, there is a negative correlation between relationship conflicts and employee affective reactions, where employee affective reactions and relationship conflicts adversely affect organizational conflict. Task conflicts do not affect employee's affective reactions negatively
09	Slabbert, (2004)	The findings of this study are based on the Thomas Killman Conflict Mode Instrument which has been used to select 50 junior and middle managers in the banking industry of South Africa. The results of the study indicated that there were significant differences between the two groups. Middle management prefers the assertive styles (competing and collaborating) with scant attention to cooperation, while junior management primarily uses the avoiding style, which is both uncooperative and unassertive
10	Behfar et al., (2008)	Findings indicated linkages between strategies for managing different types of conflict and group performance and satisfaction as the study focuses the conflict resolution among the teams. This is a qualitative study using 57 autonomous teams which suggests that groups that improve or maintain top performance over time share three conflict resolution tendencies such as (a) focusing on the content of interpersonal interactions rather than delivery style, (b) explicitly discussing reasons behind any decisions reached in accepting and distributing work assignments, and (c) assigning work to members who have the relevant task expertise rather than assigning by other common means such as volunteering, default, or convenience. The authors' results also suggest that teams that are successful over time are likely to be both proactive in anticipating the need for conflict resolution and pluralistic in developing conflict resolution strategies that apply to all group members
11	Oudenhoven et al., (1998)	The purpose of this study was to examine managerial conflict management in Denmark, the United Kingdom, the Netherlands, Spain, and Belgium. According to the findings, Danish managers require a more constructive approach to conflict management than those in Belgium. Power distance may cause conflicts among supervisors in the same countries. Other three countries represented intermediate positions. Denmark and Netherlands managers are highly constructive than managers from more masculine nations when it comes to the conflict handling process

continues on following page

Table 1. Continued

	Authors	Findings
12	Vivar, (2006)	The study focuses on conflict management through the use of a nursing case study. As nursing organizations deal with a variety of difficulties and stress levels, conflict management is of paramount importance. Findings indicated that power conflict as a key aspect of tension among nursing units. Therefore, management of that aspect indicated proper conflict management among the nursing organizations
13	Kozan and Ergin, (1999)	In this study, cross-cultural conflict management research was extended to an intra-cultural level. The data was collected from 435 employees in 40 different organizations in Turkey. Avoidance conflict management styles was found to be common by those having strong tradition and conformity values. Forcing style seemed to be high among those who have more power levels
14	Kure, (2010)	Narrative practices were expanded in the field of organizational mediation. Presented a conceptual framework for organizational conflict as a hierarchical discursive field. According to the paper, narrative mediators can serve four major purposes in conflict resolution: stimulating a sense of contingency; externalizing the conflict; discovering hidden organizational experiences; and building alternative narratives about organizational practices.
15	Olekalns, (1997)	This study examined the effects of conflict, peace, negotiation, and mediation on developmental and cross-cultural aspects of conflict management. Through the Kabanoff (1991) typology, it linked framework and micro-level issues and identified two main research perspectives: 1) the importance of establishing relationships between organizational types and conflict management styles; and 2) the importance of considering how these relationships impact disputant outcomes.
16	Ongori, (2009)	To enhance organizational performance, this study identified the causes, effects, types, and strategies for managing conflicts within organizations effectively. The purpose of this study was to develop unique strategies on how to manage conflicts in organizations using a sample of 130 managers from government departments, parastatals, and private companies in Botswana. The findings indicated that the major cause for most organizational conflict as the unavailability of the resources
17	Mele, (2011)	This study focused action research methodology based on a five-year case study of a firm operating in the Information and Communication (IT) industry. Three types of conflicts been identified as (i) types, (ii) timing (iii) effects. These dimensions facilitate the management of conflicts for the strategic level and operational level
18	Grieves et al., (2006)	This paper focused the barriers to learning and identified certain thematic constructs. Data were collected using a survey to investigate the managers' views (36 representing 36 organizations) and identified most significant obstacles to organizational learning. The performance enhancement is done using clear clarification of the problems and resolution through Action Research
19	Posthuma et al., (2011)	According to the findings, task conflict is positively related to innovative behaviors and knowledge sharing behaviors. There is a negative correlation between relationship conflicts and individual-directed organizational citizenship behaviors and knowledge sharing behaviors. It appears that the innovation building process and the rewarding process are moderating factors in relation to task and relationship conflicts. In Shanghai, China, part-time MBA students from a variety of industries were used to collect data
20	Greer et al., (2012)	There are three types of conflict, namely task-related conflicts, process-related conflicts, and relationship-related conflicts. There is a negative relationship between task and process conflicts and the functioning of a team. It should be noted, however, that the negative effects of task conflicts on the team functioning aspect can vary and decrease depending on the situation.
21	Lupu and Sloman, (1997)	According to this study, different techniques were used to identify the importance of conflicts for users and when to ignore conflicts due to precedence relationships with policies. It was discussed in this paper how to reduce potential conflicts that a user may have to resolve and how to prevent undesired changes to the policy specification or domain membership

continues on following page

Table 1. Continued

	Authors	Findings
22	Opatha and Ismail, (2001)	A comprehension of worker grievance handling was provided by focusing on three key areas: grievance policy, grievance procedure, and grievance practice. Paper has given and agenda consisting of 21 points of actions for senior management as clearly stating the purpose in grievance handling policies such as; accepting the worker rights
23	Iddagoda et al., (2017)	The purpose of this paper was to discuss how labour management relations can be measured empirically in organizations. To measure labour-management relations, seventeen criteria have been identified, and two approaches have been proposed: the passive approach based on secondary data, and the active approach based on primary data
24	Akuratiyagamage and Opatha, (2004)	The purpose of this paper was to examine the grievances suffered by the managers of commercial bank branches in Colombo, Sri Lanka. There was a particular focus on identifying grievance causes, as well as other related factors such as grievance handling procedures used by banks and branch managers' satisfaction with current practices for grievance handling. Data were collected from 100 branch managers in five commercial banks in Colombo district.
25	Sharma and Samantara, (1994)	The study evaluated the efficacy in conflict management strategies focusing superior-subordinator relationship. The study analyzed eight ways to handle conflicts as avoiding arguments, following rules, accommodating, consulting, smoothing, forcing, compromise and confrontation. It is also revealed that confrontation and smoothing effects are associated with effectiveness while accommodative behaviours emerge as the most ineffective method of conflict resolution
26	Karen, (1994)	The study examined the benefits and disadvantages of emotional and task-related conflict among work groups. Group value consensus (GVC), group value fit (GVF), been hypothesized to decrease conflict. Data were collected from 88 workgroups performing comparable organizational tasks, and the major findings indicated that there are low levels of value similarity among members and between the group and governing superiors including higher levels of conflict and high levels of value similarity. Group performance and satisfaction were negatively associated with emotional conflict, but positively associated with task conflict. Full-time and part-time employees and students from Midwestern business schools make up the study sample
27	Karen, (1997)	Using a generalized conflict model, this paper explored daily conflicts among six organizational work teams. The model evaluation revealed that relationship conflicts negatively impact performance and satisfaction; consequently, process conflicts negatively impact performance; and task conflicts negatively impact performance based on specified dimensions. Further, emotions reduce effectiveness, while resolution potential and ability to conform to norms increase effectiveness and importance. Groups with norms that accept task but not relationship conflict are most effective. The model and findings broaden the current knowledge levels on organizational conflicts and suggest ways in which it can either be alleviated or wisely encouraged
28	Nikku, (2004)	The study is based on the Telugu Ganga Canal, which is a conflict-ridden river diversion project in India. The paper suggests a model of multi stakeholder institution recognizing different users and their needs and frame governance rules and implements them through collective action
29	Samantara and Sharma, (2016)	The study reviewed organizational conflict literature in an integrated framework. It also analyzed basic issues related to organizational conflict as conceptual meaning and definitions of conflict, antecedent conditions, and determinants of conflict. This also focused on the internal dynamics of a conflict. This highlighted the fact that conflict can have either functional or pathological which is solely based on the management. The findings highlighted that the levels of conflict and styles of handling conflict are different from organization to another organization
30	Cooke and Jing, (2009)	The paper outlined major sources of work life conflicts encountered by workers in China against a context of marketisation of the economy, the rapid growth of the private sector and a trend of work intensification across occupational groups.

Source: Developed by the authors

DISCUSSION OF THE FINDINGS

Based on the above comprehensive literature review four main future research gaps were identified. There is a first major gap, which relates to the fact that several researchers have studied the topic of organisational conflict management in the fields of organizational behaviour and occupational psychology. In spite of the fact that organisational conflict is a topic that falls under Human Resource Management (HRM), based on the research conducted over a long period in organizational behaviour and occupational psychology, it has been found that the researchers within the field of Human Resource Management have a lack of focus on the management of organizational conflict. Based on the agency theory, effective corporate governance must balance the conflict of interests between shareholders and managers. According to Wirtz (2011), the board of directors is one of the governance mechanisms that has received the most attention in governance research. Therefore, various characteristics related to board structure and composition are considered by many studies to be the main characteristics of an effective corporate governance that is capable of boosting business performance.

Secondly, most of these studies have focused on Western and European countries with relatively little attention being paid to the Asian context and emerging economies (Riaz & Junaid, 2013). The analysis on basic issues related to organizational conflict as conceptual meaning and definitions of conflict, antecedent conditions, and determinants of conflict is less evident in the prevailing literature. Furthermore, internal dynamics of a conflict can have either functional or pathological which is solely based on the management. The findings highlighted that the levels of conflict and styles of handling conflict are different from organization to another organization. As part of the study by Chen and Ayoko, the authors examined the influence of three emotions (enthusiasm, excitement, and behavioural guilt) on three types of conflict (task, relationship, and process) in three different settings. As part of their study, a sample of employed graduate business students from several countries was selected (South Africa, Norway, China, Singapore, Malaysia, Mexico, Persia, Scotland, the US, Germany, and New Zealand). It appears that enthusiasm is positively correlated with task conflict in the study. There was no correlation between excitement and task conflict, however. It is important to note, however, that both relationship conflict and process conflict were positively associated with both excitement and enthusiasm.

Third and fourth gaps were identified based on the above Table 1. In the majority of studies that have been conducted, monomethod quantitative or monomethod qualitative methodology has been used incorporating a single data collection instrument. In a few studies, mixed research methodologies were used to investigate the scenarios with more accurate results. Due to these factors, it is necessary to conduct more future research that incorporates both quantitative and qualitative methods (Both quantitative and qualitative approaches). There is a fourth gap in the literature, as fewer studies provided an unbiased outcome by analysing both employee and employer perspectives. Majority of the existing studies used the perspective of either employee or the employer which is inadequate to draw a complete picture of the scenario.

CONCLUSION

Organizational conflict management in emerging economies is an interesting research area for both organisational psychology and human resource management. The main objective of this study is to explore the research gaps to facilitate future researchers through a comprehensive literature review. Researchers identified three research gaps which can be categorized as both empirical gaps and theoretical gaps. Research gap 1 and research gap 2 in this article can be categorized as empirical gaps. Research gap 3 is a theoretical gap. The findings of this paper provide useful insights to future researchers to conduct their studies on organisational conflict management with special reference to emerging economies.

REFERENCES

Abdalla, A. (2001). Principles of Islamic interpersonal conflict intervention: A search within Islam and western literature. *The Journal of Law and Religion*, *15*(1), 151–184.

Akuratiyagamage, V. M., & Opatha, H. H. D. N. P. (2004). Grievances of middle managers: An empirical investigation into perceptions of commercial bank branch managers in Sri Lanka. *Journal of Management Research*, *4*(2), 99–112.

Behfar, K. J., Peterson, R. S., Mannix, E. A., & Trochim, W. M. (2008). The critical role of conflict resolution in teams: A close look at the links between conflict type, conflict management strategies, and team outcomes. *The Journal of Applied Psychology*, *93*(1), 170–188. doi:10.1037/0021-9010.93.1.170 PMID:18211143

Boakye-Sarpong, K. (1998). Bureaucracy and development in the emerging nations: An ecological approach. *Institute of African Studies Research Review*, *14*(1), 1–15.

Cerni, T., Curtis, G. J., & Colmar, S. H. (2012). Cognitive-experiential self theory and conflict-handling styles: Rational and constructive experiential systems are related to the integrating and compromising conflict-handling styles. *International Journal of Conflict Management*, *23*(4), 362–381. doi:10.1108/10444061211267263

Cooke, F. L., & Jing, X. (2009). Work-life balance in China: Sources of conflicts and coping strategies. *NHRD Network Journal*, *2*(6), 18–28. doi:10.1177/0974173920090603

Custance, P., Walley, K., & Jiang, D. (2012). Crisis brand management in emerging markets: Insight from the Chinese infant milk powder scandal. *Marketing Intelligence & Planning*, *30*(1), 18–32. doi:10.1108/02634501211193895

De Dreu, C. K. (2008). The virtue and vice of workplace conflict: Food for (pessimistic) thought. *Journal of Organizational Behavior: The International Journal of Industrial. Occupational and Organizational Psychology and Behavior*, *29*(1), 5–18. doi:10.1002/job.474

Greer, S., Saygi, O., Aaldering, H., & de Dreu, C. K. W. (2012). Conflict in medical teams: Opportunity or danger? *Medical Education*, *46*(10), 935–942. doi:10.1111/j.1365-2923.2012.04321.x PMID:22989127

Grieves, J., McMillan, J., & Wilding, P. (2006). Barriers to learning: Conflicts that occur between and within organisational systems. *International Journal of Learning Intellectual Capital*, *3*(1), 86–103. doi:10.1504/IJLIC.2006.009212

Hau-siu Chow, I., & Ding, D. Z. Q. (2002). Moral judgement and conflict handling styles among Chinese in Hong Kong and PRC. *Journal of Management Development*, *21*(9), 666–679. doi:10.1108/02621710210441667

Holt, J., & DeVore, C. J. (2005). Culture, gender, organizational role, and styles of conflict resolution: A meta-analysis. *International Journal of Intercultural Relations*, *29*(2), 165–196. doi:10.1016/j.ijintrel.2005.06.002

Iddagoda, A., Opatha, H. H. P., & Gunawardana, K. (2016). Towards a Conceptualization and an Operationalization of the Construct of Employee Engagement. *International Business Research*, *9*(2), 1–14. doi:10.5539/ibr.v9n2p85

Jehn, K. A. (1994). Enhancing effectiveness: An investigation of advantages and disadvantages of value-based intragroup conflict. *International Journal of Conflict Management*, *5*(3), 223–238. doi:10.1108/eb022744

Jehn, K. A. (1995). A multimethod examination of the benefits and detriments of intragroup conflict. *Administrative Science Quarterly*, *40*(2), 256–282. doi:10.2307/2393638

Jehn, K. A. (1997). A qualitative analysis of conflict types and dimensions in organizational groups. *Administrative Science Quarterly*, *42*(3), 530–557. doi:10.2307/2393737

Kamil Kozan, M., & Ergin, C. (1999). The influence of intra-cultural value differences on conflict management practices. *International Journal of Conflict Management, 10*(3), 249–267. doi:10.1108/eb022826

Kure, N. (2010). Narrative mediation and discursive positioning in organisational conflicts. *Explorations: An E-Journal of Narrative Practice*, *2*(10), 24–35.

Lu, L., Zhou, F., & Leung, K. (2011). Effects of task and relationship conflicts on individual work behaviors. *International Journal of Conflict Management, 22*(2), 131–150. doi:10.1108/10444061111126675

Lupu, E., & Sloman, M. (1997). Conflict analysis for management policies. In *Integrated Network Management V: Integrated management in a virtual world Proceedings of the Fifth IFIP/IEEE International Symposium on Integrated Network Management San Diego, California, USA, May 12–16, 1997* (pp. 430-443). Springer US. 10.1007/978-0-387-35180-3_32

McKenna, S., & Richardson, J. (1995). Business values, management, and conflict handling: Issues in contemporary Singapore. *Journal of Management Development, 14*(4), 56–70. doi:10.1108/02621719510084202

Medina, D. M., Munduate, L., Martínez, I., & Cisneros, I. (2002). *Types of conflict and personal and organizational consequences.* Paper presented at the Comunicación presentada a la Internacional Association for Conflict Management Conference.

Medina, F. J., Munduate, L., Dorado, M. A., Martínez, I., & Guerra, J. M. (2005). Types of intragroup conflict and affective reactions. *Journal of Managerial Psychology, 20*(3/4), 219–230. doi:10.1108/02683940510589019

Mele, C. (2011). Conflicts and value co-creation in project networks. *Industrial Marketing Management, 40*(8), 1377–1385. doi:10.1016/j.indmarman.2011.06.033

Mohr, J., & Spekman, R. (1994). Characteristics of partnership success: Partnership attributes, communication behavior, and conflict resolution techniques. *Strategic Management Journal, 15*(2), 135–152. doi:10.1002mj.4250150205

Ndubisi. (2011). Conflict handling, trust and commitment in outsourcing relationship: A Chinese and Indian study. *Industrial Marketing Management, 40*(1), 109-117.

Nikku, B. R. (2004, August). Water rights, conflicts and collective action-Case of the Telugu Ganga project, India. In *The tenth biennial conference of the International Association for the Study of Common Property (IASCP).* The Instituto de Investigaciones Sociales, Universitad Nacional Autonoma de México.

Odetunde, O. J. (2013). Influence of transformational and transactional leaderships, and leaders' sex on organisational conflict management behaviour. *Gender & Behaviour*, *11*(1), 5323–5335.

Olekalns, M. (1997). Conflict at work: Defining and resolving organisational conflicts. *Australian Psychologist*, *32*(1), 56–61. doi:10.1080/00050069708259618

Opatha, H. H. D. N. P., & Ismail, Z. (2001). Towards effective worker grievance handling: Some reflections. *Analisis*, *8*(1/2), 111–127.

Oudenhoven, J. P., Mechelse, L., & De Dreu, C. (1998). Managerial conflict management in five European countries: The importance of power distance, uncertainty avoidance, and masculinity. *Applied Psychology*, *47*(3), 439–455. doi:10.1111/j.1464-0597.1998.tb00037.x

Rahim, A., & Bonoma, T. V. (1979). Managing organizational conflict: A model for diagnosis and intervention. *Psychological Reports*, *44*(3, suppl), 1323–1344. doi:10.2466/pr0.1979.44.3c.1323

Randeree, K. (2008). Organisational Justice. *Journal of Law and Governance*, *3*(4), 57–68.

Randeree, K., & El Faramawy, A. T. (2011). Islamic perspectives on conflict management within project managed environments. *International Journal of Project Management*, *29*(1), 26–32. doi:10.1016/j.ijproman.2010.01.013

Riaz, M. K., & Junaid, F. A. (2013). Workplace conflict: Constructive or destructive. *Muhammad Khan Riaz & Fatima Ali Juniad (2014). Workplace Conflict: Constructive or Destructive. SRM–IMT Journal of Business & Management Research*, *3*(1), 84–90.

Rugman, A., Verbeke, A., Collinson, S., & Morgan, G. (2009). The Regional Dimension of Multinationals and the End of "Varieties of Capitalism". *Images of the Multinational Firm*, 23-44.

Samantara, R., & Sharma, N. (2016). Organisational conflict literature: A Review. *KIIT Journal of Management*, *12*(2), 158–179.

Sharma, R. A., & Samantara, R. (1994). Conflict management in an Indian firm: A case study. *Decision (Washington, D.C.)*, *21*(4), 235.

Slabbert, A. D. (2004). Conflict management styles in traditional organisations. *The Social Science Journal*, *41*(1), 83–92. doi:10.1016/j.soscij.2003.10.007

Song, X. M., Xie, J., & Dyer, B. (2000). Antecedents and consequences of marketing managers' conflict-handling behaviors. *Journal of Marketing*, *64*(1), 50–66. doi:10.1509/jmkg.64.1.50.17989

Tang, S. F., & Kirkbride, P. S. (1986). Developing conflict management skills in Hong Kong: An analysis of some cross-cultural implications. *Management Education and Development*, *17*(3), 287–301. doi:10.1177/135050768601700315

Van de Vliert, E., Nauta, A., Giebels, E., & Janssen, O. (1999). Constructive conflict at work. *Journal of Organizational Behavior: The International Journal of Industrial. Occupational and Organizational Psychology and Behavior*, *20*(4), 475–491. doi:10.1002/(SICI)1099-1379(199907)20:4<475::AID-JOB897>3.0.CO;2-G

Vivar, C. G. (2006). Putting conflict management into practice: A nursing case study. *Journal of Nursing Management*, *14*(3), 201–206. doi:10.1111/j.1365-2934.2006.00554.x PMID:16600008

Wirtz, P. (2011). The cognitive dimension of corporate governance in fast growing entrepreneurial firms. *European Management Journal*, *29*(6), 431–447. doi:10.1016/j.emj.2011.06.004

Zapf, D. (1999). Organisational, work group related and personal causes of mobbing/bullying at work. *International Journal of Manpower*, *20*(1/2), 70–85. doi:10.1108/01437729910268669

Chapter 9
The Role of Organizational Culture on Women's Leadership in Organizations in Switzerland

Silvena Dencheva Yordanova
Varna University of Management, Bulgaria

Vahid Asghari
Varna University of Management, Bulgaria

ABSTRACT

Each organization is defined by its own culture, formed by the key stakeholders. For some companies, it is considered as male culture being aggressive, whereas other companies tolerate different organizational beliefs. For sure, the organizational culture reflects on the values of all its members. It affects human resource practices also. How people are selected in interviews and how their career planning is performed reflects also the company values. It is considered that the performance of the companies measured by the revenues and turnover of staff depend on the leaders in the organization. The following hypotheses have been formulated: 1. Women's leadership positively affects the organizational culture of organizations based in Switzerland. 2. Women's leadership positively affects organizational values of organizations in Switzerland. 3. Women's leadership positively affects organizational conditions of organizations in Switzerland. 4. Women's leadership positively affects the organizational environment of organizations based in Switzerland.

DOI: 10.4018/978-1-6684-6567-7.ch009

INTRODUCTION

Each organization is defined by its own culture, formed by the key stakeholders. For some companies, it is considered as male culture being aggressive, whereas other companies tolerate different organizational beliefs. For sure, the organizational culture reflects on the values of all its members as it affects on human resource practices too. How people are selected on interviews and how their career planning is performed shows the current organizational culture also. It is considered that the performance of the companies measured by the revenues, turnover of staff depend on the leaders in the organization. The contribution of its members is perceived through the lens of the company values. Then arises the question how the organizational cultura impacts on the performance of its members? Does it matter if managers are women or men? All these questions are addressed in the current chapter.

The following hypotheses have been formulated:

1. Women's leadership positively affects on the organizational culture of Organizations based in Switzerland.
2. Women's leadership positively affects on on organizational values of organizations in Switzerland.
3. Women's leadership positively affects on organizational conditions of organizations in Switzerland.
4. Women's leadership positively affects on the organizational environment of organizations based in Switzerland.

MAIN BODY

Women constitute half of society and their participation can be effective in its development and progress. The chapter is focused on providing understanding on the essence of women leadership and how it impacts the organizational culture in organizations based in Switzerland. For this purpose, a profound literature review with a focus on the sociological and management theories has been carried. What is more, the goal of the chapter is to present the influence that women leaders in Switzerland have on the organizations. Does the gender play role regarding company's performance? In order to understand this a survey has been used in a form of offline questionnaire among 150 managers and employees in organizations based in Switzerland.

Self-report method has been used to complete this research questionnaire. The study shows that the majority of respondents, 80% of the participants find their work environment as desirable. 94% of the participants describe it as average and good the organizational culture. More than 70% of the participants describe as desirable and good their organizational values and more than 74% of the participants have declared positive attitudes towards gender-based leadership. Research hypothesis test has been confirmed that women's leadership affect positively and significantly on the organizational culture, on organizational values and working conditions and organizational environment in organizations based in Switzerland. To sum it up, women's leadership in organizations based in Switzerland has been able to have a positive effect on the controlled organizations.

The progress of the companies depends on leader and its ability to adapt and be proactive. However, their influence depends on their gender, whether male or female. The influence of a female manager differs significantly from having a male manager as the studies conducted across the globe show that female leaders have a distinct influence on organizational, values, culture, and climate compared to male managers (GENEVA, 2019; MEGAN, 2020). However, studies have yet to be conducted concerning the influence of women's leadership on the organizational culture of organizations based in Switzerland.

When it comes to work environment, only 24 companies of the Fortune Global 500 (i.e., 4.8%) have female CEOs, according to Steffens et al., 2019. The statistics for Europe shows that women on top managerial positions at the top 100 companies represent just 15% (Steffens et al., 2019. The effects of different gender compositions at the top-level of organizations on a whole range of potentially important outcome variables by studying the consequences of balanced gender compositions as well as male or female majorities for female leaders have been highlighted by Steffens et al., 2019 as women are considered of being warm and caring, while men are associated with agentic traits such as being competent and assertive (Steffens et al., 2019).

Organizations with women leaders have a positive environment. Due to many positive characteristics, including empathy, mindfulness, multitasking, open communication, and open-mindedness, women can easily sync with their team (MEGAN, 2020). The stereotypes about genders assumes that leadership is more associated with men, as they are supposed to possess power and other agentic qualities, and to be incongruent with the female gender role (Eagly and Karau, 2002; Koenig et al., 2011).

However, women unlike men possess emotional intelligence, can solve many problems at one time and are motivated which is required for a successful leader. It is clear that women are more emotional and empathic that men so that they can be useful and innovative for the companies they lead by transforming the organizational management style, thus enhancing the organization's effectiveness. Women in leadership positions bring moral perspectives and values to the organization (Ashgari, 2023). It is considered that women leaders perform their leadership roles by being honest, transparent in their management, and are ethically responsible decision-makers (Nakamura et al., 2022).

To sum up, there are many reasons why women on leadership positions should be part of organizations based in Switzerland (Ashgari, 2023). Powerful women can take risks, learn from mistakes, and fight for what they believe in. Also, it is essential to note that women possess similar characteristics as their male counterparts; they are able to adapt, persevere and ignore bad advice (Council, 2017).

The chapter presents results from a study on the impact that women managers and leaders have on the organization's environmental culture and values and to the extent they influence organizational leadership in Switzerland. In this regard, the study also deals with the changes that women leaders introduce in the companies they lead. For this purpose, offline questionnaires are used in order to provide understanding on how women's leadership in organizations based in Switzerland impacts on the environmental culture and values and how women leaders can change the future of corporate leadership. The study also seeks to investigate the changes that women leaders make in organizations based in Switzerland and whether this only applies to organizations in Switzerland. This study investigates this problem by assuming that women leaders have the ability to influence environmental culture and values of organizations in a positive way (Ashgari, 2023).

It is considered that women are not suitable for middle managerial and top level positions as result of cultural stereotypes (Zenger &Folkman, 2021). Furthermore, Minkov (2011), proves that it is especially true as perception in some of the developing countries - such as Brazil, where high level of gender inequality exists that women leaders are perceived as unsuitable to be occupied by women. What is more, the role incredulity states that "a form of gender bias where women are mistakenly assumed to be in a support or stereotypically female role rather than a leadership or stereotypically male role (Beatriz, 2023).

Women leaders are perceived and portrayed as emotional, which affects them when making decisions (Brescoll, 2016). What is more the researchers Zenger and Folkman (2012, 2019) point that better leadership skills are possessed by women, who are portrayed as being competent and productive as men, and in some cases outperform them occupying leadership positions (Beatriz, 2023). Emotional intelligence as Yordanova, 2023 states is represented by self-awareness, empathy, self-motivation ability of the individual, all skills that women possess.

Other researchers Feitosa et al. (2019) stated that women perform better to balance between work and life, facing the difficulties of the gender bias met in the leadership(Beatriz, 2023).

It became clear that in uncertain times as covid crisis women leaders performed better in managing teams. In this regard, Carter et al. (2022) analyzed what traits were used to do hard things while still being "good human beings" such as being wise and compassionate defined as very important skills. The analysis showed that in spite of the big number of women who lost their job in the covid crisis, the majority of women possessed these traits which helped them to outperform men (Beatriz, 2023).

An explanation about leadership is provided by sociological and management theories focusing on specific traits and behavior possessed by leaders. In this regard, the behavioral theory suggests that the behavior of leaders can be set as an example and thus copied by their followers. The theory postulates that leaders are trained and educated by transferring different leadership skills in their followers (Khan et al., 2020). In this regard, women on leadership positions impact on other women in the companies they lead as in Switzerland, the women managers have a big impact not only on the companies they manage, but also on the society. This is due to their better performance as they feel they are well-represented in managerial positions. Lastly, the traits of women in leadership of organizations based in Switzerland affect positively on their staff. Hence, women in the leadership of organizations based in Switzerland impact on the organizational culture of their companies (Asghari, 2023).

The leadership can be viewed from many perspectives. As the leader is the person driving the organization to change and having a strong impact on other individuals by motivating them and imposing the will of the leader onto others to induce obedience, respect, loyalty and cooperation (Moore, 1927; Eklund, Barry and Grunberg, 2017)-through the behavior, by motivation or setting an example to be followed so that the group or team where all can benefit (Appelbaum et al.2019).

In this regard, Callahan and Grunberg (2016) identified a conceptual "FourCe-PITO" framework that describes today's leader by the Four C's ("FourCe"), Character, Competence, Context, and Communication, occur across four different psychological levels--Personal, Interpersonal, Team, and Organizational (PITO) as described by Appelbaum et al.2019.

The leadership style of women can be further explained with Hofstede's theory focusing on different dimensions of organizational culture in multicultural aspect such as:

Process-Oriented vs. Results-Oriented

The dominating organizational culture can vary from process-oriented culture, expressed by technical and bureaucratic routines that may discourage women to rise to leadership position. On the other hand, results-oriented organizational culture is more concerned with the outcomes (Hofstede, 2011).

Job-Oriented vs. Employee-Oriented

Job-oriented organizational culture refers to employees doing their best while performing their duties and responsibilities. On the other hand, employee-oriented culture is oriented to taking care for the whole well-being of all employees on behalf of the company. In both cultures there is a group responsibility and all employees support each other to achieve a common goal (Hofstede, 2011).

Professional vs. Parochial

In the professional organizational culture the employees identify themselves with the profession they perform while in the parochial culture, whereas in the parochial culture the employees identify with the organization they work. In other words, all employees are provided with equal opportunities to become leaders in the organization they work (Hofstede, 2011).

Open Systems vs. Closed Systems

Open systems organizational culture allows fluent communication inside and outside of the company whereas in the closed systems the communication is mainly internally oriented. Only few people have the authority to communicate with external audiences. (Hofstede, 2011).

Tight vs. Loose Control

A tight organizational culture relies on many rules and strict regulations whereas in the loose, the organizational control is less (Hofstede, 2011).

Pragmatic vs. Normative

A pragmatic organizational culture gives employees flexibility when working on their tasks whereas the normative one is more focused on applying specific organizational rules and policies when working on specific work tasks(Ashgari, 2023).

The leadership style is also affected by the work environment of the specific company. In other words, a positive work environment results in positive organizational culture and the opposite. The environment of the workplace greatly influences the quality of work and innovation in the organization (Asghari, 2023).

According to studies, women work better if the working environment is positive as they feel more motivated and recognized in such working conditions. When managers are motivated to work, there is an improvement in the organizational culture of the organization (Bobe & Kober, 2020).

The type of structure recognizing the accomplishment of women employees has been discussed by Koland (2015) as such a structure would recognize and reward women in the same way for the same types of accomplishments as men would favour equality in the workplace. It is also interesting to note that masculinity of women could allow them to be compared to the males and thus, be more successful as leaders. Thus, the organizations should focus on developing programs to help women create these characteristics and leadership traits, with the help of men mentoring them how to use of power, emotions, negotiations, politics and competition (Appelbaum et al.2019).

The researchers by the moment have focused on feminine and masculine characteristics and how they impacted on the styles of leadership of women in men in organizations. However, the latest studies show that today's executives may have started to adapt both of the gender-linked traits in order to become successful leaders. No doubt that women succeed as leaders depending on the culture and context. 'Modern organizations are working towards and actually needing a modern leadership style that is characterized by more stereotypically female qualities, such as concern for others'' (Appelbaum et al.2019). However, "there are still very few women in leadership positions despite persuasive evidence of their positive effect on profitability.'' Although the picture has gradually changed in terms of female representation in top leadership positions, the question remains; when will the barriers that women face when trying to climb to the top echelons of the corporate world disappear? (Appelbaum, et al. 2013b)

The studies showed that if employees are working in a positive working environment, it will affect them positively, thus strengthening organizational values (Kuenzi et al., 2019). The working environment created by the leaders is considered as part of the organizational culture. In such situations, then leaders feel comfortable and gain zeal to work more effectively (Sihombing et al., 2018). Working in a friendly organizational environment makes employees more motivated and increases their level of loyalty towards the organization and leaves no room for laziness in the organization. The positive working climate affects well on employees and confirms organizational values. The studies shows that women work better in a positive organizational climate (Kuenzi et al., 2020) as they are more motivated to perform their tasks feeling safe and well (Ashikali et al., 2021). To sum up, empirical studies confirmed that female leaders' organizational climate will have an influence on the organizational values of the organization (Ashgari, 2023). The negative perceptions of men towards women taking managerial and leadership positions still exists. On the other side, women with a positive attitude believe that organizational, social and cultural factors prevent them from achieving a career development and becoming managers. Also, husbands' attitude towards women's management is related to employees' attitude towards women's specific issues and information barriers (Kajbaf et al., 2008).

To sum up, existing negative stereotypes that women are not suitable to work on leadership positions have provoked us to carry the current study and understand how organizational culture affects on women leaderships of organizations based in Swizerland. Before we present our study, we shall discuss the context of gender equality as it is now in Swizerland.

The organizational culture in Switzerland is affected by the business culture among Swiss people, who are known for their diversity, creativity, and innovativeness. Switzerland business culture is famous with its strict planning, aversion of risks, and formality https://golookexplore.com/.

Being punctual is a rule number one, required by all Swiss companies as it is the most important aspect of the business culture of people in this country https://golookexplore.com/

Switzerland is leading in female labor force participation in Europe, together with the Netherlands and the Nordic countries as 61.9% of working-age women in Switzerland work, 10.5 percentage points fewer than men. However, when it comes to women who are employed full time, Switzerland is lagging behind European countries as 3 in 5 employed women in Switzerland work part-time, as opposed to less than 1 in 5 men. The data of BCG show that more women in Switzerland are joining the workforce due to the rising levels of educational attainment (Globaldata.com). Women in this country are now attending higher education institutions, including universities, in large numbers. Gender analysis shows that the number of women joining technical courses has risen from 13.5 to 31.3 percent in seven years (Canada, 2019). Gender diversity on Switzerland boards has risen to 55 percent in recent years.

According to Global data report women held 47.1% of the labor force in Switzerland and the proportion of the female labor force in Switzerland increased by 0.2% compared to the previous year in 2021so that between 2010-2021, the proportion of the female labor force in Switzerland increased by 2.4% (Globaldata.com).

According to the 2021 Global Gender Gap Report, Swiss is among the top countries with a narrow gender gap. Besides Swiss ranking high in gender equality, there is a need to fix the gender gap that exists in leadership positions because women bring substantial benefits to the organization (ESGHUB, 2022). Women prefer flex working opportunities and 2 in 5 underemployed women would like to work full-time. The remainder - 3 in 5 - would like to increase part-time work, especially mothers who work. 2 in 5 women would refuse an attractive job offer if they had a negative experience during the hiring process. Women care about the job content and more women in Switzerland (30%) than abroad (23%) want to work on interesting products and topics, especially those highly educated (43%) and managers (36%) as showed by BCG/The Network proprietary web survey).

The data of BCG show that for the first time in history, 52% of the 100 largest publicly listed companies in Switzerland have at least 3 women on their supervisory board.

In this regard, Switzerland is presenting lower results compared to European peers. However, the Swiss Labor Force survey shows that women are generally employed in lower positions than men and more often in non-managerial positions. For example, significantly more women than men – 65% as opposed to 50% – occupy positions without a supervisory role.

It is interesting to note that the majority of women (75%) in Switzerland value stable jobs that leave time for family, friends and hobbies. This tendency remains the same for men (63%) and is not affected by age or education levels. It becomes clear that Swiss women prefer mainly stable part-time job than their global peers. Generally, men and women in Switzerland show a lower willingness to progress to leadership positions (17% women vs 26% men) relative to their global peers (39% women vs 43% men). However, women who already work at any management level want to progress in their career as they wish to advance in their companies (28%) is higher compared to the general Swiss results. Moreover, they expect less regarding work-life balance - 8 percentage points less compared to the average result for all women in Switzerland. Female managers are also less likely to want to work part-time compared to their non-manager peers (BCG/ The Network proprietary web survey).

In this regard, attention should be paid to the specific indicator introduced by the World economic forum is the The Global Gender Gap Index that measures per year the current state and evolution of gender parity across four key dimensions (Economic Participation and Opportunity, Educational Attainment, Health and Survival, and Political Empowerment). The index presents the progress of countries' efforts towards closing these gaps over time, since its inception in 2006. It is worth to note that there is significant variance among this indicator per countries in different geographic regions. For example, the gender parity in Europe (76.3%) is higher compared to the parity level in North America (75%) this year to rank first of eight geographic regions. Closely behind Europe and North America is Latin America and the Caribbean, with 74.3% parity. It is interesting also to note that Europe has the highest gender parity of all regions at 76.3%, with one-third of countries in the region ranking in the top 20 and 20 out of 36 countries with at least 75% parity. Iceland, Norway and Finland are the best-performing countries, both in the region and in the world, while Hungary, Czech Republic and Cyprus rank at the bottom of the region. Overall, there is a decline of 0.2 percentage points in the regional score based on the constant sample of countries. At the current rate of progress, Europe is projected to attain gender parity in 67 years https:// www.weforum.org/ The index show several dimensions such as women as active part in the labour force. For this indicator,: Women have been (re-)entering the workforce at a slightly higher rate than men, resulting in a modest recovery from last year's low. Between the 2022 and 2023 edition, parity in the labour-force participation rate increased from 63% to 64%. However, the recovery in women's labour-force participation remains unfinished, as parity is still at the second-lowest point since the first edition of the index in 2006 (https://www.weforum.org)/.

In this ranking, Switzerland takes the 21st position with a score of 0,783 which is close to the rank of Estonia that occupies the 22nd position. Thi indicator composes of several sub indexes such as: Economic Participation and Opportunity, Educational Attainment, Health and Survival, and Political Empowerment.

In this regard, wages for similar work, the only countries in which the gender gap is perceived as more than 80% closed are Albania (85.8%) and Burundi (84.1%). Almost 1/4 of the 146 economies included in this year's edition score between 70%-80% on

Table 1. Key figures on income differences between women and men, 2012-2021, in %

	2012	2013	2014	2015	2016	2017	2018	2019	2020	2021
Gender Overall Earnings Gap (GOEG)	…	…	44,9	…	43,3	…	43,2	…	…	
Gender pay gap (arithmetic mean / average)	19,3	…	18,1	…	18,3	…	19,0	…	18,0	…
Gender Pension Gap	…	…	33,5	31,2	31,9	31,6	30,9	33,1	34,6	,8

… Unknown since data has not (yet) been gathered

Sources: Swiss Labour Force Survey (SLFS), Swiss Earnings Structure Survey (ESS), Central Compensation Office (CCO),

Old Age and Survivors' Insurance (OASI), Statistics on Income and living Conditions (SILC)

© FSO

Informations: Information center, Section Demography and Migration

this indicator including some of the most well developed economies, such as Iceland (78.4% of gap closed), Singapore (78.3%), United Arab Emirates (77.6%), United States (77.3%), Finland (76.3%), Qatar (74.5%), Saudi Arabia (74.1%), Lithuania (74.1%), Slovenia (73.5%), Bahrain (72.8%), Estonia (71.4%), Barbados (71.2%), Luxembourg (70.4%), New Zealand (70.4%), Switzerland (70.3%), and Latvia (70.1%)https://www.weforum.org/.

Women's paid employment is different from men's in various respects based on their work-time percentage and position they occupy. What is more, while women's economic activity rate is lower than men's, their unemployment rate based on ILO definition is higher https://www.bfs.admin.ch/.

Figure1. Economic activity of women in Switzerland

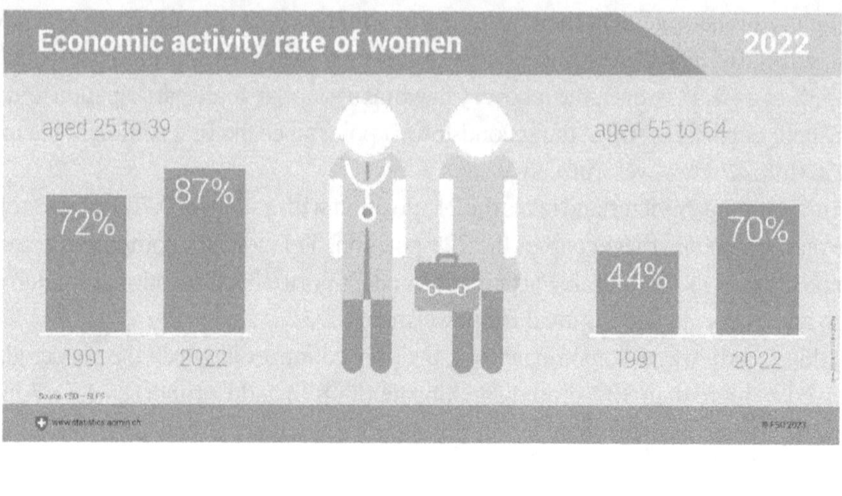

The differences between women and men regarding paid employment should be taken into account from the perspectives of paid and unpaid work between the sexes. When it comes to characteristics of female paid employment, such as part-time work, should be considered in the context of women's balance between family and work and, consequently, the amount of work they do at home, because women still do most of the housework https://www.bfs.admin.ch/.

As it can be seen from Figure 1, there is a significant increase in the economic activity of women aged 5 5to 64 years from 1991 year to 2022 year. It can be also noted that the positive shift from women aged 25 to 39 as they have also increased their economic activity through years as shown on Figure 1. On the other side, the wages are still different form genders as it is obvious from Figure 2. There is still 19,5 % gender gap as depicted on Figure 2.

According to data of FSO in Swizerland, 60.1% of people receiving a gross monthly wage of less than CHF 4000 for a full-time job were women. Conversely, more men

Figure 2. Average pay and gender pay gap in Switzerland for 2020 year

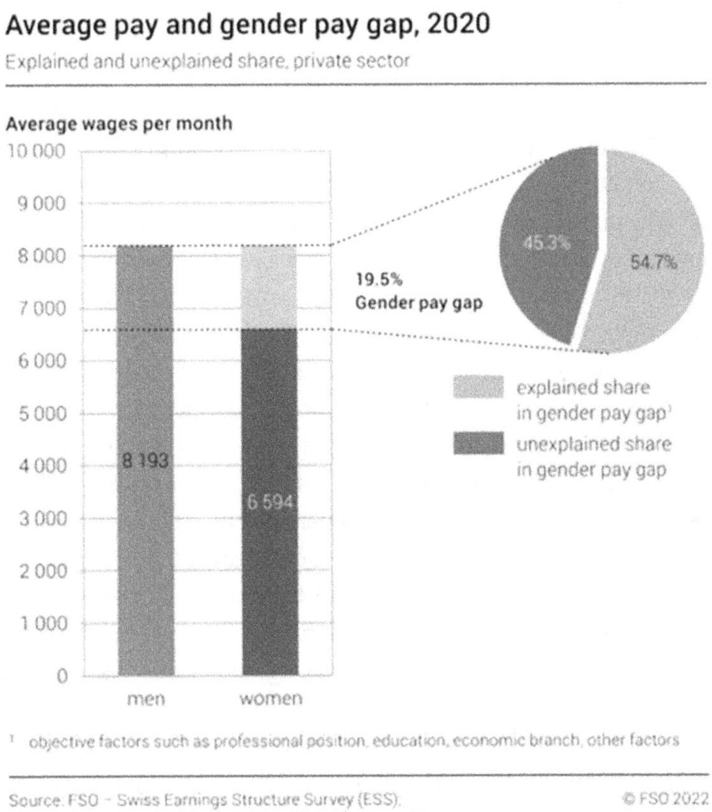

received top wages, accounting for 78.5% of employees earning a gross monthly salary of more than CHF 16 000 (2018: 81.2%). As a whole, the overall gender pay gap decreased by 1% from 19.0% in 2018 to 18.0% in 2020 (private and public sectors together). 47.8% of the pay gap remains unexplained, according to the Federal Statistical Office (FSO).

The data of FASO showed that if women and men have the same skill level, wages of women are lower than men's: and wage gaps vary between 12% and 19% depending on the skill level, education and cossupied position in the organizations women work. To sum up, women receive less wages than men even when they have the same education and the same occupational position. Depending on their educational level, they earn between almost 2% (elementary school teaching certificate) and 18% (university) less than men. In the same occupational position, women's salaries are 7% (no management responsibilities) and 17% (top, upper and middle management) lower than men's (FSO).

Methodology

The method of the present research is cross-sectional survey. Since the purpose of this research is to describe and investigate the effect of women's leadership on the organizational culture of Organizations based in Switzerland, the method of this research is descriptive-correlational study of case type. This type of research looks for relationships between variables. It is applied research in terms of purpose and survey research in terms of conduction. In this research, data collection has been done through field survey method (Asghari, 2023).

The study conducts quantitative research in form of self-administered off-line questionnaire. The questionnaire is developed in English language to ensure universal understanding and is distributed among both managers and non-managerial staffs of organization ns based in Switzerland. The questions are focused on provide understanding and study the impact that women leadership has on the organizational culture of organizations based in Switzerland. The study seeks personal information from the potential respondents and again strictly maintaining confidentiality and anonymity in information gathering (Asghari, 2023).

The study uses a convenient sample size of 150 people from different sectors, industries, factories and service related organizations as well as the NGOs based in Switzerland. The sample size is within a convenient locality that the researcher is more familiar with because all questionnaires administered in hand or free return envelope. The study sampling is based on one-to-one interaction and is going to cover a specific location to cut commuting costs, including parking lots, waiting bay in factories and social places (Asghari, 2023).

The study aims to study how women's leadership affects on organizational culture of organizations based in Switzerland. The study hypothesis stated that women leaders have an impact on the organizational culture of organizations based in Switzerland. Also, the study hypothesis stated that women leaders have an impact on the organizational values. The last hypothesis is that women leaders have an impact on the organizational climate of organizations based in Switzerland.

The normality of the data was examined using SPSS data analysis mechanism which normalized the perception of women leadership influence on organization culture, values, and work environment. In all categories, the questionnaires achieved a Cronbach's Alpha of >0.7 on average, which indicates that the analysis is good and their scale is internally consistent.

According to Table 2, 12.7% of the respondents are under 25 years old. 23.3% of the respondents are between 25 and 34 years old. 16.7% of them are 35 to 44 years old. 24.7% of them are 45 to 50 years old and 22.7% of the respondents are 51 and more than 51 years old. More than three quarters of the respondents are 50 and less than 50 years old.

The results from study show that 2% of the respondents have considered their organizational environment completely undesirable whereas just 3.3% of them have evaluated it as undesirable. At the same time, 14.7% of the respondents have described that their organization and work environment is on average level and 31.3% of them have defined their organizational and work environment as desirable and good. To sum up, the majority of the respondents have considered their work environment as desirable and good.

The results from study show that 3.1% of the respondents have declared that the organizational culture of their work place is completely undesirable whereas 21.3% of them have described it as an average. 47.4% of them believe that the organizational culture of their work place was desirable and 25.3% of them have said that the organizational culture of their office was completely desirable. To sum up, again the data showed that the majority of the respondents have considered the organizational culture of their office as desirable (Asghari, 2023)..

Table 2. Frequency distribution of respondent's age

Respondent's Ages	Numbers	Percentages	Cumulative Percentages
Less than 25 years old	19	12.7	12.7
25 to 34 years old	35	23.3	36.0
35 to 44 years old	25	16.7	52.7
45 to 50 years old	37	24.7	77.3
51 and more than 51 years old	34	22.7	100.0
Total	150	100.0	

Source: (Asghari, 2023)

Table 3. Frequency distribution of respondent's attitude towards the gender-based leadership

	Completely Undesirable	Undesirable	Average	Desirable	Completely Desirable
Numbers	3	7	29	78	33
Percentage	2.0	4.7	19.3	52.0	22.0

The results from study show that 2% of the respondents have declared that the organizational values of their work place were completely unacceptable whereas just 4% of them have considered the organizational values of their office as desirable. 23.3% of them have claimed that the organizational values of their work place were at an average level. 48% of them or in other words half of them have considered the organizational values of their work place as desirable and 22.7% of them have said that the organizational values of their work place were completely good and desirable (Asghari, 2023).

The results from study show that 2.7% of the respondents have described the organizational conditions of their office as undesirable whereas just 3.3% of them have evaluated them as undesirable and 14.7% of them have defined the organizational conditions of their office at an average level. 50.7% of the respondents have claimed that the organizational conditions of their work place were desirable and 28.7% of them have said that the organizational conditions of their office were completely desirable. If we sum up, the majority of the respondents have stated that the organizational conditions of their office are desirable(Asghari, 2023).

The results from study show that only 2% of respondents have had completely opposite attitude towards management and leadership based on the gender compared to 4.7% of them also have had opposite attitude towards it. 19.3% of the respondents have had an average attitude towards the gender-based leadership. 52% of the respondents have said that their attitude towards the gender-based management was agreeable. 22% of them have claimed that their attitude towards to the management and leadership based on the gender was completely agreeable. To sum up, the majority of the respondents have had agreeable attitude towards the gender-based leadership(Asghari, 2023)..

Hypothesis 1: Women's leadership has a positive effect on the organizational culture of Organizations based in Switzerland.

For this purposes, Pearson's correlation coefficient was used and the correlation coefficient between the two variables of women's leadership in organizations and organizational culture in Organizations based in Switzerland is equal to 0.621 and its significance level is equal to 0.001. To sum it up, the first hypothesis has been confirmed so that women's leadership impacts positively on the organizational culture in Organizations based in Switzerland and this result can be generalized to the statistical population of the research with error probability of one percent (

Hypothesis 2: Women's leadership has a positive effect on organizational values of organizations in Switzerland.

For this purposes Pearson's correlation coefficient was used and the correlation coefficient between women's leadership in organizations and organizational values in Switzerland is equal to 0.595 and its significance level is equal to 0.001. So the second hypothesis has been also confirmed that women leaders have a positive impact on the organizational values in organizations in Switzerland (Asghari, 2023).

Hypothesis 3: Women's leadership has a positive effect on organizational conditions of organizations in Switzerland.

For this purposes Pearson's correlation coefficient was used the results showed that the third hypothesis has been confirmed. It means that women leaders have positive impact on the working conditions of Swiss organizations as the correlation coefficient between women's leadership in the organization and organizational conditions of organizations in Switzerland is equal to 0.786 and its significance level is equal to 0.001.

Hypothesis 4: Women's leadership has a positive effect on the organizational environment of Organizations based in Switzerland.

For this purposes Pearson's correlation coefficient was used to test this hypothesis and the correlation coefficient between women's leadership in organizations and organizational environment of organizations in Switzerland is equal to 0.417 and its significance level is equal to 0.000 that is significant in the level of 1%. Therefore, according to error probability of 1%, that the fourth hypothesis has been again confirmed (Asghari, 2023)..

CONCLUSION

The current chapter showed that leadership of women is very different based on the context and culture. Thus the Hofstede and Minkov's theory has been confirmed that in different countries the role of men and women are various and values differ accordingly. In patriarchal societies, more dominating values are to take good position in the society, and monetary rewards prevail. In different society exists differences among perceptions and roles of different genders as it became clear from all existing gender stereotypes. It is considered that Germany and Austria are highly ranked as patriarchal countries because they value incomes, approval, progress and controversy.

The study results confirmed the hypotheses that women leaders have a positive impact on the organizational culture. Positivity is achieved through use of empathy and applying emotional intelligence to employees. The results indicated that what motivates employees is the good working environment and positive relationship among employees on the working place.

In other words, employees prefer positive organizational climate that motivates them and affects also on their loyalty to the organizations. It became clear that women leaders affect also positively on the organizational values as through clear values, these leaders can dramatically improve employees' relationships in the workplace and help them live with these values (Ashgari, 2023).

REFERENCES

Andrews, R., Boyne, G. A., & Walker, R. M. (2006). Strategy content and organizational performance: An empirical analysis. *Public Administration Review*, *66*(1), 52–63. doi:10.1111/j.1540-6210.2006.00555.x

Appelbaum, D'Antico, & Daoussis. (2019). Women as Leaders The More Things Change, the More It's the Same Thing. *International Journal of Management and Business*, *10*(1).

Asghari, V. (2023). *Influence of women's leadership on the organizational culture of organizations based in Switzerland* [MBA dissertation].

Ashikali, T., Groeneveld, S., & Kuipers, B. (2021). The role of inclusive leadership in supporting an inclusive climate in diverse public sector teams. *Review of Public Personnel Administration*, *41*(3), 497–519. doi:10.1177/0734371X19899722

Batliwala, S., & Dhanraj, D. (2007). Gender myths that instrumentalize women: a view from the Indian front line. *Feminisms in development: Contradictions, contestations and challenges, 35*(4), 11-18.

Bieri, S., & Sancar, A. (2009). *Power and poverty. Reducing gender inequality by ways of rural employment?* Academic Press.

Bloomfield, J., & Fisher, M. J. (2019). Quantitative research design. *Journal of the Australasian Rehabilitation Nurses Association*, *22*(2), 27–30. doi:10.33235/jarna.22.2.27-30

Bobe, B. J., & Kober, R. (2020). Does gender matter? The association between gender and the use of management control systems and performance measures. *Accounting and Finance*, *60*(3), 2063–2098. doi:10.1111/acfi.12365

Boyne, G. A., & Walker, R. M. (2004). Strategy content and public service organizations. *Journal of Public Administration: Research and Theory*, *14*(2), 231–252. doi:10.1093/jopart/muh015

Canada, G. A. (2019). *Gender Analysis*. https://www.international.gc.ca/world-monde/funding-financement/gender_analysis-analyse_comparative.aspx?lang=eng

Chattopadhyay, R., & Duflo, E. (2001). Women as policy makers: Evidence from a randomized policy experiment in India. *Econometrica*, *72*(5), 1409–1443. doi:10.1111/j.1468-0262.2004.00539.x

Council, Y. E. (2017). *Eight Traits Every Powerful Female Leader Possesses*. https://www.forbes.com/sites/yec/2017/10/03/eight-traits-every-powerful-female-leader-possesses/?sh=40d794a5608f

David, A., Joan, M., Seth, O., & Reeve, V. (2001). The glass ceiling effect. *Social Forces*, *80*(2), 655–681. doi:10.1353of.2001.0091

Devereux, S., & Solomon, C. (2006). *Employment creation programmes: The international experience*. ILO.

Eagly, A. H., & Sczesny, S. (2009). *Stereotypes about women, men, and leaders: Have times changed?* American Psychological Association.

Elson, D. (2010). Gender and the global economic crisis in developing countries: A framework for analysis. *Gender and Development*, *18*(2), 201–212. doi:10.1080/13552074.2010.491321

ESGHUB. (2022). *The role of Women in Business Management in Switzerland*. https://esghub.ch/the-role-of-women-in-business-management-in-switzerland/

FDFA. (2020). *Switzerland's commitment to women's rights worldwide*. https://www.eda.admin.ch/eda/en/fdfa/fdfa/aktuell/newsuebersicht/2020/03/csw.html

Galbreath, J. (2011). Are there gender-related influences on corporate sustainability? A study of women on boards of directors. *Journal of Management & Organization*, *17*(1), 17–38. doi:10.5172/jmo.2011.17.1.17

Geneva. (2023, March 8). *Women in leadership bring better business performance*. International Labor Organization. https://www.ilo.org/global/about-the-ilo/newsroom/news/WCMS_701767/lang--en/index.htm

Geneva, I. (2017). *Gender in employment policies and programmes: What works for women?* https://www.ilo.org/wcmsp5/groups/public/---ed_emp/documents/publication/wcms_613536.pdf

Geng, F., Redcay, E., & Riggins, T. (2019). The influence of age and performance on hippocampal function and the encoding of contextual information in early childhood. *NeuroImage, 195*, 433–443. doi:10.1016/j.neuroimage.2019.03.035 PMID:30905835

Goldkuhl, G., & Cronholm, S. (2010). Adding theoretical grounding to grounded theory: Toward multi-grounded theory. *International Journal of Qualitative Methods, 9*(2), 187–205. doi:10.1177/160940691000900205

Guerrero, S., Chênevert, D., Vandenberghe, C., Tremblay, M., & Ben Ayed, A. K. (2018). Employees' psychological empowerment and performance: How customer feedback substitutes for leadership. *Journal of Services Marketing, 32*(7), 868–879. doi:10.1108/JSM-09-2017-0325

Hobfoll, S. E. (2001). The influence of culture, community, and the nested-self in the stress process: Advancing conservation of resources theory. *Applied Psychology, 50*(3), 337–421. doi:10.1111/1464-0597.00062

Hofstede, G. (2011). Dimensionalizing Cultures: T he Hofstede Model in Context. *Online Readings in Psychology and Culture, 2*(1).

Jencks, C., & Phillips, M. (2011). *The Black-White test score gap*. Brookings Institution Press.

Jhpiego. (2016). *Gender analysis toolkit for health systems*. https://gender.jhpiego.org/analysistoolkit/gender-analysis-framework/

Johansen, M. S. (2007). The effect of female strategic managers on organizational performance. *Public Organization Review, 7*(3), 269–279. doi:10.100711115-007-0036-1

Kajbaf, K., & Sadat, M. (2008). Investigating the attitude of Isfahan Education Organization employees towards women's management and obstacles to promoting women to management positions. *Social Psychological Studies of Women, 6*(3), 133-147.

Kanter, R. M. (1977). *Men and women of the corporation*. Academic Press.

Karsten, M. F. (2006). *Management, gender, and race in the 21st century*. University Press of Amer.

Khan, H., Rehmat, M., Butt, T. H., Farooqi, S., & Asim, J. (2020). Impact of transformational leadership on work performance, burnout and social loafing: A mediation model. *Future Business Journal, 6*(1), 1–13. doi:10.118643093-020-00043-8

Kuenzi, M., Brown, M. E., Mayer, D. M., & Priesemuth, M. (2019). Supervisor-subordinate (dis) agreement on ethical leadership: An investigation of its antecedents and relationship to organizational deviance. *Business Ethics Quarterly*, *29*(1), 25–53. doi:10.1017/beq.2018.14

Kuenzi, M., Mayer, D. M., & Greenbaum, R. L. (2020). Creating an ethical organizational environment: The relationship between ethical leadership, ethical organizational climate, and unethical behavior. *Personnel Psychology*, *73*(1), 43–71. doi:10.1111/peps.12356

Lahti, E. (2013). *Women and leadership: factors that influence women's career success: female leaders' reflections on their career development and leadership*. Academic Press.

McAdam, R., & Henderson, J. (2004). Influencing the future of TQM: Internal and external driving factors. *International Journal of Quality & Reliability Management*, *21*(1), 51–71. doi:10.1108/02656710410511696

MEGAN. A. (2020). *Highlighting Importance Of Women Leadership In Your Organization*. https://witi.com/articles/1843/Highlighting-Importance-Of-Women-Leadership-In-YourOrganization/#:~:text=When%20women%20become%20leaders%2C%20they,is%20really%20going%20on%20underneath

Meier, K. J., & O'Toole, L. J. Jr. (2005). Managerial networking: Issues of measurement and research design. *Administration & Society*, *37*(5), 523–541. doi:10.1177/0095399705277142

Nakamura, Y. T., Hinshaw, J., & Burns, R. (2022). Developing Women's Authenticity in Leadership. *Merits*, *2*(4), 408–426. doi:10.3390/merits2040029

Nasser, F. F. (2019). *Factors affecting the principles of organizational management in improving the actions of managers and employees to separate men and women in service organizations (case study: service organizations ofTabriz city)*. Academic Press.

Natural, H. R. (2021). *10 reasons why the world needs more women in leadership roles*. https://www.naturalhr.com/2021/03/23/10-reasons-why-the-world-needs-more-women-in-leadership-roles/

Nielsen, M. W., & Börjeson, L. (2019). Gender diversity in the management field: Does it matter for research outcomes? *Research Policy*, *48*(7), 1617–1632. doi:10.1016/j.respol.2019.03.006

Oh, N., & Lee, J. (2020). Changing landscape of emergency management research: A systematic review with bibliometric analysis. *International Journal of Disaster Risk Reduction*, *49*, 101658. doi:10.1016/j.ijdrr.2020.101658

Opie, T., & Henn, C. (2013). Work-family conflict and totalitas kerja among mothers: Conscientiousness and neuroticism as moderators. *SA Journal of Industrial Psychology, 39*(1). Advance online publication. doi:10.4102ajip.v39i1.1082

Parker, K., Horowitz, J. M., & Rohal, M. (2015). *Women and leadership: Public says women are equally qualified, but barriers persist.* Pew Research Center.

Priser, J., & Bernard, D. (2021). The Collections of Scientific Instruments of the Faculty of Sciences of Rennes: A Tool for School Education and for the Training of Students and Teachers. In *Historical Scientific Instruments in Contemporary Education* (pp. 84–104). Brill.

Ray, P., Reddy, S. S., & Banerjee, T. (2021). Various dimension reduction techniques for high dimensional data analysis: A review. *Artificial Intelligence Review, 54*(5), 3473–3515. doi:10.100710462-020-09928-0

Reza, N. J. (2015). *Comparing organizational success in organizations with male and female managers.* Tehran University.

Rosener, J. B. (1995). *America's competitive secret: Women managers.* Oxford University Press on Demand.

Sihombing, S., Astuti, E. S., Al Musadieq, M., Hamied, D., & Rahardjo, K. (2018). The effect of servant leadership on rewards, organizational culture and its implication for employee's performance. *International Journal of Law and Management.*

Steffens, M., Vladot, M., & Scheifele, C. (2019). *Male Majority, Female Majority, or Gender Diversity in Organizations: How Do Proportions Affect Gender Stereotyping and Women Leaders' Well-Being?* (Vol. 10). Front. Psychol., Sec. Organizational Psychology. doi:10.3389/fpsyg.2019.01037

Yordanova, S. (2023). *Emotional intelligence of the leader-is it needed?* Academic Press.

Chapter 10
The Effect of Work and Family Conflict on Life Satisfaction:
Gender Concept

Selda Coşkuner Aktaş
https://orcid.org/0000-0003-4040-2939
Hacettepe University, Turkey

ABSTRACT

The purpose of this study is to examine the effect of gendered aspects of work and family conflict on life satisfaction. The data were collected from two major public universities in Turkey, and 349 dual-earner family members were reached by using random sampling method. The study employed linear regression analysis to predict the effect of work and family conflict on women's and men's life satisfaction. The regression analysis model explained 21% of the life satisfaction of women while it explained 20% of the life satisfaction of men. According to the findings, women's life satisfaction was predicted by both strain-based work-to-family conflict and strain-based family-to-work conflict. The life satisfaction of men, however, was only predicted by strain-based family-to-work conflict. In light of the results, the contribution of the study to the literature was highlighted.

DOI: 10.4018/978-1-6684-6567-7.ch010

INTRODUCTION

Work and family occupy a large part of an individuals life. Since work and family are often physically and temporally separate, early research considered work and family systems as two independent operating systems. However, by the 1970s, research findings on work and family life revealed that events at work affect family life, and events at family affect work life that started to reflect an open system approach and the permeability between them (Clark, 2000; Katz & Kahn, 1978).

It is well established in the work and family literature that this permeability between family and work creates work and family conflict. That is, participation in the work (family) role makes it difficult to participate in the family (work) role. The conflict occurs "when time devoted to the requirements of one role makes it difficult to fulfill the requirements of another, strain from participation in one role makes it difficult to fulfill the requirements of another and specific behaviors required by one role make it difficult to fulfill the requirements of another." (Greenhaus & Beutell, 1985).

Work and family conflict is bidirectional, from work to family and from family to work (Frone et al., 1992). Low spouse support, young children, and spouse employment are one of the most important factors in the conflict coming from the family domain (family-to-work conflict) excessive work hours, inflexibility of the work schedule, and work overload are the most important ones in the conflict coming from the work domain (work-to-family conflict) (Greenhaus & Beutell, 1985).

Previous research has shown that work and family conflict generates negative consequences on individuals' life, which is consistently found to be one of the factors impacting life satisfaction (Yucel, 2017). The study conducted by Coşkuner (2013) showed that conflict experienced in both work and family areas negatively affects life satisfaction. Accordingly, the time devoted to work and the perceived workload negatively affect life satisfaction through work-to-family conflict while the perceived family burden undermines the life satisfaction through family-to-work conflict. Yucel's study (2017) found a negative correlatoon between that work-to-family conflict and life satisfaction.

It can be said that the most researched variable in relation to conflict in the work and family literature is sex (Jones & Mckenna, 2002; Reynolds, 2005). The reason for this is the traditional gender roles approach. Behind this approach lies the reflection of biological sex-based characteristics on the roles of men and women, thus resulting in culturally and socially constructed sex roles. According to this, while the primary responsibility of the man is to provide for the economic life of the house and to meet the needs; the primary responsibility of women is limited to the home and is responsible for the care of children and household activities. (Parsons & Bales, 1955). From this point of view, the gender roles approach assumes that the nature of the role demands varies in men and women (Barnett et al., 1995). For this reason, women's employment and their involvement in work life are considered to be the most important cause of work and family conflict. Because even if the woman works, her responsibilities at home do not disappear or decrease; feel their responsibilities about home and family much more than men (Watkins, 1995). This situation increases the role burden of working women. Women, who have primary responsibilities both at home and at work, may face an excessive role load while trying to fulfill these responsibilities at the same time, and this may cause women to experience work and family conflict (expecially family-to-work) more than men (Bacharach et al., 1991).

Therefore, this study was conducted in order to examine both aspects of the work and family conflict (work-to-family conflict and family-to-work conflict) on the basis of sex, and to determine to what extent this conflict has an impact on the life satisfaction of male and female participants. In this sense, the questions to be answered in this study are as follows:

1) Does sex affect the level of work-to-family conflict?
2) Does sex affect the level of family-to-work conflict?
3) What is the effect of the work-to-family conflict and family-to-work conflict on life satisfaction of women?
4) What is the effect of the work-to-family conflict and family-to-work conflict on life satisfaction of men?

BACKGROUND

The relationship between work and family has attracted the attention of various sciences and fields of study (organizational behavior and human resources management, industrial and organizational psychology, clinical psychology, population science, family sociology, family science, gerontology, occupational psychology, etc.) for many years (Voydanoff, 2008). In the relationship between work and family, the "non-relationship" view had an important place in the past. The advocate of this view, Kanter (1977), argued that work and family are independent fields and that there is no relationship between them, and defended this view under the name of the Myth of Separate Worlds. This view is that work and family are two separate worlds governed by their own rules; therefore, he argues that these two areas should be examined separately, independently of each other. (Huang et al., 2004). In this view, with the traditional approach, the family, which is the paradise of peace and comfort, is the place of the woman, while the work environment, where there is competition and tension, was seen as a man's world. (Piotrkowski et al., 1987). According to

Voydanoff (1987), this view is a product of gender role ideology, and according to this ideology, men work outside the home in a paid job to support their family; the woman, on the other hand, carries out the domestic activities as a wife and mother.

The Myth of Separate Worlds was later replaced by the acceptance that work and family are not two separate worlds from research results that the relationship between them is dynamic and reciprocal due to the increase in the number of dual-income families (Gordon & Kambeyer, 1980; Johnson, 1980) in parallel with the increase in the number of working women with the industrial revolution, and with the impact of changes in expectations about individual satisfaction (Yankelovich, 1981). This view argues that changes in the family (work) should examine with the changes at work (family) (Huang et al., 2004).

After the view that there is a reciprocal relationship between work and family was supported by studies, subsequent research focused on how the family and work area affect each other, and the view that work and family roles affect each other negatively has been widely accepted. This view includes adjustment disorder between work and family roles (Cartwright, 1978), work and family interaction problems (Burke et al., 1980), work and family incompatibility (Jones & Butler, 1980), work and family tension (Kelly & Voydanoff, 1985) and finally work and family conflict (Greenhaus & Beutell, 1985).

The view that work and family roles compete with each other is generally supported by the *Role Strain Theory* (Goode, 1960) and *Role Conflict* (Kahn et al., 1964). Role strain is the difficulty experienced in fulfilling role responsibilities. This difficulty arises because of the lack of resources (e.g. time, energy) required to meet the demands of the roles, the role responsibilities that can only be fulfilled at a certain time and a certain place, the behaviors required by the roles conflict with each other, the fulfillment of the responsibilities of one role make it difficult to fulfill the responsibilities of the other role, and the role creates a wide variety of behavioral demands (Goode, 1960). Role conflict is the simultaneous occurrence of compliance with one of two or more role expectations in a way that makes it difficult to comply with the other. Greenhaus and Beutell (1985) defined family and work conflict as a type of interrole conflict in which role expectations related to work and family fields are mutually incompatible in some aspects. They stated that there are three basic types of work and family conflict. These are time-based, strain-based, and behavior-based conflicts (Greenhaus & Beutell, 1985).

Time-based conflict arises from multiple roles competing with each other in terms of time. Time spent on the requirements of one role cannot be spent on the requirements of another role. Strain-based conflict is when a stressful situation in one role negatively affects the performance of the other role. In this case, the pressure in one role makes it difficult to adapt to the demands of the other role, and in this way the roles become incompatible with each other. Behavior-based conflict is when the specific behavior patterns of one role are incompatible with the behavior expectations of the other role (Greenhaus & Beutell, 1985). Later, another conflict type was added to these 3 conflict types and named as psychological conflict. Psychologically-based conflict is when an individual is mentally busy with another role while physically fulfilling a role, and this situation negatively affects the activities in the physically fulfilled role (Van Steenbergen et al., 2007). An individual can experience only one of these conflict types, or they can experience all of them at the same time depending on the conditions they are in. Work and family conflict is bidirectional, from work to family and from family to work. Work-to-family conflict is the conflict from work to family that occurs as a result of the interference of work with the family while family-to-work conflict is the is the conflict from family to work that occurs as a result of the interference of family with the work (Frone et al., 1992).

METHOD

Procedure and Sample

In this study, it was planned to determine the effect of work and family conflict on life satisfaction of women and men and to discuss the results of the study in terms of gender roles. The population of the research consisted of dual-earner family members from two major public university employees. The study was conducted with 349 participants using the Simple Random Sampling Method.

Measures

The data of the research were collected through interviews with the participants who voluntarily agreed to participate in the research through a questionnaire. The questionnaire form included demographic information about the participants (sex, age, education level, number of children, etc.), Work and Family Conflict Scale to determine the level of work and family conflict, and Life Satisfaction Scale to determine life satisfaction of the participants.

Work and Family Conflict: In order to measure the work and family conflict levels of the participants, the work-family conflict items of the "Work and Family Relationship Scale" developed by Van Stenbergen et al. (2007) were used. The scale consists of 18 items including 3 dimensions (time based, strain based and psychological based) from work to family and from family to work. Items were measured using 5-point scales (1= strongly disagree, 5= strongly agree). High scores on the scale indicate high work and family conflict. Internal reliability of dimensions for time-based work-to-family conflict, .77; strain-based work-to-family conflict, .88;

psychological-based work-to-family conflict .88; time-based family-to-work conflict, .74; strain-based family-to-work conflict, .92; psychological-based family-to-work conflict, .82 (Van Stenbergen et al., 2007). In this study, the internal reliability of the sub-dimensions was .77 for time based work-to-family conflict; strain based work-to-family conflict, .88; psychological based work-to-family conflict .88; time based family-to-work conflict, .74; strain based family-to-work conflict, .92; and psychological based family-to-work conflict was found to be .82.

Life Satisfaction: The Satisfaction with Life Scale (SWLS), developed by Diener et al. (1985), was used to measure the life satisfaction of participants. Items were measured using 5-point scales (1= strongly disagree, 5= strongly agree). High scores on the scale indicate high life satisfaction. The internal reliability of the scale was reported as .87 by the researchers (Diener et al., 1985). In this study, the internal reliability of the scale was found to be .90.

Data Analysis

The data of the research were evaluated in SPSS.21 program. Demographic and descriptive information about the participants are presented with descriptive statistics such as frequency, percentage, mean and standard deviation. In order to determine whether the participants' work and family conflict and its sub-dimensions differ according to sex, the Two Sample T-test was applied. Multiple Linear Regression Analysis was performed to determine the effects of work-family conflict on life satisfaction of women and men.

RESULTS

Demographic Characteristics of Participants

Of the 349 individuals participating in the study, 61.0% were female and 39.0% were male. The mean age of the participants was =40.6 ±7.8. Among the participants, those with a graduate degree are leading with 46.7%, followed by those who stated that they have undergraduate degrees with 29.2%, high school and less with 13.6%, and associate degree with 10.6%. When the participants were examined in terms of job classification, staff comprised 56.7% of the participants and 43.3% of the faculty. While the average number of children the participants had was =1.65 ±0.7, the mean age of the youngest child they had was found to be =8.72 ±6.56 (Table 1).

Table 1. Distribution of participants by demographic characteristics

Variable		f	%		Std. Deviation
Sex	Women	213	61.0		
	Men	136	39.0		
Age				40.6	7.8
Education	High school and below	47	13.5		
	Community college	37	10.6		
	Undergraduate	102	29.2		
	Graduate	163	46.7		
Job classification	Faculty	151	43.3		
	Staff	198	56.7		
Number of children				1.65	0.7
Age of the youngest child				8.72	6.56
Total		**349**	**100**		

Work and Family Conflict and Life Satifaction

The average scores of work and family conflict, sub-dimensions of conflicts and life satisfaction of the individuals participating in the study are given in Table 2. Since a low or high cut-off point is not specified for each scale and sub-dimensions, it is not possible to qualify as high or low average scores of the participants. However, it can be said that the average values in the table are not too far or too close to the minimum and maximum values (Table 2).

Table 2. Descriptive statistics on work and family conflict, sub-dimensions, and life satisfaction of the participants

Scales	Min.	Max.		Std. Deviation
Time based work-to-family conflict	3	15	8.09	3.18
Strain based work-to-family conflict	3	15	8.84	2.94
Psychological based work-to-family conflict	3	15	7.48	2.77
Work-to-family conflict	9	45	24.40	6.97
Time based family-to-work conflict	3	15	7.46	2.75
Strain based family-to-work conflict	3	15	6.77	2.58
Psychological based family-to-work conflict	3	15	7.46	2.54
Family-to-work conflict	9	45	21.70	6.36
Life satisfaction	5	25	17.54	4.48

The Relationship of Work and Family Conflit and Its Sub-Dimensions With Sex

In the study, in order to determine whether the participants' work and family conflict and its sub-dimensions differ according to sex, the Two-sample t-Test was applied.

When the work-to-family conflict average scores of the female and male participants were examined; it was seen that the averages of both sexes were quite close to each other (women: =24.38, men: =24.44). Not surprisingly, the difference between the two averages was not statistically significant ($p>0.05$). A similar situation is also valid for the sub-dimensions of the work-to-family conflict. According to this, the difference between the mean of time based work-to-family conflict, strain based work-to-family conflict and psychological based work-to-family conflict of male and female participants was not found statistically significant ($p>0.05$)

Another aspect of work and family conflict is family-to-work conflict. Table 3 shows that the average scores of both female and male participants on the family-to-work conflict scale are very close to each other. The Two-sample t-Test performed also showed that the difference in scores between the two averages was not statistically significant ($p>0.05$). This is also the case for the family-to-work conflict sub-dimensions the average scores were not statistically significant according to sex ($p>0.05$) (Table 3).

MULTIPLE LINEAR REGRESSION ANALYSIS

Predicting Effect of Work and Family Conflict on Life Satisfaction of Women

The results of the regression analysis regarding the prediction of the effect of work-to-family and family-to-work conflict on the life satisfaction of female participants are given in Table 4. As a result of the analysis, a significant regression model was obtained ($F=8.891$, $p=.000$). This means model significantly predicts life satisfaction. The independent variables in the model explain approximately 21% of the total variance in life satisfaction of female participants ($R^2=.206$). Relative order of importance of independent variables on life satisfaction according to the standardized regression coefficient strain based family-to-work conflict, strain based work-to-family conflict, psychological based family-to-work conflict, time based work-to-family conflict, psychological based work-to-family conflict and time based family-to-work conflict (Table 4).

Table 3. Two-sample t-Test results on work and family conflict and sub-dimensions of participants by sex

Work and Family Conflict	Sex		Std	t	p
Time based work-to-family conflict	Women	8.19	3.26	.748	.455
	Men	7.93	3.06		
Strain based work-to-family conflict	Women	8.74	2.96	-.754	.451
	Men	8.98	2.92		
Psychological based work-to-family conflict	Women	7.45	2.72	.-258	.796
	Men	7.53	2.86		
Work-to-family conflict	Women	24.38	7.19	-.079	.937
	Men	24.44	6.65		
Time based family-to-work conflict	Women	7.55	2.83	.786	.432
	Men	7.32	2.62		
Strain based family-to-work conflict	Women	6.76	2.62	-.135	.893
	Men	6.79	2.52		
Psychological based family-to-work conflict	Women	7.53	2.60	.609	.543
	Men	7.36	2.45		
Family-to-work conflict	Women	21.84	6.51	.529	.597
	Men	21.47	6.13		

Table 4. Multiple linear analysis results for prediction of life satisfaction of women

Model	Unstandardized Coefficients		Standardized Coefficients			Correlations	
	B	Std. Error	Beta	t	Sig.	Partial	Part
Constant	24.984	1.151		21.698	.000		
Time based work-to-family conflict	-.081	.119	-.058	-.679	.498	-.047	-.042
Strain based work-to-family conflict	-.285	.125	-.186	-2.291	.023	-.058	-.142
Psychological based work-to-family conflict	-.049	.123	-.030	-.402	.688	-.028	-.025
Time based family-to-work conflict	.043	.125	.027	.344	.732	.024	.021
Strain based family-to-work conflict	-.418	.146	-.241	-2.860	.005	-.195	-.178
Psychological based family-to-work conflict	-.165	.138	-.095	-1.195	.233	-.083	-.074

When the Two-sample t-Test results regarding the significance of the regression coefficient are examined, it is seen that strain based family-to-work conflict (B=-.418, t=-2.860, p=.005) and strain based work-to-family conflict (B=-.285)., t=-2.291, p=.023) was found to be a significant predictor of life satisfaction. Accordingly, a one-unit increase in strain based family-to-work conflict causes a decrease of .418 in life satisfaction. And, a one-unit increase in strain based work-to-family conflict causes a decrease of .285 in life satisfaction. Other variables alone do not have a statistically significant effect on life satisfaction (p>0.05) (Table 4).

Predicting Effect of Work and Family Conflict on Life Satisfaction of Men

The results of the regression analysis regarding the prediction of the effect of work-to-family and family-to-work conflict on the life satisfaction of male participants are given in Table 5. As a result of the analysis, a significant regression model was obtained (F=5.297, p=.000). This means model significantly predicts life satisfaction. The independent variables in the model explain approximately 20% of the total variance in life satisfaction of male participants (R^2=.198). Relative order of importance of independent variables on life satisfaction according to the standardized regression coefficient strain based family-to-work conflict, strain based work-to-family conflict, psychological based work-to-family conflict, psychological based family-to-work conflict, time based work-to-family conflict and time based family-to-work conflict (Table 5).

When the Two-sample t-Test results regarding the significance of the regression coefficient were examined, it was seen that strain based family-to-work conflict (B=-.731, t=-3.787, p=.000) was a significant predictor of life satisfaction. Accordingly, a one-unit increase in strain based family-to-work conflict causes a decrease of .731 in life satisfaction. Other variables alone do not have a significant effect on life satisfaction (p>0.05) (Table 5).

DISCUSSION

The overall aim of the present study was to determine the effect of the work-to-family conflict and family-to-work conflict on life satisfaction and discuss the results in the view of gender roles.

Hammer et al. (1997) argued that most men still maintain full involvement in their work because their spouse assume the responsibility for housework and caring from the point of gender roles. So, it can be said that men tend to experience more work-to-family conflict than women in relatively traditional cultures like Turkey

Table 5. Multiple linear analysis results for prediction of life satisfaction of men

Model	Unstandardized Coefficients		Standardized Coefficients			Correlations	
	B	Std. Error	Beta	t	Sig.	Partial	Part
Constant	23.070	1.495		15.428	.000		
Time based work-to-family conflict	.013	.151	.009	.083	.934	.007	.007
Strain based work-to-family conflict	-.193	.137	-.129	-1.414	.160	-.124	-.112
Psychological based work-to-family conflict	.074	.154	.048	.478	.634	.042	.038
Time based family-to-work conflict	.014	.174	.008	.080	.936	.007	.006
Strain based family-to-work conflict	-.731	.193	-.422	-3.787	.000	-.316	-.299
Psychological based family-to-work conflict	.017	.201	.086	.086	.932	.008	.007

(Hammer et al., 1997). The study results, hovever, showed that the scores of the participants in the work-to-family conflict and its sub-dimensions scale did not differ according to sex. In other words, the level of the scores of work-to-family conflict and its sub-dimensions of women and men were not statistically different from each other. The research examining the relationship between work-to-family conflict and sex has reported different results. Wang et al.'s (2020) in China showed that women experience more work-to-family conflict than men. Consistently, Antalyalı & Çarıkçı's (2007) study found a significant difference between the sexes in terms of work-to-family conflict. Accordingly, female participants experience more work-to-family conflict than males.

Time required for housework and caring for the family are one of the most important factors in family-to-work conflict, especially in families with children. So, the dual-earner couples with children tend to have more family-to-work conflict and a higher level of stress than their counterparts with no children (Michel & Hargis, 2008). Furthermore, from the view of gender roles, it can not be a surprise that women have more family-to-work conflict than men. In the present study, however, the scores of the participants in the family-to-work conflict and its sub-dimensions scale did not differ by sex. That means the level of the scores of work-to-family conflict and its sub-dimensions of women and men were not statistically different from each other. This contrary result could be due to various reasons. First, since all participants are dual-earner family members, all male participants may contribute to chores or caring to ease the burden of their working wives even though it is a help rather than a share. Second, since the youngest child of the participants is of school age (=8.72), women could have relatively less childcare responsibilities that brings less family-to-work conflict. Third, the adoption of egalitarian gender roles by spouses in the family or the paid help for housework may also the other explanations of why women's conflict scores were not higher than men. The literature is divided on this subject. In other words, while some repot that women have more work-to-family conflicts in societies with traditional gender role understanding, some studies have documented the opposite. For instance, a study conducted by Wang et al. (2020) in China, which has relatively similar characteristics to Turkey in terms of traditional gender roles found men experience more family-to-work conflict than women. Further, the study also documented individuals who held traditional gender roles have both lower work-to-family conflict and family-to-work conflict.

Research has shown that conflict from either work-to-family or family-to-work can lead to a decrease in satisfaction, including life satisfaction, marital satisfaction, and job satisfaction (Netemeyer et al., 1996). In the present study, regression analysis was applied to male and female participants separately in order to determine the effect of work and family conflict on life satisfaction according to sex. The regression model created for female participants showed that family and work conflict had an effect on women's life satisfaction. The model explained approximately 21% of women's life satisfaction. In the model, it was seen that both types of conflict based on tension (strain based work-to-family conflict and strain based family-to-work conflict) alone have an important effect on women's life satisfaction. Accordingly, both the work's intervention that creates tension for the family and the family's intervention that creates tension in the family negatively affect women's life satisfaction. The time that family members allocate for the family is affected by the working situation (Shelton, 1992). Working in a paid job in the family reduces the time and energy that she will spend on her primary responsibilities in the family due to traditional gender roles and creates tension. It is inevitable that the negative effect of tension-based conflict, which is true both from the job to the family and from the family, on life satisfaction also reduces the quality of life of women.

The regression model created for male participants showed that family and work conflict had an effect on men's life satisfaction. The model explained approximately 20% of men's life satisfaction. Within the model, it was seen that the effect of strain based family-to-work conflict on life satisfaction of men was significant. Accordingly, the intervention of family that creates tension in the work negatively affects men's life satisfaction.

CONCLUSION AND SUGGESTIONS

It is an accepted fact today that work and family roles are the two most central roles in human life, and they both affect and are affected by each other. Due to these features, it is possible that the demands for these roles sometimes conflict with each other by exceeding the resources of the individuals. In this study, it was aimed to determine what effect the work and conflict had on the life satisfaction of both women and men and whether the level of conflict between work and family roles differs according to sex. The reason why the study focused on the sex stems from traditional gender roles. Within the framework of traditional gender roles, since women's work outside the home will not remove their primary responsibilities at home, it is predicted that the level of work and family conflict of women will be higher than that of men, and their life satisfaction will be more negatively affected by work and family conflict than men. The results, hovewer, partially confirmed this prediction. The level of work and family conflict of women (work-to-family conflict and family-to-work conflict) was not statistically higher than that of the men. The effect of work and family conflict on life satisfaction is almost close to each other in both sexes. Family and work conflict explained about 21% of the variance in women's life satisfaction while it explained about 20% of the variance in men's life satisfaction. The effect of strain-based work-to-family conflict on life satisfaction is statistically significant in both sexes. Therefore, family friendly workplace arragements place an important role to ease work-to-family conflict of workers. Workplace flexibility, expansion of family leave, paid sick days can be counted among these arrangements (Trask, 2017)..

The study results also showed that the strain-based family-work-to-conflict significantly affected women's life satisfaction, not men's. The effect of the strain-based family-to-work conflict on the life satisfaction of women can be explained by the traditional gender roles mentioned above. Even if the woman has a paid job, the fact that she is still primarily responsible for the activities carried out in the family causes strain-based family-to-conflict and undermines her life satisfaction. In this sense, family support holds higher importance, especially coming from the spouse to ease the women's family burden.

The fact that there was no significant difference between the levels of both work-family conflict and family-work conflict levels of male and female participants in the study is thought to be related to the sample selection of the research. In order to ensure as much homogeneity among the participants as possible in the study, it was ensured that the participants whose spouses never worked or did not work full-time were excluded from the scope, and that the work and family conflict levels of both female and male participants were determined under equal conditions. It is thought that the method followed in this study will shed light on future studies based on sex comparisons, especially on family-to-work conflict.

LIMITATIONS

This study is not without limitations. First, the cross-sectional research design of the study fails to infer the causal relationships between the variables. Determining the causal relationships between the variables can only detect by the longitudinal research method. Second, the quantitative nature of the study has not been designed to respond to the question "how" from the participants to explore the hidden dynamics between work and family in gender base. Only qualitative research will be more effective at determining how events that occur in the work and family sphere are influenced by one another using small samples because quantitative studies have a generalization objective and are conducted on large sample groups.

REFERENCES

Antalyalı, O. I., & Çarıkçı, I. H. (2007). Gender effect on work family conflict among managers. *Journal of Suleyman Demirel University Institue of Social Sciences, 6*, 117–127.

Bacharach, S. B., Bamberger, P., & Conley, S. (1991). Work home conflict among nurses and engineers: Mediating the impact of role stress on burnout and satisfaction at work. *Journal of Organizational Behavior, 12*(1), 39–53. doi:10.1002/job.4030120104

Barnett, R. C., Raudenbush, S. W., Brennan, R. T., Pleck, J. H., & Marshall, N. L. (1995). Changes in job and marital experience and change in psychological distress: A longitudinal study of dual-earner couples. *Journal of Personality and Social Psychology, 69*(5), 839–850. doi:10.1037/0022-3514.69.5.839 PMID:7473034

Burke, R. J., Weir, T., & Duwors, R. E. Jr. (1980). Work demands on administrators and spouse well-being. *Human Relations, 33*(4), 253–278. doi:10.1177/001872678003300404

Cartwright, L. K. (1978). Career satisfaction and role harmony in a sample of young women physicians. *Journal of Vocational Behavior, 12*(2), 184–196. doi:10.1016/0001-8791(78)90033-7

Clark, S. C. (2000). Work/family border theory. *Human Relations, 53*(6), 747–770. doi:10.1177/0018726700536001

Coşkuner, S. (2013). *Work-family conflict as a mediator between work-family characteristics and marital, family and life satisfaction of faculty members* [Unpublished doctoral thesis]. Hacettepe University Graduate School of Social Sciences.

Diener, E., Emmons, R. A., Larsen, R. J., & Griffin, S. (1985). The satisfaction with life scale. *Journal of Personality Assessment, 49*(1), 71–75. doi:10.120715327752jpa4901_13 PMID:16367493

Frone, M. R., Russell, M., & Cooper, M. L. (1992). Antecedents and outcomes of work family conflict: Testing a model of the work family ınterface. *The Journal of Applied Psychology, 77*(1), 65–78. doi:10.1037/0021-9010.77.1.65 PMID:1556042

Goode, W. J. (1960). A theory of role strain. *American Sociological Review, 25*(4), 483–496. doi:10.2307/2092933

Gordon, H. A., & Kammeyer, K. C. W. (1980). The gainful employment of women with small children. *Journal of Marriage and Family, 42*(2), 327–336. doi:10.2307/351230

Greenhaus, J. H., & Beutell, N. J. (1985). Sources of conflict between work and family roles. *Academy of Management Review, 10*(1), 76–88. doi:10.2307/258214

Hammer, L. B., Allen, B., & Grigsby, T. D. (1997). Work-family conflict in dual-earner couples: Within-individual and crossover effects of work and family. *Journal of Vocational Behavior, 50*(2), 185–203. doi:10.1006/jvbe.1996.1557

Huang, Y. H., Hammer, L. B., Neal, M. B., & Perrin, N. A. (2004). The relationship between work-to-Family conflict and family-to-work conflict: A longitudinal study. *Journal of Family and Economic Issues, 25*(1), 79–100. doi:10.1023/B:JEEI.0000016724.76936.a1

Johnson, B. L. (1980). Marital and family characteristics of the labor force. *Monthly Labor Review, 103*(4), 48–52.

Jones, A. P., & Butler, M. C. (1980). A role transition approach to the stresses of organizationally-induced family role disruption. *Journal of Marriage and Family, 42*(2), 367–376. doi:10.2307/351234

Jones, W. M., & Mckenna, J. (2002). Women and work-home conflict: A dual paradigm approach. *Health Education, 102*(5), 249–259. doi:10.1108/09654280210444128

Kahn, R. L., Wolfe, D. M., Quinn, R., Snoek, J. D., & Rosenthal, R. A. (1964). *Organizational stress: Studies in role conflict and ambiguity*. Wiley.

Kanter, R. M. (1977). *Work and family in the united states: A critical review and agenda for research and policy*. Russell Sage Foundation.

Katz, D., & Kahn, R. L. (1978). The social psychology of organizations (2nd ed.). Wiley.

Michel, J. S., & Hargis, B. (2008). Linking mechanisms of work-family conflict and segmentation. *Journal of Vocational Behavior*, *73*(3), 509–522. doi:10.1016/j.jvb.2008.09.005

Netemeyer, R. G., Boles, J. S., & McMurrian, R. (1996). Development and validation of work–family conflict and family–work conflict scales. *Journal of Applied Psychology*, *81*(4), 400–410. https://doi.org/10.1037/0021-9010.81.4.400

Parsons, T. & Bales, R. F. (1955). *Family, socialization and interaction process*. Academic Press.

Piotrkowski, C. (1979). *Work and the family system*. Macmillan.

Reynolds, J. (2005). In the face of conflict: Work-life adjustments and desired work hour adjustments. *Journal of Marriage and Family*, *67*(5), 1313–1331. doi:10.1111/j.1741-3737.2005.00219.x

Shelton, B. A. (1992). *Women, men, and time: Gender a differences in paid work, housework, and leisure*. Greenwood.

Trask, B. S. (2017). Alleviating the stress on working families: Promoting family-friendly workplace policies. *National Council of Family Relations Policy Brief*, *2*(1). Retrieved June 5, 2022, from https://www.ncfr.org/sites/default/files/2017-01/ncfr_policy_brief_january_2017.pdf

Van Steenbergen, E. F., Ellemers, N., & Mooijaart, A. (2007). How work and family can facilitate each other? Distinct types of work-family facilitation and outcomes for women and men. *Journal of Occupational Health Psychology*, *12*(3), 279–300. doi:10.1037/1076-8998.12.3.279 PMID:17638494

Voydanoff, P. (1987). *Work and family life*. Sage Publications.

Voydanoff, P. (2008). A conceptual model of the work-family interface. In L. Lero, D.S. Korabik, & K. Karen (Eds.), Handbook of work-family integration: Research, theory, and best practices (pp: 37-55). Whitehead. doi:10.1016/B978-012372574-5.50006-5

Voydanoff, P., & Kelly, R. F. (1984). Determinants of Work-Related Family Problems among Employed Parents. *Journal of Marriage and Family*, *46*(4), 881. doi:10.2307/352536

Wang, H. M., Ma, A. L., & Guo, T. T. (2020). Gender concept, work pressure, and work–family conflict. *American Journal of Men's Health, 14*(5). doi:10.1177/1557988320957522

Watkins, K. E. (1995). Changing managers' defensive reasoning about work/family conflicts. *Journal of Management Development, 14*(2), 77-88.

Yankelovich, D. (1981). *New rules: Searching for self-fulfillment in a world turned upside down*. Random House.

Yucel, D. (2017). Work-to-family conflict and life satisfaction: The moderating role of type of employment. *Applied Research in Quality of Life*, *12*(3), 577–591. doi:10.100711482-016-9477-4

Chapter 11
From Resistance to Readiness:
Leveraging Neuroscience Perspectives for Successful Change Management in the Manufacturing Sector

Ashlita Florence Lopez
https://orcid.org/0009-0008-1643-5371
CHRIST University (Deemed), India

Sebin Joy
https://orcid.org/0000-0001-9007-6786
CHRIST University (Deemed), India

Arti Arun Kumar
CHRIST University (Deemed), India

ABSTRACT

Change initiatives often encounter resistance from employees, impeding successful implementation. Leveraging insights from neuroscience can provide valuable guidance in navigating this resistance and promoting readiness for change. Social experiences in a work environment affect the brain positively or negatively. By understanding the brain's response to change, change managers can create a supportive environment and communicate accordingly. This study examines the impact of social experiences on readiness to change among employees in the manufacturing sector from a neuroscience perspective. SCARF is a neuroscience-based model that evaluates five dimensions of social experiences such as status, certainty, autonomy, relatedness, and fairness. This quantitative study is based on data collected from different manufacturing organisations. The results of this study provide insights into how change managers can address these social domains to promote successful change initiatives and improve employee readiness to change.

DOI: 10.4018/978-1-6684-6567-7.ch011

INTRODUCTION

Change management is a critical process for any organisation looking to implement change. In this process, people, teams, and organisations are moved from their current states to the desired future ones using a systematic strategy. Controlling the evolution of production systems, processes, and technology is crucial in the manufacturing industry. The manufacturing sector has changed significantly in recent years as a result of globalisation, technical improvements, and changes in consumer behaviour. Manufacturers are under increasing pressure to respond to these developments in order to maintain their competitive position and meet shifting consumer expectations. They must constantly improve their practices, structures, and products if they want to remain competitive. One of the important elements of change management in the industrial sector is managing the impact of change on employees.

Workers are an essential part of the production process because labour-intensive industrial procedures are typically involved. Therefore, it is imperative to make sure that employees receive the necessary training and assistance to enable them to adapt to new practices, systems, and technology. For employees, change can be difficult and disruptive. Employees may experience fear, uncertainty, and discomfort, and these feelings may have an impact on how motivated and productive they are. Change may be challenging when humans are involved, especially when it requires stepping outside of one's usual comfort zone and into an unfamiliar environment. With changes come new positions, responsibilities, difficulties, and opposing viewpoints. As a result, the entire process must be skilfully handled. People typically become confused and fight the process when the future is unclear to them (Dhingra & Punia, 2016).

In order to ensure a smooth transition, it is crucial to manage the emotional effect of change on employees. This entails giving staff members the knowledge, resources, and support they need to comprehend the change and its effects. To promote employee engagement and buy-in, it is critical to include them in the change process and solicit their thoughts and comments.

The SCARF model is a neuroscience-based framework that describes how people react to social circumstances that cause five domains of threat or reward: Status, Certainty, Autonomy, Relatedness, and Fairness. These categories are important for change management because they frequently result in threats or rewards for employees who work in the manufacturing sector, which can affect how they emotionally react to the change. During an incident, the SCARF language may be helpful for recognising dangers as well as handling emotions. There is evidence to support the idea that labelling and revaluating emotions can aid in managing them. (Campbell et al., 2022). This research paper seeks to explore the synergistic relationship between change management and the SCARF model, delving into how incorporating SCARF principles can enhance the implementation of successful organizational change. By examining the impact of each SCARF element on employees' readiness to change, this study aims to provide valuable insights into tailoring change strategies that address psychological needs, foster engagement, and facilitate a smoother transition, ultimately contributing to the achievement of sustainable and positive change outcomes.

Research Questions

1) Is the SCARF model significant in the manufacturing industry for change management?
2) Do social experiences such as status, certainty, autonomy, relatedness, and fairness have any impact on the readiness to change?

The subject of this paper makes an effort to investigate how the SCARF model and change management among workers in the manufacturing sector interact. Each of these characteristics, coupled with demographic criteria like age, duration of experience, and role in the firm, will have an impact on how willing and proactive individuals are to participate in the process of execution. Additionally, the study seeks to pinpoint best practices and approaches that can enhance the results of change implementation and to provide suggestions for professionals on how to successfully navigate the difficulties of managing change using the SCARF model.

BACKGROUND

In the current economic situation, organisations are having to deal with larger and more frequent changes. A changing economy, an empowered workforce, and technological improvements have all contributed to a situation in which change is now the one thing that never changes (Bold, 2011). Any organization must effectively manage change if it hopes to succeed in the contemporary, intensely competitive, and ever-changing business environment (By, 2007). Numerous different approaches have been used to conceptualise, research, and analyse organisational transformation. Organizations' natural response to change is typically reactive, discontinuous, ad hoc, and frequently precipitated by an organisational crisis since the need for change is frequently unanticipated. Different types of change have, as one might anticipate, prompted various organisational responses. (Hudescu & Ilies, 2011)). Findings imply that managers must engage with five factors in order to achieve change: organisation, internal resources, outside consultants, supplier ties, and customer relations (Nguyen et al., 2015).

Importance of Change in an Organisation

In today's rapidly evolving business landscape, organizational agility is a critical factor for success and survival. Change, as an inherent part of adaptation and growth, plays a pivotal role in cultivating agility within organisations. However, change initiatives often encounter resistance and challenges, highlighting the significance of effective change leadership. In this context, all firms are starting to realise how important it is to develop the capability to change successfully and quickly (Bold, 2011). It is important to characterise organisational change and change inside an organisation in terms of both the speed and extent of organisational change. Organisational transformation, regardless of how swiftly it happens, is a company's progression from its existing plateau to its anticipated future condition in order to increase the efficiency and effectiveness of the organisation (Pryor et al., 2022). The theories will be more solid and applicable to all sorts of change, and guidance for practitioners will be more useful. (Anthony & Dibella, 2010). A crucial step any business must take to properly implement new technology in the workplace is to determine who will be affected and how, whether directly or indirectly. Since both the number of people affected and the velocity of change will continue to dramatically rise, this is a critical worry for companies as they progressively transition to data-rich, networked settings. (Fisher & Wesolkowski, 1999).

Resistance of Employees to Change

. It is becoming more and more crucial for firms to react quickly to changes in the environment (Baird & Wang, 2010). Resistance to change, preparation for change, effective leadership, employee engagement and participation in change initiatives, and the roles and competencies required to ensure the success of strategic change are among the themes that reoccur most frequently (Bateh et al., 2013). Employees at all levels have this mental model, which hinders the effective implementation of change. The relative strength of each element producing the resistance and how it varies by stakeholder group must be identified by organisations that want to overcome resistance to change. The best strategies for lessening resistance can then be used once this has been established (Schweiger et al., 2018).

There are still several differences in the resistance-related events that are viewed and, eventually, operationalized. Many authors have provided definitions that are so inclusive that they might cover practically every adverse response, force, or obstacle that opposes or limits change. These concepts have additionally suggested that resistance to change is a challenge that must be resolved or eradicated (Erwin & Garman, 2010).

The readiness of organisation members to embrace change can occasionally be influenced by prior experiences with change, particularly if those changes went poorly. Therefore, managers must integrate a variety of strategies, including education and communication, negotiation and agreement, participation and involvement, and explicit and implicit coercion, to manage resistant situations. At the organisational level, organisational culture, external variables, leadership style, and technological impact all have an impact on how change-ready an organisation is (Alolabi et al., 2021).

The study found that readiness for change significantly mediated the relationship between transformational leadership and employee performance, and that readiness for change also significantly influenced the relationship between transformational leadership and employee performance (Asbari et al., 2021). It is asserted that aware individuals are better able to overcome cognitive distortions, anticipate opportunities rather than threats in change, deal with paradoxes, and control the negative arousal that frequently accompanies organisational change. On the organisational level, it is suggested that organising processes create organisational cultures that are more receptive to learning, open communication, supportive working relationships, and participatory decision-making, which increase readiness (Gartner, 2013).

Although, any change process will inevitably encounter resistance. Resistance may be better understood as an effort to rediscover purpose or to preserve what was valuable in the past, as opposed to being interpreted negatively. The various experiences and meanings of change are usually ignored in discussions of it. Change may be both a threat and an opportunity, a reason for sadness and joy, unexpected and expected, regulated and uncontrolled. (Antonacopoulou & Gabriel, 2001).

Effects of Change Management in the Manufacturing Sector

Two aspects of the current business climate are the escalating worldwide competition and the quickening development of manufacturing technologies. Quality, cost-effectiveness, and responsiveness to market changes have become the business's strategic priority as a result of these factors working together. Manufacturers are increasingly realising that effective human resource management and proper positioning of advanced manufacturing technology (AMT) are essential to successfully competing in the global market (Co et al., 1998). Managers must be aware of the phase in which they should anticipate exceptional circumstances, issues, and opposition to change. The most effective organisations are those that can quickly adapt to changing circumstances. The primary components of the change management process that enhance organisational performance have been recognised as planning for change, managing change through a plan to manage resistance, and reinforcing change. (Kuzhda, 2006) The degree to which organisational members accept a change can be significantly impacted by different communication strategies used at different stages of the change process.(Klein, 1996). The vast quantity of these approaches and their claimed low success rates make it difficult for a business to evaluate and ultimately select a change strategy. However, it has been shown that the success or failure of a change attempt depends on how well change tactics are used (Hudescu & Ilies, 2011). Manufacturing companies may need to understand why some employees reject technological change while others welcome and assist it. The findings advise management to effectively involve workers in decision-making and, if possible, pick technologies that will raise workers' skill requirements in order to prevent worker resistance to such changes (Kimhi, et al, 2019)

SCARF Model and Neuroscience

The SCARF model, developed by David Rock, provides a framework for understanding and leveraging social factors that influence human behaviour. This model aligns with neuroscience research, which has explored the neural processes underlying social experiences and their impact on individuals' responses.

Status: Neuroscience research supports the significance of social status. A study by Zink et al. (2008) using fMRI showed that perceived social status activates the brain's reward system, leading to increased motivation and positive emotions. This aligns with the SCARF model's emphasis on recognizing and affirming individuals' status within an organization.

Certainty: Neuroscientific studies highlight the brain's preference for certainty. In a study by Harris et al. (2007), uncertainty activated the amygdala, a brain region associated with threat response. Conversely, providing clear information and reducing uncertainty activated reward-related brain regions, as demonstrated by Kringelbach et al. (2008).

Autonomy: Research on autonomy aligns with the SCARF model's emphasis on providing individuals with a sense of control. Deci and Ryan (2000) demonstrated that autonomy-supportive environments activate reward-related brain regions, leading to intrinsic motivation and engagement. This supports the SCARF model's suggestion to grant autonomy and decision-making opportunities during change initiatives.

Relatedness: Neuroscientific studies on social connectedness and relatedness align with the SCARF model's focus on fostering positive relationships. According to research by Eisenberger et al. from 2003, social inclusion stimulated reward-related brain areas while social exclusion stimulated pain centers in the brain. Cikara et al. (2011) demonstrated that empathy and connectedness positively influence social behaviour.

Fairness: Neuroscience research highlights the brain's sensitivity to fairness. A study by Fehr and Camerer (2007) showed that unfair treatment activated brain regions associated with negative emotional responses. On the other hand, fairness and equity activated reward-related brain regions, as demonstrated by Tabibnia et al. (2008).

The SCARF helps in understanding human behaviour and responses to social and organisational stimuli. SCARF, which encompasses Status, Certainty, Autonomy, Relatedness, and Fairness, provides a framework to explore the psychological factors that shape individuals' reactions to change and social interactions. Neuroscience complements this model by unravelling the underlying neural mechanisms behind emotional responses, decision-making, and cognitive processes during change. We gain a deeper appreciation of how the brain processes social threats and rewards, how emotions impact change readiness, and how leaders can leverage neuroscientific findings to design change management strategies that foster inclusivity, mitigate resistance, and promote a supportive environment for successful change implementation. This neuroscience mode SCARF offers a powerful lens to optimise change efforts, creating opportunities for more adaptive and engaged individuals and organisations.

SCARF Model in Change Management

These five domains of SCARF model trigger the brain's "primary reward" or "primary threat" circuitry (together with related networks). The model makes it easier for people to recall, recognise, and maybe change the fundamental social domains that govern human activity. (Rock, 2012). The SCARF model helps people become more capable of comprehending and, ultimately, changing their own and other people's behaviour in social settings, making them more adaptable. The prototype is particularly pertinent to leaders and managers in organisations, specialists in organisational learning and development, facilitators, trainers, coaches, consultants, and teachers, as well as social workers, volunteers in the community, or anybody trying to persuade others. These people are what we refer to as "change agents" in general. SCARF is beneficial for understanding and enhancing the calibre of interactions with co-workers, friends, and family on a daily basis (Rock et al., 2012).

SCARF features three fundamental operations that work in practically all circumstances. They include explanation, regulation, and prediction. Understanding the SCARF domains before an organisational event where personnel will be exposed to change can assist anticipate the possible hazards in a social environment and help in adapting methods and activities to reduce risks and maximise profits. The SCARF language could be useful for identifying threats and controlling emotions during an incident. There is proof in favour of the claim that identifying and reassessing emotions can help with managing them. (Campbell et al., 2022). The relationship between two crucial organisational success variables (individual innovativeness and the quality of supervisor-subordinate relationships) and commitment to change is fostered in large part by work autonomy, one of the less studied ideas (Kpinpuo et al., 2023). The SCARF model suggests strategies for facilitating change and provides some insight into why change can be so challenging. An organisational change that is not effectively handled is likely to affect many different people's performance across all five SCARF domains. When managing a change carefully, one would use the offsetting effect (Rock, Dixon, & Ochsner, 2010) to provide the impression that there have been increases in the areas where these increases are most easily implemented. By giving individuals a say in some part of the process, for instance, a team rearranging functions could reduce the threat of SCARF and give them a greater sense of autonomy. Moreover, information regarding the bigger picture might be offered so that people feel more certain. (Rock et al., 2012). The integration of neuroscience research with the SCARF model provides a deeper understanding of the neural processes underlying social experiences and their impact on individuals' motivation and readiness to change. The alignment between neuroscience findings and the SCARF model's principles suggests that leveraging social factors can contribute to effective change management strategies.

RESEARCH DESIGN

The primary objective of the study is to find out the impact of SCARF social dimensions on employees' readiness to change. Also, it looks into the socio-demographic differences of employees. In order to arrive at the result based on the objectives a descriptive research approach was designed with the help of quantitative methodology.

Conceptual Framework

The goal of the research is to learn more about the relationship and impact of the SCARF model (Status, certainty, autonomy, relatedness and fairness) on the readiness to change employees in the manufacturing industry. As (figure 1) shows in this conceptual model; Status, Certainty, Autonomy, Relatedness and fairness are taken as the independent variables and readiness to change as the dependent variable.

Figure 1. Conceptual model

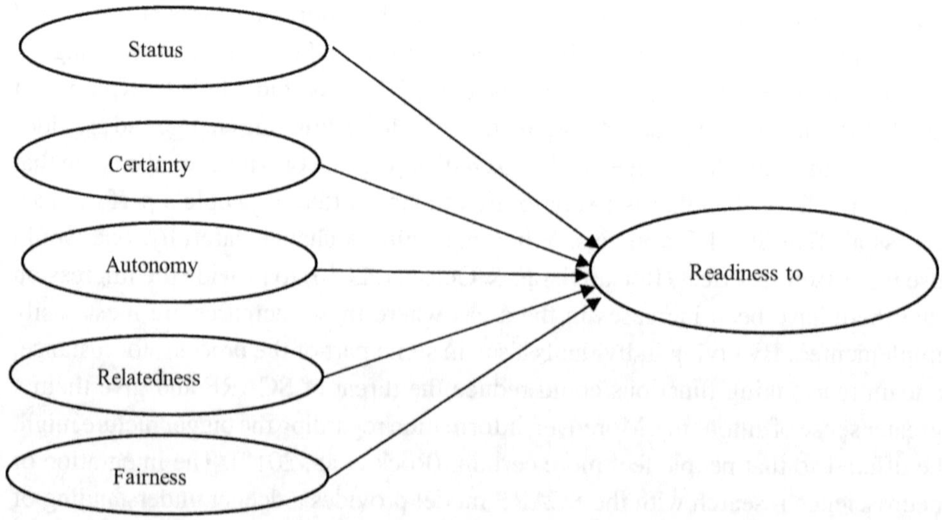

Objectives of the Research

1) To determine the relationship between each of the domains of SCARF (Status, Certainty, Autonomy, Relatedness and Fairness) with readiness to change
2) To evaluate the impact of the domains of SCARF model (Status, Certainty, Autonomy, Relatedness and Fairness) on change management in employees in the manufacturing industry.
3) To analyse the significant impact of the domains of SCARF model (Status, Certainty, Autonomy, Relatedness and Fairness) on readiness to change in employees.

Instruments

The data was collected using structured questionnaires. The questionnaire consisted of three parts. First part asked demographical questions, second part used SCARF scale and third part aimed to understand employees readiness to change. The researchers adapted the SCARF assessment items developed by the Neuroleadership Institute (2018) to measure the five dimensions of social experience and Employees readiness to change was measured by change management scale (O'Berry, 2009).

The reliability of the questionnaire was analysed during the pilot and the scale returned a Cronbach's alpha score greater than 0.7.

Participants

The final dataset comprised 170 complete responses by participants from different manufacturing industries. 51.8% are between the ages of 21 and 30, 15.5% are between the ages of 31 and 40, and 41 and 50 are represented by 17.3% of respondents. A sizable portion of responders, about 50%, had one to five years of experience. 22.7% of people have 16 years or more of job experience, followed by 13.6% by 5 to 10 years and then 10-15 years. Among the population 21.8% are in management roles, 15.5% in management trainee roles, 8.2% in production manager roles, and the rest people in production worker and R&D manager jobs and other roles.

Data Analysis

The collected data was first coded in Excel and then transferred to IBM SPSS for the final analysis. The distribution of the data was first analysed to ensure that parametric tests could be used.

ANALYSIS AND INTERPRETATION

Descriptive Statistics

Table 1. Descriptive analysis

	Minimum	Maximum	Mean	Std. Deviation
Status	1.00	5.00	4.0636	.83440
Certainty	1.00	5.00	3.8788	81989
Autonomy	1.75	5.00	3.6818	.73409
Relatedness	1.00	5.00	3.9212	.92306
Fairness	1.00	5.00	4.1091	.87755
Readiness to change	1.00	5.00	3.9500	.75404

From Table 1, which represents descriptive statistics, the following information can be inferred.

Status: For status, the mean score is 4.0636 with a standard deviation of .83440. This suggests that, on average, individuals in the sample perceive themselves as having relatively high levels of status.

Certainty: The mean score given is 3.8788 with a standard deviation of .81989. This suggests that individuals in the sample may not be entirely certain about their beliefs or behaviours.

Autonomy: The mean score was 3.6818 with a standard deviation of .73409. This suggests that individuals in the sample may require relatively low levels of autonomy.

Relatedness: The mean score was 3.9212 with a standard deviation of .92306. This suggests that individuals in the sample may require relatively low levels of relatedness to others

Fairness: The mean score was 4.1091 with a standard deviation of .87755. This suggests that, on average, individuals in the sample require higher levels of fairness.

Correlation Analysis

The first hypothesis is to study if there is any relation between the domains of SCARF (Status, Certainty, Autonomy, Relatedness and Fairness) with the readiness to change. The correlation study's advantage is that it quantifies the degree of dependency or relationship between two variables. The Pearson correlation coefficient, which measures how strongly two variables are related, ranges in value from -1 to +1. The strength of their linear relationship is measured, and as a result, it shows whether one variable rises or falls when the other rises or falls. Table 2 shows the correlation analysis between SCARF dimensions and readiness to change.

Table 2. Correlation analysis

		Readiness to Change
Status	Pearson Correlation	.627**
	Sig. (2-tailed)	.000
Certainty	Pearson Correlation	.685**
	Sig. (2-tailed)	.000
Autonomy	Pearson Correlation	.566**
	Sig. (2-tailed)	.000
Relatedness	Pearson Correlation	.662**
	Sig. (2-tailed)	.000
Fairness	Pearson Correlation	.641**
	Sig. (2-tailed)	.000

Ho: There is no relation between Status and readiness to change in employees
Ha: There is a relation between Status and readiness to change in employees.

With a correlation coefficient of 0.627, there is a strong correlation between status and readiness to change. When the first variable's value rises, the second variable's value also tends to increase, and vice versa. This correlation provides valuable insight for change management strategies. Understanding that employees in higher-status positions are more likely to exhibit greater readiness to change can help change managers tailor their approaches and engage employees effectively. It underscores the importance of involving employees at different status levels in the change process and addressing any resistance that may arise from employees in lower-status positions.

Ho: There is a no relation between Certainty and readiness to change in employees
Ha: There is a relation between Certainty and readiness to change in employees.

The correlation coefficient of 0.685 indicates a strong positive correlation between certainty and readiness to change. This means that as the level of certainty increases, an individual's readiness to embrace change also tends to increase, and vice versa. Recognizing that higher levels of certainty are associated with greater readiness to change can guide change managers in fostering an environment that promotes certainty, such as providing clear and transparent communication about the change, addressing concerns and doubts, and offering support and resources to build confidence. By addressing and enhancing certainty, change managers can positively impact employees' readiness to embrace change and facilitate smoother transitions.

Ho: There is a no correlation between Autonomy and readiness to change in employees
Ha: There is a correlation between Autonomy and readiness to change in employees.

The correlation coefficient of 0.566 indicates a strong positive correlation between readiness to change and autonomy. This correlation provides valuable insights for change management strategies. Recognizing that autonomy is associated with greater readiness to change can guide change managers in empowering employees by granting them a certain level of autonomy and decision-making power during the change process. This involvement can increase their sense of ownership, motivation, and commitment to embracing and supporting the change. By fostering a culture of autonomy and involving employees in decision-making processes, change managers can enhance readiness to change, facilitate employee engagement, and ultimately increase the likelihood of successful change implementation.

Ho: There is a no correlation between Relatedness and readiness to change in employees

Ha: There is a correlation between Relatedness and readiness to change in employees.

The correlation coefficient between relatedness and readiness to change is 0.662, indicating a strong positive correlation between these two variables. This means that as the level of relatedness increases, individuals' readiness to embrace change also tends to increase, and vice versa. The sense of relatedness is associated with greater readiness to change can guide change managers in fostering a supportive and inclusive environment. This can be achieved through team-building activities, encouraging collaboration and open communication, and promoting a sense of belonging within the organization. By addressing the relatedness aspect and creating a positive social environment, change managers can enhance individuals' readiness to embrace change, improve teamwork and cooperation, and ultimately facilitate successful change implementation.

Ho: There is no correlation between Fairness and readiness to change in employees

Ha: There is a correlation between Fairness and readiness to change in employees.

The correlation coefficient between fairness and readiness to change is 0.641, indicating a strong positive correlation between these two variables. Understanding that fairness is associated with greater readiness to change can guide change managers in promoting a fair and transparent change process. Employee participation in decision-making, fair participation opportunities, clear and consistent communication, and timely resolution of complaints are all ways to do this. By promoting fairness in the change management process, change managers can enhance individuals' readiness to embrace change, build trust and commitment, and create a positive work environment conducive to successful change implementation.

The strong positive correlation between the SCARF domains and readiness to change suggests that there is a relationship between them. The significance level (Sig.) of 0.000 suggests that all the correlations are statistically significant.

Regression Analysis

Since the domains and readiness to change are related, it is necessary to further assess how each of these domains; status, certainty, autonomy, relatedness, and fairness affects readiness to change. The below tables (Tables 3,4,5) explains the regression analysis.

Table 3. Regression model

Model	R	R Square	Adjusted R Square	Std. Error of the Estimate
1	.731[a]	.534	.511	.52703

a. Dependent Variable: Readiness to Change
b. Predictors: (Constant), Status, Autonomy, Certainty, Relatedness, Fairness

Table 4. ANOVA

Model		Sum of Squares	df	Mean Square	F	Sig.
1	Regression	33.088	5	6.618	23.825	.000[b]
	Residual	28.887	104	.278		
	Total	61.975	109			

A. Dependent Variable: Readiness to Change
B. Predictors: (Constant), Status, Autonomy, Certainty, Relatedness, Faireness

Table 5. Coefficients

Model		Unstandardized Coefficients		Standardized Coefficients	t	Sig.
		B	Std. Error	Beta		
	(Constant)	.962	.309		3.114	.002
	Status	.117	.108	.129	1.082	.282
	Certainty	-.048	.088	-.052	-.547	.586
	Autonomy	.195	.080	.190	2.424	.017
	Relatedness	.303	.092	.370	3.286	.001
	Fairness	.194	.093	.226	2.079	.040

a. Dependent Variable: Readiness to Change

Here the objective is to study if there is any impact of SCARF (Status, Certainty, Autonomy, Relatedness and Fairness) on readiness to change in employees.

Ho: There is no significant impact of the domains of SCARF model (Status, Certainty, Autonomy, Relatedness and Fairness) on readiness to change in employees

Ha: There is a significant impact of the domains of SCARF model (Status, Certainty, Autonomy, Relatedness and Fairness) on readiness to change in employees.

To test this hypothesis, a multi-linear regression is utilised using Change as the dependent variable and Status, Certainty, Autonomy, Relatedness, and Fairness as the independent variables. Multilinear regression analysis is used to predict the values of the dependent variable Y given a list of independent variables (X1, X2, X3, etc.).

The value of R squared, as shown in the table, is 0.534. This demonstrates that 53.4% of the difference in willingness to change can be attributed to SCARF (Status, Certainty, Autonomy, Relatedness, Fairness).

The ANOVA table displays that the significant level is 0.000. The result of $p < 0.05$ indicates the model's relevance and hence we reject the null hypothesis and accept the alternate hypothesis. Its significance reveals the type of relationship between the independent and dependent variables. If the value of is positive, then the relationship between the independent and dependent variables is positive. If the beta value is negative, the connection between the dependent and independent variables is negative.

The coefficients in the table represent the magnitude and direction of the relationships between each independent variable (Status, Certainty, Autonomy, Relatedness, Fairness) and the dependent variable (Readiness to Change). The standardized coefficients (betas) allow for a comparison of the relative importance of the variables in predicting the outcome. Based on the standardized coefficients (betas), the variables that have the strongest relationships with Readiness to Change are Relatedness (Beta = 0.370) and Autonomy (Beta = 0.190). These variables have positive relationships, indicating that higher scores on Relatedness and Autonomy are associated with higher levels of Readiness to Change. The other variables (Status, Certainty, Fairness) have smaller standardized coefficients and weaker relationships with Readiness to Change. It's important to note that the significance of the coefficients is indicated by the Sig. values. In this case, variables Autonomy, Relatedness, and Fairness have statistically significant relationships with Readiness to Change (Sig. < 0.05).

In this analysis, Certainty only has a negative value among the independent variables that are presented. Accordingly, for every unit increase in certainty, readiness to change decreases by 0.052 units, holding all other variables constant. Similarly, for each one-unit decrease in certainty, readiness to change would increase by 0.052 units. It suggests that individuals who have high levels of certainty about their beliefs or behaviours may be less likely to be open to change, while those with lower levels of certainty may be more receptive to new ideas or perspectives.

Here, additional assumptions taken here is that, as given in the above table, status, autonomy, relatedness and fairness have positive beta values, this means that the sample may be more open to change and a unit increase in these positive values will increase the overall readiness to change.

RESULTS AND DISCUSSION

Results

This study found a positive and strong correlation between each of the domains of SCARF (Status, Certainty, Autonomy, Relatedness and Fairness) and readiness to change in employees. This indicates that as status, certainty, autonomy, relatedness and fairness increase, readiness to change also increases. 53.4% of the variation in readiness to change in employees can be explained by the domains of SCARF. On a further review of the beta coefficients, it was found that every domain, aside from "certainty" (-0.547) —had a positive beta coefficient. A unit rise in certainty will cause the readiness to decline even more, according to the beta value of -.547 for this domain. A unit rise in the beta value will result in an increase in the readiness to change for the remaining domains.

SCARF has been demonstrated to be a flexible tool that can be utilised in a wide range of professional settings and with a wide range of structure and change-management tactics, with the welfare of people at its centre (Campbell et al., 2022). As an outcome, it is known from this study that SCARF (Status, certainty, autonomy, relatedness, and fairness) has an association with readiness to change and does in fact have an impact on the emotional side of readiness to change.

Significance of the Study and Managerial Implications

Despite the recognized importance of effective change management in organizations, research indicates that a significant number of change initiatives fail to achieve their intended objectives. This demonstrates the requirement for a greater comprehension of the factors that contribute to successful change implementation, as well as the barriers and challenges that hinder it. The SCARF model can help change managers understand the social domains that impact behaviour and create a change management strategy that addresses the domains of the SCARF model to create a more positive and effective change experience for employees.

The mean of replies was found to be high for status and fairness based on descriptive statistics. Therefore, the majority of respondents regard status and fairness in the workplace the most. In addition to making sure that decisions, rules, and processes are fair and reasonable, managers should look for methods to assist people to advance within the company by giving them promotions, leadership opportunities, and recognition. Regular employee evaluations can be used to pinpoint problem areas and implement the required adjustments to raise morale and increase job satisfaction. Managers can create training programmes that emphasise the acquisition of competencies that are highly appreciated by employees.

For the regression study, certainty showed a negative beta coefficient value, It can suggest that individuals who have high levels of certainty about their beliefs or behaviours may be less likely to be open to change, while those with lower levels of certainty may be more receptive to new ideas or perspectives. When people are uncertain about the benefits of a particular change or are unsure about how to make the change successfully, they may feel less motivated to take action. This can reduce readiness to change. As a practical implication, organizations and change facilitators can use the SCARF model to design change initiatives that consider the psychological needs of individuals. By promoting autonomy, fostering a sense of relatedness, and ensuring fairness, organizations can create a supportive environment that encourages readiness to change and facilitates successful change implementation. Additionally, the model can help identify potential barriers to readiness to change, such as uncertainty and status concerns, allowing for targeted strategies to address these issues.

Limitations

Some limitations of the above research include the possibility that it cannot be applied generally to other populations or contexts, as it was conducted on a specific group of respondents. Additionally, the data was collected using self-reported measures, which could contain biases or errors. The sample size may also limit the statistical power of the study, and there may be other unmeasured variables that could affect the results.

Discussion

With a focus on the SCARF model, the current study aims to analyse the factors that affect attitudes and views towards change in the workplace. This study's conclusions have a number of ramifications for both theory and practice. Initially, it was discovered that the SCARF model is an effective framework for comprehending the social domains that influence behaviour in the workplace. The current research discovered that status and fairness were the most significant areas for employees, consistent with prior studies. Therefore, in order to give employees a more effective and positive experience with change, change managers should concentrate on developing a change management strategy that addresses these domains. Managers should make sure that decisions, policies, and procedures are just and reasonable in addition to giving staff members chances to progress within the business through promotions, leadership roles, and recognition. Regular evaluations of employees can also be used to identify problem areas and put the necessary corrections into place to boost morale and boost job satisfaction. Managers can also design training programmes that have a focus on developing skills that are highly valued by their workforce.

In the SCARF model, Status refers to an individual's perception of their social standing, relative to others. If someone perceives themselves to have a higher status, they may feel more confident and motivated to make changes. However, the lack of statistical significance in this study suggests that Status might not be a strong driver of readiness to change for the participants in this particular context. Certainty relates to the predictability and control individuals have over their circumstances. When people feel uncertain about the outcomes of change, they might be more hesitant to embrace it. the regression analysis revealed that certainty had a negative beta coefficient value, indicating that people who are very certain of their beliefs or behaviours may be less likely to be open to change while people who are less certain of their beliefs or behaviours may be more receptive to novel ideas or viewpoints. This result is consistent with earlier studies that indicated those with fixed mindsets are less likely to be receptive to new information or exhibit behaviours that contradict their views (Dweck, 2006; Grant, 2013). People may feel less inspired to take action when they are doubtful of the advantages of a particular change or about how to implement the change successfully, which can lessen their readiness to change. However, the lack of statistical significance in this study implies that Certainty might not be a significant factor affecting readiness to change in this sample.

The study found that "Autonomy" had a moderate positive influence on readiness to change, and this relationship was statistically significant. When people have autonomy over the change process, they are more likely to feel motivated and committed to making the necessary adjustments. The statistically significant relationship in this study suggests that providing individuals with a sense of autonomy can enhance their readiness to change. Relatedness pertains to individuals' sense of connection and belongingness with others. The results indicated that "Relatedness" had a strong positive influence on readiness to change, and this relationship is highly statistically significant. When individuals feel supported and part of a group that is going through a change together, they are more likely to embrace the change positively. The high statistical significance of this study suggests that fostering a sense of relatedness can have a substantial impact on readiness to change. The study found that "Fairness" has a positive influence on readiness to change. Fairness is about perceived fairness and equitable treatment. When individuals believe that the change process is fair and just, they are more likely to be open to it. The statistically significant relationship in this study indicates that ensuring fairness during the change process can contribute to increased readiness to change.As this study suggests Autonomy, Relatedness, and Fairness emerged as significant factors influencing individuals' readiness to change. While Status and Certainty did not show significant effects in this study, it is essential to acknowledge that the influence of these factors may vary depending on the specific context and the individuals involved.

Our understanding of the factors influencing attitudes and beliefs at work is improved by the current study. The result that most respondents place a high value on status and fairness supports the social exchange hypothesis, which holds that people try to maximise benefits and minimise costs in their relationships with others. The regression analysis also lends credence to the notion of planned behaviour, which holds that attitudes, subjective standards, and perceived behavioural control all influence behaviour.

SOLUTIONS AND RECOMMENDATIONS

The social experiences in a working context have a great impact on change management strategies as it indirectly affects the brain of an employee either by rewarding or threatening it. Given the statistically significant positive influence of Autonomy on Readiness to Change, organisations should focus on providing employees with opportunities for decision-making and involvement in the change process. Empower individuals by allowing them to have a say in how the change is implemented and providing them with the necessary resources and support to take ownership of their roles during the transition. As Relatedness emerged as a strong positive influencer of Readiness to Change, it is crucial to promote a sense of connection and belongingness among employees. Encourage teamwork, collaboration, and open communication channels to create a supportive environment where individuals feel connected to their colleagues and the broader organisational goals. Social activities and team-building exercises can also enhance the sense of relatedness. Given the statistically significant positive impact of Fairness on Readiness to Change, it is essential to ensure transparency, equity, and fairness in the change process. Communicate the rationale behind the change, address concerns and feedback from employees, and ensure that decision-making processes are perceived as fair. Fairness can be promoted by providing clear guidelines and criteria for evaluation, involving employees in decision-making, and demonstrating consistency in treatment throughout the change initiative.

Although Status and Certainty did not show statistically significant influences on Readiness to Change, it is still important to consider these factors. To address status concerns, organisations can provide opportunities for employees to develop new skills and acquire knowledge related to the change. Recognising and valuing individual contributions during the transition can also help mitigate any potential status-related concerns. Regarding Certainty, it is crucial to communicate change-related information clearly and regularly, addressing any uncertainties or concerns that may arise. Providing support mechanisms, such as training, coaching, and regular updates, can help individuals feel more confident and prepared for the change.

Recognising the unique dynamics of each organisation and its employees, it is recommended to customise change management approaches to the specific context. Consider conducting assessments or surveys to gain insights into employees' readiness and receptiveness to change, and use the findings to customise change strategies accordingly. Involve employees in the change planning process to ensure their perspectives and needs are taken into account.

Regularly monitoring and evaluating the progress of the change initiative by track indicators of Readiness to Change, such as employees' engagement, adoption of new behaviours, and overall satisfaction with the change process also may help the change management process. Continuous monitoring allows for timely interventions and helps in ensuring the change initiative remains on track. Strong leadership and effective communication are crucial in gaining employees' buy-in and fostering their readiness to change. Offering training programs that focus on change leadership, communication, and creating an inclusive and supportive environment during times of transition is recommended. Leaders has to understand that the factors such as Autonomy, Relatedness, Fairness, Status, and Certainty can contribute to a more supportive and engaging change environment, resulting in greater employee acceptance and commitment to the change process.

FUTURE RESEARCH DIRECTIONS

Future research could aim to replicate these findings in different populations or industries and use more objective measures to collect data. Longitudinal studies could also be conducted to examine how these attitudes and beliefs change over time, and how they affect outcomes. Qualitative research could be conducted to gain a better comprehension of the fundamental causes of these generational differences and to identify potential interventions that could be used to improve workplace culture and productivity.

Developing and testing neuroscience-informed change interventions specifically for the manufacturing sector and implementing such interventions and evaluating their impact on employees' brain responses, behaviour, and readiness to change can help refine change management strategies. Evaluating the effectiveness of neurofeedback training in enhancing employees' readiness for change in the manufacturing industry. Neurofeedback can help individuals regulate their brain activity and emotional responses, potentially improving their openness to change.

By exploring these future research directions, the manufacturing sector can develop more effective and evidence-based change management strategies. Incorporating neuroscientific findings into change initiatives can lead to greater employee readiness, engagement, and successful adaptation to the evolving demands of the industry.

CONCLUSION

The study advances our knowledge of the variables affecting attitudes and beliefs at work. Fostering a brain-friendly work culture and implementing effective change management practices are vital for cultivating a thriving and innovative workplace. The social exchange theory, which contends that people aim to maximise benefits and minimise costs in their relationships with others, is supported by the conclusion that the majority of respondents place a high value on status and fairness. The theory of planned behaviour, which contends that attitudes, arbitrary standards, and perceived behavioural control all have an impact on behaviour, is also supported by the regression analysis. The post-hoc analyses advance our knowledge of generational variations at work and emphasise the significance of considering social and cultural context when examining attitudes and beliefs. To replicate these findings in various demographics and circumstances and to establish potential interventions that could be utilised to enhance workplace culture and productivity, more research is required.

The need of routine employee evaluations to identify issues and make the necessary corrections to improve morale and boost job satisfaction is stressed by the study. These evaluations can be used by managers to pinpoint the areas where staff members need more guidance or instruction and to give them performance feedback that will enable them to gain new knowledge and abilities. Managers may boost their employees' readiness to change by using these strategies and cultivating a more productive and positive workplace culture that benefits both workers and the organisation as a whole. A brain-friendly work culture combined with effective change management paves the way for long-term success and prosperity.

REFERENCES

Alhaderi, M. Dr. S. (2000). *Kotter's Eight Step Change Model for Employees' Intentional, Cognitive and Emotional Readiness for Change and Developing Regional Economy in Saudi Banking Sector's, Role of Homologous Communication, Learning Demand and Job Involvement.* Retrieved April 20, 2023, from https://www.abacademies.org/articles/kotters-eight-step-change-model-for-employees-intentionalcognitive-and-emotional-readiness-for-change-and-developing-regional-eco-12435.html

Alolabi, Y. A., Ayupp, K., & al Dwaikat, M. (2021). Issues and implications of readiness to change. *Administrative Sciences*, *11*(4), 140. Advance online publication. doi:10.3390/admsci11040140

Anthony, D., & Dibella, J. J. (2010). *Critical Perceptions of Organisational Change.* doi:10.1080/14697010701649707

Antonacopoulou, E. P., & Gabriel, Y. (2001). Emotion, learning and organizational change towards an integration of psychoanalytic and other perspectives. *Journal of Organizational Change Management*, *14*(5), 435–451. doi:10.1108/EUM0000000005874

Asbari, M., Hidayat, D., & Purwanto, A. (2021). Managing Employee Performance: From Leadership to Readiness for Change. *International Journal of Social and Management Studies.* http://www.ijosmas.org

Baird, K., & Wang, H. (2010). Employee empowerment: Extent of adoption and influential factors. *Personnel Review*, *39*(5), 574–599. doi:10.1108/00483481011064154

Bateh, J., Castaneda, M. E., & Farah, J. E. (2013). Employee Resistance to Organizational Change. *International Journal of Management & Information Systems*, *17*(2), 113–116. doi:10.19030/ijmis.v17i2.7715

Bold, E. O. (2011). *Instruments And Techniques Used In The Design And Implementation Of Change Management.* Retrieved October 5, 2022, from https://www.proquest.com/docview/887542393?pq-origsite=gscholar&fromopenview=true

Campbell, S., Prior, S., Bramble, M., & Maxwell, H. (2022). *Examining the engagement of health services staff in change management: Modifying the SCARF assessment model.* doi:10.19043/ipdj.121.005

Chambers, C. (2004). Technological advancement, learning, and the adoption of new technology. *European Journal of Operational Research*, *152*(1), 226–247. doi:10.1016/S0377-2217(02)00651-3

Chrusciel, D. (2006). Considerations of emotional intelligence (EI) in dealing with change decision management. *Management Decision*, *44*(5), 644–657. doi:10.1108/00251740610668897

Co, H. C., Patuwo, B. E., & Hu, M. Y. (1998). The human factor in advanced manufacturing technology adoption: An empirical analysis. *International Journal of Operations & Production Management*, *18*(1), 87–106. doi:10.1108/01443579810192925

Deci, E. L., & Ryan, R. M. (2000). The "what" and "why" of goal pursuits: Human needs and the self-determination of behaviour. *Psychological Inquiry*, *11*(4), 227–268. doi:10.1207/S15327965PLI1104_01

Dhingra, R., & Punia, B. K. (2016). Relational Analysis of Emotional Intelligence and Change Management: A Suggestive Model for Enriching Change Management Skills Concept Development. *Vision (Basel)*, *20*(4), 312–322. doi:10.1177/0972262916668726

Doorewaard, H., & Benschop, Y. (2003). HRM and organizational change: An emotional endeavor. *Journal of Organizational Change Management*, *16*(3), 272–286. doi:10.1108/09534810310475523

Eisenberger, N. I., Lieberman, M. D., & Williams, K. D. (2003). Does rejection hurt? An FMRI study of social exclusion. *Science*, *302*(5643), 290–292. doi:10.1126cience.1089134 PMID:14551436

Erwin, D. G., & Garman, A. N. (2010). Resistance to organizational change: Linking research and practice. *Leadership and Organization Development Journal*, *31*(1), 39–56. doi:10.1108/01437731011010371

Fehr, E., & Camerer, C. F. (2007). Social neuroeconomics: The neural circuitry of social preferences. *Trends in Cognitive Sciences*, *11*(10), 419–427. doi:10.1016/j.tics.2007.09.002 PMID:17913566

Fisher, W., & Wesolkowski, S. (1999). Tempering technostress. *IEEE Technology and Society Magazine*, *18*(1), 28–33. doi:10.1109/44.752243

Gärtner, C. (2013). *Enhancing Readiness for Change by Enhancing Mindfulness*. https://www.tandfonline.com/doi/pdf/10.1080/14697017.2013.768433

Harris, L. T., McClure, S. M., van den Bos, W., Cohen, J. D., & Fiske, S. T. (2007). Regions of the MPFC differentially tuned to social and nonsocial affective evaluation. *Cognitive, Affective & Behavioral Neuroscience*, *7*(4), 309–316. doi:10.3758/CABN.7.4.309 PMID:18189004

Helpap, S., & Bekmeier-Feuerhahn, S. (2016). Employees' emotions in change: Advancing the sensemaking approach. *Journal of Organizational Change Management*, *29*(6), 903–916. doi:10.1108/JOCM-05-2016-0088

Hudescu, L., & Ilies, L. (n.d.-b) *Challenges in Choosing an Effective Change Management Approach*. Retrieved October 5, 2022, from https://www.proquest.com/docview/1220671941?pq-origsite=gscholar&fromopenview=true

International, V., Kimhi, S., Oliel, Y., & Odemegwu Ojukwu, C. (2019). Change Management and Organizational Performance in Selected Manufacturing Companies in Anambra State, Nigeria. *The International Journal of Social Sciences and Humanities Invention*, *6*(05), 5. doi:10.18535/ijsshi/v6i5.06

Klein, S. M. (1996). A management communication strategy for change. *Journal of Organizational Change Management*, *9*(2), 32–46. doi:10.1108/09534819610113720

Kpinpuo, S. D., Akolgo, I. G., & Naimi, L. (2023). Leading change and innovation in Ghana's banking sector: The mediating role of work autonomy. *Industrial and Commercial Training*, *55*(1), 1–18. doi:10.1108/ICT-12-2021-0086

Kringelbach, M. L., Lehtonen, A., Squire, S., Harvey, A. G., Craske, M. G., Holliday, I. E., Green, A. L., Aziz, T. Z., Hansen, P. C., Cornelissen, P. L., & Stein, A. (2008). A specific and rapid neural signature for parental instinct. *PLoS One*, *3*(2), e1664. doi:10.1371/journal.pone.0001664 PMID:18301742

Kuzhda, T. (2006). *Diagnosing resistance to change in the change management process*. Retrieved October 5, 2022, from https://cyberleninka.ru/article/n/diagnosing-resistance-to-change-in-the-changemanagement-process/viewer

Nguyen, T. H., Newby, M., & Macaulay, M. J. (2015). Information technology adoption in small business: Confirmation of a proposed framework. *Journal of Small Business Management*, *53*(1), 207–227. doi:10.1111/jsbm.12058

Rock, D., Cox, C., Fellow, P., & Green, P. (2012). *SCARF in 2012: updating the social neuroscience of collaborating with others*. https://www.saskatoonhealthregion.ca/about/PFMS/Documents/Change_Leadership_Module/SCARF%20Model%20-%20Updating%20the%20Social%20Neuroscience%20of%20Collaborating%20with%20Others.pdf

Schweiger, S., Stouten, H., & Bleijenbergh, I. L. (2018). A System Dynamics Model of Resistance to Organizational Change: The Role of Participatory Strategies. *Systems Research and Behavioral Science, 35*(6), 658–674. doi:10.1002res.2509

Smollan, R. K., & Sayers, J. G. (2009). *Organizational Culture, Change and Emotions: A Qualitative Study.* doi:10.1080/14697010903360632

Tabibnia, G., Satpute, A. B., & Lieberman, M. D. (2008). The sunny side of fairness: Preference for fairness activates reward-related brain regions. *Journal of Cognitive Neuroscience, 20*(3), 414–425.

Todnem By, R. (2005). Organisational change management: A critical review. *Journal of Change Management, 5*(4), 369–380. doi:10.1080/14697010500359250

Ugoani, J. N. N. (2017). Emotional Intelligence and Successful Change Management in the Nigerian Banking Industry. *Independent Journal of Management & Production, 8*(2), 335. doi:10.14807/ijmp.v8i2.550

Zink, C. F., Tong, Y., Chen, Q., Bassett, D. S., Stein, J. L., & Meyer-Lindenberg, A. (2008). Know your place: Neural processing of social hierarchy in humans. *Neuron, 58*(2), 273–283. doi:10.1016/j.neuron.2008.01.025 PMID:18439411

KEY TERMS AND DEFINITIONS

Autonomy: It reflects the degree of control over one's own actions and decisions.

Certainty: Clarity, predictability, and sense of control over the environment.

Fairness: Equitable treatment and distribution of resources, rewards, and opportunities.

Relatedness: The feeling of connection, and belongingness in social interactions.

Social Experience: It is the collective interactions, activities, and relationships that individuals engage in within a social context.

Status: It is the relative importance of an individual in a social context.

Compilation of References

Abdalla, A. (2001). Principles of Islamic interpersonal conflict intervention: A search within Islam and western literature. *The Journal of Law and Religion*, *15*(1), 151–184.

Abernethy, K. E., Bodin, T., Olsson, P., Hilly, Z., & Schwarz, A. (2014). Two steps forward, two steps back: The role of innovation in transforming towards community-based marine resource management in Solomon Islands. *Global Environmental Change*, *28*(1), 309–321. doi:10.1016/j.gloenvcha.2014.07.008

Acemoglu, D., Cantoni, D., Johnson, S., & Robinson, J. (2011). The Consequences of Radical Reform: The French Revolution A Theory of Political Transitions. *The American Economic Review*, *101*(7), 3286–3307. doi:10.1257/aer.101.7.3286

Acemoglu, D., & Robinson, J. (2015). The rise and fall of general laws of capitalism J. *Economic Perspectives*, *29*(1), 3–28. doi:10.1257/jep.29.1.3

Acosta Guzmán, J. A. (2015). La innovación empresarial y la cultura organizacional. *3C Empresa*, *4*(3), 160-174. Retrieved from https://dialnet.unirioja.es/servlet/articulo?codigo=5165298

Aghion, P., Caroli, E., & García-Peñalosa, C. (1999). Inequality and economic growth: The perspective of the new growth theories. *Journal of Economic Literature*, *37*(4), 1615–1660. doi:10.1257/jel.37.4.1615

Aghion, P., & Howitt, P. W. (1997). *Endogenous growth theory*. MIT Press.

Akuratiyagamage, V. M., & Opatha, H. H. D. N. P. (2004). Grievances of middle managers: An empirical investigation into perceptions of commercial bank branch managers in Sri Lanka. *Journal of Management Research*, *4*(2), 99–112.

Aladwani, A. M. (2001). Change management strategies for successful ERP implementation. *Business Process Management Journal*, *7*(3), 266–275. doi:10.1108/14637150110392764

Al-Alawi, A. I., Abdulmohsen, M., Al-Malki, F. M., & Mehrotra, A. (2019). Investigating the barriers to change management in public sector educational institutions. *International Journal of Educational Management*, *33*(1), 112–148. doi:10.1108/IJEM-03-2018-0115

Aldrich, A. S., & Lotito, N. J. (2020). Pandemic Performance: Women Leaders in the Covid-19 Crisis. *Politics & Gender*, *16*(4), 1–9. doi:10.1017/S1743923X20000549

Alhaderi, M. Dr. S. (2000). *Kotter's Eight Step Change Model for Employees' Intentional, Cognitive and Emotional Readiness for Change and Developing Regional Economy in Saudi Banking Sector's, Role of Homologous Communication, Learning Demand and Job Involvement*. Retrieved April 20, 2023, from https://www.abacademies.org/articles/kotters-eight-step-change-model-for-employees-intentionalcognitive-and-emotional-readiness-for-change-and-developing-regional-eco-12435.html

Ali, M., & Kulik, C. (2014). Matching age and gender diversity: A linear and curvilinear prediction test competitive. *Journal of Business Ethics*, *125*, 497–512. doi:10.100710551-013-1930-9

Allen, T. G., & Flood, C. T. (2018). The Experiences of Women in Higher Education: Who Knew There Wasn't a Sisterhood? *Leadership and Research in Education*, *4*, 10–27.

Allison, K. (1998). Membership in the social category of stressed and oppressed. In J. Swim & C. Stangor (Eds.), *Prejudice: The Target Perspective, 145-170*. Academic Press. doi:10.1016/B978-012679130-3/50042-9

Alolabi, Y. A., Ayupp, K., & al Dwaikat, M. (2021). Issues and implications of readiness to change. *Administrative Sciences*, *11*(4), 140. Advance online publication. doi:10.3390/admsci11040140

Amable, B. (2000). Institutional complementarity and diversity of social systems of innovation and production. *Review of International Political Economy*, *7*(4), 645–687. doi:10.1080/096922900750034572

André, S. (2018). Embracing generational diversity: Reducing and managing workplace conflict. *ORNAC Journal*, *36*(4), 13–13.

Andrews, R., Boyne, G. A., & Walker, R. M. (2006). Strategy content and organizational performance: An empirical analysis. *Public Administration Review*, *66*(1), 52–63. doi:10.1111/j.1540-6210.2006.00555.x

Ansell, C. (2000). The networked polity: Regional development in Western Europe. *Governance: An International Journal of Policy, Administration and Institutions*, *12*(2), 303–333. doi:10.1111/0952-1895.00136

Antalyalı, O. I., & Çarıkçı, I. H. (2007). Gender effect on work family conflict among managers. *Journal of Suleyman Demirel University Institue of Social Sciences*, *6*, 117–127.

Anthony, D., & Dibella, J. J. (2010). *Critical Perceptions of Organisational Change*. doi:10.1080/14697010701649707

Antonacopoulou, E. P., & Gabriel, Y. (2001). Emotion, learning and organizational change: Towards an integration of psychoanalytic and other perspectives. *Journal of Organizational Change Management*, *14*(5), 435–451. doi:10.1108/EUM0000000005874

Appelbaum, D'Antico, & Daoussis. (2019). Women as Leaders The More Things Change, the More It's the Same Thing. *International Journal of Management and Business*, *10*(1).

Appelbaum, S., Serena, M., & Shapiro, B. (2005). Generation X and the Boomers: An analysis of realities and myths. *Management Research News, 28*(1), 1–33. doi:10.1108/01409170510784751

Araújo, C., & Teixeira, A. (2014). Determinants of International Technology Transfer: An Empirical Analysis of the Enterprise Europe Network. *Journal of Technology Management & Innovation, 9*(3), 120–134. doi:10.4067/S0718-27242014000300009

Arriaga, T. T., Stanley, S. L., & Lindsey, D. B. (2020). *Leading While Female: A Culturally Proficient Response for Gender Equity*. Corwin.

Arthur, B. (1989). Competing technologies, increasing returns, and lock-in by historical events. *Economic Journal (London), 1989*(99), 116–131. doi:10.2307/2234208

Asbari, M., Hidayat, D., & Purwanto, A. (2021). Managing Employee Performance: From Leadership to Readiness for Change. *International Journal of Social and Management Studies.* http://www.ijosmas.org

Asghari, V. (2023). *Influence of women's leadership on the organizational culture of organizations based in Switzerland* [MBA dissertation].

Ashikali, T., Groeneveld, S., & Kuipers, B. (2021). The role of inclusive leadership in supporting an inclusive climate in diverse public sector teams. *Review of Public Personnel Administration, 41*(3), 497–519. doi:10.1177/0734371X19899722

Audretsch, B. D., & Link, N. A. (2012, February). Entrepeneurship and innovation: Public policy frameworks. *The Journal of Technology Transfer, 37*(1), 1–17. doi:10.100710961-011-9240-9

Bacharach, S. B., Bamberger, P., & Conley, S. (1991). Work home conflict among nurses and engineers: Mediating the impact of role stress on burnout and satisfaction at work. *Journal of Organizational Behavior, 12*(1), 39–53. doi:10.1002/job.4030120104

Baerlein, T., Kasymov, U., & Zikos, D. (2015). Self-Governance and Sustainable Common Pool Resource Management in Kyrgyzstan. *Sustainability, 7*(1), 496–521. doi:10.3390u7010496

Bagilhole, B. (2019). Against the odds: Women academics' research opportunities. In *Gender, teaching and research in higher education* (pp. 46–56). Routledge. doi:10.4324/9781315254548-5

Baharuddin, M. F., Masrek, M. N., & Shuhidan, S. M. (2019). Innovative Work Behaviour of School Teachers: a Conceptual Framework. *International E-Journal of Advances in Education,* S(14), 213-221. 10.1876B/ijaedu.593851

Bailes, L. P., & Guthery, S. (2020). Held Down and Held Back: Systematically Delayed Principal Promotions by Race and Gender. *AERA Open, 6*(2). doi:10.1177/2332858420929298

Baird, K., & Wang, H. (2010). Employee empowerment: Extent of adoption and influential factors. *Personnel Review, 39*(5), 574–599. doi:10.1108/00483481011064154

Banks, J. A., & McGee Banks, C. A. (2004). *Handbook of research on multicultural education* (2nd ed.). Jossey-Bass.

Barba, I., & Iraizoz, B. (2020). Effect of the Great Crisis on Sectoral Female Employment in Europe: A Structural Decomposition Analysis. *Economies*, *8*(3), 64. doi:10.3390/economies8030064

Barnett, R. (1990). *The idea of higher education*. McGraw-Hill Education.

Barnett, R. C., Raudenbush, S. W., Brennan, R. T., Pleck, J. H., & Marshall, N. L. (1995). Changes in job and marital experience and change in psychological distress: A longitudinal study of dual-earner couples. *Journal of Personality and Social Psychology*, *69*(5), 839–850. doi:10.1037/0022-3514.69.5.839 PMID:7473034

Barro, R. (1991). Economic growth in a cross-section of countries. *The Quarterly Journal of Economics*, *106*(2), 407–443. doi:10.2307/2937943

Barro, R. (1997). *Determinants of Economic Growth. A cross-country empirical study*. MIT Press.

Barro, R., & Beckerg, G. (1989). Fertility Choice in a Model of Economic Growth. *Econometrica*, *57*(2), 481–501. doi:10.2307/1912563

Bateh, J., Castaneda, M. E., & Farah, J. E. (2013). Employee Resistance to Organizational Change. *International Journal of Management & Information Systems*, *17*(2), 113–116. doi:10.19030/ijmis.v17i2.7715

Batliwala, S., & Dhanraj, D. (2007). Gender myths that instrumentalize women: a view from the Indian front line. *Feminisms in development: Contradictions, contestations and challenges*, *35*(4), 11-18.

Battilana, J., & Casciaro, T. (2012). Change agents, networks, and institutions: A contingency theory of organizational change. *Academy of Management Journal*, *55*(2), 381–398. doi:10.5465/amj.2009.0891

Battilana, J., & D'Aunno, T. (2009). Institutional work and the paradox of embedded agency. In T. B. Lawrence, R. Suddaby, & B. Leca (Eds.), *Institutional work: Actors and agency in institutional studies of organizations* (p. 3158). Cambridge University Press. doi:10.1017/CBO9780511596605.002

Battilana, J., Leca, B., & Boxenbaum, E. (2009). How actors change institutions: Towards a theory of institutional entrepreneurship. *The Academy of Management Annals*, *3*(1), 65–107. doi:10.5465/19416520903053598

Bauer, N. M., & Taylor, T. (2022). Selling them short? Differences in news coverage of female and male candidate qualifications. *Political Research Quarterly*.

Baumgartner, F. R., & Jones, B. D. (2009). *Agendas and Instability in American Poli-tics* (2nd ed.). University of Chicago Press. (Original work published 1993)

Baumgartner, F., & Jones, B. (1991). Agenda dynamics and policy sub-systems. *The Journal of Politics*, *53*(4), 1044–1074. doi:10.2307/2131866

Behfar, K. J., Peterson, R. S., Mannix, E. A., & Trochim, W. M. (2008). The critical role of conflict resolution in teams: A close look at the links between conflict type, conflict management strategies, and team outcomes. *The Journal of Applied Psychology*, *93*(1), 170–188. doi:10.1037/0021-9010.93.1.170 PMID:18211143

Bellini, M. I., Graham, Y., Hayes, C., Zakeri, R., Parks, R., & Papalois, V. (2019). A woman's place is in theatre: Women's perceptions and experiences of working in surgery from the Association of Surgeons of Great Britain and Ireland women in surgery working group. *BMJ Open*, *9*(1), e024349. doi:10.1136/bmjopen-2018-024349 PMID:30617103

Bell, S., & Feng, H. (2007). Made in China: IT infrastructure policy and the politics of trade opening in post-WTO China. *Review of International Political Economy*, *14*(1), 49–76. doi:10.1080/09692290601081343

Benslimane, M., & Moustaghfir, K. (2020). Career development practices and gender equity in higher education. *International Journal of Management Education*, *14*(2), 183–211.

Benziman, Y. (2020). "Winning" the "battle" and "beating" the COVID-19 "enemy": Leaders' use of war frames to define the pandemic. *Peace and Conflict*, *26*(3), 247–256. doi:10.1037/pac0000494

Berger, P., & Luckmann, T. (1966). *The social construction of reality: A treatise in the sociology of knowledge*. Anchor Books.

Berthon, P. (1993). Psychological Type And Corporate Culture: Relationship And Dynamics. *Omega*, *21*(3), 329–344. doi:10.1016/0305-0483(93)90090-8

Bessant, J., & Rush, H. (1995). Building bridges for innovation: The role of consultants in technology transfer. *Research Policy*, *24*(1), 97–115. doi:10.1016/0048-7333(93)00751-E

Beugelsdijk, S., & Mudambi, R. (2013). MNEs as border-crossing multi-location enterprises: The role of discontinuities in geographic space. *Journal of International Business Studies*, *44*(5), 413–426. doi:10.1057/jibs.2013.23

Bévort, F., & Suddaby, R. (2016). Scripting professional identities: How individuals make sense of contradictory institutional logics. *Journal of Professions and Organization*, *3*(1), 17–38. doi:10.1093/jpo/jov007

Bieri, S., & Sancar, A. (2009). *Power and poverty. Reducing gender inequality by ways of rural employment?* Academic Press.

Bils, M., & Klenow, P. (2000). Does schooling cause growth? *The American Economic Review*, *90*(5), 1160–1183. doi:10.1257/aer.90.5.1160

Binz, C., Harris-Lovett, S., Kiparsky, M., Sedlak, D. L., & Truffer, B. (2016). The thorny road to technology legitimation-institutional work for potable water reuse in california. *Technological Forecasting and Social Change*, *103*(February), 249–263. doi:10.1016/j.techfore.2015.10.005

Bishop, C. (2012). *Artificial Hells: Participatory Art and the Politics of Spectatorship*. Verso. Print

Bitektine, A., & Haack, P. (2015). The "macro" and the "micro" of legitimacy: Toward a multilevel theory of the legitimacy process. *Academy of Management Review*, *40*(1), 49–75. doi:10.5465/amr.2013.0318

Blanning, T. C. (1986). *The origins of the French revolutionary wars*. Longman Group Limited.

Bloomfield, J., & Fisher, M. J. (2019). Quantitative research design. *Journal of the Australasian Rehabilitation Nurses Association*, *22*(2), 27–30. doi:10.33235/jarna.22.2.27-30

Blythe, J., Baumann, A., Zeytinoglu, I., Denton, M., Akhtar-Danesh, N., Davies, S., & Kolotylo, C. (2008). Nursing generations in the contemporary workplace. *Public Personnel Management*, *37*(2), 137–159. doi:10.1177/009102600803700201

Blyth, M. (2002). *Great Transformations: Economic Ideas and Institutional Change in the Twentieth Century*. Cambridge University Press. doi:10.1017/CBO9781139087230

Blyth, M., Hodgson, G. M., Lewis, O., & Steinmo, S. (2011). Introduction to the Special Issue on the Evolution of Institutions. *Journal of Institutional Economics*, *7*(3), 299–315. doi:10.1017/S1744137411000270

Boakye-Sarpong, K. (1998). Bureaucracy and development in the emerging nations: An ecological approach. *Institute of African Studies Research Review*, *14*(1), 1–15.

Bobe, B. J., & Kober, R. (2020). Does gender matter? The association between gender and the use of management control systems and performance measures. *Accounting and Finance*, *60*(3), 2063–2098. doi:10.1111/acfi.12365

Boix, C. (2003). *Democracy and Redistribution*. Cambridge University Press. doi:10.1017/CBO9780511804960

Bold, E. O. (2011). *Instruments And Techniques Used In The Design And Implementation Of Change Management*. Retrieved October 5, 2022, from https://www.proquest.com/docview/887542393?pq-origsite=gscholar&fromopenview=true

Bontekoning, A. C. (2007). *Generations in organizations* [Generaties in Organisaties. Een onderzoek naar generatieverschillen en de effecten daarvan op de ontwikkeling van organisaties] [Doctoral thesis]. University of Tilburg.

Boughey, C. (2009). *A meta-analysis of teaching and learning at five research-intensive South African universities*. Research Commissioned by the Higher Education Quality Committee. Unpublished.

Bourdieu, P. (1977). *Outline of a Theory of Practice*. Cambridge University Press. doi:10.1017/CBO9780511812507

Bowen, E., Lloyd, S., & Thomas, S. (2004). Changing Cultural Attitudes towards Graduates in SMEs to Stimulate Regional Innovation. *Industry and Higher Education*, *18*(6), 385–390. doi:10.5367/0000000042683575

Boyne, G. A., & Walker, R. M. (2004). Strategy content and public service organizations. *Journal of Public Administration: Research and Theory*, *14*(2), 231–252. doi:10.1093/jopart/muh015

Bozeman, B., & Papadakis, M. (1995). Company interactions with federal laboratories: What they do and why they do it. *The Journal of Technology Transfer*, *20*(3-4), 64–74. doi:10.1007/BF02280349

Bright, A., Acosta, S., & Parker, B. (2020). Humility Matters: Interrogating Our Positionality, Power, and Privilege Through Collaboration. In Handbook of Research on Diversity and Social Justice in Higher Education (pp. 19-40). IGI Global.

Broda, P. (2020). Institutions, economy and politics: The debate between Commons and North. *European Journal of the History of Economic Thought*, *22*(October). Advance online publication. doi:10.1080/09672567.2020.1837197

Bromley, D. W. (1989). Institutional Change and Economic Efficiency. *Journal of Economic Issues*, *23*(3), 735–759. doi:10.1080/00213624.1989.11504936

Bromley, D. W., & Anderson, G. (2012). *Vulnerable People, Vulnerable States: Redefining the Development Challenge*. Routledge. doi:10.4324/9780203113325

Brousseau, E., Dedeurwaerdere, T., & Siebenhüner, B. (2012). *Reflexive Governance for Global Public Goods*. MIT Press. doi:10.7551/mitpress/9780262017244.001.0001

Brown, H. (2013). The new security state. In P. McPhee (Ed.), *A companion to the French Revolution* (pp. 343–358). Blackwell Publishing Ltd.

Buchanan, J. M. (1979). Natural and artifactual man. In The Collected Works of James M. Buchanan, Volume 1: The Logical Foundations of Constitutional Liberty. Indianapolis: Liberty Fund, Inc.

Burke, P. J., & Crozier, G. (2014). Higher education pedagogies: Gendered formations, mis/recognition and emotion. *Journal of Research in Gender Studies*, *4*(2), 52.

Burke, R. J., Weir, T., & Duwors, R. E. Jr. (1980). Work demands on administrators and spouse well-being. *Human Relations*, *33*(4), 253–278. doi:10.1177/001872678003300404

Butler, R. (1987). *Ageism: The enclyclopedia of Aging*. Springer.

Bygstad, B., Øvrelid, E., Ludvigsen, S., & Dæhlen, M. (2021). Dual Digitalisation – a Framework for Digital Transformation of Higher Education NOS-HS Workshop 1, 30-31 March 2021 - Understanding digital transformations of teaching and learning in Nordic higher education and beyond. University of Agder (Norway), Aarhus University (Denmark) and KTH Royal Institute of Technology (Sweden).

Cahdriyana, R. A., Richardo, R., Fahmi, S., & Setyawan, F. (2019, March). Pseudo-thinking process in solving logic problem. *Journal of Physics: Conference Series*, *1188*(1), 012090. doi:10.1088/1742-6596/1188/1/012090

Calderón, H. G., & Serna, G. H. M. (2009). Relaciones entre recursos humanos y cultura organizacional. un estudio empírico. *Acta Colombiana de Psicologia*, *12*(2), 97–114. https://www.redalyc.org/pdf/798/79815640010.pdf

Cambridge University Press. (2023). https://dictionary.cambridge.org/es/diccionario/ingles/ultimate

Cameron, K. S., & Quinn, R. E. (2006). Diagnosing and changing organizational culture: based on the competing values framework. Jossey-Bass.

Cameron, K. S., & Quinn, R. E. (2010). Diagnosing and changing organizational culture: based on the competing values framework. Jossey-Bass.

Cameron, K. S., & Quinn, R. E. (2011). *Diagnosing and changing organizational culture: Based on the competing values framework*. John Wiley & Sons. doi:10.1002/9780470661628

Cameron, P. (1969). Age parameters of young, middle-aged, and elderly adults. *Journal of Gerontology*, *24*(2), 201–202. doi:10.1093/geronj/24.2.201 PMID:5789257

Campbell, S., Prior, S., Bramble, M., & Maxwell, H. (2022). *Examining the engagement of health services staff in change management: Modifying the SCARF assessment model*. doi:10.19043/ipdj.121.005

Campbell, J. L. (1998). Institutional analysis and the role of ideas in political economy. *Theory and Society*, *27*(3), 377–409. doi:10.1023/A:1006871114987

Campbell, J. L. (2004). *Institutional Change and Globalization*. Princeton University Press. doi:10.1515/9780691216348

Canaan, J. E., & Shumar, W. (Eds.). (2008). *Structure and agency in the neoliberal university* (Vol. 15). Routledge. doi:10.4324/9780203927687

Canada, G. A. (2019). *Gender Analysis*. https://www.international.gc.ca/world-monde/funding-financement/gender_analysis-analyse_comparative.aspx?lang=eng

Carbado, D. W., Crenshaw, K. W., Mays, V. M., & Tomlinson, B. (2013). Intersectonality: Mapping the movements of a theory. *Du Bois Review*, *10*, 303–312. doi:10.1017/S1742058X13000349 PMID:25285150

Cardel, M. I., Dhurandhar, E., Yarar-Fisher, C., Foster, M., Hidalgo, B., McClure, L. A., ... Willig, A. L. (2020). Turning chutes into ladders for women faculty: A review and roadmap for equity in academia. *Journal of Women's Health*, *29*(5), 721–733. doi:10.1089/jwh.2019.8027 PMID:32043918

Carlisle, K., & Gruby, R. L. (2019). Polycentric systems of governance: A theoretical model for the commons. *Policy Studies Journal: the Journal of the Policy Studies Organization*, *47*(4), 927–952. doi:10.1111/psj.12212

Carrillo, J. (2007). Maquiladoras en México: ¿Evolución o agotamiento? *Revista Comercio Exterior, 57*(8), 668-681. Retrieved from http://revistas.bancomext.gob.mx/rce/magazines/106/5/Carrillo.pdf

Cartwright, L. K. (1978). Career satisfaction and role harmony in a sample of young women physicians. *Journal of Vocational Behavior, 12*(2), 184–196. doi:10.1016/0001-8791(78)90033-7

Castelblanco, J., & Robledo, J. (2014). Relación entre el PIB y algunos indicadores de Ciencia y Tecnología: Colombia vs. Corea del Sur. *Revista Escenarios: Empresa y territorio, 3*, 79-99. https://repositorio.esumer.edu.co/jspui/bitstream/esumer/326/2/Esumer_relacion.pdf

Celermajer, D. (2019). The Tick-Tick-Ticking Time Bomb and Erosion of Human Rights Institutions. *Angelaki, 24*(4), 87–102. doi:10.1080/0969725X.2019.1635829

Cennamo, L., & Gardner, D. (2008). Generational differences in work values, outcomes, and person organization values. *Journal of Managerial Psychology, 23*(8), 891–906. doi:10.1108/02683940810904385

Cerna, L. (2013). *The Nature of Policy Change and Implementation: A Review of Different Theoretical Approaches.* OECD.

Cerni, T., Curtis, G. J., & Colmar, S. H. (2012). Cognitive-experiential self theory and conflict-handling styles: Rational and constructive experiential systems are related to the integrating and compromising conflict-handling styles. *International Journal of Conflict Management, 23*(4), 362–381. doi:10.1108/10444061211267263

Cetron, M., & Davies, O. (2003). Trends that shape the future: Technological, labor, management and institutional trends. *The Futurist, 37*(2), 30–43.

Chaffin, B. C., Gosnell, H., & Cosens, B. A. (2014). A decade of adaptive governance scholarship: Synthesis and future directions. *Ecology and Society, 19*(3), 56. doi:10.5751/ES-06824-190356

Chaffin, B. C., & Gunderson, L. H. (2016). Emergence, institutionalization, and renewal: Rhythms of adaptive governance in complex social-ecological systems. *Journal of Environmental Management, 165*, 81–87. doi:10.1016/j.jenvman.2015.09.003 PMID:26426283

Chambers, C. (2004). Technological advancement, learning, and the adoption of new technology. *European Journal of Operational Research, 152*(1), 226–247. doi:10.1016/S0377-2217(02)00651-3

Chappell, L., & Waylen, G. (2013). Gender and the Hidden Life of Institutions. *Public Administration, 91*(3), 599–615. doi:10.1111/j.1467-9299.2012.02104.x

Charness, N., & Czaja, S. J. (2006). *Training Older Workers: What We Know and What We Don't Know. # 2006-22*. AARP.

Chattopadhyay, R., & Duflo, E. (2001). Women as policy makers: Evidence from a randomized policy experiment in India. *Econometrica, 72*(5), 1409–1443. doi:10.1111/j.1468-0262.2004.00539.x

Chavance, B. (2012). John Commons's organizational theory of institutions: A discussion. *Journal of Institutional Economics*, *8*(1), 27–47. doi:10.1017/S1744137411000336

Chen, L. (2008). Institutional inertia, adjustment, and change: Japan as a case of a coordinated market economy. *Review of International Political Economy*, *15*(3), 460–479. doi:10.1080/09692290801931404

Chiang, C. F. (2010). Perceived organizational change in the hotel industry: An implication of change schema. *International Journal of Hospitality Management*, *29*(1), 157–167. doi:10.1016/j.ijhm.2009.08.002

Chiu, W., Chan, A., Snape, E., & Redman, T. (2001). Age stereotypes and discrimination attitudes towards older workers: An east-west comparison. *Human Relations*, *54*, 629–661. doi:10.1177/0018726701545004

Cho, S., Crenshaw, K. W., & McCall, L. (Eds.). (2013). Toward a field of intersectionality studies: theory, applications, and praxis. Theory Signs, 38, 785–810. doi:10.1086/669608

Choudhury, P. (2021). Our work-from-anywhere future. *Harvard Business Review*. Retrieved November 30, 2021, from https://hbr.org/2020/11/our-work-from-anywhere-future

Chrusciel, D. (2006). Considerations of emotional intelligence (EI) in dealing with change decision management. *Management Decision*, *44*(5), 644–657. doi:10.1108/00251740610668897

Clark, S. C. (2000). Work/family border theory. *Human Relations*, *53*(6), 747–770. doi:10.1177/0018726700536001

Clemens, E. (1997). *The People's Lobby: Organizational Innovation and the Rise of Interest Group Politics in the United States*. University of Chicago Press.

Clemens, E. S., & Cook, J. M. (1999). Politics and Institutionalism: Explaining Durability and Change. *Annual Review of Sociology*, *25*(1), 441–466. doi:10.1146/annurev.soc.25.1.441

Cloutier, C., & Langley, A. (2013). The Logic of Institutional Logics: Insights From French Pragmatist Sociology. *Journal of Management Inquiry*, *22*(4), 360–380. doi:10.1177/1056492612469057

Co, H. C., Patuwo, B. E., & Hu, M. Y. (1998). The human factor in advanced manufacturing technology adoption: An empirical analysis. *International Journal of Operations & Production Management*, *18*(1), 87–106. doi:10.1108/01443579810192925

Collins, P. H. (1990). *2000. Black Feminist Thought: Knowledge, Consciousness, and the Politics of Empowerment*. Routledge.

Commons, J. R. (1934/1961). *Institutional Economics. Its Place in Political Economy* (Vols. 1–2). The University of Wisconsin Press.

CONACYT. (2004). *Informe General del Estado de la Ciencia y la Tecnología (IGECYT), México*. Retrieved from https://www.siicyt.gob.mx/index.php/transparencia/informes-conacyt/informe-general-del-estado-de-la-ciencia-tecnologia-e-innovacion/informe-general-2004

Cooke, R., & Lafferty, J. (1989). Organizational Culture Inventory (OCI). Human Synergistics.

Cooke, F. L., & Jing, X. (2009). Work-life balance in China: Sources of conflicts and coping strategies. *NHRD Network Journal*, *2*(6), 18–28. doi:10.1177/0974173920090603

Cosens, B. (2013). Legitimacy, adaptation, and resilience in ecosystem management. *Ecology and Society*, *18*(1), 3. doi:10.5751/ES-05093-180103

Cosens, B. A., Gunderson, L. H., & Chaffin, B. C. (2014). The adaptive water governance project: Assessing law, resilience and governance in regional socio-ecological water systems facing a changing climate. Ida. *Law Rev. Nat. Resour. Environ. Law Ed*, *51*, 1–28.

Coşkuner, S. (2013). *Work-family conflict as a mediator between work-family characteristics and marital, family and life satisfaction of faculty members* [Unpublished doctoral thesis]. Hacettepe University Graduate School of Social Sciences.

Council, Y. E. (2017). *Eight Traits Every Powerful Female Leader Possesses*. https://www.forbes.com/sites/yec/2017/10/03/eight-traits-every-powerful-female-leader-possesses/?sh=40d794a5608f

Covaleski, M. A., Dirsmith, M. W., Heian, J. B., & Samuel, S. (1998). The calculated and the avowed: Techniques of discipline and struggles over identity in Big Six public accounting firms. *Administrative Science Quarterly*, *43*(2), 293–327. doi:10.2307/2393854

Crouch, C., & Farrell, H. (2004). Breaking the path of institutional development? Alternatives to the new determinism. *Rationality and Society*, *16*(1), 5–43. doi:10.1177/1043463104039874

Crow, M., & Bozeman, B. (1998). *Limited by Design: R & D Laboratories in the U.S. National Innovation System*. Columbia University Press.

Cummings, T. G., & Worley, C. G. (2014). *Organization development and change*. Cengage Learning.

Custance, P., Walley, K., & Jiang, D. (2012). Crisis brand management in emerging markets: Insight from the Chinese infant milk powder scandal. *Marketing Intelligence & Planning*, *30*(1), 18–32. doi:10.1108/02634501211193895

Dahl, R. A. (1957). The concept of power. *Behavioral Science*, *2*(3), 201-215. doi:10.1002/bs.3830020303

Dasgupta, P. (2005). The Economics of Social Capital. *The Economic Record*, *81*(s1), 2–21. doi:10.1111/j.1475-4932.2005.00245.x

David, A., Joan, M., Seth, O., & Reeve, V. (2001). The glass ceiling effect. *Social Forces*, *80*(2), 655–681. doi:10.1353of.2001.0091

David, P. (1985). Clio and the economics of QWERTY. *The American Economic Review*, *1985*(7), 332–337.

Davis, G. F., McAdam, D., Scott, W. R., & Zald, M. N. (Eds.). (2005). *Social movements and organization theory*. Cambridge University Press. doi:10.1017/CBO9780511791000

Davis, K. (2008). Intersectionality as buzzword: A sociology of science perspective on what makes a feminist theory successful. *Feminist Theory*, *9*(1), 67–85. doi:10.1177/1464700108086364

De Dreu, C. K. (2008). The virtue and vice of workplace conflict: Food for (pessimistic) thought. *Journal of Organizational Behavior: The International Journal of Industrial. Occupational and Organizational Psychology and Behavior*, *29*(1), 5–18. doi:10.1002/job.474

de León, L. J., Pérez, R. J. V., & Boza, C. J. (2016). *Introducción a las Técnicas de Muestreo*. Ediciones Pirámide.

Deal, J., Altman, D., & Rogelberg, S. (2010). Millennials at work: What we know and what we need to do. *Journal of Business and Psychology*, *25*(2), 191–199. doi:10.100710869-010-9177-2

Deci, E. L., & Ryan, R. M. (2000). The "what" and "why" of goal pursuits: Human needs and the self-determination of behaviour. *Psychological Inquiry*, *11*(4), 227–268. doi:10.1207/S15327965PLI1104_01

Dedeurwaerdere, T. (2013). Transdisciplinary Sustainability Science at Higher Education Institutions: Science Policy Tools for Incremental Institutional Change. *Sustainability*, *5*(9), 3783–3801. doi:10.3390u5093783

Denison, D. (1996). What is the difference between organizational culture and organizational climate? A native's point of view on a decade of paradigm wars. *Academy of Management Review*, *21*(3), 619–654. doi:10.2307/258997

Denison, D. R. (2012). *Corporate culture and organizational effectiveness*. John Wiley & Sons. doi:10.1002/9781119205472

Devereux, S., & Solomon, C. (2006). *Employment creation programmes: The international experience*. ILO.

Dewey, J. (1933). *How We Think A Restatement of the Relation of Reflective Thinking to the Educative Process*. Heath & Co Publishers.

Dextras-Gauthier, J. (2014). *Culture organisationnelle et santé mentale au travail. Université de Montréal*. Philosophiae. Faculté des Études Supérieures et Postdoctorales. Retrieved from https://papyrus.bib.umontreal.ca/xmlui/handle/1866/12019

Dhingra, R., & Punia, B. K. (2016). Relational Analysis of Emotional Intelligence and Change Management: A Suggestive Model for Enriching Change Management Skills Concept Development. *Vision (Basel)*, *20*(4), 312–322. doi:10.1177/0972262916668726

Diener, E., Emmons, R. A., Larsen, R. J., & Griffin, S. (1985). The satisfaction with life scale. *Journal of Personality Assessment*, *49*(1), 71–75. doi:10.120715327752jpa4901_13 PMID:16367493

Dilnot, C. (2018). The relationship between A-level subject choice and league table score of university attended: The 'facilitating', the 'less suitable', and the counter-intuitive. *Oxford Review of Education*, *44*(1), 118–137. doi:10.1080/03054985.2018.1409976

DiMaggio, P. (1988). Interest and agency in institutional theor y. In L. Zucker (Ed.), *Research on institutional patterns: Environment and culture* (pp. 3–21). Ballinger Publishing Co.

DiMaggio, P. (1988). Interest and agency in institutional theory. In L. Zucker (Ed.), *Institutional Patterns and Organizations: Culture and Environment: 3–22*. Ballinger.

DiMaggio, P. (1991). Constructing an organizational field as a professional Project: U.S. art museums, 1920–1940. In P. DiMaggio & W. Powell (Eds.), *The New Institutionalism in Organizational Analysis: 267–292*. University of Chicago Press.

DiMaggio, P. J. (1988). Interest and Agency in Institutional Theory. In L. G. Zucker (Ed.), *Institutional Patterns and Organizations: Culture and Environment* (pp. 3–22). Ballinger.

Dishman, L. (2021). *This is how each generation is feeling about returning to the office*. Fast Company. Retrieved December 1, 2021, from https://www.fastcompany.com/90673558/this-is-howeach-generation-is-feeling-about-returning-to-the-office

Dolowitz, D. P., & Marsh, D. (1996). Who Learns What from Whom? A Review of the Policy Transfer Literature. *Political Studies*, *44*(2), 343–357. doi:10.1111/j.1467-9248.1996.tb00334.x

Donkin, R. (2014). *Future of work*. Palgrave Macmillan.

Doorewaard, H., & Benschop, Y. (2003). HRM and organizational change: An emotional endeavor. *Journal of Organizational Change Management*, *16*(3), 272–286. doi:10.1108/09534810310475523

Dowding, K. (1995). Model or metaphor? A critical review of the policy network approach. *Political Studies*, *43*(1), 136–158. doi:10.1111/j.1467-9248.1995.tb01705.x

Eagly, A. H., & Sczesny, S. (2009). *Stereotypes about women, men, and leaders: Have times changed?* American Psychological Association.

Edgar, H. S. (1996). Three Cultures of Management: The Keyto Organizational Learning. *Sloan Management Review*, *38*(1), 9. http://cmapspublic.ihmc.us/rid=1255442538593_81326613_21696/Three cultures of management schein.pdf

Edman, J. (2016). Cultivating Foreignness: How Organizations Maintain and Leverage Minority Identities. *Journal of Management Studies*, *53*(1), 55–88. doi:10.1111/joms.12129

Edwards, A. (2013). El diagnóstico de la cultura organizacional o las culturas de la cultura. *Global Media Journal México, 6*(11), 67-81. https://gmjmexico.uanl.mx/index.php/GMJ_EI/article/view/79/78

Eisenberger, N. I., Lieberman, M. D., & Williams, K. D. (2003). Does rejection hurt? An FMRI study of social exclusion. *Science*, *302*(5643), 290–292. doi:10.1126cience.1089134 PMID:14551436

El-Besomey, D. A. M. (2020). The Contemporary Vision of Universal Strategic Planning for Facing (COVID-19) Crisis in the Field of Higher Education Via Virtual Learning-Training. *European Journal of Education*, *3*(2), 151–164. doi:10.26417/869dvb85y

Elsbach, K. D., & Stigliani, I. (2018). Design thinking and organizational culture: A review and framework for future research. *Journal of Management*, *44*(6), 2274–2306. doi:10.1177/0149206317744252

Elsdon, R., & Lyer, S. (1999). Creating Value and Improving Retention Through Employee Development: The Sun Microsystems Experience. *Human Resources Planning, 22*(2), 39-40.

Elson, D. (2010). Gender and the global economic crisis in developing countries: A framework for analysis. *Gender and Development*, *18*(2), 201–212. doi:10.1080/13552074.2010.491321

Emirbayer, M., & Goldberg, C. A. (2005). Pragmatism, Bourdieu, and collective emotions in contentious politics. *Theory and Society*, *34*(5-6), 469–518. doi:10.100711186-005-1619-x

Eriksson-Zetterquist, U., Lindberg, K., & Styhre, A. (2009). When the good times are over: Professionals encountering new technology. *Human Relations*, *62*(8), 1145–1170. doi:10.1177/0018726709334879

Erwin, D. G., & Garman, A. N. (2010). Resistance to organizational change: Linking research and practice. *Leadership and Organization Development Journal*, *31*(1), 39–56. doi:10.1108/01437731011010371

ESGHUB. (2022). *The role of Women in Business Management in Switzerland*. https://esghub.ch/the-role-of-women-in-business-management-in-switzerland/

Estrin, S., & Prevezer, M. (2011). The role of informal institutions in corporate governance: Brazil, Russia, India, and China compared. *Asia Pacific Journal of Management*, *28*(1), 41–67. doi:10.100710490-010-9229-1

Farr, J., Tesluk, P., & Klein, S. (1998). Organizational structure of the workplace and the older worker. In Impact of work on older adults (Vol. 19, pp. 143-206). Springer.

Favero, M., Gatto, P., Deutsch, N., & Pettenella, D. (2016). Conflict or synergy? Understanding interaction between municipalities and village commons (regole) in polycentric governance of mountain areas in the Veneto Region, Italy. *The International Journal of the Commons*, *10*(2), 821–853. doi:10.18352/ijc.470

FDFA. (2020). *Switzerland's commitment to women's rights worldwide*. https://www.eda.admin.ch/eda/en/fdfa/fdfa/aktuell/newsuebersicht/2020/03/csw.html

Fehr, E., & Camerer, C. F. (2007). Social neuroeconomics: The neural circuitry of social preferences. *Trends in Cognitive Sciences*, *11*(10), 419–427. doi:10.1016/j.tics.2007.09.002 PMID:17913566

Fischhendler, I. (2015). The securitization of water discourse: Theoretical foundations and research gaps. Int. Environ. Agreem. *Politics Law Econ*, *2015*(15), 245–2.

Fisher, W., & Wesolkowski, S. (1999). Tempering technostress. *IEEE Technology and Society Magazine*, *18*(1), 28–33. doi:10.1109/44.752243

Fitzgerald, T. (2020). Mapping the terrain of leadership: Gender and leadership in higher education. *Irish Educational Studies*, *39*(2), 1–12. doi:10.1080/03323315.2020.1729222

Foucault, M. (1978). *The History of Sexuality* (Vol. 1). Vantage Books, Random House.

Fox, M. F., & Fonesca, C. (2006). Gender and mentoring of faculty in science and engineering: Individual and organisational factors. *International Journal of Learning and Change*, *1*(4), 460–483. doi:10.1504/IJLC.2006.013912

Frantzeskaki, N., Broto, V. C., Coenen, L., & Loorbach, D. (2017). *Urban Sustainability Transitions* (1st ed.). Routledge. doi:10.4324/9781315228389

French, J. R. P., Jr., & Raven, B. (1959). The bases of social power. In D. Cartwright (Ed.), Studies in social power (pp. 150-167). Ann Arbor, MI: University of Michigan Press.

Friedland, R. (2013). Review: The institutional logics perspective: An innovative approach to culture, structure, and process. *M@n@gement, 15*(5), 583-595.

Frone, M. R., Russell, M., & Cooper, M. L. (1992). Antecedents and outcomes of work family conflict: Testing a model of the work family ınterface. *The Journal of Applied Psychology*, *77*(1), 65–78. doi:10.1037/0021-9010.77.1.65 PMID:1556042

Fuenfschilling, L. (2019). *An Institutional perspective on sustainability transitions Handbook of Sustainable Innovation.* Edward Elgar Publishing. https://www.elgaronline.com/view/edcoll/9781788112567/9781788112567.00020.xml

Fuenfschilling, L., & Truffer, B. (2014). The structuration of socio-technical regimes-conceptual foundations from institutional theory. *Research Policy*, *43*(4), 772–791. doi:10.1016/j.respol.2013.10.010

Furet, F. (1980/2006). The French Revolution Revisited. In G. Kates (Ed.), *The French Revolution, recent Debates and New Controversies* (2nd ed., pp. 53–567). Routledge.

Gabriele, A. (2002). S&T policies and technical progress in China's industry. *Review of International Political Economy*, *9*(2), 333–373. doi:10.1080/09692290110126137

Gabrielova, K., & Buchko, A. A. (2021). Here comes generation Z: Millennials as managers. *Business Horizons*, *64*(4), 489–499. doi:10.1016/j.bushor.2021.02.013

Galbreath, J. (2011). Are there gender-related influences on corporate sustainability? A study of women on boards of directors. *Journal of Management & Organization*, *17*(1), 17–38. doi:10.5172/jmo.2011.17.1.17

García, L., Hernández, R., Vargas, B., & Cuevas, H. (2012). Diagnóstico de la cultura organizacional en universidades tecnológicas bajo el Modelo de Valores en Competencia. *Estudios en Ciencias Sociales y Administrativas. Universidad de Celaya, 2*, 9-29. Retrieved from https://www.researchgate.net/profile/Hector-Cuevas-Vargas/publication/282353614_Diagnostico_de_la_cultura_organizacional_en_universidades_tecnologicas_bajo_el_Modelo_de_Valores_en_Competencia/links/560d7ac308ae6cf68153f578/Diagnostico-de-la-cultura-organizacional-en-universidades-tecnologicas-bajo-el-Modelo-de-Valores-en-Competencia.pdf

Gardner, H. (1995). *Leading Minds*. Harper Collins.

Gärtner, C. (2013). *Enhancing Readiness for Change by Enhancing Mindfulness*. https://www.tandfonline.com/doi/pdf/10.1080/14697017.2013.768433

Gelleard, C., & Higgs, P. (2005). *Aging contexts: cohort class and community*. Polity Press.

Geneva, I. (2017). *Gender in employment policies and programmes: What works for women?* https://www.ilo.org/wcmsp5/groups/public/---ed_emp/documents/publication/wcms_613536.pdf

Geneva. (2023, March 8). *Women in leadership bring better business performance*. International Labor Organization. https://www.ilo.org/global/about-the-ilo/newsroom/news/WCMS_701767/lang--en/index.htm

Geng, F., Redcay, E., & Riggins, T. (2019). The influence of age and performance on hippocampal function and the encoding of contextual information in early childhood. *NeuroImage, 195*, 433–443. doi:10.1016/j.neuroimage.2019.03.035 PMID:30905835

Gök, A., Karaulova, M., & Shapira, P. (2016). Dynamics of Transition in Core-Periphery Structures in Global Research System. Presented at the *EU-SPRI Conference, Lund*, Sweden.

Goldkuhl, G., & Cronholm, S. (2010). Adding theoretical grounding to grounded theory: Toward multi-grounded theory. *International Journal of Qualitative Methods, 9*(2), 187–205. doi:10.1177/160940691000900205

Goldstone, J. (2009). Rethinking Revolutions: Integrating Origins, Processes, and Outcomes. *Comparative Studies of South Asia, Africa and the Middle East, 29*(1), 18–32. doi:10.1215/1089201X-2008-040

Goleman, D. (2017). *Leadership that gets results (Harvard business review classics)*. Harvard Business Press.

Gómez, C., & Sánchez, J. (2005). HR's strategic role within MNCs: Helping build social capital in Latin America. *International Journal of Human Resource Management, 16*(12), 2189–2200. doi:10.1080/09585190500358596

Goode, W. J. (1960). A theory of role strain. *American Sociological Review, 25*(4), 483–496. doi:10.2307/2092933

Goodman, E., & Loh, L. (2011). Organizational change: A critical challenge for team effectiveness. *Business Information Review, 28*(4), 242–250. doi:10.1177/0266382111427087

Goodstein, J. D., & Velamuri, S. R. (2009). States, power, legitimacy, and maintaining institutional control: The battle for private sector telecommunication services in Zimbabwe. *Organization Studies*, *30*(5), 489–508. doi:10.1177/0170840609104395

Göransson, K. E., Ehnfors, M., Fonteyn, M. E., & Ehrenberg, A. (2008). Thinking strategies used by Registered Nurses during emergency department triage. *Journal of Advanced Nursing*, *61*(2), 163–172. doi:10.1111/j.1365-2648.2007.04473.x PMID:18186908

Gordon, H. A., & Kammeyer, K. C. W. (1980). The gainful employment of women with small children. *Journal of Marriage and Family*, *42*(2), 327–336. doi:10.2307/351230

Gornitzka, A., Kyvik, S., & Stensaker, B. (2005). Implementation analysis in higher education. In A. Gornitzka, M. Kogan, & A. Amaral (Eds.), *Reform and change in higher education: analyzing policy implementation* (pp. 35–56). Springer. doi:10.1007/1-4020-3411-3_3

Graham, L. R. (2010). *What Have We Learned About Science and Technology from the Russian Experience?* Stanford University Press.

Greene, H. W. (2012). *Econometric Analysis*. Pearson.

Greener, I. (2002). Understanding NHS reform: The policy-transfer, social learning and path-dependency perspectives. *Governance: An International Journal of Policy, Administration and Institutions*, *15*(2), 161–183. doi:10.1111/1468-0491.00184

Greenhaus, J. H., & Beutell, N. J. (1985). Sources of conflict between work and family roles. *Academy of Management Review*, *10*(1), 76–88. doi:10.2307/258214

Green, M. (2007). *Change management masterclass: A step-by-step guide to successful change management*. Kogan Page Publishers.

Greenwood, R., Diaz, A. M., Li, S. X., & Lorente, J. C. (2010). The Multiplicity of Institutional Logics and the Heterogeneity of Organizational Responses. *Organization Science*, *21*(2), 521–539. doi:10.1287/orsc.1090.0453

Greenwood, R., Raynard, M., Kodeih, F., Micelotta, E. R., & Lounsbury, M. (2011). Institutional complexity and organizational responses. *The Academy of Management Annals*, *5*(1), 317–371. doi:10.5465/19416520.2011.590299

Greenwood, R., Suddaby, R., & Hinings, C. R. (2002). Theorizing Change: The Role of Professional Associations in the Transformation of Institutionalized Fields. *Academy of Management Journal*, *45*(1), 58–80. doi:10.2307/3069285

Greer, S., Saygi, O., Aaldering, H., & de Dreu, C. K. W. (2012). Conflict in medical teams: Opportunity or danger? *Medical Education*, *46*(10), 935–942. doi:10.1111/j.1365-2923.2012.04321.x PMID:22989127

Greif, A. (1998). Self-enforcing political systems and economic growth: Late medieval Genoa. In R. Bates, A. Greif, M. Levi, J. L. Rosenthal, & B. Weingast (Eds.), *Analytical Narratives: 23–63*. Princeton University Press. doi:10.2139srn.49207

Grieves, J., McMillan, J., & Wilding, P. (2006). Barriers to learning: Conflicts that occur between and within organisational systems. *International Journal of Learning Intellectual Capital*, *3*(1), 86–103. doi:10.1504/IJLIC.2006.009212

Grimson, J., & Grimson, W. (2019). Eliminating gender inequality in engineering, industry, and academia. In *The Engineering-Business Nexus* (pp. 315–339). Springer. doi:10.1007/978-3-319-99636-3_15

Grosse, R. (1996). International technology transfer in services. *Journal of International Business Studies*, *27*(4), 781–800. doi:10.1057/palgrave.jibs.8490153

Grzymala-Busse, A. (2010). The best laid plans: The impact of informal rules on formal institutions in transitional regimes. *Studies in Comparative International Development*, *45*(3), 311–333. doi:10.100712116-010-9071-y

Guberman, N., Fournier, D., Belleau, J., Beeman, J., & Gervais, L. (1994). Des questions sur la culture organisationnelle des organismes communautaires. *Nouvelles Pratiques Sociales*, *7*(1), 45–62. doi:10.7202/301251ar

Guerrero, S., Chênevert, D., Vandenberghe, C., Tremblay, M., & Ben Ayed, A. K. (2018). Employees' psychological empowerment and performance: How customer feedback substitutes for leadership. *Journal of Services Marketing*, *32*(7), 868–879. doi:10.1108/JSM-09-2017-0325

Guisán, M., & Neira, I. (2001). Capital humano y capital físico en la OCDE, su importancia en el crecimiento económico en el período 1965-95. *Estudios Económicos de Desarrollo Internacional*, *1*, 1-13. Retrieved from https://www.usc.gal/economet/reviews/eedi123.pdf

Gujarati, D., & Porter, D. (2010). *Econometría (Quinta edición)*. McGraw Hill.

Guo, C. (2019). *Synergy mechanism and empirical research of manufacturing and producer services in China from the perspective of Global Value Chain* [Ph.D. Thesis]. Shanghai Academy of Social Sciences.

Gutiérrez, M., & Herráiz, G. (2009). Intergenerational Grandparents School Program. *Espai Social, Revista del Colegio Oficial d'Educadores i Eeducadors Socials de la Comunitat Valenciana*, *9*, 41-44.

Hackler, N. (2022). Managing masculinity in public organizations. Handbook on gender and public administration. doi:10.4337/9781789904734.00014

Haller, T., & Merten, S. (2008). "We are Zambians—Don't tell us how to fish!" institutional change, power relations and conflicts in the Kafue flats fisheries in Zambia. *Human Ecology*, *36*(5), 699–715. doi:10.100710745-008-9191-4

Hall, P., & Soskice, D. (2001). *Varieties of Capitalism: The Institutional Foundations of Comparative Advantage*. Oxford University Press. doi:10.1093/0199247757.001.0001

Hall, P., & Taylor, R. (1996). Political science and the three new institutionalisms. *Political Studies*, *44*(5), 936–957. doi:10.1111/j.1467-9248.1996.tb00343.x

Hammer, L. B., Allen, B., & Grigsby, T. D. (1997). Work-family conflict in dual-earner couples: Within-individual and crossover effects of work and family. *Journal of Vocational Behavior*, *50*(2), 185–203. doi:10.1006/jvbe.1996.1557

Hansen, M. (2018). *Cultivating change: The relationship between organizational culture, leadership style and communication style with organizational change* [Doctoral dissertation]. Marquette University.

Hanushek, E. A., & Luque, J. A. (2003). Efficiency and equity in schools around the world. *Economics of Education Review*, *22*(5), 481–502. doi:10.1016/S0272-7757(03)00038-4

Harding, S. G. (1986). *The Science Question in Feminism*. Cornell University Press.

Harding, S. G. (1991). *Whose Science? Whose knowledge? Thinking From Women's Lives*. Cornell University Press.

Harmon, D. J. (2019). When the Fed speaks: Arguments, emotions, and the microfoundations of institutions. *Administrative Science Quarterly*, *64*(3), 542–575. doi:10.1177/0001839218777475

Harris, M. C. (2015). *Exploring different generations: A phenomenological study on conflict management in the workplace* (Order No. 3722198). Available from ABI/INFORM Collection; ProQuest Central; ProQuest Dissertations & Theses Global. (1728126657)

Harris, L. T., McClure, S. M., van den Bos, W., Cohen, J. D., & Fiske, S. T. (2007). Regions of the MPFC differentially tuned to social and nonsocial affective evaluation. *Cognitive, Affective & Behavioral Neuroscience*, *7*(4), 309–316. doi:10.3758/CABN.7.4.309 PMID:18189004

Hau siu Chow, I., & Ding, D. Z. Q. (2002). Moral judgement and conflict handling styles among Chinese in Hong Kong and PRC. *Journal of Management Development*, *21*(9), 666–679. doi:10.1108/02621710210441667

Hayes, C., & Graham, Y. N. (2020). Prophylaxis in Action:# MeToo for Women of Medical and Surgical Disciplines. In Gender Equity in the Medical Profession (pp. 270-279). IGI Global.

Helpap, S., & Bekmeier-Feuerhahn, S. (2016). Employees' emotions in change: Advancing the sensemaking approach. *Journal of Organizational Change Management*, *29*(6), 903–916. doi:10.1108/JOCM-05-2016-0088

Henderson, M., Sullivan, A., Anders, J., & Moulton, V. (2018). Social class, gender and ethnic differences in subjects taken at age 14. *Curriculum Journal*, *29*(3), 298–318. doi:10.1080/09585176.2017.1406810

Henley, J., & Roy, E. A. (2020). Are female leaders more successful at managing the coronavirus crisis. *Guardian*. https://www. theguardian. com/world/2020/apr/25/why-do-female-leadersseem-to-be-more-successful-at-managing-the-coronavirus-crisis

Herepath, A., & Kitchener, M. (2016). When small bandages fail: The field-level repair of severe and protracted institutional breaches. *Organization Studies*, *37*(8), 1113–1139. doi:10.1177/0170840615622065

Hernandez, D. (2011). *Young people and intergenerational dialogue in community transformation and social*. Center for Psychological and Sociological Research.

Hernández, R., Fernández, C., & Baptista, M. P. (2010). *Metodología de la Investigación*. Mc. Graw Hill.

Hewitt, P. (2006). Electronic mail and internal communication: A three-factor model. *Corporate Communications, 11*(1), 78–92. doi:10.1108/13563280610643570

Heymann, J., Levy, J. K., Bose, B., Ríos-Salas, V., Mekonen, Y., Swaminathan, H., ... Darmstadt, G. L. (2019). Improving health with programmatic, legal, and policy approaches to reduce gender inequality and change restrictive gender norms. *Lancet, 393*(10190), 2522–2534. doi:10.1016/S0140-6736(19)30656-7 PMID:31155271

Heyns, E., Eldermire, E., & Howard, H. (2019). Unsubstantiated Conclusions: A Scoping Review on Generational Differences of Leadership in Academic Libraries. *Journal of Academic Librarianship, 45*(5), 102054. doi:10.1016/j.acalib.2019.102054

Hicks, D. (1993). University-industry research links in Japan. *Policy Sciences, 26*(4), 361–395. https://www.jstor.org/stable/4532299. doi:10.1007/BF00999478

Hirschman, A. (1982). *Shifting Involvements, Private Interest and Public Action*. Princeton University Press.

Hitt, M. A., Xu, K., & Carnes, C. M. (2016). Resource based theory in operations management research. *J. Operat. Manag., 41*, 77–94. doi: .2015.11.002 doi:10.1016/j.jom

Hobfoll, S. E. (2001). The influence of culture, community, and the nested-self in the stress process: Advancing conservation of resources theory. *Applied Psychology, 50*(3), 337–421. doi:10.1111/1464-0597.00062

Hochschild, A. R. (2016). *Strangers in Their Own Land: Anger and Mourning on the American Right*. The New Press.

Hodgson, G. (2017). 1688 and all that: Property rights, the Glorious Revolution, and the rise of British capitalism. *Journal of Institutional and Theoretical Economics, 13*(1), 79–107. doi:10.1017/S1744137416000266

Hofstede, G. (2011). Dimensionalizing Cultures: T he Hofstede Model in Context. *Online Readings in Psychology and Culture, 2*(1).

Höllerer, M. A. (2013). From taken-for-granted to explicit commitment: The rise of CSR in a corporatist country. *Journal of Management Studies, 50*(4), 573–606. doi:10.1111/joms.12029

Holt, J., & DeVore, C. J. (2005). Culture, gender, organizational role, and styles of conflict resolution: A meta-analysis. *International Journal of Intercultural Relations, 29*(2), 165–196. doi:10.1016/j.ijintrel.2005.06.002

Hooghe, L., & Marks, G. (2003). Unraveling the central state, but how? Types of multi-level governance. *The American Political Science Review*, *97*(2), 233–243.

Hounkonnou, D., Kossou, D., Kuyper, T. W., Leeuwis, C., Nederlof, S., Roling, N., Dawson, O. S., Traore, M., & Huis, V. A. (2012). An innovation systems approach to institutional change: Smallholder development in West Africa. *Agricultural Systems*, *108*, 74–83. doi:10.1016/j.agsy.2012.01.007

Huang, Y. H., Hammer, L. B., Neal, M. B., & Perrin, N. A. (2004). The relationship between work-to-Family conflict and family-to-work conflict: A longitudinal study. *Journal of Family and Economic Issues*, *25*(1), 79–100. doi:10.1023/B:JEEI.0000016724.76936.a1

Hudescu, L., & Ilies, L. (n.d.-b) *Challenges in Choosing an Effective Change Management Approach*. Retrieved October 5, 2022, from https://www.proquest.com/docview/1220671941?pq-origsite=gscholar&fromopenview=true

Hughes, M. (2014). *Managing change: A critical perspective* (2nd ed.). CIPD.

Huitema, M., & Egas, M. (2009). Adaptive water governance: Assessing the institutional prescriptions of adaptive (co-) management from a governance perspective and defining a research agenda. *Ecology and Society*, *14*(1), 26. doi:10.5751/ES-02827-140126

Hummert, M. (1999). A social cognitive perspective on age stereotypes. In *Social Cognition and Aging (pp. 175-196)*. Academic Press. doi:10.1016/B978-012345260-3/50009-4

Hutchings, K. (2006). *Diversity and HRD*. Pearson.

Icard, E., & Drumctz, F. (1994). Développement des Marchés de Titres et Financement de l'Économie Française. Bulletin de la Banque de France, 6.

Iddagoda, A., Opatha, H. H. P., & Gunawardana, K. (2016). Towards a Conceptualization and an Operationalization of the Construct of Employee Engagement. *International Business Research*, *9*(2), 1–14. doi:10.5539/ibr.v9n2p85

Ide, T. (2015). Why Do Conflicts Over Scarce Renewable Resources Turn Violent? A qualitative comparative analysis. *Global Environmental Change*, *2015*(33), 61–70. doi:10.1016/j.gloenvcha.2015.04.008

Immergut, E. (1992). *Health Politics: Interests and Institution in Western Europe*. Academic Press.

Indajang, K., Halim, F., & Sudirman, A. (2021). The Effectiveness of Teacher Performance in Terms of the Aspects of Principal Leadership, Organizational Culture, and Teacher Competence. *Proceedings of the 2nd Annual Conference on Blended Learning, Educational Technology and Innovation (ACBLETI 2020), 560*, 402-408. https://www.atlantis-press.com/article/125957871.pdf

Ingram, P., & Clay, K. (2000). The choice-within-constraints new institutionalism and implications for sociology. *Annual Review of Sociology*, *26*(1), 525–546. doi:10.1146/annurev.soc.26.1.525

Inman, A. G. (2020). Culture and Positionality: Academy and Mentorship. *Women & Therapy*, *43*(1-2), 112–124. doi:10.1080/02703149.2019.1684678

Instituto Nacional de Estadística y Geografía. (2015). *Encuesta Intercensal 2015*. Recuperado de https://www.inegi.org.mx/programas/intercensal/2015

International Labour Organization. (2011). *Skills and Occupational Needs in Renewable Energy*. Geneva: European Commission. Retrieved from https://www.ilo.org/wcmsp5/groups/public/---ed_emp/---ifp_skills/documents/publication/wcms_166823.pdf

International, V., Kimhi, S., Oliel, Y., & Odemegwu Ojukwu, C. (2019). Change Management and Organizational Performance in Selected Manufacturing Companies in Anambra State, Nigeria. *The International Journal of Social Sciences and Humanities Invention*, *6*(05), 5. doi:10.18535/ijsshi/v6i5.06

Iorgulescu, M. C. (2016). Generation Z and its perception of work. *CrossCultural Management Journal*, *18*(1), 47–54.

Jackson, G. (2005). Contested boundaries: ambiguity and creativity in the evolution of German codetermination. In Beyond Continuity: Institutional Change in Advanced Political Economies. Oxford University Press.

Jacometti, M. (2013). *Institutional Work na conformação do conhecimento difundido em redes interorganizacionais: estudo de APLs no Estado do Paraná*. Tese (Doutorado em Administração). Universidade Federal do Paraná, PR, 2013. Diponível em: https://acervodigital.ufpr.br/handle/1884/34682

Jamali, A., Bhutto, A., Khaskhely, M., & Sethar, W. (2022). Impact of leadership styles on faculty performance: Moderating role of organizational culture in higher education. *Management Science Letters*, *12*(1), 1–20. doi:10.5267/j.msl.2021.8.005

Jamali, D. (2005). Changing management paradigms: Implications for educational institutions. *Journal of Management Development*, *24*(2), 104–115. doi:10.1108/02621710510579473

Jameson, J. (Ed.). (2019). *International perspectives on leadership in higher education: Critical thinking for global challenges*. Routledge. doi:10.4324/9781315122410

Jandrić, P., Hayes, D., Truelove, I., Levinson, P., Mayo, P., Ryberg, T., ... Jackson, L. (2020). Teaching in the Age of Covid-19. *Postdigital Science and Education*, 1-162.

Jehn, K. A. (1994). Enhancing effectiveness: An investigation of advantages and disadvantages of value-based intragroup conflict. *International Journal of Conflict Management*, *5*(3), 223–238. doi:10.1108/eb022744

Jehn, K. A. (1995). A multimethod examination of the benefits and detriments of intragroup conflict. *Administrative Science Quarterly*, *40*(2), 256–282. doi:10.2307/2393638

Jehn, K. A. (1997). A qualitative analysis of conflict types and dimensions in organizational groups. *Administrative Science Quarterly*, *42*(3), 530–557. doi:10.2307/2393737

Jencks, C., & Phillips, M. (2011). *The Black-White test score gap*. Brookings Institution Press.

Jhpiego. (2016). *Gender analysis toolkit for health systems*. https://gender.jhpiego.org/analysistoolkit/gender-analysis-framework/

Johannessen, J. A. (2021). How can we reduce resistance to changes within organisations? In *Continuous Change and Communication in Knowledge Management* (pp. 57–73). Emerald Publishing Limited. doi:10.1108/978-1-80117-033-820211003

Johansen, M. S. (2007). The effect of female strategic managers on organizational performance. *Public Organization Review*, *7*(3), 269–279. doi:10.100711115-007-0036-1

Johnson, A. (2001). *Functions in innovation system approaches*. Retrieved June 26, 2015, from https://www.druid.dk/uploads/tx_picturedb/ds2001-205.pdf

Johnson, B. L. (1980). Marital and family characteristics of the labor force. *Monthly Labor Review*, *103*(4), 48–52.

Jones, A. P., & Butler, M. C. (1980). A role transition approach to the stresses of organizationally-induced family role disruption. *Journal of Marriage and Family*, *42*(2), 367–376. doi:10.2307/351234

Jones, C. (2006). Bourgeois revolution revivified: 1789 and social change. In G. Kates (Ed.), *The French Revolution, recent Debates and New Controversies* (2nd ed., pp. 87–112). Routledge.

Jones, J., Murray, S., & Tapp, S. (2018). Generational Differences in the Workplace. *Journal of Business Diversity*, *18*(2), 88–97.

Jones, W. M., & Mckenna, J. (2002). Women and work-home conflict: A dual paradigm approach. *Health Education*, *102*(5), 249–259. doi:10.1108/09654280210444128

Kahn, R. L., Wolfe, D. M., Quinn, R., Snoek, J. D., & Rosenthal, R. A. (1964). *Organizational stress: Studies in role conflict and ambiguity*. Wiley.

Kajbaf, K., & Sadat, M. (2008). Investigating the attitude of Isfahan Education Organization employees towards women's management and obstacles to promoting women to management positions. *Social Psychological Studies of Women, 6*(3), 133-147.

Kamil Kozan, M., & Ergin, C. (1999). The influence of intra-cultural value differences on conflict management practices. *International Journal of Conflict Management*, *10*(3), 249–267. doi:10.1108/eb022826

Kanter, R. M. (1977). *Men and women of the corporation*. Academic Press.

Kanter, R. M. (1977). *Men and women of the corporation*. Basic Books.

Kanter, R. M. (1977). *Work and family in the united states: A critical review and agenda for research and policy*. Russell Sage Foundation.

Kanter, R. M. (2012). Ten reasons people resist change. *Harvard Business Review*, 74.

Kapur, D., & Lewis, P. (1997). *Webb R: The World Bank: Its First Half Century*. Brookings Institution Press.

Karam, C. M., & Jamali, D. (2013). Gendering CSR in the Arab Middle East: An institutional perspective. *Business Ethics Quarterly*, *23*(1), 31–68. doi:10.5840/beq20132312

Karsten, M. F. (2006). *Management, gender, and race in the 21st century*. University Press of Amer.

Katz, D., & Kahn, R. L. (1978). The social psychology of organizations (2nd ed.). Wiley.

Kennedy, M. T., & Fiss, P. C. (2013). An ontological turn in categories research: From standards of legitimacy to evidence of actuality. *Journal of Management Studies*, *50*(6), 1138–1154. doi:10.1111/joms.12031

Kenny, M. (2007). Gender, Institutions and Power: A Critical Review. *Politics*, *27*(2), 91–100. doi:10.1111/j.1467-9256.2007.00284.x

Keogh, W., & Galloway, L. (2004). Teaching enterprise in vocational disciplines: Reflecting on positive experience. *Management Decision*, *42*(3/4), 531–541. doi:10.1108/00251740410519001

Kern, F., & Howlett, M. (2009). Implementing transition management as policy reforms: A case study of the Dutch energy sector. *Policy Sciences*, *42*(4), 391–408. doi:10.100711077-009-9099-x

Khan, H., Rehmat, M., Butt, T. H., Farooqi, S., & Asim, J. (2020). Impact of transformational leadership on work performance, burnout and social loafing: A mediation model. *Future Business Journal*, *6*(1), 1–13. doi:10.118643093-020-00043-8

Khurram, J., Wandschneider, K., & Wunnava, P. V. (2007). The effect of political regimes and technology on economic growth. *Applied Economics*, *39*(11), 1425–1432. doi:10.1080/00036840500447906

Kim, T.-Y., Shin, D., Oh, H., & Jeong, Y.-C. (2007). Inside the Iron Cage: Organizational Political Dynamics and Institutional Changes in Presidential Selection Systems in Korean Universities, 1985–2002. *Administrative Science Quarterly*, *52*(2), 286–323. doi:10.2189/asqu.52.2.286

Kingdon, J. W. (2011). *Agendas, Alternatives, and Public Policies*. Little, Brown. (Original work published 1984)

King, P. M., & Kitchener, K. S. (2004). Reflective judgment: Theory and research on the development of epistemic assumptions through adulthood. *Educational Psychologist*, *39*(1), 5–18. doi:10.120715326985ep3901_2

Klein, S. M. (1996). A management communication strategy for change. *Journal of Organizational Change Management*, *9*(2), 32–46. doi:10.1108/09534819610113720

Knight, J. (1992). *Institutions and Social Conflict*. Cambridge University Press. doi:10.1017/CBO9780511528170

Kodeih, F., & Greenwood, R. (2014). Responding to Institutional Complexity: The Role of Identity. *Organization Studies*, *35*(1), 7–39. doi:10.1177/0170840613495333

Kohler-Koch, B., & Eising, R. (Eds.). (1999). The transformation of governance in the European Union. Routledge.

Kohli, M. (1994). Work and retirement: a comparative perspective. In Age and structural retardation. Wiley.

Kornai J. (1991). *The Soviet Union's Road to a free economy, comments of an outside observer.* Tanner Lecture (part II), delivered at Leningrad University.

Kostoff, R. J., Antonio del Río, J., Cortés, H. D., Smith, C., Smith, A., Wagner, C., Leydesdorff, L., Karypis, G., Malpohl, G., & Tshiteya, R. (2005). The structure and infrastructure of Mexico's science and technology. *Technological Forecasting and Social Change, 72*(7), 798–814. doi:10.1016/j.techfore.2005.02.001

Kostova, T., & Roth, K. (2002). Adoption of an organizational practice by subsidiaries of multinational corporations: Institutional and relational effects. *Academy of Management Journal, 45*(1), 215–233. doi:10.2307/3069293

Kotter, J. (2014). *The 8-step process for leading change.* The Kotter International Home Page. Retrieved July 20, 2023, from https://www.kotterinc.com/methodology/8-steps/

Kotter, J., & Heskett, J. (1992). *Corporate culture and performance.* Free Press.

Kowske, B., Rasch, R., & Wiley, J. (2010). Millennials' (lack of) attitude problem: An empirical examination of generational effects on work attitudes. *Journal of Business and Psychology, 25*(2), 265–279. doi:10.100710869-010-9171-8

Kpinpuo, S. D., Akolgo, I. G., & Naimi, L. (2023). Leading change and innovation in Ghana's banking sector: The mediating role of work autonomy. *Industrial and Commercial Training, 55*(1), 1–18. doi:10.1108/ICT-12-2021-0086

Kraatz, M. S., & Block, E. (2008). Organizational implications of institutional pluralism. In R. Greenwood, C. Oliver, K. Sahlin-Andersson, & R. Suddaby (Eds.), *The Sage handbook of organizational institutionalism.* Sage. doi:10.4135/9781849200387.n10

Kringelbach, M. L., Lehtonen, A., Squire, S., Harvey, A. G., Craske, M. G., Holliday, I. E., Green, A. L., Aziz, T. Z., Hansen, P. C., Cornelissen, P. L., & Stein, A. (2008). A specific and rapid neural signature for parental instinct. *PLoS One, 3*(2), e1664. doi:10.1371/journal.pone.0001664 PMID:18301742

Krook, M. L., & Mackay, L. (2010). *Gender, Politics, and Institutions: Towards a Feminist Institutionalism.* Palgrave Macmillan.

Kuenzi, M., Brown, M. E., Mayer, D. M., & Priesemuth, M. (2019). Supervisor-subordinate (dis) agreement on ethical leadership: An investigation of its antecedents and relationship to organizational deviance. *Business Ethics Quarterly, 29*(1), 25–53. doi:10.1017/beq.2018.14

Kuenzi, M., Mayer, D. M., & Greenbaum, R. L. (2020). Creating an ethical organizational environment: The relationship between ethical leadership, ethical organizational climate, and unethical behavior. *Personnel Psychology*, *73*(1), 43–71. doi:10.1111/peps.12356

Kungl, G., & Geels, F. G. (2018). Sequence and alignment of external pressures in industry destabilisation: Understanding the downfall of incumbent utilities in the German energy transition (1998–2015). *Environmental Innovation and Societal Transitions*, *26*(March), 78–100. doi:10.1016/j.eist.2017.05.003

Kure, N. (2010). Narrative mediation and discursive positioning in organisational conflicts. *Explorations: An E-Journal of Narrative Practice*, *2*(10), 24–35.

Kuzhda, T. (2006). *Diagnosing resistance to change in the change management process*. Retrieved October 5, 2022, from https://cyberleninka.ru/article/n/diagnosing-resistance-to-change-in-the-changemanagement-process/viewer

Lago, E. C. (2020). *Wandembruck. Trabalho institucional na implementação do roteiro turístico Sentidos do Campo no Estado do Paraná* (Dissertação Mestrado em Administração). Universidade Tecnológica Federal do Paraná, Curitiba, PR, 2018. Disponível em: http://repositorio.utfpr.edu.br/jspui/handle/1/3890

Lahti, E. (2013). *Women and leadership: factors that influence women's career success: female leaders' reflections on their career development and leadership*. Academic Press.

Lange, L. (2020). Transformation Revisited Twenty Years of Higher Education Policy in South Africa In: Transforming Universities in South Africa. African Higher Education: Developments and Perspectives, 6. doi:10.1163/9789004437043_003

Lannelli, C., & Duta, A. (2018). Inequalities in school leavers' labour market outcomes: Do school subject choices matter? *Oxford Review of Education*, *44*(1), 56–74. doi:10.1080/03054985.2018.1409970

Lawrence, T. B., & Suddaby, R. (2006). Institutions and institutional work. In *Sage Handbook of organization studies* (2nd ed., pp. 215-254). Sage. https://www.researchgate.net/publication/242437344_Institutions_and_institutional_w ork/link/550aa6900cf290bdc10fdad3/download

Lawrence, T., & Suddaby, R. (2006). Institutions and institutional work. In S. Clegg, C. Hardy, T. Lawrence & W. Nord (Eds.), Sage handbook of organization studies (2nd ed. pp. 215–254). Sage. doi:10.4135/9781848608030.n7

Lawrence, B. (1996). Organization Age Standards: Why is it so hard to know one when you see one? *The Gerontologist*, *36*(2), 209–220. doi:10.1093/geront/36.2.209 PMID:8920090

Lawrence, T. B., & Phillips, N. (2004). From Moby Dick to Free Willy: Macro-cultural discourse and institutional entrepreneurship in emerging institutional fields. *Organization*, *11*(5), 689–711. doi:10.1177/1350508404046457

Leblebici, H., Salancik, G., Copay, A., & King, T. (1991). Institutional change and the transformation of interorganizational fields: An organizational history of the U.S. broadcasting industry. *Administrative Science Quarterly, 36*(3), 333–363. doi:10.2307/2393200

Leca, B., & Naccache, P. (2006). A Critical Realist Approach to Institutional Entrepreneurship. *Organization, 13*(5), 627–651. doi:10.1177/1350508406067007

Leccardi & Feixa. (2011). The concept of generation in theories on youth. *Last Decade, 34*, 11-32.

Lee, M.-D. P., & Lounsbury, M. (2015). Filtering Institutional Logics: Community Logic Variation and Differential Responses to the Institutional Complexity of Toxic Waste. *Organization Science, 26*(3), 847–866. doi:10.1287/orsc.2014.0959

Lester, S., Standifer, R., Schultz, N., Windsor, J., & Gerhardt, M. (2012). Actual Versus. Perceived Generational Differences at Work: An Empirical Examination. *Journal of Leadership & Organizational Studies, 19*(3), 341–354. doi:10.1177/1548051812442747

Levi, M. (1997). A model, a method, and a map: rational choice in comparative and historical analysis. In M. Lichbach & A. Zuckerman (Eds.), *Comparative Politics: Rationality, Culture, and Structure* (pp. 19–41). Cambridge University Press.

Lima-Cruz, C. M., Fleith de Medeiros, J., Carvalho-Tatim, D., & Mara-Meurer, A. (2013). Interfaces entre cultura organizacional e comunicação organizacional: um estudo multicasos em universidades. *Análise A Revista Acadêmica da FACE, Porto Alegre, 24*(1), 92-103. Retrieved from https://revistaseletronicas.pucrs.br/ojs/index.php/face/article/view/18340

Lipton, B. (2015). A New" ERA" of Women and Leadership: The Gendered Impact of Quality Assurance in Australian Higher Education. *Australian Universities Review, 57*(2), 60–70.

Lockwood, M. (2016). Creating protective space for innovation in electricity distribution networks in Great Britain: The politics of institutional change. *Environmental Innovation and Societal Transitions, 18*, 111-127. https://www.sciencedirect.com/science/article/pii/S2210422415000453 doi:10.1016/j.eist.2015.05.007

Lopez-de-Silanes, F., La Porta, R., & Shleifer, A. (1998). Law and Finance. *Journal of Political Economy, 106*(6), 1113–1155. doi:10.1086/250042

Lubell, M., Mewhirter, J., & Berardo, R. (2020). The Origins of Conflict in Polycentric Governance Systems. *Public Administration Review, 80*(2), 222–233. doi:10.1111/puar.13159

Lucas, R. Jr. (1988). On the mechanics of economic development. *Journal of Monetary Economics, 22*(1), 3–42. doi:10.1016/0304-3932(88)90168-7

Lu, L., Zhou, F., & Leung, K. (2011). Effects of task and relationship conflicts on individual work behaviors. *International Journal of Conflict Management, 22*(2), 131–150. doi:10.1108/10444061111126675

Lupu, E., & Sloman, M. (1997). Conflict analysis for management policies. In *Integrated Network Management V: Integrated management in a virtual world Proceedings of the Fifth IFIP/IEEE International Symposium on Integrated Network Management San Diego, California, USA, May 12–16, 1997* (pp. 430-443). Springer US. 10.1007/978-0-387-35180-3_32

Maas, B., Grogan, K. E., Chirango, Y., Harris, N., Liévano-Latorre, L. F., McGuire, K. L., ... Primack, R. B. (2020). Academic leaders must support inclusive scientific communities during COVID-19. *Nature Ecology & Evolution, 4*(8), 1–2. doi:10.103841559-020-1233-3 PMID:32493950

Mackay, F., Kenny, M., & Chappell, L. (2010). New Institutionalism through a Gender Lens: Towards a Feminist Institutionalism? *International Political Science Review, 31*(5), 573–588. doi:10.1177/0192512110388788

Mahoney, J. & Thelen. (Eds.). (2010). *Explaining Institutional Change*. New York: Cambridge University Press.

Mahoney, J., & Thelen, K. (2010). A theory of gradual institutional change. In J. Mahoney & K. Thelen (Eds.), *Explaining institutional change: ambiguity, agency, and power* (pp. 1–37). Cambridge University Press.

Malsch, B., & Gendron, Y. (2013). Re-theorizing change: Institutional experimentation and the struggle for domination in the field of public accounting. *Journal of Management Studies, 50*(5), 870–899. doi:10.1111/joms.12006

Mankiw, N. G., Romer, D., & Weil, D. N. (1992). A contribution to the empirics of economic growth. *The Quarterly Journal of Economics, 107*(2), 407–437. doi:10.2307/2118477

Mann, M. (1986). *The Sources of Social Power, A history of power from the beginning to A.D. 1760* (Vol. I). Cambridge University Press.

Marcondes-Leite, B., & Cristiane de Oliveira, H. (2014). *Rotatividade de Pessoal, a partir do problema de cultura e clima organizacional, Faculdade de Pindamonhangaba*. Retrieved from https://www.educaedu-brasil.com/centros/faculdade-de-pindamonhangaba--fapi-uni2843

Marini, M. (1984). Age and sequence norms in the transition to adulthood. *Social Forces, 63*(1), 229–244. doi:10.2307/2578867

Martí, I., & Mair, J. (2009). Bringing change into the lives of the poor: Entrepreneurship outside traditional boundaries. In T. Lawrence, R. Suddaby & B. Leca (Eds.), Institutional work: Actors and agency in institutional studies of organizations (pp. 92–119). Cambridge University Press.

Martí, G. (2017). New Concepts for New Dynamics: Generating Theory for the Study of Religious Innovation and Social Change. *Journal for the Scientific Study of Religion, 56*(1), 6–18. doi:10.1111/jssr.12325

Martínez, M. A. (2010). Relaciones entre cultura y desempeño organizacional en una muestra de empresas colombianas: reflexiones sobre la utilización del modelo de Denison. *Cuadernos de Administración, 23*(40), 163-190.

Martín, X., Segredo, A., & Perdomo, I. (2013). Capital humano, gestión académica y desarrollo organizacional. *Educación Médica Superior*, *27*(3), 288–295. http://scielo.sld.cu/pdf/ems/v27n3/ems14313.pdf

Mathews, B., & Linski, C. M. (2016). Shifting the paradigm: Reevaluating resistance to organizational change. *Journal of Organizational Change Management*, *29*(6), 963–972. doi:10.1108/JOCM-03-2016-0058

Mayer & Tuma. (1990). *Life history analysis in life course research (Comp). University of Wisconsin*. Press.

Mayer, K., & Schoepflin, U. (1989). The state and course of life. *Sociology Annual Review,* 187-209.

McAdam, R., & Henderson, J. (2004). Influencing the future of TQM: Internal and external driving factors. *International Journal of Quality & Reliability Management*, *21*(1), 51–71. doi:10.1108/02656710410511696

McEvoy, G., & Cascio, W. (1989). Employee and job performance. *Journal of Applied Psychology,* 11.

McKenna, S., & Richardson, J. (1995). Business values, management, and conflict handling: Issues in contemporary Singapore. *Journal of Management Development*, *14*(4), 56–70. doi:10.1108/02621719510084202

McLaughlin, M. W. (1987). Learning from experience: Lessons from policy implementation. *Educational Evaluation and Policy Analysis*, *9*(2), 171–178. doi:10.3102/01623737009002171

McNair, T. B., Bensimon, E. M., & Malcom-Piqueux, L. (2020). *From equity talk to equity walk: Expanding practitioner knowledge for racial justice in higher education*. John Wiley & Sons. doi:10.1002/9781119428725

Medina, D. M., Munduate, L., Martínez, I., & Cisneros, I. (2002). *Types of conflict and personal and organizational consequences.* Paper presented at the Comunicación presentada a la Internacional Association for Conflict Management Conference.

Medina, F. J., Munduate, L., Dorado, M. A., Martínez, I., & Guerra, J. M. (2005). Types of intragroup conflict and affective reactions. *Journal of Managerial Psychology*, *20*(3/4), 219–230. doi:10.1108/02683940510589019

MEGAN. A. (2020). *Highlighting Importance Of Women Leadership In Your Organization.* https://witi.com/articles/1843/Highlighting-Importance-Of-Women-Leadership-In-YourOrganization/#:~:text=When%20women%20become%20leaders%2C%20they,is%20really%20going%20on%20underneath

Mehta, J. (2013). Why American education fails and how lessons from abroad could improve it. *Foreign Affairs*, *92*(3), 72–79.

Meier, K. J., & O'Toole, L. J. Jr. (2005). Managerial networking: Issues of measurement and research design. *Administration & Society*, *37*(5), 523–541. doi:10.1177/0095399705277142

Mele, C. (2011). Conflicts and value co-creation in project networks. *Industrial Marketing Management, 40*(8), 1377–1385. doi:10.1016/j.indmarman.2011.06.033

Meletiadou, E. (2022). The lived experiences of female educational leaders in higher education in the UK: Academic resilience and gender. In *Handbook of Research on Practices for Advancing Diversity and Inclusion in Higher Education* (pp. 1–19). IGI Global. doi:10.4018/978-1-7998-9628-9.ch001

Men, L. R., Neill, M., & Yue, C. A. (2020). Examining the effects of symmetrical internal communication and employee engagement on organizational change outcomes. *The Public Relations Journal, 13*(4), 1–19.

Meyer, J. P., Srinivas, E. S., Lal, J. B., & Topolnytsky, L. (2007). Employee commitment and support for an organizational change: Test of the three-component model in two cultures. *Journal of Occupational and Organizational Psychology, 80*(2), 185–211. doi:10.1348/096317906X118685

Meyer, J., & Rowan, B. (1977). Institutionalized organizations: Formal structure as myth and ceremony. *American Journal of Sociology, 83*(2), 340–363. doi:10.1086/226550

Meyers, M. (2013). The war on academic women: Reflections on post-feminism in the neoliberal academy. *The Journal of Communication Inquiry, 37*(4), 274–283. doi:10.1177/0196859913505619

Mezias, J. (2002). Identifying liabilities of foreignness and strategies to minimize their effects: The case of labor lawsuit judgments in the United States. *Strategic Management Journal, 23*(3), 229–244. doi:10.1002mj.220

Mezirow, J. (2009). Transformative learning theory. In J. Mezirow & E. W. Taylor (Eds.), *Transformative Learning in Practise: Insights from Community, 39 Workplace, and Higher Education* (pp. 18–32). Jossey Bass.

Michel, J. S., & Hargis, B. (2008). Linking mechanisms of work-family conflict and segmentation. *Journal of Vocational Behavior, 73*(3), 509–522. doi:10.1016/j.jvb.2008.09.005

Miller, C., & Major, B. (1998). Dealing with stigma and prejudice. In Prejudice: The Target Perspective (pp. 243-272). Academic Press.

Milovanović, A., Kostić, M., Zorić, A., Đorđević, A., Pešić, M., Bugarski, J., Todorović, D., Sokolović, N., & Josifovski, A. (2020). Transferring COVID-19 Challenges into Learning Potentials: Online Workshops in Architectural Education. *Sustainability, 12*(17), 7024. doi:10.3390u12177024

Mintzberg, H. (1979). *The structuring of organizations*. Prentice Hall.

Moe, T. (2015). Vested interests and political institutions. *Political Science Quarterly, 130*(2), 277–318. doi:10.1002/polq.12321

Mohamed, Collier, Sutton, Davern, & Leech. (2013). Enhancing the business value of business intelligence: the role of knowledge sharing and assimilation. *Journal of Information Systems, 27*(2), 87–105. doi:10.2308/isys-50563

Mohr, J. W., & Bogdanov, P. (2013, December). Introduction—Topic models: What they are and why they matter. *Poetics*, *41*(6), 545–569. doi:10.1016/j.poetic.2013.10.001

Mohr, J., & Spekman, R. (1994). Characteristics of partnership success: Partnership attributes, communication behavior, and conflict resolution techniques. *Strategic Management Journal*, *15*(2), 135–152. doi:10.1002mj.4250150205

Moon, Y. J., & Kym, H. G. (2006). A Model for the Value of Intellectual Capital. *Canadian Journal of Administrative Sciences*, *23*(3), 253–269. doi:10.1111/j.1936-4490.2006.tb00630.x

Morrill, C. (2005). Institutional change and interstitial emergence: The growth of alternative dispute resolution in American law, 1965–1995. In W. Powell & D. Jones (Eds.), *How Institutions Change*. University of Chicago Press.

Motoyama, Y., Cao, C., & Appelbaum, R. (2014). Observing regional divergence of Chinese nanotechnology centers. *Technological Forecasting and Social Change*, *81*, 11–21. doi:10.1016/j.techfore.2013.02.013

Muller, E. (2009). *Innovation system and policies*. Retrieved June 26, 2015, from: http://www.evoreg.eu/doc/files/lete/200912.Emmanuel_Muller_Innovation _systems _and_ policies.pdf

Mullins, L. J. (2007). *Management and organisational behaviour*. Pearson education.

Munive, A., Donville, J. & Darmstadt, G. L. (2023). Public leadership for gender equality: A framework and capacity development approach for gender transformative policy change. *eClinicalMedicine, 56*, 101798. doi:10.1016/j.eclinm.2022.0179

Murmann, J. P. (2003). *Knowledge and competitive advantage: The co-evolution of firms, technology, and national institutions*. Cambridge University Press. doi:10.1017/CBO9780511510953

Nakamura, Y. T., Hinshaw, J., & Burns, R. (2022). Developing Women's Authenticity in Leadership. *Merits*, *2*(4), 408–426. doi:10.3390/merits2040029

Nasser, F. F. (2019). *Factors affecting the principles of organizational management in improving the actions of managers and employees to separate men and women in service organizations (case study: service organizations of Tabriz city)*. Academic Press.

Nataraajan, R., & Chawla, S. K. (1994). Random transfer of technology: An unexplored phenomenon. *The Journal of Technology Transfer*, *19*(1), 27–32. doi:10.1007/BF02373668

National Economic Council. (2011). *A strategy for American innovation: securing our economic growth and prosperity.* Council of Economic Advisers, and Office of Science and Technology Policy. Retrieved from https://obamawhitehouse.archives.gov/sites/default/files/uploads/InnovationStrategy.pdf

Natural, H. R. (2021). *10 reasons why the world needs more women in leadership roles*. https://www.naturalhr.com/2021/03/23/10-reasons-why-the-world-needs-more-women-in-leadership-roles/

Nay, O. (2012). What drives reforms in international organizations? External pressure and bureaucratic entrepreneurs in the UN response to AIDS. *Governance: An International Journal of Policy, Administration and Institutions*, *2012*(24), 71–88.

Nazarian, A., Atkinson, P., & Foroudi, P. (2017). Influence of national culture and balanced organizational culture on the hotel industry's performance. *International Journal of Hospitality Management*, *63*, 22–32. doi:10.1016/j.ijhm.2017.01.003

Ndubisi. (2011). Conflict handling, trust and commitment in outsourcing relationship: A Chinese and Indian study. *Industrial Marketing Management, 40*(1), 109-117.

Neira Gómez, I. (2007). Capital humano y desarrollo económico mundial: Modelos econométricos y perspectivas. *Estudios Económicos de Desarrollo Internacional, 7*(2), 53-80. Retrieved from https://www.redalyc.org/pdf/165/16570203.pdf

Netemeyer, R. G., Boles, J. S., & McMurrian, R. (1996). Development and validation of work–family conflict and family–work conflict scales. *Journal of Applied Psychology*, *81*(4), 400–410. https://doi.org/10.1037/0021-9010.81.4.400

Nguyen, T. H., Newby, M., & Macaulay, M. J. (2015). Information technology adoption in small business: Confirmation of a proposed framework. *Journal of Small Business Management*, *53*(1), 207–227. doi:10.1111/jsbm.12058

Nielsen, M. W., & Börjeson, L. (2019). Gender diversity in the management field: Does it matter for research outcomes? *Research Policy*, *48*(7), 1617–1632. doi:10.1016/j.respol.2019.03.006

Nikku, B. R. (2004, August). Water rights, conflicts and collective action-Case of the Telugu Ganga project, India. In *The tenth biennial conference of the International Association for the Study of Common Property (IASCP).* The Instituto de Investigaciones Sociales, Universitad Nacional Autonoma de México.

Noble, S., & Schewe, C. (2003). Cohort segmentation: An exploration of its validity. *Journal of Business Research*, *56*(12), 979–987. doi:10.1016/S0148-2963(02)00268-0

North, D. C. & Weingast, B. R. (1989). Constitutions and Commitment: The Evolution of Institutions Governing Public Choice in Seventeenth Century England. *The Journal of Economic History, 49*(4), 803-832.

North, D. C. & Weingast, B. R. (1989). Constitutions and Commitment: The Evolution of Institutions Governing Public Choice in Seventeenth-Century England. *The Journal of Economic History, 49*(4), 803-832.

North, D., Wallis, J., Webb, S., & Weingast, B. (Eds.). (2013). In the Shadow of Violence, Politics, Economics, and the Problems of Development. Cambridge University Press.

North, D. (1981). *Structure and change in economic history*. W.W. Norton and Company.

North, D. (1990a). *Institutions, Institutional Change and Economic Performance*. Cambridge University Press. doi:10.1017/CBO9780511808678

North, D. (1990b). A Transaction Cost Theory of Politics. *Journal of Theoretical Politics*, *2*(4), 355–367. doi:10.1177/0951692890002004001

North, D., Qallis, J., & Weingast, B. (2009). *Violence and social orders: A conceptual framework for interpreting recorded human history*. Cambridge University Press. doi:10.1017/CBO9780511575839

O'Connor, P. (2019). Gender imbalance in senior positions in higher education: What is the problem? What can be done? *Policy Reviews in Higher Education*, *3*(1), 28–50. doi:10.1080/23322969.2018.1552084

O'Connor, P. (2020). Creating gendered change in Irish higher education: Is managerial leadership up to the task? *Irish Educational Studies*, *39*(2), 139–155. doi:10.1080/03323315.2019.1697951

O'Connor, P. J., Jimmieson, N. L., Bergin, A. J., Wiewiora, A., & McColl, L. (2022). Leader tolerance of ambiguity: Implications for follower performance outcomes in high and low ambiguous work situations. *The Journal of Applied Behavioral Science*, *58*(1), 65–96. doi:10.1177/00218863211053676

O'Reilly, B., & Vella-Zarb, K. (2000). *Meet the Future. The Sociological Outlook: A text with readings* (7th ed.). Collegiate Publishing Group.

O'Toole, L. Jr. (1995). Rational choice and policy implementation: Implications for interorganizational network management. *American Review of Public Administration*, *25*(1), 43–57. doi:10.1177/027507409502500103

Odetunde, O. J. (2013). Influence of transformational and transactional leaderships, and leaders' sex on organisational conflict management behaviour. *Gender & Behaviour*, *11*(1), 5323–5335.

OECD. (1999). *Managing national innovation system*. Organization for Economic & Cooperation Development.

OGT. (2020). *Management of intergenerational teams.* Obtained from Generation and Talent Observatory: https://observatoriorh.com/revista/31/la-gesti-ó-n-de equipos-intergeneracionales-veteranos-boomers-xers-y-nets

Oh, N., & Lee, J. (2020). Changing landscape of emergency management research: A systematic review with bibliometric analysis. *International Journal of Disaster Risk Reduction*, *49*, 101658. doi:10.1016/j.ijdrr.2020.101658

Okoli, G. N., Moore, T. A., Thomas, S. L., & Allen, T. T. (2020). Minority Women in Educational Leadership. *Handbook on Promoting Social Justice in Education*, 1711-1727.

Olekalns, M. (1997). Conflict at work: Defining and resolving organisational conflicts. *Australian Psychologist*, *32*(1), 56–61. doi:10.1080/00050069708259618

Oliver, C. (1991). Strategic Responses to Institutional Processes. *Academy of Management Review*, *16*(1), 145–179. doi:10.2307/258610

Oliver, C. (1992). The antecedents of deinstitutionalization. *Organization Studies*, *13*(4), 563–588. doi:10.1177/017084069201300403

Olsson, P., Gunderson, L. H., Carpenter, S. R., Ryan, P., Lebel, L., Folke, C., & Holling, C. S. (2006). Shooting the rapids: Navigating transitions to adaptive governance of social-ecological systems. *Ecology and Society*, *11*(1), 18. doi:10.5751/ES-01595-110118

ONU. (2005). *La juventud y los objetivos de desarrollo del milenio. Desafíos y Oportunidades para su Implementación*. Reporte Final del Grupo de Trabajo Ad Hoc para la Juventud y los ODM's, Centro de Información de las Naciones Unidas (CINU). Retrieved from https://www.unicef.org/venezuela/media/961/file/La%20juventud%20y%20los%20objetivos%20de%20desarrollo%20del%20milenio.pdf

Opatha, H. H. D. N. P., & Ismail, Z. (2001). Towards effective worker grievance handling: Some reflections. *Analisis*, *8*(1/2), 111–127.

Opie, T., & Henn, C. (2013). Work-family conflict and totalitas kerja among mothers: Conscientiousness and neuroticism as moderators. *SA Journal of Industrial Psychology*, *39*(1). Advance online publication. doi:10.4102ajip.v39i1.1082

Ormiston, G. C., & DeLong, D. W. (2013). How Cisco Systems manages strategic alliances for innovation and growth. *Harvard Business Review*, *91*(3), 1–9. doi:10.2139srn.2229271

Orren, K., & Skowronek, S. (1994). Beyond the iconography of order: Notes for a 'New Institutionalism. In L. Dodd & C. Jilson (Eds.), *The Dynamics of American Politics*. Westview.

Ostrom, E. (1990). *Governing the Commons: The Evolution of Institutions for Collective Action*. Cambridge University Press. doi:10.1017/CBO9780511807763

Ostrom, E. (1992). *Crafting Institutions for Self-Governing Irrigation Systems*. ICS Press.

Ostrom, E. (2005). *Understanding Institutional Diversity*. Princeton University Press.

Oudenhoven, J. P., Mechelse, L., & De Dreu, C. (1998). Managerial conflict management in five European countries: The importance of power distance, uncertainty avoidance, and masculinity. *Applied Psychology*, *47*(3), 439–455. doi:10.1111/j.1464-0597.1998.tb00037.x

Parker, K., Horowitz, J. M., & Rohal, M. (2015). *Women and leadership: Public says women are equally qualified, but barriers persist*. Pew Research Center.

Parsons, T. & Bales, R. F. (1955). *Family, socialization and interaction process*. Academic Press.

Patrickson, M., & Hartmann, L. (1995). Australia's aging population: Implications for human resource management. *International Journal of Manpower*, *15*(5), 34–46. doi:10.1108/01437729510095935

Patriotta, G., & Lanzara, G. F. (2006). Identity, institutions, and new work roles: The case of a green field automotive factory. *The American Behavioral Scientist*, *49*(7), 987–999. doi:10.1177/0002764205285180

Pelikan, P. (2003). Bringing institutions into evolutionary economics: Another view with links to changes in physical and social technologies. *Journal of Evolutionary Economics*, *13*(3), 237–258. doi:10.100700191-003-0157-9

Pellegrini, M., Uskov, V., & Casalino, N. (2020). Reimagining and Re-Designing the Post-COVID-19 Higher Education Organizations to Address New Challenges and Responses for Safe and Effective Teaching Activities. Law and Economics Yearly Review Journal, 9(part 1), 219-248.

Peltzman, S. (1989). The economic theory of regulation after a decade of deregulation. In *Brookings Papers: Microeconomics* (pp. 1–41). Brookings Institution. doi:10.2307/2534719

Pemberton, C. (1995). Organizational Culture and Equalities Work. In J. Shaw & D. Perrons (Eds.), *Making Equal Opportunities* (pp. 108–123). Open University Press.

Peng, M. W., & Heath, P. S. (1996). The growth of the firm in planned economies in transition: Institutions, organizations, and strategic choice. *Academy of Management Review*, *21*(2), 492–528. doi:10.2307/258670

Pérez, C. (2017). *Muestreo estadístico a través de ejemplos*. Garceta Grupo Editorial.

Peters, B. G. (2012). *Institutional Theory in Political Science* (3rd ed.). Continuum. doi:10.5040/9781501397813

Peters, M. A., Rizvi, F., McCulloch, G., Gibbs, P., Gorur, R., Hong, M., ... Quay, J. (2020). Reimagining the new pedagogical possibilities for universities post-Covid-19: An EPAT Collective Project. *Educational Philosophy and Theory*, 1–44.

Pettigrew, A. M., Woodman, R. W., & Cameron, K. S. (2001). Studying organizational change and development: Challenges for future research. *Academy of Management Journal*, *44*(4), 697–713. doi:10.2307/3069411

Pfeffer, J. (1981). *Power in organizations*. Pitman.

Philips, D. (2009). *Reforming the World Bank: Twenty Years of Trial – and Error*. Cambridge University Press. doi:10.1017/CBO9780511814327

Pierson, P. (2000). *Increasing returns, path dependence, and the study of politics*. Academic Press.

Pierson, P. (2004). *Politics in Time: History, Institutions, and Social Analysis*. Princeton University Press. doi:10.1515/9781400841080

Piketty, T. (2014). *Capital in the Twenty-First Century*. Harvard University Press. doi:10.4159/9780674369542

Piotrkowski, C. (1979). *Work and the family system*. Macmillan.

Polanyi, M. (1951). *The Logic of Liberty. Reflections and Rejoinders*. University of Chicago Press.

Popescu, D. I., & Popa, I. (2012). Managing Organizational Change and Innovation: IV. Success Factors in Change and Innovation. *Calitatea*, *13*(130), 99.

Powell, W. W., & Colyvas, J. A. (2007). *Microfoundations of Institutional Theory*. Academic Press.

Power, K. (2020). The COVID-19 pandemic has increased the care burden of women and families. *Sustainability: Science. Practice and Policy*, *16*(1), 67–73.

Priser, J., & Bernard, D. (2021). The Collections of Scientific Instruments of the Faculty of Sciences of Rennes: A Tool for School Education and for the Training of Students and Teachers. In *Historical Scientific Instruments in Contemporary Education* (pp. 84–104). Brill.

Rahim, A., & Bonoma, T. V. (1979). Managing organizational conflict: A model for diagnosis and intervention. *Psychological Reports*, *44*(3, suppl), 1323–1344. doi:10.2466/pr0.1979.44.3c.1323

Randeree, K. (2008). Organisational Justice. *Journal of Law and Governance*, *3*(4), 57–68.

Randeree, K., & El Faramawy, A. T. (2011). Islamic perspectives on conflict management within project managed environments. *International Journal of Project Management*, *29*(1), 26–32. doi:10.1016/j.ijproman.2010.01.013

Rapanta, C., Botturi, L., Goodyear, P., Guàrdia, L., & Koole, M. (2020). Online university teaching during and after the Covid-19 crisis: Refocusing teacher presence and learning activity. *Postdigital Science and Education*, 1-23.

Raynard, M. (2016). Deconstructing complexity: Configurations of institutional complexity and structural hybridity. *Strategic Organization*, *14*(4), 310–335. doi:10.1177/1476127016634639

Ray, P., Reddy, S. S., & Banerjee, T. (2021). Various dimension reduction techniques for high dimensional data analysis: A review. *Artificial Intelligence Review*, *54*(5), 3473–3515. doi:10.100710462-020-09928-0

Reay, D. (2004, January). Cultural capitalists and academic habitus: Classed and gendered labour in UK higher education. *Women's Studies International Forum*, *27*(1), 31–39. doi:10.1016/j.wsif.2003.12.006

Reynolds, J. (2005). In the face of conflict: Work-life adjustments and desired work hour adjustments. *Journal of Marriage and Family*, *67*(5), 1313–1331. doi:10.1111/j.1741-3737.2005.00219.x

Reza, N. J. (2015). *Comparing organizational success in organizations with male and female managers*. Tehran University.

Riaz, M. K., & Junaid, F. A. (2013). Workplace conflict: Constructive or destructive. *Muhammad Khan Riaz & Fatima Ali Juniad (2014). Workplace Conflict: Constructive or Destructive. SRM-IMT Journal of Business & Management Research*, *3*(1), 84–90.

Rijke, J., Farrelly, M., Brown, R., & Zevenbergen, C. (2013). Configuring transformative governance to enhance resilient urban water systems. *Environmental Science & Policy*, *25*, 62–72. doi:10.1016/j.envsci.2012.09.012

Rip, A., & van der Meulen, J. R. (1996). The post-modern research system. *Science & Public Policy*, *23*, 343–352.

Robbins, P., & Coulter, M. (2005). *Management* (8th ed.). Pearson Prentice Hall.

Rock, D., Cox, C., Fellow, P., & Green, P. (2012). *SCARF in 2012: updating the social neuroscience of collaborating with others*. https://www.saskatoonhealthregion.ca/about/PFMS/Documents/Change_Leadership_Module/SCARF%20Model%20-%20Updating%20the%20Social%20Neuroscience%20of%20Collaborating%20with%20Others.pdf

Roe, M. (2003). *Political Determinants of Corporate Governance*. Oxford Oxford University Press.

Rogiest, S., Segers, J., & van Witteloostuijn, A. (2015). Climate, communication and participation impacting commitment to change. *Journal of Organizational Change Management, 28*(6), 1094–1106. doi:10.1108/JOCM-06-2015-0101

Roling, N., Hounkonnou, D., Kossou, D., Kuyper, T.W., Nederlof, S., Dawson, O. S., Traoré, M., & Huis, A. V. (2012). Diagnosing the scope for innovation: Linking smallholder practices and institutional context Introduction to the special issue. *Wageningen Journal of Life Science, 60-63*, 1-6. .njas.2012.06.004 doi:10.1016/j

Romer, P. (1990b). Capital, labour, and productivity. In *Brookings Papers on Economic Activity*. Brookings Institution Press. Retrieved from https://www.brookings.edu/wp-content/uploads/1990/01/1990_bpeamicro_romer.pdf

Romero, E. J. (2008). AACSB accreditation: Addressing faculty concerns. *Academy of Management Learning & Education, 7*(2), 245–255. doi:10.5465/amle.2008.32712622

Romer, P. (1986). Increasing returns and long run growth. *Journal of Political Economy, 94*(5), 1002–1037. doi:10.1086/261420

Romer, P. (1990a). ¿Are non convexities important for understanding growth? *The American Economic Review, 80*(2), 97–103. https://www.jstor.org/stable/2006550

Rosenbloom, D., & Rinscheid, A. (2020). Deliberate decline: An emerging frontier for the study and practice of decarbonization. *Wiley Interdisciplinary Reviews: Climate Change, 11*(6), e669. doi:10.1002/wcc.669

Rosener, J. B. (1995). *America's competitive secret: Women managers*. Oxford University Press on Demand.

Rose, R. (1990). Inheritance before choice in public policy. *Journal of Theoretical Politics, 1990*(2), 263–291. doi:10.1177/0951692890002003002

Ruben, B., Mahon, G., & Shapiro, K. (2022). Academic Leader Selection, Development, Evaluation, and Recognition: Four Critical Higher Education Challenges. In International Perspectives on Leadership in Higher Education (Vol. 15, pp. 115-138). Emerald Publishing Limited.

Rubio, A., & Aragón, A. (2002). Factores explicativos del éxito competitivo. Un estudio empírico en la PYME. *Cuadernos de Gestión, 2*(1), 49–63. https://ojs.ehu.eus/index.php/CG/article/view/19218

Rudolph, C. W., Rauvola, R. S., Costanza, D. P., & Zacher, H. (2021). Generations and generational differences: Debunking myths in organizational science and practice and paving new paths forward. *Journal of Business and Psychology*, *36*(6), 945–967. doi:10.100710869-020-09715-2 PMID:32901173

Rugman, A., Verbeke, A., Collinson, S., & Morgan, G. (2009). The Regional Dimension of Multinationals and the End of "Varieties of Capitalism". *Images of the Multinational Firm*, 23-44.

Runhaar, H., Fünfschilling, L., Dasselaar, A. P. V., Moors, E. H. M., Temmink, R., & Hekkert, M. (2020). Endogenous regime change: Lessons from transition pathways in dutch dairy farming. *Environmental Innovation and Societal Transitions*, *36*(September), 137–150. doi:10.1016/j.eist.2020.06.001

Saavedra, M., & Hernández, Y. (2008). Caracterización e importancia de las MIPYMES en Latinoamérica: Un estudio comparativo. *Actualidad Contable*, *17*, 122-134. Retrieved from https://www.redalyc.org/pdf/257/25711784011.pdf

Sala-I-Martin, X. (2009). The Global Competitiveness Index: Measuring the Productive Potential of Nations. *World Economic Forum*. Retrieved from https://relooney.com/NS3040/0_New_3044.pdf

Samantara, R., & Sharma, N. (2016). Organisational conflict literature: A Review. *KIIT Journal of Management*, *12*(2), 158–179.

Sanchez-Sandoval, Y., & Verdugo, L. (2016). Development and validation of the Future Expectations Scale in Adolescence (EEFA). *Anales de Psicologia/ Annals of Psychology*, *32*(2), 545-554.

Sarkar, S. (2020). The idea of a university in India. *Economic and Political Weekly*, *55*(14).

Schein, E. H. (2010). *Organizational culture and leadership* (Vol. 2). John Wiley & Sons. doi:10.1002/9781119212043

Schewe, G. (1994). Successful innovation management: An integrative perspective. *Journal of Engineering and Technology Management*, *11*(1), 25–53. doi:10.1016/0923-4748(94)90023-X

Schiefele, U., & Schaffner, E. (2015). Teacher interests, mastery goals, and self-efficacy as predictors of instructional practices and student motivation. *Contemporary Educational Psychology*, *42*, 159–171. doi:10.1016/j.cedpsych.2015.06.005

Schneider, B. (1987). The people make the place. *Personnel Psychology*, *40*(3), 437–453. doi:10.1111/j.1744-6570.1987.tb00609.x

Schultz, L., Folke, C., Österblom, H., & Olsson, P. (2015). Adaptive governance, ecosystem management, and natural capital. *Proceedings of the National Academy of Sciences of the United States of America*, *112*(24), 7369–7374. doi:10.1073/pnas.1406493112 PMID:26082542

Schuman, H., & Scott, J. (1989). Generations and collective memories. *American Sociological Review*, *54*(3), 359–381. doi:10.2307/2095611

Schumpeter, J. A. (1951). *Capitalism, Socialism, and Democracy*. George Allen & Unwin.

Schweiger, S., Stouten, H., & Bleijenbergh, I. L. (2018). A System Dynamics Model of Resistance to Organizational Change: The Role of Participatory Strategies. *Systems Research and Behavioral Science*, *35*(6), 658–674. doi:10.1002res.2509

Scott, R. (2005). Organizaciones. Características duraderas y cambiantes. *Gestión y Política Pública*, *3*, 439–463. https://www.redalyc.org/articulo.oa?id=13314302

Scott, T., Mannion, R., Davies, H., & Marshall, M. (2003). The quantitative measurement of the organizational culture in health care. A view of an available instruments (Methods). *Health Services Research*, *38*(3), 923–946. doi:10.1111/1475-6773.00154 PMID:12822919

Secretaría de Educación Pública. (2018). *Sistema Educativo de los Estados Unidos Mexicanos*. Principales cifras ciclo escolar 2017-2018. Recuperado de https://www.planeacion.sep.gob.mx/Doc/estadistica_e_indicadores/principales_cifras/principales_cifras_2017_2018_bolsillo.pdf

Secretaría de Educación Pública. (2019). *Principales Cifras del Sistema Educativo Nacional 2018-2019*. Recuperado de https://www.planeacion.sep.gob.mx/Doc/estadistica_e_indicadores/principales_cifras/principales_cifras_2018_2019_bolsillo.pdf

Seedsman, T. (2017). Building a humane society for older people: Compassionate policy making for integration, participation positive ageing within a framework of intergenerational solidarity. *J Intergender Relationsh.*, *15*(3), 204–220. doi:10.1080/15350770.2017.1329582

Selznick, P. (1996). Institucionalism ‘old’ and ‘new’. *Administrative Science Quarterly*, *41*(2), 270–277. doi:10.2307/2393719

Seo, M. G., & Creed, W. E. D. (2002). Institutional Contradictions, Praxis, and Institutional Change: A Dialectical Perspective. *Academy of Management Review*, *27*(2), 222–247. doi:10.2307/4134353

Seo, M. G., Taylor, M. S., Hill, N. S., Zhang, X., Tesluk, P. E., & Lorinkova, N. M. (2012). The role of affect and leadership during organizational change. *Personnel Psychology*, *65*(1), 121–165. doi:10.1111/j.1744-6570.2011.01240.x

Serrate, A., Portuondo, A., Sánchez, N., & Suarez, R. (2014). Evaluación de la cultura organizacional y su incidencia en la efectividad grupal. *Ingeniería Industrial, 35*(1), 2-12. Retrieved from http://scielo.sld.cu/pdf/rii/v35n1/rii02114.pdf

Sharma, R. A., & Samantara, R. (1994). Conflict management in an Indian firm: A case study. *Decision (Washington, D.C.)*, *21*(4), 235.

Shelton, B. A. (1992). *Women, men, and time: Gender a differences in paid work, housework, and leisure*. Greenwood.

Sherwin, R. J. (2019). Character is a Sacred Bond: Reflections on Sovereignty, Grace, and Resistance. *Angelaki*, *24*(4), 70–86. doi:10.1080/0969725X.2019.1635828

Shulman, L. S. (2005). Signature pedagogies in the professions. *Daedalus*, *134*(3), 52–59. doi:10.1162/0011526054622015

Sihombing, S., Astuti, E. S., Al Musadieq, M., Hamied, D., & Rahardjo, K. (2018). The effect of servant leadership on rewards, organizational culture and its implication for employee's performance. *International Journal of Law and Management*.

Sims, R. R. (2000). Changing an organization's culture under new leadership. *Journal of Business Ethics*, *25*(1), 65–78. doi:10.1023/A:1006093713658

Skocpol, T. (1995). *Protecting Soldiers and Mothers: The Political Origins of Social Policy in the United States*. Harvard University Press. doi:10.2307/j.ctvjz81v6

Slabbert, A. D. (2004). Conflict management styles in traditional organisations. *The Social Science Journal*, *41*(1), 83–92. doi:10.1016/j.soscij.2003.10.007

Slager, R., Gond, J.-P., & Moon, J. (2012). Standardization as institutional work: The regulatory power of a responsible investment standard. *Organization Studies*, *33*(5–6), 763–790. doi:10.1177/0170840612443628

Slater, A. (2010). Altering authoritarianism: institutional complexity and autocratic agency in Indonesia. In Explaining Institutional Change. Cambridge University Press.

Smets, M., & Jarzabkowski, P. (2013). Reconstructing institutional complexity in practice: A relational model of institutional work and complexity. *Human Relations*, *66*(10), 12791309. doi:10.1177/0018726712471407

Smollan, R. K., & Sayers, J. G. (2009). *Organizational Culture, Change and Emotions: A Qualitative Study*. doi:10.1080/14697010903360632

Soboul, A. (1982). *La Révolution française*. Gallimard, Tel.

Song, X. M., Xie, J., & Dyer, B. (2000). Antecedents and consequences of marketing managers' conflict-handling behaviors. *Journal of Marketing*, *64*(1), 50–66. doi:10.1509/jmkg.64.1.50.17989

Squires, V. R., & Qi, L. (2017). *Sustainable Land Management in Greater Central Asia: An Integrated and Regional Perspective*. Routledge. doi:10.9774/gleaf.9781315679396

Staab, S., & Waylen, G. (2020). Institutional change in constrained circumstances: Gender, resistance, and critical actors in the Chilean executive. *Latin American Politics and Society*, *62*(4), 50–74. doi:10.1017/lap.2020.15

Stahl, A. (2021, May 10). How gen-Z is bringing a fresh perspective to the world of work. *Forbes*. Retrieved November 30, 2021, from https://www.forbes.com/sites/ashleystahl/2021/05/04/how-gen-z-isbringing-a-fresh-perspective-to-the-world-of-work/

Steele, C., & Aronson, J. (1995). Stereotype threat and intellectual test performance of African Americans. *Journal of Personality and Social Psychology*, *69*(5), 789–811. doi:10.1037/0022-3514.69.5.797 PMID:7473032

Steffens, M., Vladot, M., & Scheifele, C. (2019). *Male Majority, Female Majority, or Gender Diversity in Organizations: How Do Proportions Affect Gender Stereotyping and Women Leaders' Well-Being?* (Vol. 10). Front. Psychol., Sec. Organizational Psychology. doi:10.3389/fpsyg.2019.01037

Stephens, A. C. (2016). The affective atmospheres of nationalism. *Cultural Geographies, 23*(2), 181-198. doi:10.1177/1474474015569994

Stephens, A. C. (2019). National Atmospheres and the 'Brexit' Revolt." *Society and Space.* societyandspace.org/2016/08/23/national-atmospheres-and-the-brexit-revolt-angharad-closs-stephens/

Stijns, J.-P. (2006). Natural Resource Abundance and Human Capital Accumulation. *World Development, 34*(6), 1060–1083. doi:10.1016/j.worlddev.2005.11.005

Strambach, S., & Pflitsch, G. (2020). Transition topology: Capturing institutional dynamics in regional development paths to sustainability. *Research Policy, 49*(7), 104006. Advance online publication. doi:10.1016/j.respol.2020.104006

Streeck, W., & Thelen, K. (2005). Introduction: institutional change in advanced political economies. In *Beyond Continuity: Institutional Change in Advanced Political Economies* (pp. 1–39). Oxford University Press.

Sune, A., & Gibb, J. (2015). Dynamic capabilities as patterns of organizational change: An empirical study on transforming a firm's resource base. *Journal of Organizational Change Management, 28*(2), 213–231. doi:10.1108/JOCM-01-2015-0019

Syed, M. (2019). Rebel Ideas: The power of diverse thinking. Hachette UK.

Syeda-Masooda, M., Oakey, R., & Kippling, M. (1999). Utilisation of science and technology graduates by the small and medium-sized enterprise sector. *International Journal of Entrepreneurial Behaviour & Research, 5*(3), 126–143. doi:10.1108/13552559910284083

Tabibnia, G., Satpute, A. B., & Lieberman, M. D. (2008). The sunny side of fairness: Preference for fairness activates reward-related brain regions. *Journal of Cognitive Neuroscience, 20*(3), 414–425.

Tang, L., & Shapira, P. (2011). Regional development and interregional collaboration in the growth of nanotechnology research in China. *Scientometrics, 86*(2), 299–315. doi:10.100711192-010-0274-9

Tang, S. F., & Kirkbride, P. S. (1986). Developing conflict management skills in Hong Kong: An analysis of some cross-cultural implications. *Management Education and Development, 17*(3), 287–301. doi:10.1177/135050768601700315

Tanova, C., Karatas-Özkan, M., & Inal, G. (2008). The process of choosing a management career: Evaluation of gender and contextual dynamics in a comparative study of six countries: Hungary, Israel, North Cyprus, Turkey, UK and the USA. *Career Development International, 13*(4), 291–305. doi:10.1108/13620430810880790

Taylor, L. L., Beck, M. I., Lahey, J. N., & Froyd, J. E. (2017). Reducing inequality in higher education: The link between faculty empowerment and climate and retention. *Innovative Higher Education, 42*(5-6), 391–405. doi:10.100710755-017-9391-1

Taylor, P., & Walker, A. (1994). The aging workforce: Employer attitudes toward old people. *Work, Employment and Society, 8*(4), 569–591. doi:10.1177/095001709484005

Teelken, C., & Deem, R. (2013). All are equal, but some are more equal than others: Managerialism and gender equality in higher education in comparative perspective. *Comparative Education, 49*(4), 520–535. doi:10.1080/03050068.2013.807642

The Commonwealth Secretariat. (2016). *Advancing gender equality: case studies from across Commonwealth.* The Commonwealth Secretariat. https://www.oecd-ilibrary.org/content/publication/9781848599451-en

Thelen, K. (2003). How Institutions Evolve. In J. Mahoney & D. Rueschemeyer (Eds.), *Comparative Historical Analysis in the Social Sciences* (pp. 208–234). Cambridge University Press. doi:10.1017/CBO9780511803963.007

Thomas, S. (2020). Women in Higher Education Administration Leadership and the Role of Institutional Support. In *Accessibility and Diversity in the 21st Century University* (pp. 234–249). IGI Global. doi:10.4018/978-1-7998-2783-2.ch012

Thomson, K. (2020). By the light of the corona (virus): Revealing hegemonic masculinity and the double bind for men in responding to crises. *Health Sociology Review, 29*(2), 149–157. doi:10.1080/14461242.2020.1784773 PMID:33411649

Thornton, P. H., & Ocasio, W. (2008). Institutional Logics. In R. Greenwood, C. Oliver, K. Sahlin, & R. Suddaby (Eds.), *The SAGE Handbook of Organizational Institutionalism* (pp. 99–129). Sage Publications Ltd. doi:10.4135/9781849200387.n4

Thornton, P. H., Ocasio, W., & Lounsbury, M. (2012). *The institutional logics perspective: A new approach to culture, structure and process.* Oxford University Press. doi:10.1093/acprof:oso/9780199601936.001.0001

Tiwary, A. R., & Gupta, T. (2022). Stereotypical Barriers Affecting Women Aspiring High-ranking Leadership Role in Higher Education. In *Role of Leaders in Managing Higher Education* (Vol. 48, pp. 99–116). Emerald Publishing Limited. doi:10.1108/S2055-364120220000048007

Tobío, C. (2010). Demographic change, intergenerational solidarity, and social policy. *J Intergener Relationsh., 8*(4), 431–433. doi:10.1080/15350770.2010.521098

Todnem By, R. (2005). Organisational change management: A critical review. *Journal of Change Management, 5*(4), 369–380. doi:10.1080/14697010500359250

Torre, F. (2014). Contribución de la Ciencia e Ingeniería en el desarrollo económico. *The Twelfth Latin American and Caribbean Conference for Engineering and Technology.* Retrieved from https://laccei.org/LACCEI2014-Guayaquil/RefereedPapers/RP080.pdf

Tortorella, G., Nascimento, D., Caiado, R., Arrieta Posada, J. G., & Sawhney, R. (2019). How do different generations contribute to the development of a learning organization in companies undergoing a lean production implementation? *The Learning Organization*, *27*(2), 101–115. doi:10.1108/TLO-02-2019-0035

Trask, B. S. (2017). Alleviating the stress on working families: Promoting family-friendly workplace policies. *National Council of Family Relations Policy Brief, 2*(1). Retrieved June 5, 2022, from https://www.ncfr.org/sites/default/files/2017-01/ncfr_policy_brief_january_2017.pdf

Trent, R. J. (2020). *Women's Perspectives on the Role of Organizational Culture in Their Career Advancement to Leadership Positions: A Generic Inquiry* [Doctoral dissertation]. Capella University.

Tsebelis, G. (2002). *Veto Players: How Political Institutions Work.* Princeton University Press. doi:10.1515/9781400831456

Tshivhase, M. (2020). Personhood: Implications for Moral Status and Uniqueness of Women. Handbook of African Philosophy of Difference, 347-360.

Tulgan, B. (1996). *Managing Generation X: How to Bring Out the Best in Young Talent.* Oxford: Capstone.

Tversky, A., & Kahneman, D. (1974). Judgment under uncertainty: Heuristics and biases. *Science, 185*(4157), 1124-1131.

Twenge, J. (2010). A review of the empirical evidence on generational differences in work attitudes. *Journal of Business and Psychology*, *25*(2), 201–210.

Ugoani, J. N. N. (2017). Emotional Intelligence and Successful Change Management in the Nigerian Banking Industry. *Independent Journal of Management & Production*, *8*(2), 335. doi:10.14807/ijmp.v8i2.550

UNAIDS. (n.d.). *Technical Support Facilities.* UNAIDS Press.

UNESCO. (2012b). *Shaping the Education of Tomorrow: 2012 Report on the UN Decade of Education for Sustainable Development, Abridged.* Retrieved from https://sustainabledevelopment.un.org/content/documents/919unesco1.pdf

United Nations. (1987). *Report of the World Commission on Environment and Development: Our Common Future.* Retrieved from https://www.are.admin.ch/are/en/home/media/publications/sustainable-development/brundtland-report.html

Unruh, G. (2000). Understanding carbon lock-in. *Energy Policy*, *28*(12), 817–830. doi:10.1016/S0301-4215(00)00070-7

Urick, M., Hollensbe, E., Masterson, S., & Lyons, S. (2017). Understanding and managing intergenerational conflict: An examination of influences and strategies. *Work, Aging and Retirement*, *3*(2), 166–185.

Van Dam, K., Oreg, S., & Schyns, B. (2008). Daily work contexts and resistance to organisational change: The role of leader–member exchange, development climate, and change process characteristics. *Applied Psychology*, *57*(2), 313–334. doi:10.1111/j.1464-0597.2007.00311.x

Van de Vliert, E., Nauta, A., Giebels, E., & Janssen, O. (1999). Constructive conflict at work. *Journal of Organizational Behavior: The International Journal of Industrial. Occupational and Organizational Psychology and Behavior*, *20*(4), 475–491. doi:10.1002/(SICI)1099-1379(199907)20:4<475::AID-JOB897>3.0.CO;2-G

Van der Leeuw, S., Wiek, A., Harlow, J., & Buizer, J. (2012). How much time do we have? Urgency and rhetoric in sustainability science. *Sustainability Science*, *7*(S1), 115–120. doi:10.100711625-011-0153-1

Van der Post, W. Z., de Coning, T. J., & Smit, E. M. (1997). An instrument to measure organizational culture. *South African Journal of Business Management*, *28*(4), 147–168. doi:10.4102ajbm.v28i4.800

Van Maanen, J. (2012). *Organizations in action: Social science bases of administrative theory*. Transaction Publishers. doi:10.4324/9781315006252

Van Steenbergen, E. F., Ellemers, N., & Mooijaart, A. (2007). How work and family can facilitate each other? Distinct types of work-family facilitation and outcomes for women and men. *Journal of Occupational Health Psychology*, *12*(3), 279–300. doi:10.1037/1076-8998.12.3.279 PMID:17638494

Vandenkendelaere, T. (2013). Intergenerational solidarity: A two-way street that needs new paving. *Eur View.*, *12*, 235-242.

Vatn, A. (2005). Rationality, Institutions and Environmental Policy. *Ecological Economics*, *55*(2), 203–217. doi:10.1016/j.ecolecon.2004.12.001

Vatn, A. (2015b). *Environmental Governance: Institutions, Policies and Actions*. Edward Elgar.

Veblen T. (1899/1994). *The Theory of the Leisure Class: An Economic Study in the Evolution of Institutions*. Macmillan.

Villiers, C. (2019). Boardroom Culture: An Argument for Compassionate Leadership. *European Business Law Review*, *30*(2), 253–278. doi:10.54648/EULR2019012

Vivar, C. G. (2006). Putting conflict management into practice: A nursing case study. *Journal of Nursing Management*, *14*(3), 201–206. doi:10.1111/j.1365-2934.2006.00554.x PMID:16600008

Voronov, M., & Vince, R. (2012). Integrating emotions into the analysis of institutional work. *Academy of Management Review*, *37*, 58–81.

Voydanoff, P. (2008). A conceptual model of the work-family interface. In L. Lero, D.S. Korabik, & K. Karen (Eds.), Handbook of work-family integration: Research, theory, and best practices (pp: 37-55). Whitehead. doi:10.1016/B978-012372574-5.50006-5

Voydanoff, P. (1987). *Work and family life*. Sage Publications.

Voydanoff, P., & Kelly, R. F. (1984). Determinants of Work-Related Family Problems among Employed Parents. *Journal of Marriage and Family*, *46*(4), 881. doi:10.2307/352536

Wade, R. (2001). Showdown at the World Bank. *New Left Review*, *2001*(7), 124–137.

Wallenburg, I., Hopmans, C. J., Buljac-Samardzic, M., den Hoed, P. T., & IJzermans, J. N. M. (2016). Repairing reforms and transforming professional practices: A mixed-methods analysis of surgical training reform. *Journal of Professions and Organization*, *3*(1), 86–102. doi:10.1093/jpo/jov012

Wang, H. M., Ma, A. L., & Guo, T. T. (2020). Gender concept, work pressure, and work–family conflict. *American Journal of Men's Health*, *14*(5). doi:10.1177/1557988320957522

Wang, W., & Xiong, J. (2020). Research on institutional supply effect in innovation development of manufacturing industry. *Technoeconomics & Management Research.*, *2020*(5), 117–121.

Watkins, K. E. (1995). Changing managers' defensive reasoning about work/family conflicts. *Journal of Management Development*, *14*(2), 77-88.

Webber, D. J. (2002). Policies to stimulate growth: Should we invest in health or education? *Applied Economics*, *34*(13), 1633–1643. doi:10.1080/00036840110115109

Weber, K., Heinze, K., & DeSoucey, M. (2008). Forage for thought: Mobilizing codes in the movement for grass-fed meat and dairy products. *Administrative Science Quarterly*, *53*(3), 529567. doi:10.2189/asqu.53.3.529

Weber, K., Rao, H., & Thomas, L. G. (2009). From streets to suites: How the anti-biotech movement affected German pharmaceutical firms. *American Sociological Review*, *74*(2), 106127. doi:10.1177/000312240907400106

Welch, F. (1970). Education in production. *Journal of Political Economy*, *78*(1), 35–59. doi:10.1086/259599

Wenham, C., Smith, J., & Morgan, R. (2020). COVID-19: The gendered impacts of the outbreak. *Lancet*, *395*(10227), 846–848. doi:10.1016/S0140-6736(20)30526-2 PMID:32151325

Wheaton, M. M., & Kezar, A. (2019). Interlocking systems of oppression: Women navigating higher education leadership. In *Challenges and opportunities for women in higher education leadership* (pp. 61–83). IGI Global. doi:10.4018/978-1-5225-7056-1.ch005

Whitty-Collins, G. (2020). *Why Men Win at Work:...and How to Make Inequality History*. Luath Press Ltd.

Wiek, A., Withycombe, L., & Redman, C. L. (2011). Key competencies in sustainability: A reference framework for academic program development. *Sustainability Science*, *6*(2), 203–218. doi:10.100711625-011-0132-6

Wijayanti, F., Dyah, S., Saparita, R., & Abbas, A. (2016). Institutional Transformation of Local Innovation Systems in Farmer Community of Belu, East Nusa Tenggara. *Journal of STI Policy and Management, 1*(2), 137–151. doi:10.14203/STIPM.2016.51

Wilsford, D. (1994). Path dependency, or why history makes it difficult but not impossible to reform health care systems in a big way. *Journal of Public Policy, 14*(3), 251–283. doi:10.1017/S0143814X00007285

Wirtz, P. (2011). The cognitive dimension of corporate governance in fast growing entrepreneurial firms. *European Management Journal, 29*(6), 431–447. doi:10.1016/j.emj.2011.06.004

Wiser, R. (2002). *Innovation, renewable energy, and state investment: Case studies of leading clean energy funds.* Lawrence Berkeley National Laboratory. Retrieved from https://eta-publications.lbl.gov/sites/default/files/report-lbnl-51493.pdf

World Health Organization. (2020). COVID-19 and violence against women: what the health sector/system can do, 7 April 2020 (No. WHO/SRH/20.04). World Health Organization.

Wu, J. Y. (2008). A General Behavior Model and New Definitions of Organizational Cultures. *Journal of Socio-Economics, 37*(6), 2535–2545. doi:10.1016/j.socec.2007.10.002

Wyborn, C. (2015). Co-productive governance: A relational framework for adaptive governance. *Global Environmental Change, 30*, 56–67. doi:10.1016/j.gloenvcha.2014.10.009

Xiao, Q., & Klarin, A. (2019). Subordinate actors' institutional maintenance in response to coercive reforms. *Journal of Management Inquiry, 30*(1), 24–39. doi:10.1177/1056492619868027

Yankelovich, D. (1981). *New rules: Searching for self-fulfillment in a world turned upside down.* Random House.

Yin, R. K. (1994). *Case Study Research Design and Methods* (2nd ed.). Sage Publication.

Yordanova, S. (2023). *Emotional intelligence of the leader-is it needed?* Academic Press.

Yucel, D. (2017). Work-to-family conflict and life satisfaction: The moderating role of type of employment. *Applied Research in Quality of Life, 12*(3), 577–591. doi:10.100711482-016-9477-4

Zapf, D. (1999). Organisational, work group related and personal causes of mobbing/bullying at work. *International Journal of Manpower, 20*(1/2), 70–85. doi:10.1108/01437729910268669

Zeinali, Z., Muraya, K., Govender, V., Molyneux, S., & Morgan, R. (2019). Intersectionality and global health leadership: Parity is not enough. *Human Resources for Health, 17*(1), 29. doi:10.118612960-019-0367-3 PMID:31029139

Zhao, Y., Li, Y., & Sun, X. (2019). The realizing mechanism of the synergy between technological innovation and institutional innovation to drive the evolution of a manufacturing enterprise: A longitudinal grounded analysis of guangming furniture. *Journal of Management Case Studies, 12*(2), 188–180.

Zikos, D. (2020). Revisiting the Role of Institutions in Transformative Contexts: Institutional Change and Conflicts. *Sustainability*, *12*(21), 9036. doi:10.3390u12219036

Zikos, D., & Hagedorn, K. (2017). Competition for Water Resources from the European Perspective. In J. R. Ziolkowska & J. M. Peterson (Eds.), *Competition for Water Resources: Experiences and Management Approaches in the US and Europe* (pp. 19–35). Elsevier. doi:10.1016/B978-0-12-803237-4.00002-1

Zikos, D., & Thiel, A. (2013). Action Research's Potential to Foster Institutional Change for Urban Water Management. *Water (Basel)*, *5*(2), 356–378. doi:10.3390/w5020356

Zink, C. F., Tong, Y., Chen, Q., Bassett, D. S., Stein, J. L., & Meyer-Lindenberg, A. (2008). Know your place: Neural processing of social hierarchy in humans. *Neuron*, *58*(2), 273–283. doi:10.1016/j.neuron.2008.01.025 PMID:18439411

Zucker, L. (1977). The role of institutionalization in cultural persistence. *American Sociological Review*, *42*(5), 726–743. doi:10.2307/2094862

About the Contributors

Gerardo Reyes Ruiz is an Actuary by training from the Faculty of Sciences-UNAM; he studied a Specialty in Econometrics in the Postgraduate Studies Division of the Faculty of Economics-UNAM; He obtained a Master's and Doctorate (with a scholarship from CONACYT and the Carolina Foundation) in Business Studies (actuarial profile) from the Faculty of Economics and Business of the University of Barcelona, Spain. In the Doctorate he graduated with the highest honors awarded to a thesis of this nature, that is, he obtained the qualification of Excellent Cum Laude. Later he did a postdoctoral stay at the Center for Economic, Administrative, and Social Studies (CIECAS) of the National Polytechnic Institute (IPN). His work experience has been in public education institutions (UNAM, UAEM, IPN, Centro de Estudios Superiores Navales-CESNAV) where he has taught classes in Bachelor's, Specialty, Master, and Doctorate degrees. In some of these institutions, he developed several research projects, including Basic Science, forming and creating Research Networks (both nationally and internationally). All this accumulated experience allowed him to enter the National System of Researchers (SNI), Social Area, of Mexico (he has the appointment of Level I National Researcher). He is currently attached to the Center for Superior Naval Studies (CESNAV), in Mexico.

* * *

Selda Coşkuner Aktaş is an associate professor at Hacettepe University, Faculty of Economics and Administrative Sciences, Department of Family and Consumer Sciences. Dr. Coşkuner Aktaş has been working at Hacettepe University, Faculty of Economics and Administrative Sciences, Department of Family and Consumer Sciences since 2004. She was visiting scholar at North Carolina State University (NCSU) between 2011-2012. She was also a researcher at the same university in July-September 2015. Dr. Coşkuner Aktaş's research interests include role balance, family and work roles, family and work conflict, family and work facilitation, and gender roles.

Catherine Hayes is Professor of Health Professions Pedagogy and Scholarship at the University of Sunderland, UK. She is a UK National Teaching Fellow and Principal Fellow of the UK Higher Education Academy. As a graduate of Podiatric Medicine in 1992, Catherine was a Founding Fellow of the Faculty of Podiatric Medicine at the Royal College of Physicians and Surgeons (Glasgow) in 2012 and was awarded Fellowship of the Royal College of Podiatry (London) in 2010. She is currently Programme Leader of the University of Sunderland's Professional Doctorate pathways for the DBA, EdD, DPM and DProf.

Darshana Jayawardena completed his BSc in Business Management with Honours specializing in Logistics from NSBM Green University, Sri Lanka. He is reading the PCJT software engineering qualification. His research interests includes operations management, human resource management and conflict resolution.

Nirma Sadamali Jayawardena is an Assistant Professor at O P Jindal Global University, India. Her PhD is from Griffith University, Australia. She completed BSc in Business Management with a first-class honours from National School of Business Management, Green University, Sri Lanka, and completed MBA in international business from University of Colombo, Sri Lanka. Her research interests include social cognition, consumer visual memory, and advertising.

K. S. S. Kanhaiya (Orcid: 0000-0001-9117-1654) received his graduation degree in Electrical Engineering from Ranchi University, India in 1987. In 1988 he joined Steel Authority of India where he is Chief General Manager currently. He received MBA, LLB, MA (App. Psychology) and PhD (Management) degrees besides some diplomas from different universities. He is Fellow of Institution of Engineers (India), Senior Member of Computer Society of India, and Member of Indian Science Congress Association and Indian Institute of Materials Management. He writes, presents and publishes on General Management, Leadership, Strategy, OB, HRD, Business Ethics, IT and ESG issues and has authored three books. He is Patron and Senior Advisor to the Governing Council of DESC, India and Vice President of their National Executive Council. He is a Govt. of India certified Independent Director for boards of companies.

Omar Vargas-González is Professor and Head of Systems and Computing Department at Tecnologico Nacional de Mexico Campus Ciudad Guzman, professor at Telematic Engineering at Centro Universitario del Sur Universidad de Guadalajara with a master degree in Computer Systems. Has been trained in Innovation and Multidisciplinary Entrepreneurship at Arizona State University (2018) and a Generation of Ecosystems of Innovation, Entrepreneurship and Sustainability for Jalisco course by Harvard University T.H. Chan School of Health. At present conduct research on diverse fields such as Entrepreneurship, Economy, Statistics, Mathematics and Information and Computer Sciences. Has collaborated in the publication of over 20 scientific articles and conducted diverse Innovation and Technological Development projects.

Silvena Yordanova is an associate professor in Social management. Having more than 10 years experience as lecturer in Management, Strategic management, Organizational behavior. Consultant and lecturer in Electronic marketing. Scientific interests- electronic commerce, virtual communities in tourism. Monograph published "Virtual communities in tourism", 2016. Graduated University of economics-Varna, Bulgaria. Ph.D. in Social Management. Lectured Electronic commerce in Italy, Norway, Finland. Lecturing in English, Bulgarian. Speaks Bulgarian, English, Russian.

Index

A

Adaptation Strategy 157, 159, 168
Autonomy 41-42, 44, 88-89, 152, 168, 222-223, 227-229, 232-241, 246

C

Change Management 60, 142, 157, 222-224, 226, 228-230, 233-234, 237-238, 240-242
Critical Reflection 64, 85
Critical Reflexivity 64, 73, 77, 85
Culture Outcome-Oriented Strategy 168

E

Emotional Labour 60, 62, 77, 85

F

Fairness 151, 222-223, 228-229, 232, 234-242, 246
Family-to-Work Conflict 205-207, 209-210, 212, 214-217
Flat Power Structure 152, 168

G

Gender Gap 72, 187, 192-194
Gender Inequality 63, 188

H

Hierarchical Power Structure 151, 168
Human Capital 1-3, 10-11, 13-14, 24-25, 60

I

Institutional Analysis 110
Institutional Change 35, 37-38, 40-41, 43-48, 107-115, 117-121
Institutionalization 107-108, 111, 115-117, 119-120
Intergenerational Conflict 86-87, 91, 93, 97, 99-100, 106

L

Life Satisfaction 205-207, 209-212, 214, 216-217
Literature Review 107, 170, 172, 179-180, 186

M

Manufacturing 2, 6, 10, 13-14, 19-20, 45, 94-95, 106, 133-134, 139, 222-224, 226-227, 229, 231, 241-242
Masculinity 69-70, 75, 191
Matrix Power Structure 152, 168

N

Neoliberalism 60, 69, 85

O

Organisational Level 226
Organizational Change 132-134, 138-139, 141-143, 224
Organizational Change Models 132-134
Organizational Culture 1-6, 9-15, 18, 22, 24-27, 133, 135, 137-138, 142, 146-147, 149-151, 155-158, 161-165, 168-169, 185-192, 196-199
Organizational Culture Strategy 164, 169
Organizational Values 133, 185-186, 191-192, 196-200
Outcome-Oriented Strategy 168

P

People-Oriented Strategy 169
Policymaking 35, 37, 44-47, 109, 115
Positionality 61-62, 72, 85
Power Structure 146-152, 164-165, 168-169
Preservation Strategy 156, 159, 169
Public Policy 1, 24, 36

R

Readiness to Change 222, 224, 229-230, 232-242
Relatedness 222-223, 227-229, 232, 234-241, 246
Resistance to Change 137, 151, 225

S

SCARF 222-224, 227-230, 232, 234-239
Science and Technology 2-3, 14-15, 19, 25, 76
Signature Pedagogy 71, 85
SMEs 1-4, 10, 15-19, 25-26
Social Experience 230, 246

T

Transformation Strategy 157, 160, 169

W

Women Leadership 70-71, 186, 196

www.ingramcontent.com/pod-product-compliance
Lightning Source LLC
LaVergne TN
LVHW081333300926
849161LV00008B/1956
* 9 7 8 1 6 6 8 4 6 5 6 7 7 *